ISBN 978-0-483-68460-7
PIBN 10044117

This book is a reproduction of an important historical work. Forgotten Books uses
state-of-the-art technology to digitally reconstruct the work, preserving the original format
whilst repairing imperfections present in the aged copy. In rare cases, an imperfection in
the original, such as a blemish or missing page, may be replicated in our edition. We do,
however, repair the vast majority of imperfections successfully; any imperfections that
remain are intentionally left to preserve the state of such historical works.

OLD PLAYS.

VOLUME II.

GAMMER GURTON'S NEEDLE.
ALEXANDER AND CAMPASPE.
TANCRED AND GISMUNDA.
CORNELIA.
EDWARD II.

M.DCCC.XXV.

A

SELECT COLLECTION

OF

OLD PLAYS.

IN TWELVE VOLUMES.

VOL. II.

A NEW EDITION:

WITH

ADDITIONAL NOTES AND CORRECTIONS,

BY THE LATE

ISAAC REED, OCTAVIUS GILCHRIST,

AND THE EDITOR.

LONDON:

SEPTIMUS PROWETT, 23, OLD BOND STREET.

M.DCCC.XXV,

PROSPECTUS

OF A

NEW EDITION

OF

DODSLEY'S OLD PLAYS:

WITH

ADDITIONAL NOTES AND CORRECTIONS,

BY THE LATE

ISAAC REED, OCTAVIUS GILCHRIST,

AND

THE EDITOR.

IT is necessary briefly to preface the present edition of " Dodsley's Old Plays."

It is acknowledged on all hands that such a re-publication has been long wanted, and more than ten years ago the late Mr. Octavius Gilchrist printed a prospectus of the undertaking. For this task he was well qualified, not only by his own extensive knowledge of old English writers, but by the possession of a copy of the reprint of 1780, with the last notes and corrections of Mr. Isaac Reed. This copy, with various additional illustrations by Mr. Gilchrist, having devolved into the hands of the publisher of the present edition, he determined to avail himself of the valuable materials thus furnished, and of all the information supplied by the recent ardent pursuit of old English poetry.

It is needless at this time of day to dwell on the peculiar merits and attractions of our Drama, as it existed during the reigns of Elizabeth, James, and Charles; but it may be right to observe that the work known as Dodsley's Old Plays, has not hitherto included any performances by Thomas Nash, Robert Greene, Thomas Lodge, or George Peele, the contemporaries, and some of them at least, the predecessors and examples of Shakespeare. The long promised publication of the works of Shirley, and the forth-coming new edition of those of Ford, both under the superintendence of perhaps the most competent critic and illustrator it was ever the good fortune of old poet to meet with, has rendered it expedient now to reject three plays by the former and one by the latter hitherto embraced in this collection. Room will thus be afforded for productions by the four distinguished poets whose works, as above stated, have been wholly omitted. Thus a considerable additional value will be given to the present republication, and the stores of our ancient drama being rich as they are inexhaustible, it will be followed by a Supplement upon the same plan, including first-rate specimens, never reprinted and only in the hands of collectors. It is proposed, likewise, to add a volume of Masques and Pageants, of which neither Mr. Dodsley nor Mr. Reed furnished any examples, and which, independently of other attractions, include some of the best lyric poetry in our language.

Correctness of text will be the first great object: the additional notes and illustrations of Reed and Gilchrist to such plays as were reprinted in 1780, will generally be sufficient in the way of verbal criticism, and in the productions now for the first time included in any collection the Editor will be especially careful not to burden the page with useless annotations and " the ostentation of vain learning."—If a word require explanation it can usually be given as well by one apposite reference to a contemporary author, as by a hundred. The biographical matter will be short but full, and accurate, omitting nothing of importance that modern research or the diligent reading of the Editor can supply. In the volume now printed will be found some matter new even to the most industrious of our literary antiquaries.

The first volume has been reserved for the purpose of rendering the preliminary matter as complete as possible, by the end of the publication, which (as far as regards the work known as " Dodsley's Old Plays") will be finished in a year, a volume being regularly delivered to the public every month. Altogether it is hoped that the enterprise will furnish a specimen of the union of accuracy, industry, and correct taste.

It may be fit to mention that the new notes and illustrations are thus marked: I. R. for those of

Mr. Isaac Reed; O. G. for those of Mr. Octavius Gilchrist; and C. for those added by the present Editor.

This Work will be beautifully printed upon yellow laid paper, crown 8vo. price 9s. each volume, uniformly with the recent edition of Tyrwhitt's Chaucer, and the Plays and Poems of Shakespeare now publishing in eleven volumes.

A few copies have been taken off on large paper, price 14s. each volume, uniformly with Mr. Boswell's edition of Malone's Shakespeare and Gifford's Ben Jonson, &c.

28, Old Bond Street, 30th April, 1825.

GAMMER GURTON'S NEEDLE.

VOL. II.

THIS Dramatic Piece is the first performance which appeared in England under the 'name of a Comedy*. As a former Editor of it (Mr. Hawkins) observes, " There is a vein of familiar humour in this play, and " a kind of grotesque imagery not unlike some parts " of Aristophanes, but without those graces of language " and metre for which the Greek Comedian was emi- " nently distinguished." The present edition is from a copy printed in the year 1575†.

* There are reasons sufficiently conclusive to induce a belief, that John Still was the author of '' Gammer Gurton's Needle.''
He was the son of William Still of Grantham in Lincolnshire, was rector of Hadleigh in Suffolk, and was commissioned one of the Deans of Bocking in 1572; was installed canon of the 7th stall in the church of Westminster, and archdeacon of Sudbury, Mar. 28, 1576. He was first master of St. John's, then of Trinity College, Cambridge. While master of the latter he was promoted to the see of Bath and Wells, and was consecrated in Feb. 1592. He died Feb. 26, and was buried in the Cathedral Church of his diocese, 1607, leaving by testament 500l. to the alms-house in Wells.
He was twice married, and left behind him several children.

O. G.

† Although Gammer Gurton's Needle may be the first perform-ance which appeared in England under the *name* of a comedy, yet it is in all probability *not the first comedy*, properly so called, in our language. Not long since a copy, unfortunately without a title-page, of the play of " Rauf Roister Doister" was discovered, and it is now in the library of Eton College. In 1566 Thomas Hacket had a licence for " a play entitled Rauf Ruyster Duster," but as this was the only notice of its existence, it has been supposed that it was never printed. We have now, however, the play itself, and we are able to furnish the name of its author—Nicholas Udall. They are both matters of considerable curiosity, as Udall's performance is not only older than Gammer Gurton's Needle, but it is not a comedy of low country life, but the adventures of a rake frequently gulled and laughed at by his friend Matthew Merry Greek.
The evidence to prove that it was written by Nicholas Udall is very conclusive, and it serves also to show the age of his work. The play contains, in A. III. S. 3. a long letter from Ralph Roister Doister to his mistress, which is quoted by T. Wilson in his Art of Logic, printed by Grafton in 1551, as " an example of doubtful writing, taken from an enterlude made by Nicolas Vdall." Udall died about the year 1557, and Bishop Still, the author of Gammer Gurton's Needle, was then only fourteen years old, having been born in 1543. Hence we may decide, almost with certainty, that " Rauf Roister Doister" is older than Gammer Gurton's Needle. The former is a regular comedy divided into acts and scenes, and interspersed with songs. C.

NAMES OF THE SPEAKERS OF THIS COMEDIE.

DICCON[1], *the Bedlem*[2].
HODGE, *Gammer Gurton's Servante.*
TYB, *Gammer Gurton's Mayde.*
Gammer GURTON.
COCK, *Gammer Gurton's Boye.*
Dame CHATTE.
Doctor RAT, *the Curate.*
Mayster BAILYE.
DOLL, *Dame Chat's Mayde*
SCAPETHRYFT, *Mayster Bailye's servante.*

MUTES.

[1] *Diccon, the Bedlam.*] Diccon is the ancient abbreviation of Richard. See Mr. Steevens's Note on *Richard* III. A. 5. S. 3.

[2] *the Bedlam.*] After the dissolution of the religious houses where the poor of every denomination were provided for, there was for many years no settled or fixed provision made to supply the want of that care which those bodies appear always to have taken of their distressed brethren. In consequence of this neglect, the idle and dissolute were suffered to wander about the country, assuming such characters as they imagined were most likely to insure success to their frauds, and security from detection. Among other disguises many affected madness, and were distinguished by the name of *Bedlam Beggars.* These are mentioned by Edgar, in *King Lear:*

" The country gives me proof and precedent,
" Of *Bedlam* beggars who, with roaring voices,
" Stick in their numb'd and mortify'd bare arms
" Pins, wooden pricks, nails, sprigs of rosemary,
" And with this horrible object from low farms,
" Poor pelting villages, sheep-cotes, and mills,
" Sometime with lunatic bans, sometime with prayer,
" Inforce their charity."

In Dekker's *Bellman of London,* 1616, all the different species of beggars are enumerated. Amongst the rest are mentioned *Tom of Bedlam's* band of mad caps, otherwise called Poor Tom's flock of wild geese (whom here thou seest by his black and blue naked arms to be a man beaten to the world), and those wild geese, or hair brains, are called Abraham men. An Abraham man is afterwards described in this manner: " Of all the mad rascals " (that are of this wing) the *Abraham-man* is the most fantastick. " The fellow (quoth this old Lady of the Lake unto me) that sate " half naked (at table to-day) from the girdle upward, is the best " *Abraham-man* that ever came to my house, and the notablest " villain : he swears he hath been in Bedlam, and will talk fran- " tickly of purpose : you see pins stuck in sundry places of his " naked flesh, especially in his arms, which pain he gladly puts " himself to (being indeed no torment at all, his skin is either so " dead with some foul disease, or so hardened with weather, only " to make you believe he is out of his wits) : he calls himself by " the name of *Poor Tom,* and coming near any body cries out, " Poor Tom is a cold. Of these *Abraham-men,* some be exceeding " merry, and do nothing but sing songs, fashioned out of their own " brains, some will dance ; others will do nothing but either laugh " or weep ; others are dogged, and are sullen both in look and " speech, that, spying but a small company in a house, they boldly " and bluntly enter, compelling the servants through fear to give " them what they demand, which is commonly *Bacon,* or something " that will yield ready money."

Of this respectable fraternity Diccon seems to have been a member.

Massinger mentions them in *A new way to pay old Debts,* A. 2 S. 1.—" Are they padders, or *Abraham-men,* that are your consorts ?'

PROLOGUE.

As Gammer Gurton, with manye a wyde styche,
Sat pesynge and patching of Hodg her man's briche
By chance or misfortune, as shee her geare tost,
In Hodge lether bryches her needle shee lost.
When Diccon the bedlam had hard by report,
That good Gammer Gurton was robde in thys sorte,
He quyetly perswaded with her in that stound,
Dame Chat her deare gossyp this needle had found.
Yet knew shee no more of this matter (alas)
Then knoeth Tom our clarke what the priest saith at
      masse.
Hereof there ensued so fearfull a fraye,
Mas Doctor was sent for, these gossyps to staye;
Because he was curate, and estemed full wyse,
Who found that he sought not, by Diccon's device.
When all thinges were tombled and cleane out of fassion,
Whether it were by fortune, or some other constellacion,
Sodenlye the neele Hodge found by the prickynge,
And drew out of his bottocke, where he found it
      stickynge.
Theyr hartes then at rest with perfect securytie,
With a pot of good nale they stroake up theyr plauditie.

GAMMER GURTON'S NEEDLE.

THE FYRST ACTE.

THE FYRST SCEANE.

Diccon. MANY a myle have I walked, divers and
     sundry waies,
And many a good man's house have I bin at in my dais.
Many a gossip's cup in my tyme have I tasted,
And many a broche and spyt have I both turned and
     basted,
Many a peece of bacon have I had out of thir balkes[3],
In ronnyng over the countrey, with long and were
     walkes.
Yet came my foote never within those doore cheekes,
To seek flesh or fysh, garlyke, onyons or leekes,
That ever I saw a sorte in such a plyght[4],
As here within this house appereth to my syght,

[3] *—out of thir balkes,*] The summer beam or dorman. Poles
laid over a stable, or other building. Ray's *Collection of English
Words,* p. 167.

   [4] *That ever I saw a sorte in such a plyght,*] *A sort* is a company. So, in Johnson's *Every Man out of his Humour,* A. 2. S. 3.
" I speek it not gloriously, nor out of affectation, but there's he
" and the count Frugale, signior Illustre, signior Luculento, and *a
" sort* of them," &c.

   Also, in Pierce *Pennilesse's Supplication to the Devil,* 1592, p. 6.
" I know a great *sort* of good fellows that would venture," &c.

   Again, in the *Vocacyon of Johan Bale,* 1533 : "—in parell of
" pyrates, robbers, and murthirors, and a great *sort* more."

   And, in Skelton's Works, edit. 1736, p. 136.

        " Another *sorte* of sluttes
        " Some brought walnutes."

   See also Dr. Johnson and Mr. Steevens's Notes on Shakspeare,
vol. III. p. 69.

There is howlynge and schowlyng, all cast in a dumpe,
With whewling and pewling, as though they had lost
    a trump.
Syghing and sobbing, they weepe and they wayle.
I marvel in my mynd, what the devil they ayle.
The olde trot syts groning, with alas, and alas[5],
And Tib wringes her hands, and takes on in worse case.
With poore Cocke theyr boye, they be dryven in such
    fyts
I feare mee the folkes be not well in theyr wyts.
Aske them what they ayle, or who brought them in
    this staye?
They aunswer not at all, but alacke and welaway.
When I saw it booted not, out at doores I hyed mee,
And caught a slyp of bacon, when I saw none spyed
    mee,
Which I intend not far hence, unles my purpose fayle,
Shall serve for a shoing horne to draw on two pots of
    ale[6].

[5] *The olde* trot *syts groning, with alas, and alas*,] An old *trot*, or *trat*, Dr. Gray says, signifies a decrepid old woman, or an old drab. In which sense it is used in Gawin Douglas' Virgil's Ænead, B. 4. p. 96, 97.
    Out on the *old trat* agit wyffe or dame.
And p. 122. 39.
    Thus said D*ido*, and the tother with that,
    Hyit or furth with slow pase like *ane trot.*
And Shakspeare: " Why give her gold enough, and marry him " to a puppet, an aglet baby, or an *old trot* with ne'er a tooth in her " head." *Taming of the Shrew*, A. 1. S. 5. Critical Notes on Shakspeare, vol. I. p. 118.
    It is also used by Churchyard:
    Away young Frie that gives leawd counsell nowe,
    Awaie *old trotts*, that sets young flesh to sale, &c.
                        Challenge, 1593, p. 250.
And by Gascoigne:
    Go! that gunpowder consume the old *trot.*
                        Supposes, A. 3. S. 5.
Again, in Nashe's *Lenten Stuff*, 1599: "— a cage or pigeon house, " roomsome enough to comprehend her, and the toothless *trot* her " nurse, who was her only chat mate and chamber maid," &c.
    See also Mr. Steevens's Notes on Shakspeare, vol. II. p. 93.
  [6] *Shall serve for a shoing horne to draw on two pots of ale.*] So, in Pierce *Pennilesse's Supplication*, p. 23. " — wee have generall rules

THE FYRST ACTE.

THE SECOND SCEANE.

HODGE. DICCON.

Hodge. See so cham arayed with dablynge in the durt!
She that set me to ditchinge, ich wold she had the
    squirt.
Was never poore soule that such a life had?
Gog's bones, thys vilthy glaye hase drest mee too bad.
God's soule, see how this stuffe teares!
Iche were better to bee a bearward, and set to keepe
    beares.
By the masse, here is a gashe, a shamefull hole indeade,
And one stytch teare furder, a man may thruste in his
    heade.
    Diccon. By my father's soule, Hodge, if I shulde
    now be sworne,
I cannot chuse but say thy breech is foule betorne.
But the next remedye in such a case and hap,
Is to plaunche* on a piece as brode as thy cap.
    Hodge. Gog's soule man, 'tis not yet two dayes fully
    ended,
Synce my dame Gurton (cham sure) these breches
    amended.

" and injunctions as good as printed precepts, or statutes set downe
" by acte of parliament, that goe from drunkard to drunkard as
" still to keepe your first man, not to leave anie flockes in the bottom
" of the cup, to knock the glasse on your thumbe when you have
" done, to have some *shooring horne* to pull on your wine, as a
" rasher of the coles, or a redde herring."
    Again in Nash's Lenten Stuff, 1599, " —— which being double
" roasted, and dried as it is, not only sucks up all the rheumatick
" inundations, but is a *shoeing horn* for a pint of wine overplus."
    * *Plaunche* on a piece as brode as thy cap.] A *plaunch* is a plank
of wood. To *plaunch* therefore is a verb formed from it. See
Measure for Measure, vol. 2. edit. 1778, p. 106. S.
    The above note but ill explains its meaning; the word will be
better illustrated by the following description of the fortification of
Ypres by Holinshed.
    " It was fensed with a mighty rampire, and a thicke hedge,
trimlie *plashed*, and woond with thornes, &c."
                   Chron. 2. 759. *Ed.* 1807. O. G.

But cham made such[7] a drudge to trudge at every
          neede,
Chwold rend it, though it were stitched wath sturdy
          packthreede.

  Diccon. Hodge[8], let thy breeches go, and speake
          and tell mee soone,
What devil ayleth gammer Gurton, and Tib her mayd
          to frowne.

  Hodge. Tush, man, th'art deceyved, 'tys theyr dayly
          looke:
[9]They coure so over the coles, theyr eyes be blear'd
          with smooke.

  Diccon. Nay, by the masse, I perfectly perceved as
          I came hether,
That eyther Tib and her dame hath ben by the eares
          together,
Or els as great a matter, as thou shalt shortly see.

  Hodge. Now iche beseeche our Lord they never
          better agree.

  Diccon. By Gog's soule, there they syt as still as
          stones in the streite,
As though they had ben taken with fairies, or els with
          some il spreet.

  Hodge. Gog's hart, I durst have layd my cap to a
          crowne,
Ch'would learn of some prancome as soon as ich came
          to town.

  Diccon. Why, Hodge, art thou inspyred? or dedst
          thou thereof here?

  Hodge. Nay, but ich saw such a wonder, as ich saw
          nat this seven yere.

---

 [7] succ.

 [8] Hoge

 [9] *They coure*] This is the reading of the first edition, which in
all the subsequent ones is very improperly altered to *cover.* To
coure, is to bend, stoop, hang or lean over. See Beaumont and
Fletcher's *Monsieur Thomas,* A. 4. S. 6. and Pierce *Pennilesse's
Supplication to the Devil,* 1592, p. 8.

 Again,
  " He much rejoyst, and *cour'd* it tenderly,
  " As chicken newly hatcht, from dreaded destiny."
       Spenser's *Fairy Queen,* B. 2. c. 8. S. 9.

Tome Tannkard's cow (be gog's bones) she set me up
    her sail,

And flynging about his halse aker*, fysking with her
    taile,

As though there had been in her ars a swarme of
    bees;

And chad not cryed tphrowh hoore, shea'd lept out of
    his lees.

    Diccon. Why, Hodg, lies the connyng in Tom
      Tankard's cowe's tail?

    Hodge. Well, ich chave hard some say such tokens
      do not fayle.

But ca'st thou not tell, in faith, Diccon, why she frowns,
    or whereat?

10 Hath no man stolen her ducks, or henes, or gelded
    Gyb her cat?

    Diccon. What devyll can I tell, man, I cold not
      have one word,

They gave no more hede to my talke then thou woldst
    to a lord.

    Hodge. Iche cannot styll but muse, what mervaylous
      thinge it is:

Chyll in and know my selfe what matters are amys.

    So in Shakspeare's *King Henry VI.* Part 2. vol. 6. p. 362,
edit. 1778.

        " The splitting rocks *cowr'd* in the sinking sand." S.
  Again,

    " As thus he spake, each bird and beast behold
    " Approaching two and two, these *cow'ring* low
    " With blandishment, each bird stoop'd on his wing."
                    Paradise Lost, B. 8. l. 349.

  * *His halse aker.*] I believe we should read *halse anchor*, or
anker, as it was anciently spelt; a naval phrase. The *halse* or
halser was a particular kind of cable. Shakspeare, in his *Antony
and Cleopatra*, has an image similar to this.

    " The brize upon her, like a *cow* in June,
    " Hoists sail and flies." S.

10 *Hath no man stolne her ducks, or henes, or gelded* Gyb *her cat!*]
Gyb was the name by which all male or ram cats were distin-
guished. See Mr. Warton's Note on the first part of *Henry IV.*
A. I. S. 2.

Diccon. Then fare well, Hodge, a while, synce thou
        doest inward hast,
For I will into the good wyfe Chat's, to feele how the
        ale does tast.

THE FYRST ACTE.

THE THYRD SCEANE.

HODGE. TYB.

Hodge. Cham agast, by the masse, ich wot not what
        to do.
Chad nede blesse me well before ich go them to.
Perchaunce some fellon sprit may haunt our house
        indeed.
And then chwere but a noddy to venter where cha no
        neede.
Tyb. Cham worse then mad, by the masse, to be at
        this staye,
Cham chyd, cham blamd, and beaton all th'ours on
        the daye.
Lamed and hunger storved, prycked up all in jagges,
Havyng no patch to hyde my backe, save a few rotten
        ragges.
Hodge. [11] I say, Tyb, if thou be Tyb, as I trow sure
        thou bee,
What devyll make-a-doe is this betweene our dame
        and thee?

---

[11] *I say, Tyb, if thou be Tyb, as I* trow *sure thou bee,*] *Trow* is an
old word, which signifies *believe.* As in A. 5. S. 2.
    This prose I *trow* may serve, though no word spoke.
Again,
    A false knave bi Gods pitie ye were but a foole to *trow* him.
Again,
    I *trow* he'll come no more at my house. *Wily beguiled,* 1606.
Again,
    " And that is best I *trowe* in warre, to let it go, and not to
        stoppe it."   Ascham's *Toxophilus.*

Tib. Gog's breade, Hodge, thou had a good turn
  thou wart not here this while.
It had ben better for some of us to have bén hence a
  myle.
My Gammer is so out of course, and frantyke all at ones,
That Cocke, our boy, and I poore wench, have felt it
  on our bones.
  Hodge. What is the matter, say on, Tib, whereat
    she taketh so on ?
  Tib. She is undone, she sayth, (alas) her joye and
    life is gone.
If shee here not of some comfort, shee sayth[12] she is
  but dead,
Shall never come within her lyps, one inch of meate ne
  bread.
  Hodge. By'r ladie, cham not very glad to see her in
    this dumpe ;
Cholde a noble her stole hath fallen, and shee hath
  broke her rumpe.
  Tib. Nay, and that were the worst, we wold not
    greatly care,
For bursting * of her huckle bone, or breakyng of her
  chaire,
But greater, greater, is her grief, as Hodge we shall
  all feele.
  Hodge. Gog's woundes, Tyb, my gammer has never
    lost her neele ?
  Tib. Her neele.
  Hodge. Her neele ?

---

[12] She is sayth but dead.

 * *For bursting.*] i. e. breaking. See note on *King Henry IV.*
Part 2d. edit 1778. vol. 5, p. 537. S.

 From the following passage, in a letter from Mr. Sterne, dated
August 11, 1767, it appears that the word is still used in the same
sense among the common people in the north of England. . " My
" postilion has set me a-ground for a week, by one of my pistols
" bursting in his hand, which he taking for granted to be quite shot
" off—he instantly fell upon his knees, and said, ' Our Father
" which art in heaven, hallowed be thy name,' at which, like a
" good christian, he stopped, not remembering any more of it—
" the affair was not so bad as he at first thought, for it has only
" *bursten* two of his fingers, he says."

Tib. Her neele; by him that made me, it is true,
    Hodge, I tell thee.

Hodge. Gog's sacrament! I would she had lost
    th'arte out of her bellie.

The devill, or els his dame, they ought her sure a shame,

How a murryon came this chaunce, (say, Tib) unto
    our dame?

Tib. My gammer sat her down on her pes*, and bad
    me reach thy breches,

And by and by a vengeance in it or she had take two
    stitches,

To clout a clout upon thine ars, by chaunce asyde she
    lears,

And Gyb our cat, in the milke-pan, she spied over head
    and eares.

Ah hore, out these, she cryd aloud, and swapt the
    breches downe,

Up went her staffe, and out leapt Gyb at doors into
    the towne.

And synce that time was never wyght cold set their
    eies upon it.

[13] Gog's malison, chave Cocke and I, byd twenty times
    light on it.

Hodge. And is not then my breches sewid up, to
    morow that I shuld were?

Tib. No, in faith, Hodge, thy breches lie, for all
    this never the nere.

Hodge. Now a vengeance light on al the sort, that
    better shold have kept it;

The cat, the house, and Tib our maid, that better shold
    have swept it.

Se where she cometh crawling! come on, in twenty
    devils way;

Ye have made a fayre daie's worke, have you not?
    pray you say.

---

* *on 'her pes*] I know not what word *pes* can signify, unless
it be derived from the old French *paisse* or *paisseau*, a perch, or seat.
It may however mean the *pes* of cloth, with which, as the prologue
says, she was

    " *pesynge* and patching of Hodge her man's *briche.*"   S.

[13] *Gog's malison,*] i. e. God's curse. Glossary to Peter Langtoft.

THE FYRST ACTE.

THE FOURTH SCEANE.

GAMMER.　HODGE.　TIB.　COCKE.

Gammer. Alas, alas, I may well curse and ban
This daie, that ever I saw it, with Gyb and the milke pan.
For these, and ll lucke togather, as knoweth Cocke
　　my boie,
Have stacke [14] away my deare neele, and rob'd me of
　　my joye.
My fayre long strayght neele, that was myne onely
　　treasure,
The fyrst day of my sorow is, and last end of my pleasure.
　Hodge. Might ha kept it when ye had it; but fooles
　　will be fooles styll:
Lose that is vast in your handes? ye neede not, but
　　ye will.
　Gammer. Go hie thee, Tib, and run thou hoore to
　　th' end here of the towne.
Didst cary out dust in thy lap? seeke wher thou porest
　　it downe [15];
And as thou sawest me roking in the ashes where
　　I morned,
So see in all the heape of dust thou leave no straw
　　unturned.
　[16] *Tib.* That chal, Gammer, swythe and tyte, and
　　sone be here agayne.
　Gammer. Tib, stoope and loke downe to the ground
　　to it, and take some paine.

---

[14] *Have* stacke, &c.] Mr. Dodsley, in the former edition, reads *tacke.*

[15] dowde.

[16] *That chai Gammer, swythe and tyte, and sone be here agayne.*]
Swythe and tyte, swiftly and directly.
　　　Kyng Estmere threwe the harpe asyde
　　　　And *swith* he drew his brand;
　　　And Estmere he and Alder yonge,
　　　　Right stiffe in stour can stand.
　　　Percy's *Reliques of Ancient Poetry,* vol. I. p. 75.

Hodge. Here is a pretty matter, to see this gere how
    it goes :
By gog's soul, I thenk you wold loes your arse, and it
    were loose.
Your neele lost? it is pitie you shold lack care and
    endlesse sorow.
Gog's deth, how shall my breches be sewid? shall I
    go thus to morow?
    Gammer. Ah, Hodge, Hodge, if that ich cold find
    my neele, by the reed,
Ch'ould sow thy breches ich promise the, with full
    good double threed,
And set a patch on either knee, shuld last this monethes
    twaine,
Now God and good saint Sithe *, I praye to send it
    home [17] againe.
    Hodge. Wherto served your hands and eies, but this
    your neele to kepe?
What devill had you els to do? ye keep, ich wot, no
    sheepe.
Cham faine abrode to dyg and delve, in water, myre,
    and claye,
Sossing and possing in the durte styll from day to daye.
A hundred thinges that be abrode, cham set to see
    them weele :
And foure of you syt idle at home, and cannot keepe
    a neele.
    Gammer. My neele, alas, ich lost it, Hodge, what time
    ich me up hasted,
To save milke set up for the, which Gib our cat hath
    wasted.
    Hodge. The devill he burst both Gib and Tib, with
    all the rest ;
Cham alwayes sure of the worst end, whoever have the
    best.

Hence *swythe* to Doctor Rat bye the that thou were gone.
                          A. 3. S. 3.
Thou shalt fynd lyeng an inche of whyte tallow candell
Lyght it, and brynge it *tite* away. A. 1. S. 4.
* *Saint Sithe.*]· Perhaps a corruption of Saint Swithen. S.
[17] *home*] Mr. Dodsley reads, back again.

Where ha you ben fidging abrode, since you your
    neele lost?

    Gammer. Within the house, and at the dore, sitting
        by this same post;

Wher I was loking a long howre, before these folks
    came here;

But, welaway! all was in vayne, my neele is never the nere.

    Hodge. Set me a candle, let me seeke, and grope
        where ever it bee.

Gog's heart, ye be folish (ich thinke) you knowe it not
    when you it see.

    Gammer. Come hether, Cocke, what Cocke, I say.

    Cocke. Howe, Gammer?

    Gammer. Goe, hye thee soone, and grope behynd the
        old brasse pan,

Whych thing when thou hast done,

Ther shalt thou fynd an old shooe, wherein, if thou
    looke well,

Thou shalt fynd lyeng an inche of whyte tallow candell;

Lyght it, and brynge it tite awaye.

    Cocke. That shal be done anone.

    Gammer. Nay, tary, Hodge, till thou hast light, and
        then weele seke ech one.

    Hodge. Cum away, ye horson boy, are ye asleepe?
        ye must have a crier.

    Cocke. Ich cannot get the candel light, here is
        almost no fier.

    Hodge. Chil hold the a peny, chil make thee come
    if that ich may catch thine cares.

Art deffe, thou horson boy? Cocke, I say, why canst
    not hear's?

    Gammer. Beate hym not, Hodge, but helpe the boy,
    and come you two together.

THE FIRST ACTE.

THE FIFTH SCEANE.

GAMMER. TYB. COCKE. HODGE.

Gammer. How now, Tyb! quicke, lets here what
    newes thou hast brought hether?

Tib. Chave tost and tumbled yender heap over and
    over againe,

And winowed it through my fingers, as men wold
    winow grain;

Not so much as a hen's turd, but in pieces I tare it.

Or what so ever clod or clay I found, I did not spare it.

Lokyng within and eke without, to find your neele (alas)

But all in vaine, and without help, your neele is where
    it was.

Gammer. [18] Alas, my neele we shall never meete!
    adue, adue for aye.

Tib. Not so, Gammer, we myght it fynde, if we
    knew where it laye.

Cocke. Gog's crosse, Gammer, if ye will laugh,
    looke in but at the doore,

And see how Hodge lieth tomblynge and tossing amids
    the floure,

Rakyng there, some fyre to find amonge the ashes dead,

Where there is not one sparke so byg as a pyn's head:

At last in a darke corner two sparkes he thought he sees,

Which where indede nought els, but Gyb our cat's
    two eyes.

---

[18] *Alas, my neele we shall never mete! adue, adue for aye.*] Adieu,
adieu *for ever.* As in the following instances:
> For *aye* to be in shady cloister mew'd.
>> *Midsummer Night's Dream*, A. 1.
> And sit *for aye* enthronized in heaven.
>> Marlow's *Edward* II.
> Whereas the other makes us live *for aye.*
>> *Tragedy of Cræsus*, 1604.
> —Let this pernicious hour,
> Stand *aye* accursed in the Calendar.

See Mr. Steevens's Shakspeare, vol. III. p. 7. vol. IV. p. 565.

Puffe, quod Hodge, thinking thereby to have fyre
    without doubt;
With that Gyb shut her two eyes, and so the fyre
    was out;
And by and by them opened, even as they were before,
With that the sparkes appered even as they had done
    of yore;
And even as Hodge blew the fire as he did thincke,
Gyb, as she felt the blast, strayght way began to
    wyncke;
Till Hodge fell of swering, as came best to his turne,
The fier was sure bewicht, and therfore wold not burne:
At last Gyb up the stayers, among the old postes and
    pinnes,
And Hodge he hied him after, til broke were both his
    shinnes:
Cursynge and sweering otbs, were never of his makyng,
That Gyb wold fyre the house, if that shee were not
    taken.
    Gammer. See here is all the thought that the foolish
      urchyn taketh!
And Tyb methinke at his elbowe, almost as mery
    maketh.
This is all the wyt ye have when others make their
    mone.
Come downe Hodge, where art thou? and let the cat
    alone.
    Hodge. Gogs harte, help and come up, Gyb in her
      tayle hath fyre,
And is like to burne all if she get a lytle hier:
[19] Cum downe (quoth you?) nay, then you might count
    me a patch,
The house cometh down on your heads if it take ons
    the thatch.

---

[19] *Cum downe (quoth you?) nay, then you might count me* a patch,]
" This term, says Mr. Malone, came into use from the name of a
" celebrated fool. This I learn from Wilson's *Art of Rhetorique*,
" 1553: ' A word making, called of the Grecians Onomatopœia,

Gammer. It is the cat's eyes, foole, that shineth in
the darke.

Hodge. Hath the cat, do you thinke, in every eye a
sparke?

Gammer. No, but they shyne as lyke fyre as ever
man see.

Hodge. By the masse, and she burne all, yoush
beare the blame for mee.

Gammer. Cum downe and help to seeke here our
neele that it were found;

Downe, Tyb on *thy* knees, I say, downe Cocke to
the ground,

[20] To God I make a vowe, and so to good saint Anne,

A candell shall they have a peece, get it where I can,

If I may my neele finde in one place or in other.

Hodge. Now a vengeaunce on Gib lyght, on Gyb
and Gyb's mother,

" is when we make words of our own mind, such as be derived
" from the nature of things.'—As to call one *patche*, or cowlson,
" whom we see to do a thing, foolishly; because these two in
" their time were notable fools.

" Probably the dress which the celebrated *patch* wore was in
" allusion to his name, patched or parti-coloured. Hence the
" stage-fool has ever since been exhibited in a motley coat. In
" Rowley's *When you see me you know me; or, Hist. of King
" Henry* VIII 1632, Cardinal Wolsey's Fool *Patch* is introduced.
" Perhaps he was the original *patch* of whom Wilson speaks."

Note on *Merchant of Venice*, A. 2. S. 5.

In Chaloner's Translation of the *Praise of Folly*, by Erasmus,
1549, is the following passage : " And by the fayeth ye owe to the
" immortal godds, may any thing to an indifferent considerer be
" deemed more happie and blisful than is this kinde of men whome
" commonly ye call fooles, poltes, ideotes, and *patches* ?"

Again, " I have subtraied these my selie *patchs*, who not onelye
" themselves are ever mery, playing, singing, and laughing, but
" also whatever they doo, are provokers of others lykewyse to
" pleasure, sporte, and laughter, as who sayeth ordeyned herefore
" by the Godds of theyr benevolence to recreate the sadnesse of
" mens lyves."

[20] *To God I make a vowe, and so to good saint Anne,*

A candell shall they have a peece, get it where I can,] In all
cases of distress, and whenever the assistance of a superior power

And all the generacion of cats both far and nere.
Looke on the ground, horson, thinks thou the neele is
    here?

  Cocke. By my trouth, Gammar, me thought your
    neele here I saw,
But when my fyngers toucht it, I felt it was a straw.

   Tib. See, Hodge, what's tys; may it not be within it?

  Hodge. Breake it, foole, with thy hand, and see and
    thou canst fynde it.

   Tib. Nay, breake it you, Hodge, accordyng to your
    word.

  Hodge. Gog's sydes, fie! it styncks: it is a cat's
    tourd:
It were well done to make thee eate it, by the masse.

  Gammer. This matter amendeth not, my neele is
    still where it wasse.
Our candle is at an ende, let us all in quight,
And come another tyme, when we have more lyght.

THE SECOND ACTE.

Firste a SONGE.

Back and syde go bare, go bare,
  booth foote and hande go colde:
But belley, God sende thee good ale ynoughe,
  whether it be newe or olde.

was necessary, it was usual with the Roman Catholicks to promise
their tutelary saints to light up candles at their altars, to induce
them to be propituous to such applications as were made to them.
The reader will see a very ridiculous story of this kind in the first
volume of Lord Oxford's Collection of Voyages, p 771, quoted in
Dr. Gray's Notes on Shakspeare, vol. I. p. 7. Erasmus has a
story to the same purpose in his *Naufragium.*

I CAN not cate, but lytle meat,
  my stomacke is not good;
But sure I thinke, that I can drynk
  With him that weares a hood.[21]
Thoughe I go bare, take ye no care,
  I am nothinge a colde;
I stuffe my skyn so full within,
  of joly good ale and olde.
Back and syde, go bare, go bare,
  booth foote and hand go colde:
But belly, God send the good ale inoughe,
  whether it be new or olde.

[22] I love no rost, but a nut-brown toste,
  and a crab layde in the fyre,
A lytle bread shall do me stead,
  much breade I not desyre.

[21] Alluding to the drunkenness of the Fryars.

[22] *I love no rost, but a nut-brown toste,*
  and a crab *layde in the fyre,*] So, in the 3d Act. 4th Scene:
" A cup of ale had in his hand, and *a crab* lay in the fyer."
Again:
" Now *a crab* in the fire were woorth a good grote,
" That I might quaffe with my captn. Tom tospot."
     Like will to like, c. 2.
Again:
" And sometime lurk I in a gossip's bowl,
" In very likeness of a *roasted crab.*"
     Midsummer Night's Dream, A. 2. S. 1.
Upon this last passage, Mr. Steevens has given the following examples of the use of this word:
" Yet we will have in store *a crab* in the fire,
" With nut brown ale."   *Henry V. Anon.*
" And sit down in my chaire by my faire Alison,
" And turn a *crabbe* in the fire as merry as Pope Joan.
     Damon and Pithias, vol. I.
" —— sitting in a corner turning *crabs,*
" Or coughing o'er a warmed pot of ale."
    Description of Christmas in Summer's last Will and Testament, by Nash, 1600.

No froste nor snow, no winde, I trow,
　can hurte mee if I wolde,
I am so wrapt, and throwly lapt
　of joly good ale and olde.
Back and side go bare, &c.

And Tyb my wyfe, that as her lyfe
　loveth well good ale to seeke,
Full ofte drinkes shee, tyll ye may see
　the teares run down her cheekes ;
[23] Then dooth she trowle to mee the bowle,
　even as a mault worme shuld ;
And sayth, sweet hart, I tooke my part
　of this joly good ale and olde.
Back and side go bare, &c.

Now let them drynke, tyll they nod and winke,
　even as good felowes shoulde doe,
They shall not mysse to have the blisse
　good ale doth bringe men to :

[23] *Then dooth she trowle to mee the bowle*,]　" *Trowle*, or *trole the*
" *bowl*, was a common phrase in drinking for passing the vessel
" about, as appears by the following beginning of an old Catch :
　" *Trole*, *trole* the bowl to me,
　" And I will *trole* the same again to thee."
And in this other, in Hilton's Collection :
　" Tom Bouls, Tom Bouls,
　" Seest thou not how merrily this good ale *trowles ?*"
　　　　　Sir John Hawkins's *History of Musick*, vol. III. 22.
Again :
　Sirra Shakebagge, canst thou remember
　Since we *trould the boule* at Sittingburn.
　　　　　　　　Arden of Feversham, 1592.
　Giv't us weele pledge, nor shall a man that lives
　In charity refuse it, I will not be so old
　As not be grac't to honour Cupid, giv't us full,
　When we were young, we could ha *trold* it off,
　Drunke down a Dutchman.
　　　　　　　Marston's Parasitaster or Fawne, A. 5.
　Now the cups *trole* about to wet the gossips whistles,
　It pours down I faith they never think of payment.
　　　　　　　A Chast Mayd in Cheap-side, p. 34.

And all poor soules that have scowred boules,
　　or have them lustely trolde,
God save the lyves of them and their wyves,
　　whether they be yonge or olde.
Back and side go bare, &c.

The Fyrst Sceane.

DICCON.　HODGE.

Diccon. Well done, by Gog's malt, well songe and
　　well sayde :
Come on, mother Chat ,as thou art [24] *a* true mayde.
One fresh pot of ale let's see, to make an ende
Agaynst this colde wether, my naked armes[25] to de-
　　fende :
This gere it warms the soule, now wind blow on thy
　　worst,
And let us drink and swill till that our bellies burste,
Now were he a wyse man, by cunnynge colde defyne
Which way my journey lyeth, or where Diccon will
　　dyne :
But one good turne I have, be it by nyght or daye,
South, east, north or west, I am never out of my waye.
　　Hodge. Chym goodly rewarded, cham I not, do you
　　　　thyncke?
[26] Chad a goodly dynner for all my sweate and swyncke;

---

[24] Add.

[25] *nuked armes*]   See Dekker's Description of an Abraham-man,
p. 4.

[26] *sweate and swyncke;*]   To *swynke* is to work or labour ; as in
Spenser's *Fairy Queen*, B. 2. Cant. 7. St. 8 .
　　" For which men *swink* and sweat incessantly."
Again in *Comus*, by Milton, l. 293 :
　　" And the *swinkt* hedger at his supper sat ,"

Neyther butter, cheese, mylk, onyons, fleshe nor fyshe,
Save thys pece of barly bread, tis a pleasant costly
dishe.

Diccon. Haile, fellow Hodge, and [27] *well* to fare with
thy meat, if you have any :
But by thy words, as I them smelled, thy daintrels be
not manie.

Hodge. Daintrels, Diccon ! Gogs soule man, save
this pece of dry horsbred,
Chat byt no byt this lyve-longe daie, no crome come
in my hed :
My gutts they yawle, crawle, and all my belly rumbleth,
The puddyinges cannot lye still, ech one over other
tumbleth.
By Gog's harte cham so vexte, and in my belly pende,
Chould one peece were at the spittlehouse, another at
the castel's ende.

Diccon. Why Hodge, was there none at home thy
dinner for to set ?

Hodge. Gogs [28] bread, Diccon, ich came to late,
was nothing ther to get :
Gib (a fowle feind might on her light) lickt the milke
pan so clene ;
See Diccon, 'twas not so well washt this seven yere, as
ich wene.

Also, in Chaucer's *Canterbury Tales*, Prol. l. 184 :
  " What shulde he studie, make himselven wood,
  " Upon a book in cloistre alway to pore,
  " Or *swinken* with his hondes, and laboure,
  " As Austin bit? how shal the world be served ?
  " Let Austin have his *swink* to him reserved."
And, in *Pierce Plowman's Vision* :
  " Hermets an heape with hoked staves,
  " Wenten to Walsingham, and her wenches after
  " Great loubees and long, that loth were to *swinke*,
  " Clothed hem in copes, to be knowen from other."

[27] will.

[28] Gogs.

A pestilence lyght on all ill lucke, chad thought yet
    for all this
Of a morsell of bacon behynde the dore, at worst shuld
    not misse :
But when ich sought a slyp to cut, as ich was wont
    to do,
Gogs souls, Diccon, Gyb our cat had eate the bacon to !
    ⌊*Which bacon Diccon stole, as is declared before.*

Diccon. Ill luck, quod he ? mary swere it, Hodg,
    this day the trueth tel,
Thou rose not on thy right syde, or els blest thee not
    wel.
Thy mylk slopt up ! thy bacon filtched ! that was to
    bad luck, Hodg.

Hodge. Nay, nay, ther was a fowler fault, my Gam-
    mer ga me the dodge :
Seest not how cham rent and torn, my heels, my knees,
    and my breech ?
Chad thought as ich sat by the fire, help here and
    there a stitch ;
But there ich was powpte indeed.

Diccon. Why, Hodge ?

Hodge. Bootes not, man, to tell,
Cham so drest amongst a sorte of fooles, chad better
    be in hell,
My Gammar (cham ashamed to say) by God, served
    me not weele.

Diccon. How so, Hodge ?

Hodge. Hase she not gone, trowest now thou, and
    lost her neele ?

Diccon. Her eele, Hodge ! who fysht of late ? that
    was a dainty dysh.

Hodge. Tush, tush, her neele, her neele, her neele,
    man, tys neither flesh nor fysh,
A lytle thing with an hole in the end, as bright as
    any syller,
Small, longe, sharpe at the poynt, and straight as
    any pyller.

Diccon. I know not what a devil thou menest, thou
  bringst me more in doubt.

Hodge. Knowest not with what Tom tailer's man
  sits broching throughe a clout?
A neele, a neele, a neele, my Gammer's neele is gone.

Diccon. Her neele! Hodge, now I smel thee, that
  was a chaunce alone:
By the masse thou hadst a shameful losse, and it were
  but for thy breches.

Hodge. Gog's soule, man, chould give a crown,
  chad it but three stitches.

Diccon. How sayest thou, Hodg? what shuld he
  have again thy nedle got?

Hodge. Be'm vather's soul, and chad it, chould give
  him a new grot.

Diccon. Canst thou keepe counsaille in this case?

Hodge. Els chwold my tonge were out.

Diccon. Do thou [29] but then by my advise, and I
  wil fetch it without doubt.

Hodge. Chyll runne, chyll ryde, chyll dygge, chyll
      delve,
  chyll toyle, chyll trudge, shalt see;
Chyll hold, chyll drawe, chyll pull, chyl pynche,
  chyll kneele on my bare knee;
Chyll scrape, chyll scratche, chyll syfte, chyll seeke,
  chyll bowe, chyll bende, chyll sweate,
Chyll stoop, chyll stur, chyll cap, chyl knele,
  chyll crepe on hands and feete;
Chyll be thy bondman, Diccon, ich sweare by sunne
  and moone,
And channot sumwhat to stop this gap, cham utterly
  undone.
          [*Pointing behind to his torne breeches.*

Diccon. Why, is ther any special cause thou takest
  hereat such sorow?

Hodge. Kirstian Clack, Tom Simson's maid, by the
  masse coms hether to morrow;

29 Than.

Cham not able to say, betweene us what may hap,
She smyled on me the last Sonday when ich put of my
cap.
 Diccon. Well, Hodge, this is a matter of weight, and
  must be kept close,
30 It might els turne to both our costes, as the world
  now gose.
Shalt sware to be no blab, Hodge.
 Hodge. Chyll, Diccon.
 Diccon. Then go to,
Lay thine hand here, say after me, as thou shalt here
  me do.
Haste no booke?
 Hodge. Cha no booke, I.
 Diccon. Then needes must force us both,
Upon my breech to lay thine hand, and there to take
  thine oth.
 Hodge. I Hodge breechelesse,
Sweare to Diccon rechelesse
By the crosse that I shall kysse,
To kepe his counsaile close,
And alwayes me to dispose
To worke that his pleasure is.
    [*Here he kysseth* Diccon's *breech.*
 Diccon. Now, Hodge, see thou take heede,
And doe as I thee byd;
For so I judge it meete,
This nedle againe to win,
There is no shift therein,
But conjure up a spreete.

 30 *It might els turne to both our costes, as the world* now gose.] In
the 14th of Queen Elizabeth, 1572, an act of Parliament passed,
by which very heavy penalties were inflicted on all rogues, Vaga-
bonds, and sturdy beggars. Among others, who are therein described and directed to be deemed such, are idle persons going
about feigning themselves to have knowledge in phisnomie, pal-
mestrie, or other abused sciences, whereby they bear the people in
hand that they can tell their destinies, deaths, and fortunes, *and
such other like fantastical imaginations.* This statute seems to be
alluded to here by Diccon, and will serve to confirm the later date

Hodge. What the great devill, Diccon, I saye?
Diccon. Yea, in good faith, that is the waye,
[31] Fet with some prety charme.
Hodge. Softe, Diccon, be not to hasty yet,
By the masse, for ich begyn to sweat,
Cham afrayde of some [32] harme.
Diccon. Come hether then, and sturre the nat
One inche out of this cyrcle plat,
But stande as l thee teache.
Hodge. And shall ich be here safe from theyr clawes?
Diccon. The mayster devill with his longe pawes
Here to thee cannot reache.
Now will l settle me to this geare.
Hodge. I say Diccon, heare me, heare :
Go softely to thys matter.
Diccon. What devyll, man, art afraide of nought?
Hodge. Canst not tarrye a lytle thought
Tyll ich make a curtesie of water ?*
Diccon. Stand still to it, why shuldest thou feare
hym ?
Hodge. Gog's sydes, Diccon, me thinke ich heare
him,
And tarrye chal mare all.
Diccon. The matter is no worse then I tolde it.
Hodge. By the masse, cham able no longer to holde
it :
[33] So bad, iche must beraye the hall.
Diccon. Stand to it, Hodge, sture not, you horson.
What devyll, be thine ars stringes brusten ?
Thy selfe a while but staye,
The devill I smell hym, wyll be here anone.
Hodge. Hold him fast, Diccon, cham gone, cham
gone,
Chyll not be at that fraye.

of the Play; and at the same time prove the forgery of that assigned to it by Chetwood.
  [31] Fet] i. e. fetched.
  [32] syme.
  * *Tyll ich make a curtesie of water.*] Ut mulieres solent ad min-
gendum. S.
  [33] To.

THE SECOND ACTE.

THE SECOND SCEANE.

DICCON. CHAT.

Diccon. Fy, shytten knave, and out upon thee!
Above all other loutes, fye on thee!
Is not here a clenly prancke?
But thy matter was no better,
Nor thy presence here no sweter,
[34] To flye I con [35] thee thanke.
[36] Here is a matter worthy glosynge
Of Gammer Gurton's needle losynge,
And a foule peece of warke:
A man, I thyncke, myght make a playe
And nede no worde to this they saye,
Being but halté a clarke.

---

[34] *To flye* I con *thee thanke.*] I con him no thanks for it, occurs
in Shakspeare's *All's well that ends well,* and Mr. Steevens says it
means, " I shall not thank him in studied language." I meet
with the same expression in *Pierce Pennilesse his Supplication,* &c.
    " I believe he *will con thee little thanks for it.*"
Again, in *Wily beguiled,* 1613.
    " I *con* master Churms *thanks* for this.
Again, in *Any thing for a quiet life:* " He would not trust you with
" it, *I con* him thanks for it." To *con thanks* may indeed exactly
answer the French *sçavoir gré.* *To con* is to know.
    Cun or *con thanks,* says the Glossary to the Lancashire Dialect,
is to *give thanks* ; and in that sense only the words appear to be
used to this day in the North of England. In Erasmus's *Praise of
Folly,* by Chaloner, 1569, Sig. E 2: " But in the meane whyle ye
" ought to *conne me thanke,*" &c. and Sig. I 4: " —who nathe-
less *conned him a greate thanke,*" &c. Again, in *Pierce Pennilesse
Supplication,* p. 28 : " It is well doone " to practise thy wit, but
" (I believe) our Lord will *cun thee little* thanke for it."
    [35] Can.
    [36] *Here is a matter worthy* glosynge] i. e. glossing or commenting
upon. So, in *Pierce Plowman's Visions* :
      Glosed the Gospel as hem good liked,
      For covetous of copes construe it as thei wold.

Softe, let me alone, I will take the charge,
This matter further to enlarge
Within a tyme shorte;
If ye will marke my toyes, and note,
I will geve ye leave to cut my throte
If I make not good sporte.
Dame, Chat, I say, where be ye, within?
    Chat. Who have we there maketh such a din?
    Diccon. Here is a good fellow, maketh no great
      daunger.
    Chat. What, Diccon? come nere, ye be no straunger:
[37] We be fast set at trump, man, hard by the fyre;
Thou shalt set on the king, if thou come a little nyer.
    Diccon. Nay, nay, there is no tarying: I must be gone
      againe;
But first for you in councel* I have a word or twaine.
    Chat. Come hether Dol; Dol, sit downe and play this
      game,
And as thou sawest me do, see thou do even the same:
There is five trumps besides the queene, the hindmost
      thou shalt finde her,
Take hede of Sim Glover's wife, she hath an eie behind
      her.

[37] *We be fast set at* trump, man, *hard by the fyre;*] The common etymology of the word *trump*, as made use of in games at cards, derives it from a corruption of *triumph*; but Ben Jonson spells the word *tromp*, from which Mr. Whalley conjectures that his Author thought it was derived from the French *tromper*, to deceive. And indeed it will easily bear this acceptation. A person playing at the game thinks he shall win the trick, till his adversary takes it from him by a *tromp*; he is *trompt*, or deceived,
          Whalley Note on *The New Inn*, A. 1. S. 3.
   Trump was a game played with cards, as will appear by the following passage of Dekker's *Bellman of London*, Sig. F 2: "To "speake of all the sleights used by *card-players* in all sorts of games "would but weary you that are to read, and bee but a thanklesse "and unpleasing labour for me to set them downe. Omitting "therefore the deceipts practised (even in the fayrest and most "civill companies) at Primero, Saint Maw, *Trump*, and such like "games, I will, &c."
   * *In councel*—] i. e. in secrecy. See Note to the *Merry Wives of Windsor*, edit. 1778, vol. I. p. 228. S.

Now, Diccon, say your will.

Diccon. Nay, softe a little yet,
I wold not tell my sister, the matter is so great,
[38] There I wil have you sweare by our dere lady of Bullaine,
Saint Dunstone and saint Donnyke,* with the three
kinges of Kullaine,[39]
That ye shal keepe it secret.

---

[38] *There I wil have you sweare by our dere lady of Bullaine.*] Mr.
Hawkins says probably *Lady Ann Bullen*, than which there could
hardly have been a conjecture more wide from the meaning of the
speaker.   Our dere Lady of Bullaine is no other than the image of
the Vigin Mary at Boulogne, which was formerly held in so much
reverence, that it was one of those to which Pilgrimages used to
be made.   In Chaucer's *Canterbury Tales*, Prol. l. 465, describing
the *Wife of Bath*, he says:
   " And thries hadde she ben at Jerusaleme.
   " She hadde passed many a strange streme.
   " At Rome she hadde ben, and at *Boloine*,
   " In Galice at Seint James, and at Coloine.
The Virgin Mary was the patroness of the town of Boulogne in a
very singular manner, it being holden immediately of her: " For
" when King Lewis II. after the decease of Charles of Burgundy,
" had taken in Boulogne, anno 1477, as new Lord of the town (thus
" John de Serres relateth it), he did homage without sword or spurs
" bareheaded, and on his knee, before the Virgin Mary, offering
" unto her image an heart of massie gold, weighing 2000 crowns.
" He added also this, that he and his successors kings after him
" should hold the county of Boulogne of the said Virgin, and do
" homage unto her image in the great church of the higher town
" dedicated to her name, paying at every change of a vassal an
" heart of pure gold of the same weight."
                    Heylin's *Survey of France*, 1656, p. 193.
   * *Saint Donnyke,*] i. e. Saint Dominick. S.
[39] *— with the three kinges of Kullaine,*] The three kings of Coloyn
are supposed to have been the wise men who travelled unto our
Saviour by the direction of the star.   To these kings, several
writers have given the names of Gaspar, Melchior, and Balthazar;
but Sir Thomas Browne, in his *Vulgar Errors*, has a whole chapter
concerning them, in which he doubts all the principal facts in the
account of them. See B. 7. C. 8.   The celebrated Thomas Coryat,
when at Coloyn, took some pains to collect many circumstances
relative to these kings, with which he hath filled several pages of
his Book; and to which those who are desirous of further information on the subject must be referred.

Chat. Gog's bread, that will I doo,
As secret as mine owne thought, by God and the devil
too [40]

Diccon. Here is Gammer Gurton, your neighbour, a
sad and hevy wight,
Her goodly faire red cock at home, was stole this last
night.

Chat. Gog's soul! her cock with the yelow legs, that
nightly crowded * so just?

Diccon. That cocke is stollen.

Chat. What, was he fet out of the hen's ruste?

Diccon. I can not tel where the devil he was kept,
under key or locke,
But Tib hath tykled in Gammer's eare, that you shoulde
steale the cocke.

Chat. [41] Have I? strong hoore, by brea dand salte—

Diccon. What softe, I say be styl.
Say not one word for all this geare.

Chat. By the masse, that I wyl,
I wil have the yong hore by the head, and the old trot
by the throte.

Diccon. Not one word, dame Chat, I say, not one
word for my cote.

Chat. Shall such a begar's brawle † as that, thinkest
thou, make me a theefe?
The pocks light on her hores sydes, a pestilence and
mischeefe.

[40] Two.

* *crowded*] A crowd is a small fiddle. Hence the name of
Crowdero, in Hudibras. Crowded means—made a musical noise.
See Note on Alexander and Campaspe, p. 103. S.

[41] *Have I? strong hoore* by bread and salte—] This oath occurs
again, A. 5. S. 2:
   " Yet shal we find no other wight save she *by bread and salt.*"
From the following passage, in Nash's *Lenten Stuff*, 1599, it
may be inferred that it was once customary to eat *bread and salt*
previous to the taking an oath: " Venus, for Hero was her Priest,
" and Juno Lucina the Midwife's Goddess, for she was now
" quickned, and cast away by the cruelty of Æolus, took *bread and*
" *salt*, and eat it, that they would be smartly revenged on that
" truculent, windy jailor ; &c."

† *begar's brawle*]   I suppose she means beggar's *brawling*, or
squalling infant.   See note 22, to *The Jovial Crew*, vol. 10, p. 357.

Come out, thou hungry nedy bytche; O that my nails
    be short!

   Diccon. Gog's bred, woman, hold your peace, this
    gere wil els passe sport;

I wold not for an hundred pound, this matter shuld be
    knowen

That I am auctour of this tale, or have abrode it blowen.

Did ye not sweare ye wold be ruled, before the tale I
    tolde?

I said ye must all secret keepe and ye said sure ye
    wolde.

   Chat. Wolde you suffer your selfe Diccon, such a
    sort to revile you

With slaunderous words to blot your name, and so to
    defile you?

   Diccon. No, good wife Chat, I wold be loth such
    drabs shulde blot my name;

But yet ye must so order all, that Diccon beare no
    blame.

   Chat. [42] Go to then, what is your rede, say on your
    minde, ye shall mee rule herein.

   Diccon. Godamercye dame Chat, in faith thou must
    the gere begin:

It is twenty pound to a goose turd my gammer will not
    tary.

But hether ward she comes as fast as her legs can her
    cary,

---

[42] *Go to then, what is your* rede, *say on your minde, ye shall mee* rule
herein.] *Rede,* i. e. counsel or advice. So, in A. 4. S. 2:

   Therefore I *rede* you three, go hence and within keepe close.

Again,

   Well, if ye will be ordred and do by my *reade.*

Again. A. 5. S. 2.

   And where ye sat he said ful certain, if I wold folow his *read.*

Again, in Erasmus's *Praise of Folie,* by Chaloner, Sig. D 4: " Unles
" perchaunce some would chose suche a souldier as Demosthenes,
" who folowying Archilocus, the poetes *rede* scarce lookynge his ene-
" mies in the face, threw downe his sheelde and ranne awaie as
" cowardly a warriour as he was a wyse oratour."

   The old Version of the singing Psalms also begins in this manner:

     The man is blest that hath not bent

      To wicked *rede* his ear.

To brawle with you about her cocke, for well I hard Tib
    say,
The cocke was rosted in your house, to breakfast yester-
    day:
And when ye had the carcas eaten, the fethers ye out
    fiunge,
And Doll, your maid, the legs she hid a foote depe in
    the dunge.
    Chat. O gracyous God, my heart it burstes!
    Diccon. Well, rule your self a space,
And gammer Gurton when she commeth anon into
    thys place,
Then to the queane let's see *ye* [43] tell her your mynd,
    and spare not,
So shall Diccon blamelesse bee; and then go to, I care
    not.
    Chat. Then hoore, beware her throte, I can abide no
    longer:
In faith, old witch, it shal be seene which of us two be
    stronger;
And Diccon, but at your request, I wold not stay one
    howre.
    Diccon. Well, keepe it in till she be here, and then
    out let it powre.
In the meane while get you in, and make no wordes of
    this;
More of this matter within this howre to here you shall
    not miss.
Because I know you are my friend, hide it I cold not
    doubtles:
Ye know your harm, see ye be wise about your owne
    busines,
So fare ye well.
    Chat. Nay, soft Diccon, and drynke: what, Doll, I
    say,
Bringe here a cup of the best ale, let's see, come quicly
    awaye.

[43] Addition.
Ye is an unnecessary addition. The construction is—Then let
us see to the queane, &c. S.

THE SECOND ACTE.

THE THIRD SCEANE.

HODGE.   DICCON.

Diccon. Ye see, masters, that one end tapt of this
     my short devise,
Now must we broche t'other to, before the smoke arise,
And by the time they have a while run,
          I trust ye need not crave it,
But loke what lieth in both their harts, ye ar like sure
     to have it.
Hodge. Yea, Gog's soul, art alive yet? what Diccon,
     dare ich come?
Diccon. A man is well hied to trust to thee, I wil say
     nothing but mum.
But and ye come any nearer, I pray you see all be
     sweete.
Hodge. [44] Tush man, is gammer's neele found? that
     chould gladly weete.
Diccon. She may thanke thee it is not found, for if
     you had kept thy standing,
The devil he wold have fet it out, ev'n Hodg, at thy
     commanding.
Hodge. Gog's hart! and cold he tel nothing wher
     the neele might be found?
Diccon. Ye foolysh dolt, ye were to seek, ear we had
     got our ground;
Therfore his tale so doubtfull was, that I cold not
     perceive it.
Hodge. Then ich se wel somthing was said, chope
     one day yet to have it.

---

[44] *Tush man, is gammer's neele found? that chould gladly* weete.]
i. e. gladly know. So, in Shakspeare's *Anthony and Cleopatra*,
A 1. S. 1:
          " — in which, I bind
     " On pain of punishment, the world *to weete*,
     " We stand up peerless."
The word *weet* is also used by Spenser and Fairfax.

[45] But Diccon, Diccon, did not the devill cry, ho, ho,
    ho?

    Diccon. If thou hadst taryed where thou stood'st,
        thou woldest have said so.

    Hodge. Durst swere of a boke, chard him rore,
        streight after ich was gone;

But tel me Diccon, what said the knave, let me here
    it anon.

    Diccon. The horson talked to mee, I know not well
        of what:

[46] One whyle his tonge it ran, and paltered of a cat,
Another whyle he stammered styll upon a rat;
Last of all there was nothing but every word chat,
    chat;
But this I well perceyved before I wold him rid,
Betweene chat and the rat, and the cat the nedle is
    hyd:

---

[45] *But Diccon, Diccon, did not the devill cry, ho, ho, ho?*]   In the
ancient moralities, and in many of the earliest entertainments of
the stage, the devil is introduced as a character, and it appears to
have been customary to bring him before the audience with this cry
of *ho, ho, ho.*   See particularly the *Devil is an Ass,* by Ben Jonson,
A. 1. S. 1.   From the following passages, in *Wily beguiled,* 1606,
we learn the manner in which the character used to be dressed:
" Tush! fear not the dodge: I'll rather put on my flashing red
" nose and my flaming face, and come wrap'd in a calf's skin, and
" cry, *ho, ho,* &c."   Again, " I'll put me on my great carnation
" nose, and wrap me in a rowsing calf's skin suit, and come like
" some hobgoblin, or some devil ascended from the grisly pit of
" hell; and like a scarbabe make him take his legs: I'll play the
" devil I warrant ye."

[46] *One whyle his tonge it ran, and* paltered *of a cat,*]   To *palter,* is,
as Dr. Johnson explains it, *to shuffle,* with ambiguous expressions.
Thus,
       " And be these juggling fiends no more believ'd,
       " That *palter* with us in a double sense."
                         Macbeth, A. 5. S. 7.
In confirmation of Dr. Johnson's explanation, Mr. Steevens pro-
duces the following instances:
       " Now fortune frown, and *palter* if thou please."
                    Marius and Sylla, 1594.
         " — Romans that have spoke the word,
      " And will not *palter.*"
Englishmen for money, C. 3.   O. G.

Now wether Gib our cat have eate it in her mawe,
Or doctor Rat our curat have found it in the straw,
Or this dame Chat your neighbour have stollen it God
    hee knoweth,
But by the morrow at this time, we shal learn how the
    matter goeth.
    Hodge. Canst not learn to night man, seest not what
    is here ?
              [*Pointyng behind to his torne breeches.*
Diccon. Tys not possyble to make it sooner appere.
Hodge. Alas Diccon, then chave no shyft ; but least
    ich tary to longe,
Hye me to Sym Glover's shop, theare to seeke for a
    thonge,
Therwith this breech to tatche and tye as ich may.
    Diccon. To morow, Hodg, if we chaunce to meete,
    shall see what I will say.

THE SECOND ACTE.

THE FOURTH SCEANE.

DICCON.   GAMMER.

Diccon. Now this gere must forward goe, for here
    my Gammer commeth :
Be still a while and say nothing, make here a little
    romth.*
    Gammer. Good lord ! shall never be my lucke my
    neelĕ agayne to spye?
Alas the whyle, tys past my helpe ; where 'tis, still it
    must lye.
    Diccon. Now, Jesus, gammer Gurton, what driveth
    you to this sadnes?
I feare me, by my conscience, you will sure fall to
    madnes.

---

* *a little romth.*]   I suppose he means to say—a little *room* ; and
therefore retires till Gammer Gurton has uttered her complaint. S.

Gammer. Who is that? what Diccon? cham lost,
　　man : fye, fye.

Diccon. Mary, fye on them that be worthy; but
　　what shuld be your troble?

Gammer. Alas, the more ich thinke on it, my sorow
　　it waxeth double.

My goodly tossing* Sporyar's neele†, chave lost ich
　　not where.

Diccon. Your neele! whan?

Gammer. My neele (alas!) ich myght full it spare,

As God himselfe he knoweth nere one besyde chave.

　　Diccon. If this be all, good gammer, I warrant you
　　all is save.

Gammer. Why, know you any tydings which way my
　　neele is gone?

Diccon. Yea, that I do, doubtlesse, as ye shall here
　　anone,

A see a thing this matter toucheth, within these twenty
　　howres,

Even at this gate, before my face, by a neyghbour of
　　yours;

She stooped me downe, and up she toke up a needle or
　　a pyn,

I durst be sworne it was even yours, by all my mother's
　　kyn.

　　Gammer. It was my neele, Diccon, ich wot; for here
　　even by this poste

Ich sat, what time as ich up starte, and so my neele it
　　loste:

* *tossing*] I imagine this word was formerly used to signify
sharp. So in *The Woman's Prize*, by Beaumont and Fletcher, A. 2.
S.5 :

　　" They heave ye stool on stool, and fling main pot-lids
　　" Like massy rocks, dart ladles, tossing irons
　　" And tongs like thunder-bolts, till overlaid
　　" They fall beneath the weight."

In the two last editions of these authors, the word *tossing* is, I
think very improperly altered by Mr. Sympson to toasting.　S.

　　† *Sporyar's neele,*] The ancient spurs were fixed into straps of
leather. Spurriers of course would be obliged to use very strong
needles. S.

Who was it, leive son? speke ich pray the, and
  quickly tell me that.
Diccon. A suttle queane as any in this towne,
  your neyghboure here, dame Chat.
Gammer. Dame Chat! Diccon, let me be gone, chil
  thyther in post haste.
Diccon. [48] Take my councell yet, or ye go, for feare
  ye walke in wast.
It is a murrion crafty drab, and froward to be pleased,
And ye take not the better way, your [49] nedle yet ye
  lose it:
For when she tooke it up, even here before your doores,
What soft, dame Chat (quoth I) that same is none of
  yours.
Avaunt (quoth she) syr knave, what pratest thou of that
  I fynd?
I wold thou hadst kist me I wot whear: (she ment I
  know behind)

[47] *Who was it, leive son?*] Who was it dear son? So, in the
Ballad of Adam Bell, Clym of the Clough, and William of Cloudesly:
  Ye myght have asked towres and townes,
    Parkes and forestes plente,
  But none soe pleasant to my pay, shee sayd;
    Nor none so *lefe* to me.   Percy's *Reliques,* vol. I. 167.
[48] *Take my councell, or ye go,*] i. e. ere ye go. As in the follow-
ing instances:
  A. 3. S. 2 :
" Ich know who found it, and tooke it up shalt see *or* it be longe."
  A. 4. S. 2 :
" That *or* ye cold go twyce to church, I warrant you here news."
  Ibid.
  " But *or* all came to an ende, I set her in a dumpe."
Hall's *Chronicle, Henry* IV. 1550, p. 8 :
  " But *or* this deposition was executed in time he came to West-
" minster, &c."
  Ibid. p. 28 :
  " Wherof the kyng beyng advertysed, caused a great army to be
" assembled and marched toward his enemies, but *or* the kyng came
" to Notyngbam, &c."
Ascham's *Toxophilus:*
  " For first, as it is manye a yeare *or* they begin to be great
" shooters, &c."
        See also Mr. Steevens's Shakspeare, vol. V. p. 101.
[49] *your*] our, first edition.

[50] And home she went as brag as it had ben a bodelouce,
And I after her, as bold as it had ben the goodman of
    the house:
But there and ye had hard her, how she began to
    scolde,
The tonge it went on patins, by hym that Judas solde;
Ech other worde I was a knave, and you a hore of
    hores,
Because I spake in your behalfe, and sayde the neele
    was yours.

> *Gammer.* [51] Gogs bread! and thinks the callet thus
> to kepe my neele me fro?
>
> *Diccon.* Let her alone, and she minds non other, but
> even to dresse you so.
>
> *Gammer.* By the masse, chil rather spend the cote
> that is on my backe.

Thinks the false quean by such a slight [52] that chill my
    neele lacke?

> *Diccon.* Slip not your [53] gere, I counsell you, but of
> this take good hede,

Let not be knowen I told you of it, how well soever ye
    spede.

---

[50] *And home she went as brag as it had ben a bodelouce,*] " As brisk
" as a body-louse was formerly proverbial."

See Ray's *Proverbs*, 1742, p. 219.

[51] *Gogs bread! and thinks the* callet *thus to kepe my neele me fro?*]
" Callet a lewd woman, a drab, perhaps so called from the French
" *calote,* which was a sort of head-dress worn by country girls."

See Glossary to *Urry's Chaucer.*

So, in the *Supposes,* by Geo Gascoigne, A. 5. S. 6: " Come
" hither you old *callat,* you tattling huswife: that the devil cut out
" your tongue." See other instances in Dr. Grey's Notes on Shakspeare, vol. II p. 41.

Again, Ben Jonson's *Fox,* A. 4. S. 3

" Why, the callet
" You told me of here I have ta'en disguis'd."

Callett is elsewhere used for stupid, inactive:

Bid maudlin lay the cloth, take up the meat;
Look how she stirres; you sullen elfe, you *callett,*
Is this the haste you make?

Englishman for my Money, 4to. 1631.   O. G.

[52] slygh.   First Edition.
[53] Slepe not you gere.   First Edition.

Gammer. Chil in, Diccon, a cleene aperne to take,
    and set before me;
And ich may my neele once see, chil sure remember
    the.

THE SECOND ACTE.

THE FIFTH SCEANE.

Diccon. Here will the sporte begin, if these two
    once may meete,
Their chere, durst lay money, will prove scarsly sweete.
My gammer sure entends to be uppon her bones,
With staves, or with clubs, or els with coble stones.*
Dame Chat on the other syde, if she be far behynde,
I am right far deceived, she is geven to it of kynde.†
He that may tarry by it a whyle, and that but shorte,
I warrant hym trust to it, he shall see all the sporte.
Into the towne will I, my frendes to vysit there,
And hether straight againe to see th' end of this gere.
[54] In the meane time, felowes, pype upp your fiddles, I
    saie take them,
And let your freyndes here such mirth as ye can make
    them.

THE THIRD ACTE.

THE FYRST SCEANE.

Hodge. Sym Glover yet gramercy! cham meetlye
    well sped now,
Th'art even as good a felow as ever kyste a cowe.

* *coble stones*] *i. e.* pebble-stones. A *cobble*, in the north, signifies a *pebble*. To *cobble*, is to thraw stones. See Ray. S.
† *of kynde.*] *i. e.* by nature. S.
[54] *In the meane time, felowes, pype upp,* &c.] This passage evi-
dently shews, that music playing between the acts was introduced
in the earliest of our dramatic entertainments.

Here is a thynge[55] in dede, by the masse though ich
    speake it,
[56] Tom Tankard's great bald curtal, I thinke could not
    breake it.
And when he spyed my neede, to be so straight and
    hard,
Hays lent me here his naull, to set the gyb forward.*
As for my gammer's neele, the flyenge feynd go weete,
Chill not now go to the doore again with it to meete.
Chould make shyfte good enough, and chad a candels
    ende
The cheefe hole in my breeche, with these two chill
    amende.

THE THIRD ACTE.

THE SECOND SCEANE.

GAMMER.   HODGE.

Gammer. How, Hodge! mayst nowe be glad, cha
    newes to tell thee,
Ich knowe who hais my neele, ich trust soone shalt it
    see.
Hodge. The devyll thou does: hast hard gammer in
    deede, or doest but jest?
Gammer. Tys as true as steele, Hodge.
Hodge. Why, knowest well where dydst leese it?

---

[55] Mr. Dodsley altered this word to *thong.*
[56] *Tom Tankard's great bald* curtal,] *Curtal* is a *small horse;* properly one who hath his tail *docked or curtailed.* So, in Dekker's
Villanies discovered by Lanthorne and Candlelight, &c. 1620, Sig H.:
"He could shewe more crafty foxes in this wild goose chase, then
"there are white foxes in Russia; and more strange horse-trickes
"plaide by such riders, then *Bankes his curtal* did ever practise
"(whose gambals of the two were the honester)."
   * — *to set the gyb forward.*] A naval phrase. The gib is the
gib-sail. To set a sail, is also the technical term. S.

Gammer. Ich know who found it, and tooke it up,
    shalt see or it be longe.
Hodge. God's mother dere, if that be true, farwel
    both naule and thong.
But who hais it, gammer, say? one chould faine here
    it disclosed.
Gammer. That false fixen, that same dame Chat,
    that counts her selfe so honest.
Hodge. Who tolde you so?
Gammer. That same did Diccon the bedlam, which
    saw it done.
Hodge. Diccon! it is a vengeable knave, gammer,
    'tis a bonable * horson,
Can do mo things than that, els cham deceyved evil:
By the masse ich saw him of late cal up a great blacke
    devill.
O, the knave cryed ho, ho, he roared and he thundred,
And ye'ad bene here, cham sure you'ld murrenly ha
    wondred.
Gammer. Was not thou afraide, Hodge, to see him
    in this place?
Hodge. No, and chad come to me, chould have laid
    him on the face,
Chould have promised him.
Gammer. But Hodge, had he no horns to pushe?
Hodge. As long as your two armes. Saw ye never
    fryer Rushe
Painted on a cloth, with a side long cowe's tayle,
And crooked cloven feet, and many a hoked nayle?
For al the world (if I shuld judg) chould reckon him
    his brother:
[57] Loke even what face frier Rush had, the devil had
    such another.

---

* — *bonable*] I suppose he means to say *banable*, from to *ban*,
to curse; a rogue that ought to be execrated. S.
[57] *Loke even what face frier Rush had*,] *Fryar Rush* is mentioned
. in *Reginald Scot's Discoverie of Witchcraft*, 1584, p. 522: " *Frier*
" *Rush* was for all the world such another fellow as this *Hudgin*,
" and brought up even in the same schoole; to wit, in a kitchen:
" insomuch as the selfesame tale is written of the one as of the

Gammer. Now Jesus mercy, Hodge, did Diccon in
    him bring?

Hodge. Nay, gammer (heare me speke) chil tel you
    a greater thing.

The devil, when Diccon bad him (ich hard him
    wondrous weel)

Sayd plainly (here before us) that dame Chat had your
    neele.

Gammer. Then let us go, and aske her wherefore
    she minds to kepe it,

Seeing we know so much, 'tware madness now to
    slepe it.

Hodge. Go to her, gammer, see ye not where she
    stands in her doores?

Byd her geve you the neele, 'tys none of hers but yours.

THE THIRD ACTE.

THE THIRD SCBANE.

GAMMER. CHAT. HODGE.

Gammer. Dame Chat, cholde praye the fair, let me
    have that is mine,

Chil not this twenty yeres take one fart that is thyne;

Therfore give me mine owne, and let me live besyde
    the.

Chat. Why art thou crept from home hether to mine
    own doores to chide me?

Hence, doting drab, avaunt, or I shall set the further.

Intends thou and this knave, mee in my house to
    murther?

Gammer. Tush! gape not so; [58] no woman, shalt
    not yet eate mee,

Nor all the frends thou hast, in this shall not intreat
    mee;

" other concerning the skullian, which is said to have beene slaine,
" &c. For the reading whereof I referre you to *Frier Rush* his
" storie, or else to *John Wierus De præstigiis demonum.*"
   [58] me.

Mine owne Goods I will have, and aske the no [59]
    beleve :

What woman; pore folks must have right, though the
    thing you agreve.

    Chat. Give thee thy right, and hang the up, with
    all thy bagger's broode ;

What, wilt thou make me a theefe, and say I stole thy
    good ?

    Gammer. Chil say nothing (ich warrant thee) but
    that ich can prove it well,

Thou fet my good even from my doore, cham able this
    to tell.

    Chat. Did I (olde witch) steal oft was thine ? *
    how should that thing be knowen ?

    Gammer. Ich can not tell, but up thou tokest it as
    though it had bin thine own.

    Chat. Mary, fy on thee, thou old Gyb, with al my
    very hart.

    Gammer. [60] Nay, fy on thee thou rampe, thou ryg,†
    with al that take thy part.

    Chat. A vengeaunce on those lips that laieth such
    things to my charge.

    Gammer. A vengeaunce on those callats hips, whose
    conscience is so large.

    Chat. Come out, hogge.

    Gammer. Come out, hogge, and let have me right.

    Chat Thou arrant witche.

    Gammer. Thou bawdie bitche chil make thee curse
    this night.

---

[59] on.

* *oft was thine*?] i. e. aught, any thing. S,

[60] *Nay, fy on thee* thou rampe, &c.] Dr. Gabriel Harvey, in his
Pierce's Supererogation, 4to. 1593. speaking of Long Meg of Westminster, says : "Although she were a lusty, bouncing *rampe,*
" somewhat like Gallimetta, or maid Marian, yet was she not
" such a roinish rannel, such a dissolute flirt gillian," &c.

† *ryg,*] i. e. thou strumpet. See Note on *Antony and Cleopatra,*
Shaks. 1778, vol. 8. p. 175. S.

So in Davies's Scourge of Folly, 12mo :

    " Or wanton *Rigg,* or letcher dissolute
    " Do stand at Powles Crosse in a sheeten sute." I. R.

Chat. A bag and a wallet.*

Gammer. A carte for a callet.

Chat. Why [61] wenest thou thus to prevaile?
I hold thee a grote,
I shall patche thy coate.

Gammer. Thou warte as good kysse my tayle;
[62]Thou slut, thou kut, thou rakes, thou jakes, will not
 shame make thee hide the [63]?

Chat. Thou skald, thou bald, thou roten,* thou
 glotton, I will no longer chyd thee:
But I will teache the to kepe home.

Gammer. Wylt thou, drunken beaste?

Hodge. Sticke to her, gammer, take her by the head,
 chil warrant you this feast.

---

* *A bag and wallet.*] *i. e.* the accoutrements of an itinerant trull.
                                                            S.

[61] — *wenest*] Thinkest or imaginest. Obsolete. It occurs
again, A. 5. S. 2:
  " *I weene*, the ende will prove this brawle did first arise
  " Upon no other ground, but only Diccon's lyes."
Again, in *Euphues*, 1581, p. 14 : " *Weenest* thou that he wil have
" no mistrust of thy faithfulnesse, when he hath had tryall of thy
" ficklenesse ?"

[62] *Thou slut, thou* kut,] *Cut* appears to have been an opprobrious term used by the vulgar when they scolded or abused each
other. It occurs again, A. 5. S. 2: " That lying *cut* is lost, that
" she is not swinged and beaten."
  A horse is sometimes called *Cut* in our ancient writers, as in the
First Part of *Henry* IV. A. 2. S. 1. and Falstaffe says : " — if I
" tell thee a lye spit in my face, and call me *horse*." *Cut* is therefore probably used in the same sense as *horse*, to which it seems to
have been synonymous. Several instances of the use of this term
are collected by Mr. Steevens, in his edition of Shakspeare ; see
vol. IV. p. 202.
  It appears probable to me that the opprobrious epithet *Cut* arose
from the practice of cutting the hair of convicted thieves; which
was anciently the custom in England, as appears from the edicts of
John de Northampton against adulterers, who thought, with Paulo
Migante, that
     " England ne'er would thrive,
     " Till all the whores were burnt alive."
              See Holinshed, vol. 9. 754, Ed. 1807.   O. G.
[63] The addition.
† *thou roten*,] *i. e.* rat. So in one of the Chester Whitsun plays :
     " Here is a *rotten*, there a mouse." S.

Smyte, I saye, gammer,

Bite, I say, gammer

I trow ye wyll be keene ;

Where be your nayls? claw her by the jawes, pull me
    out both her eyen.

Gog's bones, gammer, holde up your head.

    Chat. I trow drab, I shall dresse thee.

Tary, thou knave, I hold the a grote, I shall make
    these hands blesse thee.

Take thou this, old hore, for amends, and learn thy
    tonge well to tame,

And say thou met at this bickering, not [64] thy fellow
    but thy dame.

    Hodge. Where is the strong stued hore ? * chil ge'r a
    hore's marke.

Stand out one's way, that ich kyll none in the darke.

Up, gammer, and ye be alyve, chil feyght [65] now for us
    bothe ;

Come no nere me, thou scalde callet, to kyll the ich
    wer loth.

    Chat. Art here agayne, thou hoddypeke? † what Doll,
    bryng me out my spitte.

    Hodge. Chyll broche thee wyth this, by'm father's
    soul, chyll conjure that foule sprete.

Let dore stand, Cock, why coms indeed? keep dore,
    thou horson, boy.

    Chat. Stand to it, thou dastard, for thine eares, ise
    teche the sluttish toye.

---

[64] — *not thy fellow but thy dame.*] Not thy equal, but thy mistress.

* *strong stued hore?*] *i. e.* rank strumpet from the stews. S.

[65] *feyght*] feygh, first edition.

† *thou hoddypeke?*] *i. e.* hodmandod. S.

I find this word used in *Nashe's Anatomie of Absurditie,* 1589,
Sig. B. where it seems intended as synonymous to *cuckold.* " But
" women, through want of wisedome, are growne to such wanton-
" nesse, that uppon no occasion they will crosse the streete, to
" have a glaunce of some gallant, deeming that men by one
" looke of them shoulde be in love with them, and will not stick
" to make an errant over the way, to purchase a paramour to help
" at a pinche, who, under hur husband's, that *hoddy peekes* nose,
" must have all the destilling dew of his delicate rose, leaving him
" onely a sweet sent, good inough for such a sencelesse sotte."

Hodge. Gog's woundes, hore, chile make the avaunte,
Take heed, Cocke, pull in the latche.

Chat. I faith, sir loose breche, had ye taried ye shold
have found your match.

Gammer. [66] Now ware thy throte, losel, thouse pay
for al.

Hodge Well said, gammer, by my soule.
Hoyse her, souse her, bounce her, trounce her, pull
her throte houle.

Chat. Comst behynd me, thou withered witch ? and
I get once on foote,
Thouse pay for all, thou old tarlether, ile teach thee
what longs to it.
Take the this to make up thy mouth, til time thou
come by more.

Hodge. Up, gammer, stand on your feete, where is
the old hore ?
Faith, woulde chad her by the face,
chould cracke her callet crowne.

Gammer. Ah Hodg, Hodg, where was thy help,
when fixen had me downe !

Hodge. By the masse, Gammer, but for my staffe,
Chat had gone nye to spyl you.
Ich think the harlot had not cared, and chad not com,
to kill you.
But shall we loose our neele thus?

---

[66] *Now ware thy throte, losel, thouse pay for al*] A *losel* is a worth-
less fellow.   It is a term of contempt frequently used by Spenser.
It is likewise to be met with in the *Death of Robert Earl of Hun-
tingdon*, 1601 :
"To have the lozels company."
Again, in *The Pinner of Wakefield*, 1599 :
"Peace prating lozel, &c.
See Mr. Steevens's Notes on Shakspeare, vol. IV. p. 337.
Again, in Hall's Satires, 1753, p. 78 :
"How his enraged ghost would stamp and stare,
"That Cæsar's throne is turn'd to Peter chayre
"To see an old shorne *lozell* perched high,
"Crossing beneath a golden canopy."
See Holinshed's Chron. vol. II. 740—5 Day's Pastime, 67, 4to.
1578—Englishmen for my Money, 42—Holinshed, V. 208.

O. G.

Gammer. No, Hodge, chwarde lothe doo soo.
Thinkest thou chill take that at her hand? no Hodg,
    ich tell the no.
    Hodge. Chold yet this fray were wel take up, and
        our own neele at home,
'Twill be my chaunce els some to kil, where ever it be
    or whom.
    Gammer. We have a parson, (Hodge thou knowes)
        a man estemed wise,
Mast doctor Rat, chil for hym send, and let me here
    his advise.
[67] He will her shrive for all this gere, and geve her pe-
    naunce strait,
Wese have our neele, els dame Chat comes nere within
    heaven gate.
    Hodge. Ye mary, Gammer, that ich think best:
        wyll you now for him sende?
The sooner Doctor Rat be hère, the sooner wese ha
    an ende.
And here gammer, Dyccon's devill (as iche remember
    well)
Of Cat and Chat, and doctor Rat, a felloneus tale dyd
    tell,

---

[67] *He will* shrive *her for all this gere, and geve her penaunce strait,*]
To shrive is to confess.

    " But afterwards she gan him soft to *shrieve*,
    " And wooè with faire intreatie to disclose,
    " Which of the Nymphes his heart so sore did mieve."
                            Fairy Queen, B. 4. c. 12. § 26.
    " The King call'd downe his nobles all,
    " By one, by two, by three,
    " Earl Marshall I'le goe *shrive* the queen,
    " And thou shalt wend with mee."
                    Percy's *Reliques of Ancient Poetry,* vol. II. p. 156.
    " Oh fearful! if thou wilt not, give me leave
    " To *shrive* her; lest she should die unabsolv'd."
                    'Tis pity she's a Whore, vol. VII. A. 2.
    " And truelye Philautus thou shalt not *shrive* mee like a Ghoast-
    " lye Father, for to thee I will confesse in two thinges my extreame
    " folly."   *Euphues and his England,* 1582, p. 49.

Chold you forty pound, that is the way your neele to
    get againe.
  Gammer. Chil ha him strait; call out the boy, wese
    make him take the payne.
  Hodge. What Coke, I saye, come out; what devill
    can'st not here?
  [68] *Cocke.* How now, Hodg, how does, gammer? is
    yet the wether cleare?
What wold chave me to doo?
  Gammer. Come hither, Cocke, anon.
Hence swythe to doctor Rat, hye the that thou were gone,
And pray hym come speke with me, cham not well
    at ease,
Shalt have him at his chamber, or els at mother Bee's,
Els seeke him at Hobfylcher's shop; for, as charde it
    reported,
There is the best ale in al the towne, and now is most
    resorted.
  Cocke. And shall ich brynge him with me, Gammer?
  Gammer. Yea, by and by, good Cocke.
  [69] *Cocke.* Shalt see that shall be here anone, els let
    me have one the dock.
  Hodge. Now, gammer, shal we two go in, and tary
    for hys commynge?
What devill, woman, plucke up your hart, and leve of
    al this gloming.*
Though she were stronger at the first, as ich thinke
    ye did find her.
[70] Yet there ye drest the dronken sow, what time ye
    cam behind her.
  Gammer. Nay, nay, cham sure she lost not all, for
    set them to the beginning,
And ich doubt not, but he will make small bost of her
    winning.

---

[68] *Cocke.*] Gammer, in the first edition.
[69] *Cocke.*] Hodge, in the first edition.
* *this gloming.*] i. e. sulky, gloomy looks. It is still said, in
vulgar language, that a discontented person looks *glum.* S.
[70] This line given to Gammer Gurton in the first edition.

THE THIRD ACTE.

THE FOURTH SCEANE.

TYB.   HODGE.   GAMMER.   COCKE.

Tyb. Se gammer, gammer, Gib our cat, cham afraid
    what she ayleth,
She standes me gasping behind the doore,
       as though her winde her faileth.
Now let ich doubt what Gib shuld mean, that now she
    [71] doth so dote.

Hodge. Hold hether, ich ould twenty pound, your
    neele is in her throte.
Grope her, ich say, me thinkes ich feele it; does not
    pricke your hand?

Gammer. Ich can feele nothing.

Hodge. No! ich know that's not within this land
A muryner cat than Gyb is, betwixt the Tems and
    Tyne,
Shase as much wyt in her head almost as chave in
    mine.

Tib. Faith, shase eaten some thing, that wil not
    easely downe,
Whether she gat it at home, or abrode in the towne,
Iche cannot tell.

Gammer. Alas! ich feare it be some croked pyn,
And then farewell Gyb, she is undone, and lost al
    save the skyn.

Hodge. 'Tys[72] your neele, woman, I say; Gog's
    soule, geve me a knyfe,
And chil have it out of her mawe, or else chal lose my
    lyfe.

---

[71] — *doth so* dote.] That is, appear so mad. *To dote* and *to be
mad* were used as synonymous terms. See Barret's *Alvearie, voce
dote.*
[72] Tyb.

Gammer. What! nay, Hodg, fy, kil not our cat,
    'tis all the cats we ha now.
Hodge. By the masse, dame Chat, hays me so moved,
    iche care not what I kyll, ma God a vowe.
Go to then, Tyb, to this geare, holde up her tayle and
    take her,
Chil see what devil is in her guts, chil take the paines
    to rake her.
Gammer. Rake a Cat, Hodg! what wouldst thou do?
Hodge. What thinck'st that cham not able?
Did not Tom Tankard rake his curtal toore day stand-
    ing in the stable?
Gammer. Soft, be content, let's here what news
Cccke bringeth from maister Rat.
Cock. Gammer, chave ben ther as you bad, you wot
    wel about what.
'Twil not be long before he come, ich durst sweare of
    a booke,
He byds you see ye be at home, and there for him to
    looke.
Gammer. Where didst thou finde him, boy? was he
    not wher I told thee?
Cock. Yes, yes, even at Hobfilcher's house, by him
    that bought and solde me:
A cup of ale had in his hand, and a crab lay in the
    fyer.
Chad much a do to go and come, al was so ful of myer:
And Gammer, one thing I can tel, Hobfilcher's naule
    was loste,
And doctor Rat found it againe, hard beside the doore
    poste.
Ichould a penny can say something, your neele again
    to [73] fet.
Gammer. Cham glad to heare so much, Cocke, then
    trust he will not let

[73] *fet.*] fetched. So, in Cynthia's *Revels*, A. 1. S. 2: " Nay,
" the other is better, exceeds it much: the invention is farther *fet*
" too."
    Again, in Ascham's *Toxophile*, p. 15: " And therefore agaynst
" a desperate evill began to seeke for a desperate remedie, which

To help us herein best he can; therefore till time he
    come,
Let us goe in, if there be ought to get thou shalt have
    some.

THE FOURTH ACTE.

THE FIRST SCEANE.

DOCTOR RAT.   GAMMER GURTON.

Doctor Rat. A man were better twenty times be a
    bandog and barke,
Then here among such a sort, be parish priest or clarke.
Where he shal never be at rest, one pissing while [74] a
    day,
But he must trudge about the towne, this way, and
    that way,
Here to a drab, there to a theefe, his shoes to teare
    and rent,
And that which is worst of all, at every knave's com-
    mandment.
I had not sit the space to drink two pots of ale,
But Gammer Gurton's sory boy was straite way at my
    taile;
And she was sicke, and I must come, to do I wot not
    what:
If once her fingers end but ake, trudge, call for doctor
    Rat.
And when I come not at their call, I only therby
    loose,
For I am sure to lacke therfore a tythe pig or a goose.

"was *fet* from Rome, a shop always open to any mischief, as you
"shall perceive in these few leaves, if you marke them well."
    Again, in Lyly's *Euphues*, p. 33: " — that far *fet* and deere
"bought, is good for ladies."
    [74] — *pissing while*] A proverbial expression used by Ben Jonson
in his *Magnetic Lady*; and Shakspeare, in *The Two Gentlemen of
Verona*. See Mr. Steevens's Note on the latter; and Ray's *Collection of Proverbs*. It is also to be found in Nash's *Lenten Stuff*, 1599.

I warrant you when truth is knowen, and told they
    have their tale,
The matter where about I come, is not worth a half
    peny worth of ale:
Yet must I talke so sage and smothe, as though I were
    a glosier,
Els or the yere come at an end, I shal be sure the
    loser.
What worke ye, gammer Gurton? hoow here is your
    friend doctor Rat.
    Gammer. A good Mr. doctor, cha troubled, cha
        troubled you, chwot wel that.
    Doctor Rat. How do ye, woman? be ye lustie, or
        be ye not wel at ease?
    Gammer. [75] By gys master cham not sick, but yet
        chave a disease.
Chad a foule turne now of late, chill tell it you by gigs.
    Doctor Rat. Hath your browne cow cast hir calfe,
        or your sandy sowe her pigs?
    Gammer. No, but chad ben as good as they had,
        as this, ich wot weel.

[75] *By gys*] In Shakspeare's *Hamlet*, Ophelia sings a song, in
which this adjuration is used:
    " *By gys*, and by Saint Charity."
And it is also to be found in Gascoigne's Poems, in Cambyses, by
Preston; and in the comedy of *See me and see me not*, 1618:
    " *By gisse* I swear, were I so fairly wed, &c.
                See Mr. Steevens's Note on Hamlet.
    Dr. Ridley observes, there is not the least mention of any Saint
whose name corresponds with this either in the Roman Calendar, the
service in *Usum Sarum*, or in the benedictonary of Bishop Athel-
wold; and supposes the word to be only a corrupted abbreviation
of Jesus, the letters I H S being anciently all that was set down
to denote that sacred name on altars, the covers of books, &c.
    It occurs also in the following passage of Erasmus's *Praise of
Folie*, by Chaloner, 1549: " Lyke as many great lordes there be
" who set so muche by them, as scant they can eate their meate, or
" byde a minute without them, *by jysse* a little better than they are
" wont to doo, these frouning philosophers," &c.   Sig. G 2.
    Again, in *Euphues and his England*, 1582, p. 5: " — unto whome
" he replyed, shoaring up his eyes *by Jis* sonne I accompt the
" cheere good which mainteineth health, and the servauntes honest
" whome I finde faythfull."

Doctor Rat. What is the matter?

Gammer. Alas, alas, cha lost my good neele.

My neele, I say, and wot ye what? a drab came by
    and spied it,

And when I asked hir for the same, the filth flatly
    denied it.

Doctor Rat. What was she that——

Gammer. A dame, ich warrant you: she began to
    scold and brawle;

Alas, alas, come hether, Hodge; this wretche can tell
    you all.

THE FOURTH ACTE.

The Second Sceane.

HODGE. DOCTOR RAT. GAMMER. DICCON. CHAT.

Hodge. God morow, gaffer Vicar.

Doctor Rat. Come on fellow, let us heare.

Thy dame hath sayd to me, thou knowest of all this
    geare,

Let's see what thou canst saie?

Hodge. By'm fay, sir, that ye shall,

What matter soever here was done, ich can tell your
    maship:

My gammer Gurton heare, see now,
    sat her downe at this doore, see now,

And as she began to stirre her, see now,
    her neele fell in the floore, see now,

And while her staffe she tooke, see now,
    at Gyb her cat to flynge, see now,

Her neele was lost in the floore, see now;
    is not this a wondrous thing, see now?

Then came the queane dame Chat, see now,
    to aske for hir blacke cup, see now:

And even here at this gate, see now,
    she tooke that neele up, see now.

My gammer then she yeede[76], see now,
  hir neele again to bring, see now,
And was caught by the head, see now;
  is not this a wondrous thing, see now?
She tare my gammer's cote, see now,
  and scratched hir by the face, see now,
Chad thought sh'ad stopt hir throte, see now;
  is not this a wondrous case, see now?
When ich saw this, ich was wrothe, see now,
  and start betwene them twaine, see now,
Els ich durst take a booke othe, see now,
  my gammer had bene slaine, see now.
    Gammer. This is even the whole matter, as Hodge
      has plainly tolde.
And chould fain be quiet for my part, that chould.
But helpe us good master, beseech ye that ye doo,
Els shall we both be beaten, and lose our neele too.
    Doctor Rat. What wold ye have me to doo? tell me,
      that I were gone,
I do the best that I can, to set you both at one.
But be ye sure dame Chat hath this your neele
    found?
    Gammer. Here comes the man, that see her take it
      up of the ground,
Aske him your selfe, master Rat, if ye beleve not me,
[77] And helpe me to my neele, for God's sake, and saint
    Charitie.

---

[76] *My gammer then* she yeede, *see now,*] *She yeede,* i. e. *she went.*
So Chaucer:
    " For alli *yede* out at one ere,
    " That in that other she did lere."
                Romaunt of the Rose.
The word is also used by Spenser and Fairfax.
[77] *And helpe me to my neele, for God's sake, and* saint Charitie.]
Ophelia sings:
    By Gis and by *St. Charity,* &c.
On which Mr. Steevens observes, that *St. Charity* is a known
saint among the Roman Catholicks. Spenser mentions her,
Eclog. 5. 255:
    " Ah dear Lord and sweet *Saint Charity!*"

Doctor Rat. Come nere, Diccon, and let us heare
what thou can expresse.
Wilt thou be sworne, seest dame Chat this woman's
neele have?

Diccon. Nay, by S. Benit wil I not, then might ye
thinke me rave.[78]

Gammer. Why did'st not thou tel me so even here?
canst thou for shame deny it?

Diccon. I mary, gammer: but I said I wold not
abide by it.

Doctor Rat. Will you say a thing, and not sticke to
it to trie it?

Diccon. Stick to it, quoth you, master Rat? mary,
sir, I defy it.*
Nay, there is many an honest man, when he suche
blastes hath blowne
In his friende's ears, he woulde be lothe the same by
him were knowne:
If such a toy be used oft among the honestie,
It may beseme a simple man, of your and my degree.

Doctor Rat. Then we be never the nearer, for all
that you can tell.

Diccon. Yes, mary sir, if ye will do by mine advise
and counsaile.
If mother Chat se al us here, she knowe how the matter goes,
Therfore I red you three go hence, and within keepe
close;
And I will into dame Chat's house, and so the matter
use,
That or ye cold go twise to church, I warrant you here
news.

Again, in *The Downfall of Robert Earl of Huntington,* 1601:
    " Therefore sweet Master for *Saint Charity.*"
                                Note on *Hamlet,* A. 4. S. 5.
    [78] *rave*]   Barret, in his *Alvearie,* explains *rave,* " to talke like a
" madde bodie."
    * *I defy it*] *i. e.* I refuse, deny the charge. See Note **17,** to
The Four Prentices of London, vol. 6, p. 4·5. S.

She shall looke wel about hir, but I durst lay a pledge,
Ye shall of gammer's neele have shortly better know-
    edge.
    Gammer. Now, gentle Diccon, do so; and, good
      sir, let us trudge.
    Doctor Rat. By the masse, I may not tary so long to
      be your judge.
    Diccon. Tys but a little while man, what take so,
      much paine;
If I here no newes of it, I will come sooner againe.
    Hodge. Tary so much, good master Doctor, of your
      gentlenes.
    Doctor Rat. Then let us hie inward, and Diccon
      speede thy busines.
    Diccon. Now, sirs, do you no more, but kepe my
      counsaile juste,
And doctor Rat shall thus catch some good, I trust;
But mother Chat, my gossop, talke first with all I must,
For she must be chiefe captaine to lay the Rat in the
    dust.
God deven, dame Chat, in faith, and well met in this
    lace.
    Chat.p God deven, my friend Diccon, whether walke
      ye this pace?
    Diccon. By my truth even to you, to learne how the
      world goeth.
Hard ye no more of the other matter, say me now by
    your troth?
    Chat. O yes, Diccon: here the old hoore, and Hodge
      that great knave.
But in faith, I would thou hadst sene, O Lord! I drest
    them brave.
She bare me two or three souses behind, in the nape of
    the necke,
Till I made hir olde wesen to answere again, kecke.
And Hodge, that dirty dastard, that at hir elbow
    standes,
If one paire of legs had not bene worth two paire of
    hands,

He had had his bearde shaven, if my nayles wold hvae
    served,
And not without a cause, for the knave it well deserved.
    Diccon. By the masse, I con [79] the thank, wench,
        thou didst so wel acquite the.
    Chat. And th'adst seene him, Diccon, it wold have
        made the beshite the
For laughter: the horsen dolt at last caught up a
    club,
As though he would have slaine the master devill,
    Belsabub;
But I set him soone inwarde.
    Diccon. O Lord! there is the thing,
That Hodge is so offended, that makes him starte and
    flyng.
    Chat. Why, makes the knave any moyling,* as ye
        have seene or hard?
    Diccon. Even now I sawe him last, like a mad man
        he farde,
And sware by heaven and hell, he would a wreake his
    sorrowe,
Ad leve you never a hen alive by eight of the clocke to
    morow:
Therfore marke what I say, and my wordes see that ye
    trust,
Your hens be as good as dead, if ye leave them on the
    ruste.
    Chat. The knave dare as wel go hang himself, as go
        upon my ground.
    Diccon. Wel, yet take hede, I say, I must tel you
        my tale round:
Have you not about your house, behind your furnace
    or leade,
A hole where a crafty knave may crepe in for neade?

---

[79] *can*]   So the edition of 1575.   See Note, p. 30.
    * *any moyling*]   To *moil* signifies both to *daub with dirt* and to
weary.   The reader must explain the word standing in the passage
before us as well as he can.   S.

Chat. Yes, by the masse, a hole broke down even
  within these two dayes.
Diccon. Hodge, he intends this same night to slip in
  there awayes.
Chat. O Christ, that I were sure of it! in faith he
  shuld have his mede.[80]
Diccon. Watch wel, for the knave will be there as
  sure as is your crede;
I wold spend my selfe a shilling to have him swinged
  well.
Chat. I am as glad as a woman can be of this thing
  to here tell;
By gog's bones, when he cometh, now that I know the
  matter,
He shal sure at the first skip, to leape in scalding
  water :
With a worse turne besides, when he will, let him
  come.
Diccon. I tell you as my sister, you know what
  meaneth mum.
Now lacke I but my Doctor, to play his part againe.
And lo, where he cometh towards, peradventure to his
  paine.
Doctor Rat. What good newes, Diccon? fellow, is
  mother Chat at home?
Diccon. She is syr, and she is not; but it please her
  to whome :
Yet dyd I take her tardy, as suble as she was.
Doctor Rat. The thing that thou went'st for, hast
  thou brought it to passe?
Diccon. I have done that I have done, be it worse,
  be it better.
And dame Chat at her wyt's ende, I have almost set
  her.
Doctor Rat. Why, hast thou spied the neele? quickly
  I pray thee tell.
Diccon. I have spyed it in faith, sir, I handled my
  selfe so well;

---

[80] *mede.*] Reward. Obsolete. It is a word used by Spenser,
Shakspeare, and the chief of our ancient writers.

And yet the crafty queane had almost take my trumpe;
But or all came to an ende, I set her in a dumpe.

    Doctor Rat. How so, I pray thee, Diccon?

    Diccon. Mary, syr, will ye heare?
She was clapt downe on the backside, by Cock's mother
    dere,
And there she sat sewing a halter, or a bande,
With no other thing, but gammer's nedle in her hande :
As soone as any knocke, if the filth be in doubte,
She needes but once puffe, and her candle is out :
Now I, sir, knowing of every doore the pin,
Came nycely, and said no worde, till time I was within,
And there I sawe the neele, even with these two eyes.
Who ever say the contrary, I will sweare he lyes.

    Doctor Rat. O Diccon, that I was not there then in
    thy steade!

    Diccon. Well, if ye will be ordred, and do by my
    reade,
I will bring you to a place, as the house standes,
Where ye shall take the drab with the neele in her
    handes.

    Doctor Rat. For God's sake, do so, Diccon, and I
    will gage my gowne,
To geve thee a full pot of the best ale in the towne.

    Diccon. Follow me but a litle, and marke what I say,
Lay downe your gown beside you, go to, come on your
    way :
Se ye not what is here? a hole wherin ye may creepe
Into the house, and sodenly unwares among them
    leape ;
There shal ye finde the bich-fox, and the neele together.
Do as I bid you, man, come on your wayes hether.

    Doctor Rat. Art thou sure, Diccon, the swil-tub
    standes not here aboute?

    Diccon. I was within my selfe, man, even now, there
    is no doubt.
Go softly, make no noyse, give me your foote, sir John,
Here will I waite upon you, tyl you come out anone,

    Doctor Rat. Helpe, Diccon, out alas, I shal be slain
    among them.

Diccon. If they give you not the nedle, tel them that
 ye will hang them.
Ware that, boow my wenches, have ye caught the foxe,
That used to make revel among your hennes and
  Cocks?
Save his life yet for his order, though he susteine some
  paine.
Gog's bread, I am afraide they will beat out his braine.
 Doctor Rat. Wo worth the houre that I came heare;
And wo worth him that wrought this geare,
A sort of drabs and queans have me blest,
Was ever creature halfe so evill drest?
Who ever it wrought, and first did invent it,
He shall, I warrant him, ere long repent it.
I will spend all I have without my skinne,
But he shall be brought to the plight I am in;
Master Bayly I trow, and he be worth his eares,
Will snaffle these murderers, and all that them beares:
I will surely neither byte nor suppe,
Till I fetch him hether, this matter to take up.

THE FIFTH ACTE.

THE FIRST SCEANE.

MASTER BAYLY.   DOCTOR RAT.

Bayly. I can perceive none other, I speke it from
 my hart,
But either ye ar all in the fault, or els in the greatest
 part.
 Doctor Rat. If it be counted his fault, besides all
 his greeves,
When a poore man is spoyled, and beaten among
 theeves,
Then I confesse my fault herein, at this season;
But I hope you wil not judge so much against reason.

Bayly. And me thinkes by your owne tale, of all
    that ye name,
If any plaid the theefe, you were the very same :
The women they did nothing, as your words made
    probation,
But stootly withstood your forciable invasion.
If that a theefe at your window to enter should begin,
Wold you hold forth your hand, and helpe to pull him
    in ?
Or wold [81] you kepe him out ? I pray you answere me.
   Doctor Rat. Mary kepe him out : and a good cause
    why.
But I am no theefe, sir, but an honest learned clarke.
   Bayly. Yea, but who knoweth that, when he meets
    you in the darke ?
I am sure your learning shines not out at your nose.
Was it any marvaile, though the poore woman arose,
And start up, being afraide of that was in hir purse ?
Me thinke you may be glad that your [82] lucke was no
    worse.
   Doctor Rat. Is not this evil ynough, I pray you as
    you thinke ?   [*Showing his broken head.*
   Bayly. Yea, but a man in the darke, if chaunces do
    wincke,
As soone he smites his father as any other man,
Because, for lacke of light, descerne him he ne can.
Might it not have been your lucke with a spit to have
    been slaine ?
   Doctor Rat. I thinke I am litle better, my scalpe is
    cloven to the braine :
If there be all the remedy, I know who beares the
    knockes. [83]
   Bayly. By my troth, and well worthy besides to
    kisse the stockes.
To come in on the backe side, when ye might go about,
I know non such, unles they long to have their braines
    knockt out.

---

[81] you wold.   [82] you.   [83] kockes.

Doctor Rat. Well, wil you be so good, sir, as talke
with dame Chat,
And know what she intended, I aske no more but that.
Bayly. Let her be called, fellow, because of master
doctor,
I warrant in this case, she wil be hir owne proctor:
She will tel hir owne tale in metter or in prose,
And byd you seeke your remedy, and so go wype your
nose.

THE FIFTH ACTE.

THE SECOND SCEANE.

M. BAILY.   CHAT.   D. RAT.   GAMMER.   HODGE.
DICCON.

Baily. Dame Chat, master doctor upon you here
complaineth,
That you and your maides shuld him much disorder,
And taketh many an oth, that no word he fained,
Laying to your charge, how you thought him to
murder:
And on his part againe, that same man saith furder,
He never offended you in word nor intent;
To heare you answer hereto, we have now for you sent.
Chat. That I wold have murdered him! fye on him
wretch,
And evil mought he thee for it, our Lord I beseech.
I wil swere on al the bookes that opens and shuttes
He faineth this tale out of his owne guttes.
For this seven weekes with me, I am sure, he sat not
downe;
Nay ye have other minions in the other end of the
towne,
Where ye were liker to catch such a blow
Then any where els, as farre as I know.

Baily. Be like then, master doctor, your[84] stripe
  there ye got not.
Doctor *Rat.* [85]Thinke you I am so mad, that where
  I was bet I wot not?
Will ye beleve this queane, before she hath try'd it?
It is not the first dede she hath done, and afterward
  denide it.
Chat. What man, will you say I broke your head?
Doctor *Rat.* How canst thou prove the contrary?
Chat. Nay, how provest thou that I did the
  deade?
Doctor *Rat.* To plainly, by St. Mary.
This profe, I trow, may serve, though I no word spoke.
                          [*Showing his broken head.*
Chat. Bicause thy head is broken, was it I that it
  broke?
I saw thee, Rat, I tel thee, not once within this fort-
  night.
Doctor *Rat.* No, mary, thou sawest me not; for why?
  thou hadst no light;
But I felt thee for al the darke, beshrew thy smothe
  cheekes!
And thou groped me, this wil declare any day this six
  weekes.   [*Showing his heade.*
Bayly. Answere me to this, M. Rat, when caught
  you this harme of yours?
Doctor *Rat.* A while a go, sir, God he knoweth;
  within les then these two houres.

---

[84] you.
[85] *Thinke you I am so mad, that where I was bet* I *wot not.*] i. e. I
know not. So A. 2. S. 4:
  "My tossing sporyar's neele, chave lost it *wot* not where."
  A. 3. S. 3:
  "Gammer, chave ben there as you bad, you *wot* wel about what."
  Massinger's *Unnatural Combat,* A. 5. S. 2:
              " — this will keep me safe yet
        " From being pull'd by the sleeve, and bid remember
        " The thing I *wot* of."
  Wily beguiled:
  " I was once in good comfort to have cosen'd a wench : and
  " *wot'st* thou what I told her?"

Bayly. Dame Chat, was there none with you (confesse I faith) about that season?

What woman, let it be what it wil, 'tis neither felony
nor treason.

Chat. Yes, by my faith, master Bayly, there was a
knave not farre,

Who caught one good philup on the brow with a
dorebarre.

And well was he worthy, as it semed to mee:

But what is that to this man, since this was not hee?

Bayly. Who was it then? let's here.

Doctor Rat. Alas, sir, aske you that?

Is it not made plain inough by the owne mouth of dame
Chat?

The time agreeth, my head is broken, her tong cannot
lye;

Onely upon a bare nay, she saith it was not I.

Chat. No mary was it not indeede, ye shal here by,
this one thing.

This afternoone a friend of mine, for good-wil gave me
warning,

And bad me wel loke to my ruste, and al my capons
pennes;

For if I toke not better heede, a knave wold have
my hennes.

Then I, to save my goods, toke so much pains as him to
watch;

And as good fortune served me, it was my chance him
for to catch.

What strokes he bare away, or other what was his gaines,

I wot not, but sure I am he had something for his paines.

Bayly. Yet telles thou not who it was.

Chat. Who it was? A false theefe,

That came like a false foxe, my pullain[86] to kil and
mischeefe.

---

[86] —*pullain*] Poultry. So, in Fitzherbert's *Boke of Hubandry:*
" —gyve thy *poleyn*—meate in the morning, &c." Again, in *Your
five Gallants*, by Middleton: " —and to see how pittifully the
" *pullen* will looke, it makes me after relent, and turne my anger
" into a quick fire to roast them."

Bayly. But knowest thou not his name?

Chat. I know it, but what than?

It was that crafty [87] cullyon Hodge, my gammer Gur-
　　ton's man.

　　Bayly. Cal me the knave hether, he shall sure kysse
　　　　the stockes.

I shall teach him a lesson for filching hens or cocks.

　　Doctor Rat. I marvaile, master Bayly, so bleared be
　　　　your eyes!

An egge is not so ful of meate, as she is ful of lyes:

When she hath plaid this pranke, to excuse al this geare,

She layeth the fault on such a one, as I know was not
　　　　there.

　　Chat. Was he not theare? loke on his pate; that
　　　　shalbe his witnes.

　　Doctor Rat. I wold my head were half so hole, I
　　　　wold seeke no redresse.

　　Bayly. God blesse you, gammer Gurton.

　　Gammer. * God dylde you, master mine.

　　Bayly. Thou hast a knave within thy house, Hodge,
　　　　a servant of thine.

The tel me that busie knave is such a filching one,

That hen, pig, goose, or capon, thy neighbour can have
　　　　none.

---

[87] —*cullyon*] A base contemptible fellow. So, in *Tom Tyler and
his Wife*, 1661, p. 19:

　　　"It is an old saying, praise at the parting.
　　　"I think I have made *the cullion* to wring.
　　　"I was not beaten so black and blew,
　　　"But I am sure he has as many new."

Wily beguiled:

　　"—but to say the truth, she had little reason to take a *cullion*
　"lug loaf, milksop slave, when she may have a lawyer, a gentle-
　"man that stands upon his reputation in the country;"

Massinger's *Guardian*, A. 2. S 4:

　　　　"Love live Severino,
　　　"And perish all such *cullions* as repine
　　　"At his new monarchy."

And Bobadil, in Ben Jonson's *Every Man in his Humour*, A. 3.
S. 5. when beating, Cob exclaims:

　　　"You base *cullion* you."

* *God dylde you*] i. e. reward you. See note on *Macbeth*, edit. of
Shakspeare, 1778. vol. IV. p. 482. S.

Gammer. By god cham much ameved, to heare any
  such reporte :
Hodge was not wont, ich trow, to have him in that
  sort.
  Chat. A theevisher knave is not on live, more filching, nor more false;
[88] Many a truer man than he hase hanged up by the
  halse.
And thou his dame, of al his theft thou art the sole
  receaver ;
For Hodge to catch, and thou to kepe, I never knew
  none better.
  Gammer. Sir, reverence of your masterdome, and
  you were out a doore,
Chold be so bolde, for all hir brags, to cal hir arrant
  whoore.
And ich knew Hodge so bad as tow, ich wish me endlesse sorow,
And chould not take the pains to hang him up before
  to morow.
  Chat. What have I stolen from the or thine, thou
  ilfavor'd olde trot ?
  Gammer. A great deale more (by Gods blest) then
  chever by the got,
That thou knowest wel, I neade not say it.
  Bayly. Stoppe there I say,
And tel me here, I pray you, this matter by the way :
How chaunce Hodge is not here ? him wold I faine
  have had,
  Gammer. Alas, sir, heel be here anon ; ha be handled
  to bad.

---

[88] *Many a* truer *man than he hase hanged up by the* halse.] That is,
many an honester man than he has been hanged up by the neck.
True, in the language of the times, signified *honest ;* and a true
man was generally so called in opposition to a thief. See the
First Part of *Henry* IV. Again, Hodge says, " Ich defy them al
" that dare it say ; cham as *true* as the best." *Hals,* in the Glossary to Douglas, is thus explained, " the hawse, the throat, or
" neck, al AS and Isl. *Hals* collum, Inde to *hals* or *hawse* to
" embrace, *collo dare brachia circum.*"

Chat. Master Bayly, sir, ye be not such a foole, wel
  I know,
But ye perceive by this lingring there is a pad in the
  straw.
  [*Thinking that Hodg his head was broke, and that
    Gammer wold not let him come before them.*
Gammer. Chil shew you his face, ich warrant the,
  ——lo now where he is!
Bayly. [89] Come on, fellow; it is tolde me thou art a
  shrew I wysse;
Thy neighbour's hens thou takest, and playes the two
  legged foxe;
Their chikens, and their capons to, and now and then
  their cocks.
Hodge. Ich defy them al that dare it say; cham as
  true as the best.
Bayly. Wart not thou take within this houre in dame
  Chat's hens nest?
Hodge. Take there! no master, chould not do't for
  a house ful of gold.
Chat. Thou or the devil in thy cote; sweare this I
  dare be bold.
Doctor Rat. Sweare me no swearing, quean, the
  devill he geve the sorrow;
Al is not worth a gnat, thou canst sweare till to morow.
Where is the harme he hath? shew it; by God's bread,
Ye beat him with a witnes, but the stripes light on my
  head.
Hodge. Bet me! Gog's blessed body, chold first ich
  trow have burst the;
Ich thinke, and chad my hands, loose callet, chould
  have crust the.
Chat. Thou shitten knave, I trow, thou knowest the
  ful weight of my fist.
I am fowly deceived, onles thy head and my doore-bar
  kyste.

---

[89] *Come on, fellow; it is tolde me thou art a* shrew *I wysse;*] The
word *shrew* at present is wholly confined to the female sex. It here
appears to have been equally applied to the male, and signifies
naught or *wicked.* See Barret's *Alvearie,* voce *Shrewd.*

Hodge. Hold thy chat, whore; thou criest so loude,
 can no man els be hard?

Chat. Well, knave, and I had the alone, I wold
 surely rap thy [90] costard.

Bayly. Sir, answer me to this, Is thy head whole or
 broken?

Chat. Yea, master Baily, blest be every good token.

Hodge. Is my head whole? ich warrant you, 'tis
 neither scurvy nor scald:

What, you foule beast, does think 'tis *either pild or
 bald?

Nay, ich thanke God, chil not for al that thou maist
 spend,

That chad one scab on my narse as brode as thy
 finger's end.

Bayly. Come nearer heare.

Hodge. Yes, that iche dare.

Bayly. By our lady, here is no harme:

Hodge's head is hole ynough, for al dame Chat's
 charme.

Chat. By Gog's blest, however the thing he clockes
 or smolders,

I know the blowes he bare awaie, either with head
 or shoulders.

Camest thou not, knave, within this houre, creping into
 my pens,

And there was caught within my hous, groping among
 my hens?

Hodge. A plage both on thy hens and thee? a carte,
 whore, a carte.

Chould I were hanged as hie as a tree, and chware as
 as false as thou art.

---

[90] —*costard.*] i. e. the head.   So, in *Hicke Scorner:*
  " I wyll rappe you on the *costard* with my horne."
       Mr. Steeven's Note on *Love Labour Lost,* A. 3. S. 1.
Again, in Ben Johnson's *Tale of a Tub,* A. 2. S. 2:
  " Do you mutter! sir, snorle this way,
  " That I may hear and answer what you say,
  " With my school dagger 'bout your *costard,* sir."
* *Either piled or bald.*] See note on King Henry VI. Part I.
Shaksp. 1778, vol. 6. p. 192.   S.

Geve my gammer again * her washical thou stole away
    in thy lap.

   Gammer. Yea, master Baily, there is a thing you
    know not on mayhap:

This drab she kepes away my good, (the devil he might
    her snare)

Ich pray you, that ich might have a right action on her.

   Chat. Have I thy good, old filth, or any such old
    sowe's?

I am † as true, I wold thou knew, as skin betwene thy
    browes.

   Gammer. Many a truer hath been hanged, though
    you escape the daunger.

   Chat. Thou shalt answer (by God's pity) for this thy
    foule slaunder.

   Bayly. Why, what can you charge hir withal? to
    say so ye do not well.

   Gammer. Mary, a vengeance to hir hart, the whore
    hase stoln my neele.

   Chat. Thy nedle, old witch! how so? it were almes
    thy soul to knock;

So didst thou say, the other day, that I had stolne thy
    cock.

And rosted him to my breakfast, which shal not be
    forgotten:

The devil pul out thy lying tong, and teeth that be so
    rotten.

   Gammer. Geve me my neele; as for my cocke,
    chould be very loth,

That chuld here tel he shuld hang on thy false faith
    and troth.

   Bayly. Your talke is such, I can scarse learne who
    shuld be most in fault.

   Gammer. Yet shal ye find no other wight, save she,
    by bred and salt.

---

  * —*her washical*] a corruption of *what do you call it.* S.
  † — *as true as skin betwene thy browes.*] a Proverbial phrase, used
also by Dogberry in *Much ado about Nothing.* Shaks. 1778, vol. II.
p. 326. S.

Bayly. Kepe ye content a while, se that your tonges
　　ye holde ;

Methinkes you shuld remembre, this is no place to
　　scolde.

How knowest thou, gammer Gurton, dame Chat thy
　　nedle had ?

Gammer. To name you, sir, the party, chould not be
　　very glad.

Bayly. Yea, but we muste nedes heare it, and ther-
　　fore say it boldly.

Gammer. Such one as told the tale, full soberly and
　　coldly,

Even he that loked on, wil sweare on a booke,

What time this drunken gossip my faire long neele up
　　tooke :

Diccon (master) the bedlam, cham very sure ye know
　　him.

Bayly. A false knave, by God's pitie ! ye were but a
　　foole to trow him.

I durst aventure wel the price of my best cap,

[91] That when the end is knowen, all wil turne to a jape.

Tolde he not you that besides, she stole your cocke
　　that tyde ?

Gammer. No master, no indeede, for then he shuld
　　have lyed ;

---

[91] *That when the end is knowen, all wil turne to a jape.*] *Jape*
is generally used in an obscene sense, as in the Prologue to Grim
the Collier of Croydon, vol. XI. and Skelton's Song in Sir John
Hawkin's *History of Musick*, vol. III. p. 6.　It here signifies a *jest*
or *joke*.　So, in the Prologue to Chaucer's *Canterbury Tales*, l. 705 :
　　" Upon a day he gat him more moneie
　　" Than that the persone gat in monethes tweie.
　　" And thus with famed flattering and *japes*,
　　" He made the persone, and the peple, his apes."
And, in *Batman upon Bartholeme*, 1535, as quoted by Sir John
Hawkins, in his *History of Musick*, vol. II. p. 125 : " They kepe no
" counseyll, but they telle all that they here : sodeinly they laugh,
" " and sodenly they wepe : alwaye they crye, jangle, and *jape*,
" uneth they ben stylle whyle they slepe."
Skelton's Works, 1736, p. 236 :
　　" Nay *jape* not hym, he is no smal fole.
　　" It is a solempne syre and solayne."

My cocke is, I thanke Christ, safe and wel a fine.
   Chat. Yea, but that rogged colt, that whore, that
      Tyb of thine,
Said plainly thy cock was stolne, and in my house was
      eaten;
That lying cut is lost, that she is not swinged and
      beaten.
And yet for al my good name, it were a small amendes;
I picke not this geare (hear'st thou) out of my fingers
      endes.
But he that hard it told me, who thou of late didst
      name,
Diccon, whom al men knowes, it was the very same.
   Bayly. This is the case; you lost your nedle about
      the dores;
And she answeres againe, she hase no cocke of yours;
Thus in your talke and action, from that you do intend,
She is whole five mile wide from that she doth defend.
Will you saie she hath your cocke?
   Gammer. No, mary sir, that chil not.
   Bayly. Will you confesse hir neele?
   Chat. Will I? no, sir, will I not.
   Bayly. Then there lieth all the matter.
   Gammer. Soft master, by the way,
Ye know she could do litle, and she cold not say nay.
   Bayly. Yea, but he that made one lie about your
      cocke stealing,
Wil not sticke to make another, what time lies be in
      dealing.
I weene, the ende wil prove this brawle did first arise
Upon no other ground, but only Diccon's lyes.
   Chat. Though some be lyes, as you belike have
      espyed them;
Yet other some be true, by proofe I have wel tryed
      them.
   Bayly. What other thing beside this, dame chat?
   Chat. Mary syr, even this,
The tale I told before, the selfe same tale it was his;
He gave me, like a frende, warning against my losse,
Els had my hens be stolne eche one, by God's crosse.

He tolde me Hodge wold come, and in he came indeede;
But as the matter chaunsed, with greater hast then
    speede.
This truth was said, and true was found, as truly I
    report.
    Bayly. If doctor Rat be not deceived, it was o'
      another sort.
    Doctor *Rat.* By God's mother, thou and he be a
      cople of suttle foxes;
Betweene you and Hodge, I beare awaie the boxes.
Did not Diccon appoynt the place, wher thou shuld'st
    stand to mete him?
    Chat. Yes, by the masse; and if he came, bad me
      not sticke to speet hym.
    Doctor Rat. God's sacrament! the villain knave hath
      drest us round about;
He is the cause of all this brawle, that dyrty shitten loute,
When gammer Gurton here complained, and made a
    ruful mone,
I heard him sweare that you had gotten hir nedle that
    was gone.
And this to try he furder said, he was ful loth; how be it
He was content with small adoe to bring me where to
    see it.
And where he sat, he said ful certain, if I wold folow
    his read,
Into your house a privy waie he wold me guide and leade,
And where ye had it in your hands, sewing about a
    clowte,
And set me in the backe hole, thereby to finde you
    out:
And whiles I sought a quietnes, creping upon my knees,
I found the weight of your door-bar, for my reward and
    fees.
Such is the lucke that some men gets, while they begin
    to mel, *
In setting at one such as were out, minding to make al
    well.

---

* — *mel*] i. e. to meddle. S.

Hodge. Was not wel blest, gammer, to scape that
     scoure? and chad ben there,
Then chad ben drest, belike, as ill (by the masse)
     as gaffer vicar.

Bayly. Mary, sir, here is a sport alone; I loked for
     such an end;
If Diccon had not play'd the knave, this had ben sone
     amend.
My gammer here he made a foole, and drest hir as she
     was;
And goodwife Chat he set to scold,[92] till both partes
     cried, alas!
And doctor Rat was not behind, whiles Chat his crown
     did pare;
I wold the knave had ben starke blind, if Hodg had not
     his share.

Hodge. Cham meetly wel sped alredy among's, cham
     drest like a coult;
And chad not had the better wit, chad been made a
     doult.

Bayly. Sir knave, make hast Diccon were here; fetch
     him where ever he be.

Chat. Fie on the villain, fie, fie, that makes us thus
     agree!

Gammer. Fie on him, knave, with al my hart, now
     fie, and fie againe!

Doctor Rat. Now fie on him, may I best say, whom
     he hath almost slaine.

Bayly. Lo where he commeth at hand, belike he was
     not fare.
Diccon, heare be two or three thy company cannot spare.

Diccon. God blesse you, and you may be blest so
     manie al at once.

Chat. Come knave, it were a good deed to geld the,
     by cockes bones.
Seest not thy handiwarke? sir Rat, can ye forbeare him?

Diccon. A vengeance on those hands life, for my
     hands cam not nere hym.

[92] scole.

The horsen priest hath lift the pot in some of these
    alewyves chayres,
That his head wold not serve him, belyke, to come
    downe the stayres.
    Bayly. Nay, soft, thou maist not play the knave,
    and have this language to ;
If thou thy tong bridle a while, the better mist thou do.
Confesse the truth as I shall aske, and cease a while to
    fable,
And for thy fault, I promise the, thy handling shal be
    reasonable.
Hast thou not made a lie or two, to set these two by
    the eares?
    Diccon. What if I have ? five hundred such have I
    seene within these seven yeares :
I am sory for nothing else, but that I see not the
    sport
Which was betwene them when they met, as they
    themselves report.
    Bayly. The greatest thing, master Rat, ye se how he
    is drest.
    Diccon. What devil nede he be groping so depe
    in goodwife Chat's hen's nest ?
    Bayly. Yea, but it was thy drif to bring him into the
    briars.
    Diccon. God's bread ! hath not such an old foole
    wit to save his eares ?
He showeth himselfe herein, ye see, so very [93]a coxe,
* The cat was not so madly alured by the foxe,
To run in the snares was set for him doubtlesse ;
For he leapt in for myce, and this sir John for madnes.

---

[93] — *a coxe,*] Minshieu, in his Dictionary, 1627 (as quoted by Mr.
Tollet, in his Notes on Shakspeare, vol. V. p. 433.) says : " Na-
" tural ideots and fools have and still do accustome themselves to
" weare in their cappes, cockes feathers, or a hat with a necke
" and head of a cock on the top, &c." From this circumstance,
Diccon, probably calls Dr. Rat *a coxe;* that is, *a coxcomb, an ideot.*
    * — *the cat was not, &c.*] See the *History of Reynard the Fox,*
chap. 7, edit 1701. S.

Doctor Rat. [94] Well, and ye shift no better, ye losel,
    lyther, and lasye,
I will go neare for this to make ye leape at a dasye.
In the king's name, master Baily, I charge you set
    him fast.
   Diccon. What! fast at cardes, or fast on slepe? it is
    the king I did last.
   Doctor Rat. Nay, fast in fetters, false varlet, ac-
    cording to thy deedes.
   Bayly. Master doctor, ther is no remedy, I must in-
    treat you needs
Some other kinde of punishment.
   Doctor Rat. Nay, by all halowes,
His punishment, if I may judg, shal be naught els but
    the gallous.
   Bayly. That were to sore; a spiritual man to be so
    extreame!
   Doctor Rat. Is he worthy any better, sir? how do you
    judge and deame?
   Bayly. I graunt him worthy punishment, but in no
    wise so great.
   Gammer. It is a shame, ich tel you plaine, for such
    false knaves intreat.
He has almost undone us al, that is as true as steele.
And yet for al this great ado, cham never the nere my
    neele.
   Bayly. Can'st thou not say any thing to that Diccon,
    with least or most?
   Diccon. Yea, mary sir, thus much I can say wel, the
    nedle is lost.

---

[94] *Well, and ye shift no better, ye losel, lither, and lasie,*] *Lither* is
used sometimes for *weak* or *limber*, at other times *lean or pale.*
Several examples of the former are collected by Mr. Steevens
(Notes on Shakspeare, vol. VI. p. 263).
   Again, in *Eupheus and his England,* 1582, p. 24: " For as they
" that angle for the tortoys, having once caught him, are driven
" into such a *lythernesse,* that they loose all their spirites, being be-
" nummed so, &c." Of the latter, the following will serve as
a proof. Erasmus's *Praise of Folie,* Chaloner's translation, 1549,
Sig. F 2: " Or at lest hyre some younge Phaon for mede to dooe
" the thynge, still daube theyr *lither* cheekes with peintynge, &c."

Bayly. Nay, canst not thou tel which way that nedle
    may be found ?

D*iccon*. No, by fay, sir, though I might have an
    hundred pound.

Hodge. Thou lier lickdish, didst not say the neele
    wold be gitten ?

D*iccon*. No, Hodge ; by the same token you were
    that time beshitten,

For fear of hobgobling, you wot wel what I meane,

As long as it is sence, I feare me yet ye be scarce cleane.

Bayly. Wel, master Rat, you must both learne, and
    teach us to forgeve,

Since Diccon hath confession made, and is so cleane
    shreve :

If ye to me conscent to amend this heavie chaunce,

I wil injoyne him here some open kind of penaunce :

Of this condition, where ye know my fee is twenty pence,

For the bloodshed, I am agreed with you here to
    dispence ;

Ye shall go quite, so that ye graunt the matter now to
    run,

To end with mirth emong us al, even as it was begun.

Chat. Say yea, master vicar, and he shal sure confes
    to be your detter,

And al we that be heare present will love you much the
    better.

D*octor Rat*. My part is the worst ; but since you al
    hereon agree,

Go even to master Baily, let it be so for mee.

Bayly. How saiest thou, Diccon, art content this
    shal on me depend ?

D*iccon*. Go to, Mr. Baily, say on your mind, I know
    ye are my frend.

Bayly. Then marke ye wel ; to recompence this thy
    former action,

Because thou hast offended al, to make the satisfaction,

Before their faces here kneele downe, and as I shal the
    teach,

For thou shalt take an othe of Hodge's leather breache ;

First for master doctor, upon paine of his cursse,
Where he wil pay for al, thou never draw thy pursse :
And when ye meete at one pot, he shall have the first
          pull ;
And thou shalt never offer him the cup, but it be full.
To goodwife Chat thou shalt be sworne, even on the
          same wyse,
If she refuse thy money once, never to offer it twise.
Thou shalt be bound by the same here, as thou dost
          take it,
When thou maist drinke of free cost, thou never
          forsake it.
For gammer Gurton's sake againe sworne shalt thou be,
To helpe hir to hir nedle againe, if it do lie in thee ;
And likewise be bound, by the vertue of that,
To be of good abering to Gib, hir great cat.
Last of al for Hodge, the othe to scanne,
Thou shalt never take him for fine gentleman.

    Hodge. Come on, fellow Diccon, chalbe even with
          thee now.

    Bayly. Thou wilt not sticke to do this, Diccon, I
          trow ?

    Diccon. No, by my father's skin, my hand down
          I lay it;
Loke, as I have promised, I wil not denay it;
But, Hodge, take good heede now, thou do not be-
          shite me.

        [*And gave him a good blow on the buttocke.*

    Hodge. Gog's hart, thou false villaine, dost thou
          bite me ?

    Bayly. What, Hodge, doth he hurt the or ever
          he begin?

    Hodge. He thrust me into the buttocke with a bod-
          kin or a pin,
I saie, gammer, gammer!

    Gammer. How now, Hodge, how now !

    Hodge. God's malt, gammer Gurton ——

    Gammer. Thou art mad, ich trow.

    Hodge. Will you see the devil, gammer

Gammer. The devil, sonne! God blesse us.

Hodge. Chould iche were hanged, gammer.

Gammer. Mary, se ye might dresse us.

Hodge. Chave it, by the masse, gammer.

Gammer. What, not my neele, Hodge?

Hodge. Your neele, gammer, your neele.

Gammer. No, fie, dost but dodge.

Hodge. Cha found your neele, gammer, here in my
  hand be it.

Gammer. 95 For al the loves on earth, Hodge, let me
  see it.

Hodge. Soft, gammer.

Gammer. Good Hodge.

Hodge. Soft, ich say, tarie a while.

Gammer. Nay, sweet Hodge, say truth, and not me
  begile.

Hodge. Cham sure on it; ich warrant you, it goes
  no more astray.

Gammer. Hodge, when I speake so fair, wilt stil say
  me nay?

Hodge. Go neare the light, gammer, this wel in faith
  good lucke :

Chwas almost undone, 'twas so far in my buttocke.

---

95 *For al the loves on earth, Hodge, let me see it.*] For the love of
God, of heaven, or any thing sacred, are adjurations frequently
used at this day, and appear likewise to have been so at the time
this Play was written. From the indiscriminate use of them,
it became customary on very earnest occasions to request *of all loves,*
or *for all the loves on earth.* Of these modes of expression, Mr.
Steevens hath produced the following examples :—conjuring his wife
of all loves to prepare cheer fitting.—*Honest Whore,* p. 1.

  Desire him *of all loves* to come over quickly.
                    Plautus's Menæchmi, 1595.

  I pray thee *for all loves* be thou my mynde sens I am thyne.
                    Acolastus, 1529.

  Mrs. Arden desired him *of all loves* to come back againe.

  Holinshed's *Chronicle,* p. 1064. Notes on Shakspeare, vol. I.
p. 279.

Again,

  Speak *of all loves.*   *Midsummer's Night's Dream,* A. 2. S. 3.

Gammer. 'Tis min own deare neele, Hodge, [96] sykerly
    I wot.

Hodge. Cham I not a good sonne, gammer, cham I
    not?

Gammer. Christs blessing light on thee, hast made
    me for ever.

Hodge. Ich knew that ich must finde it, els chould a
    had it never.

Chat. By my troth, gossyp Gurton, I am even as glad,
As though I mine owne selfe as good a turne had.

Bayly. And I by my conscience, to see it so come
    forth,
Rejoyce so much at it, as three needles be worth.

Doctor Rat. I am no whit sorry to see you so rejoyce.

Diccon. Nor I much the glader for all this noyce.
Yet say gramercy, Diccon, for springing of the game.

Gammer. Gramercy, Diccon, twenty times; o how
    glad cham!
If that chould do so much, your masterdome to come
    hether,
Master Rat, goodwife Chat, and Diccon together;
Cha but one halfpeny, as far as iche know it,
And chil not rest this night, till ich bestow it.
If ever ye love me, let us go in and drinke.

Bayly. I am content, if the rest thinke as I thinke.
Master Rat, it shal be best for you if we so doo,
Then shall you warme you and drese your self too.

Diccon. Soft, syrs, take us with you, the company
    shal be the more;
As proude comes behinde, they say, as anie goes before.
But now, my good masters, since we must be gone,
And leave you behinde us here all alone:
Since at our lasting ending, thus mery we bee,
For Gammer Gurton's nedle sake, let us have a
    plaudytie.

[96] — *sykerly*] Securely or certainly. So, in Chaucer's *Troilus and
Cressida*, l. 3. l. 833:
    " The drede of lesing makith him, that he
    " May in no parfite *sikernesse* ybe."

EDITIONS.

" A Ryght Pithy, Pleasaunt and Merie Comedie :
" Intytuled *Gammer Jurton's Nedle :* Played on Stage,
" not longe ago in Christes *Colledge in Cambridge.*
" *Made by Mr. S. Master of Art.* Imprented at London
" in Fleetestreat, beneth the Conduit, at the signe of
" S. John Evangelist, by *Thomas Colwell.*" Printers
Colophon : " Imprinted at London in Fleetestreate,
" beneath the Conduite, at the signe of S. John Evan-
" gelist, by Thomas Colwell. **1575.**"

" A right Pithy, Pleasant and Merry Comedy, enti-
" tuled *Gammer Gurton's Needle ;* Played on the Stage
" near a hundred years ago, in *Christe-College* in Cam-
" bridge.   Made by Mr. S. Master of Art.   London.
" Printed by Tho. Johnson, and are to be sold by
" Nath. Brook, at the Angel in Cornhil, Francis Kirk-
" man, at the John Fletchers Head, on the back side of
" St. Clements, Tho. Johnson, at the Golden Key in
" Pauls-Church-yard, and Henry Marsh, at the Princes
" Arms in Chancery lane, near Fleet-street. **1661.**"

ALEXANDER AND CAMPASPE.

JOHN LYLY was born in the [1] Wilds of Kent[*] about the year 1553, according to the computation of Wood[2], who says, " he became a student in Magdalen-Col-" lege in the beginning of 1569, aged sixteen, or " thereabouts, and was afterwards one of the demies or " clerks of that house." He took the degree of B.A. April 27, 1573[3], and of M.A. in the year 1575[4]; and afterwards on some disgust removed to Cambridge, from whence he went to court, where he was taken notice of by Queen Elizabeth, and had expectations of being preferred to the post of Master of the Revels; which, after many years attendance, he was disappointed of[†]. In what year he died is unknown, but Wood says he was alive in the year 1597.

[1] Gildon.

[*] " The southern district of Kent, which borders on Sussex and the sea,"—these are Gibbon's words, —" was formerly overspread with the great forest Anderida, and even now retains the denomination of the Weald, or Woodland."—In this district Lilly himself informs us he was born. O. G.

[2] Athen. Oxon. 295.

[3] Fasti, 108.

[4] Ibid. 111.

[†] — *had expectations of being preferred to the post of master of the revels; which after many years attendance he was disappointed of.*] The following petitions from Lilly to Queen Elizabeth, are copied from the Harleian Manuscripts in the British Museum, No. 1877, p. 71. I believe they have not been published heretofore.

A PETICION OF JOHN LILLY TO THE QUEENE'S MAJESTIE.

Tempora si numeres quæ nos numeramus,
Non venit ante suam nostra querela diem.

Most gratious and dread soueraigne, I dare not pester your highnes with many words, and want witt to wrapp upp much matter in fewe. This age epitomies the pater noster thrust into the compasse of a penny; the world into the modell of a tennis ball; all science malted into sentence. I would I were so compendious as to expresse my hopes, my fortunes, *my ouerthirts,* in two silla-bles, as merchants do riches in fewe ciphers, but I feare to comitt the error I discomend, Tediousnes; like one that vowed to search out what tyme was, spent all his, and knewe yt not. I was en-terteyned your majesty's servant by your owne gratious fauour,

He was an Author highly esteemed by his contemporaries, by several of whom as Nash[5], Lodge[6].

strengthened with condicions, that I should ayme all my courses at the reuells (I dare not saye with a promise, but a hopefull Item to the reuercion) for which these ten yeres I have attended with an unwearyed patience, and nowe I knowe not what Crabb tooke me for an Oyster, that in the midest of your sun-shine of your most gratious aspect, hath thrust a stone betweene the shells to rate me aliue that onely liue on dead hopes. If your sacred majestie thinke me unworthy, and that, after x yeares tempest, I must att the court suffer shipwrack of my tyme, my wittes, my hopes, Vouchsafe in your neuer-erring judgment, some plank or refter to wafte me into a countrʏ, where in my sadd and settled devocion 1 may, in euery corner of a thatcht cottage, write prayers instead of plaies; prayer for your longe and prosperous life, and a repentaunce that I haue played the foole so longe, and yett like

    Quod petimus pœna est, nec etiam miser esse recuso,
      Sed precor ut possem mitius esse miser.

JOHN LILLIES SECOND PETICION TO THE QUEENE.

Most gratious and dread soueraigne, tyme cannot worke my peticions, nor my peticions the tyme. After many yeares seruice yt pleased your majestie to except against tents and toils: I wish that for tennts I might putt in tenements, so should I be eased of some toyles, some lands, some good fines or forfeitures, that should fall by the just fall of these most false traiters; that seeing nothing will come by the reuells, I may play upon the rebells. Thirteene yeres your highnes seruant, but yet nothing; twenty freinds, that though they saye theye will be sure, I finde them sure to be slowe; a thowsand hopes, but all nothing; a hundred promises but yet nothing. Thus casting upp the inven-tary of my freinds, hopes, promises, and tymes, the summa totalis amounteth to just nothing. My last will is shorter than myne invencion, but three legacies, patience to my creditors, melancholie without measure to my freinds, and beggerie without shame to my familie.

    Si placet hoc merui quod ó tua fulmina cessent
      Virgo parens princeps.

In all humilitie I entreate that I may dedicate to your sacred majestie, Lillie de tristibus, wherein shal be sene patience, labours, and misfortunes.

    Quorum si singula nostrum
    Frangere non poterant, *poterant tamen omnia mentem.*

The last and the least, that if I bee borne to haue nothing, I may haue a proteccion to pay nothinge which suite is like his that haveing followed the court tenn yeares for recompence of his service, comitted a robberie, and tooke it out in a pardon.

[5] Apology of Pierce Penniless, 4to. 1593.
Have with you to Saffron Walden, 4to. 1596.
[6] Wits Misery and Words Madness, 4to. 1596, p. 57.

Webbe[7], and others, he was much complimented. Drayton, however, seems to have given his true character, when he says:

" The noble Sidney with this last arose,
" That heroe for numbers, and for prose; †
" That thoroughly pac'd our language as to show,
" The plenteous English hand in hand might go
" With Greek and Latin, and did first reduce
" Our tongue from Lily's writing then in use;
" Talking of stones, stars, plants, of fishes, flies,
" Playing with words, and idle similies,
" As th' English apes, and very zanies be
" Of every thing that they do hear and see,
" So imitating his ridiculous tricks,
" They speak and write all like meer lunaticks."

Blount, who republished six of his Plays, speaks of him in a different manner, he says, " Our nation are " in his debt for a new English which he taught them. " *Euphues and his England* began first that language. " All our ladies were then his scollers: and that beau- " tie in court, who could not parley Euphuesme, was " as little regarded as shee which now there speakes " not French."

The principal work for which he was distinguished is, entitled " Euphues. The Anatomy of Wit, verie " pleasant for all Gentlemen to read, and most neces- " sary to remember; wherein are contained the de- " lyghts that Wit followeth in his youth by the plea- " santnesse of Love, and the happinesse he reapeth in " age by the perfectnesse of Wisedome. 4to. 1580." And this was followed by " Euphues and his England, " containing his voyage and adventures mixed with " sundrie pretie discourses of honest Love, the descrip- " tion of the Countrie, the Court, and the manners of " that Isle. Delightful to be read, and nothing hurt- " full to be regarded; wherein there is small offence

[7] Discourse of English Poetry, 4to. 1586.
‡ *That heroe for numbers and for prose ;*] A word seems to be lost out of this line. For the sake of metre, read
That heroe *both* for numbers and for prose. S.

" by lightnesse given to the wise, and lesse occasion of
" loosenesse proffered to the wanton. 4to. 1582."

He was also the Author of the following Plays:

1. Alexander and Campaspe, 1584, 4to. 1591, 4to.
2. Endimion, 4to. 1591. .
3. Sappho and Phaon, 4to. 1591.
4. Galatea, 4to. 1592.
5. Mydas, 4to. 1592.
6. Mother Bombie, 4to. 1594, 4to. 1597.
7. The Woman in the Moon, 4to. 1597.
8. The Maid her Metamorphosis, 4to. 1600.
9. Love his Metamorphosis, 4to. 1601.

The first six of these Plays were re-published by
Edward Blount, in 12mo. 1632, under the title of
" Sixe Court Comedies."

Besides these, he was the Author of a piece, published in 1593, called " Pap with a Hatchet, alias, a
" fig for my Godson, or crack me this nut, or a Coun-
" try Cuff, that is, a sound box on the ear for the
" Ideot, Martin to hold his peace. Written by one
" that dares call a Dog a Dog." Imprinted for John
Oke.

PROLOGUE AT THE BLACK FRIERS.

THEY that fear the stinging of wasps, make fans of peacocks tails, whose spots are like eyes : And Lepidus, which could not sleep for the chattering of birds, set up a beast, whose head was like a dragon : and we which stand in awe of report, are compelled to set before our owl, Pallas' shield, thinking by her virtue to cover the other's deformity. It was a sign of famine to Ægypt, when Nylus flowed less than twelve cubits, or more than eighteen : and it may threaten despair unto us, if we be less curious than you look for, or more cumbersome. But as Theseus being promised to be brought to an eagle's nest, and travelling all the day, found but a wren in a hedge, yet said this is a bird : so we hope, if the shower of our swelling mountain seeming to bring forth some elephant, perform but a mouse, you will gently say, this is a beast. Basil softly touched, yieldeth a sweet scent ; but chafed in in the hand, a rank savour. We fear even so that our labours slily glanced on, will breed some content ; but examined to the proof, small commendation. The haste in performing shall be our excuse. There went two nights to the begetting of Hercules. Feathers appear not on the phœnix under seven months, and the mulberry is twelve in budding : but our travails are like the hare's, who at one time bringeth forth, nourisheth, and engendreth again ; or like the brood of Trochilus, whose eggs in the same moment that they are laid, become birds. But howsoever we finish our work, we crave pardon, if we offend in matter; and patience if we transgress in manners. We have mixed mirth with counsel, and discipline with delight; thinking it not amiss in the same garden to sow pot-herbs, that we set flowers. But we hope, as harts that cast their horns, snakes their skins, eagles their bills, become more fresh for any other labour: so our charge being shaken off, we shall be fit for greater matters. But lest like the Myndians, we make our gates greater than our town, and that our play runs out at the preface, we here conclude : wishing, that although there be in your precise judgments an universal mislike, yet we may enjoy by your wonted courtesies* a general silence.

* Curtesies   O. G.

PROLOGUE AT THE COURT.

WE are ashamed that our bird, which fluttereth by twilight, seeming a swallow, should be proved a bat, set against the sun. But as Jupiter placed Silenus's ass among the stars, and Alcibiades covered his pictures, being owls and apes, with a curtain embroidered with lions and eagles, so are we enforced, upon a rough discourse, to draw on a smooth excuse, resembling lapidaries, who think to hide the crack in a stone, by setting it deep in gold. The gods supp'd once with poor Baucis; the Persian kings sometimes shaved sticks; our hope is, your highness will at this time lend an ear to an idle pastime. [8] Appion raising Homer from hell, demanded only who was his father; and we calling Alexander from his grave, seek only who was his love. Whatsoever we present, we wish it may be thought the dancing of Agrippa's shadows, who in the moment they were seen, were of any shape one would conceive; or Lynces, who having a quick sight to discern, have a short memory to forget. With us it is like to fare as with these torches, which giving light to others, consume themselves; and we showing delight to others, shame our selves.

[8] *Appion raising Homer from hell, demanded only who was his father;*] " Quærat aliquis, quæ sint mentiti veteres Magi, cum " adolescentibus nobis visus Apion Grammaticæ artis, prodiderit " cynocephaliam herbam, quæ in Ægypto vocaretur osyrites, divi- " nam, & contra omnia venesicia : sed si ea erueretur, statim eum " qui eruisset, mori. Seque evocasse umbras ad percontandum " Homerum, qua patria quibusque parentibus genitus esset, non " tamen ausus profiteri, quid sibi respondisse diceret." C. Plin. Nat. Hist. l. **xxx.** c. 2.

DRAMATIS PERSONÆ.

ALEXANDER,
HEPHESTION,
CLYTUS,
PARMENIO,
PLATO,
ARISTOTLE,
DIOGENES,
MELIPPUS,
CRISIPPUS,
CRATES,
CLEANTHES,
ANAXARCHUS,
APELLES,
GRANICHUS,
MANES,   } Servants to { PLATO,
PSYLLUS,   DIOGENES,
                                     APELLES.

CAMPASPE,
TIMOCLEA,
LAIS.

Scene—Athens.

ALEXANDER AND CAMPASPE.[9]

ACT. I. SCEN. I.

CLYTUS. PARMENIO. TIMOCLEA. CAMPASPE. ALEXANDER. HEPHESTION.

Clytus. Parmenio, I cannot tell whether I should more commend in Alexander's victories, courage, or courtesy; in the one being a resolution without fear, in the other a liberality above custom. Thebes is rased, the people not racked, towers thrown down, bodies not thrust aside; a conquest without conflict, and a cruel war in a mild peace.

Parmenio. Clytus, it becometh the son of Philip to be none other than Alexander is; therefore seeing in the father a full perfection, who could have doubted in the son an excellency? For as the moon can borrow nothing else of the sun but light; so of a sire, in whom nothing but virtue was, what could the child receive but singular? it is for torquois [10] to stain each other,

---

[9] The subject of this play is taken from Pliny's *Natural History,* lib. 35. c. 10.
  " Tantum erat auctoritati juris in regem, alioquin iracundum :
  " quanquam Alexander ei honorem clarissimo præbuit exemplo.
  " Namque cum dilectam sibi ex pallacis suis præcipue nomine
  " Campaspem nudam pingi ob admirationem formæ ab Apelle
  " jussissit, eumque tum pari captum amore sensisset, dono eam
  " dedit. Magnus animo, major imperio sui, nec minor hoc facto,
  " quam victoria aliqua. Quippe, se vicit nec torum tantum suum,
  " sed etiam affectum donavit artifici : ne dilectæ quidam respectu
  " motus, ut quæ modo regis fuisset, modo pictoris esset. Sunt qui
  " Venerem Anadyomenen illo pictam exemplari purant."

[10] *Turquois*] In the first edition *Turkes.* "Turquesis," says Malynes, in his *Treatise of the Canker of England's Common-wealth,*

not for diamonds; in the one to be made a difference
in goodness, in the other no comparison.

Clytus. You mistake me, Parmenio, if whilst I commend Alexander, you imagine I call Philip into question; unless haply you conjecture (which none of
judgment will conceive) that because I like the fruit,
therefore I heave at the tree; or coveting to kiss the
child, I therefore go about to poison the teat.

Parmenio. Ay, but Clytus, I perceive you are born
in the east, and never laugh but at the sun-rising;
which argueth tho' a duty where you ought, yet no
great devotion where you might.

Clytus. We will make no controversy of that which
there ought to be no question; only this shall be the
opinion of us both, that none was worthy to be the
father of Alexander but Philip, nor any meet to be the
son of Philip but Alexander.

Parmenio. Soft, Clytus, behold the spoils and prisoners! a pleasant sight to us, because profit is join'd
with honour; not much painful to them, because their
captivity is eased by mercy.

Timoclea. Fortune, thou didst never yet deceive
virtue, because virtue never yet did trust fortune.
Sword and fire will never get spoil, where wisdom and
fortitude bears sway. O Thebes, thy walls were raised
by the sweetness of the harp, but rased by the shrill-
ness of the trumpet. Alexander had never come so
near the walls, had Epaminondas walk'd about the
walls; and yet might the Thebans have been merry
in their streets, if he had been to watch their towers.
But destiny is seldom foreseen, never prevented. We
are here now captives, whose necks are yoaked by

12mo. 1601, " are found in Malabar, being of Turqueys color by
" the day time, and by night by the light, greene; they growe upon
" a black stone, whereof retaining some little blacke veines is the
better." " It is," as Mr. Steevens observes, " said of the Turkey
" stone, that it faded or brightened in its colour, as the health of
" the wearer increased or grew less." (Note on *Merchant of*
Venice, p. 118. vol. III.)   See a'so Dr. Morell's Account of it,
p. 417: of his Edition of Chaucer's *Cantei bury Tales,* 8vo. 1737.

force, but whose hearts can not yield by death. Come, Campaspe, and the rest, let us not be ashamed to cast our eyes on him, on whom we fear'd not to cast our darts.

Parmenio. Madam, you need not doubt, it is Alexander that is the conqueror.

Timoclea. Alexander hath overcome, not conquer'd.

Parmenio. To bring all under his subjection, is to conquer.

Timoclea. He cannot subdue that which is divine.

Parmenio. Thebes was not.

Timoclea. Virtue is.

Clytus. Alexander, as he tendreth virtue, so he will you; he drinketh not blood, but thirsteth after honour; he is greedy of victory, but never satisfied with mercy: In fight terrible, as becometh a captain; in conquest mild, as beseemeth a king. In all things, than which nothing can be greater, he is Alexander.

Campaspe. Then if it be such a thing to be Alexander, I hope it shall be no miserable thing to be a virgin. For if he save our honours, it is more than to restore our goods. And rather do I wish he'd preserve our fame than our lives, which if he do, we will confess there can be no greater thing than to be Alexander.

Alexander. Clytus, are these prisoners? of whence these spoils?

Clytus. Like your majesty, they are prisoners, and of Thebes

Alexander. Of what calling or reputation?

Clytus I know not, but they seem to be ladies of honour.

Alexander. I will know—Madam, of whence you are I know, but who, I cannot tell.

Timoclea. Alexander, I am the sister of Theagines, who fought a battel with thy father, before the city of Chieronte,[11] where he died, I say which none can gainsay, valiantly.

---

[11] *Chieronte*] Chieronie, in the first and second editions.

Alexander. Lady, there seem in your words sparks
of your brother's deeds, but worser fortune in your life
than his death : but fear not, for you shall live without violence, enemies, or necessity—But what are you,
fair lady, another sister to Theagines?

Campaspe. No sister to Theagines, but an humble
handmaid to Alexander, born of a mean parentage,
but to extream fortune.

Alexander. Well ladies, for so your virtues shew
you, whatsoever your births be, you shall be honourably entreated. Athens shall be your Thebes, and you
shall not be as abjects of war, but as subjects to Alexander. Parmenio, conduct these honourable ladies
into the city, charge the soldiers not so much as in
words to offer them any offence, and let all wants be
supply'd so far forth as shall be necessary for such
persons, and my prisoners.

[*Exeunt* Parmenio *and captives.*

Hephestion, it resteth now that we have as great care
to govern in peace, as conquer in war : that whilst
arms cease, arts may flourish, and joining letters with
lances we endeavour to be as good philosophers as
soldiers; knowing it no less praise to be wise, than
commendable to be valiant.

Hephestion. Your majesty therein sheweth, that you
have as great desire to rule as to subdue; and needs
must that common-wealth be fortunate, whose captain
is a philosopher, and whose philosopher is a captain.

[*Exeunt.*

ACT. I. SCEN. II.

MANES.   GRANICHUS.   PSYLLUS.

Manes. I serve instead of a master, a mouse, whose
house is a tub, whose dinner is a crust, and [12] whose
bed is a board.

[12] *Whose bed is a board.*] The first and second editions read,
whose board is a bed.

Psyllus. Then art thou in a state of life which philosophers commend.   A crumb for thy supper, a hand for thy cup, and thy cloaths for thy sheets.   For *Natura paucis contenta.*

Granichus. Manes, it is pity so proper a man should be cast away upon a philosopher; but that Diogenes, that dog, should have Manes that dog-bolt, it grieveth nature, and spiteth art; the one having found thee so dissolute, absolute I would say, in body, the other so single, singular in mind.

Manes. Are you merry? it is a sign by the trip of your tongue, and the toys of your head, that you have done that to-day, which I have not done these three days.

Psyllus. What's that?

Manes. Dined.

Granichus. I think Diogenes keeps but cold chear.

Manes. I would it were so.; but he keepeth neither hot nor cold.

Granichus. What then, luke-warm?   That made Manes run from his master the last day.

Psyllus. Manes had reason; for his name foretold as much.

Manes. My name! how so, sir boy?

Psyllus. You know that it is called *Mons à movendo,* because it stands still.

Manes. Good.

Psyllus. And thou art named Manes, *à Manendo,* because thou run'st away.

Manes. Passing reasons! I did not run away, but retire.

Psyllus. To a prison, because thou wouldst have leisure to contemplate.

Manes. I will prove that my body was immortal, because it was in prison.

Granichus. As how?

Manes. Did your masters never teach you that the soul is immortal?

Granichus. Yes.

Manes. And the body is the prison of the soul.

Granichus. True.

Manes. Why then, thus to make my body immortal, I put it in prison.

Granichus. Oh bad!

Psyllus. Excellent ill!

Manes. You may see how dull a fasting wit is: therefore, Psyllus, let us go to supper with Granichus; Plato is the best fellow of all philosophers. Give me him that reads in the morning in the school, and at noon in the kitchen.

Psyllus. And me.

Granichus. Ah, sirs, my master is a king in his parlour for the body; and a God in his study for the soul. Among all his men he commendeth one that is an excellent musician, then stand I by and clap another on the shoulder and say, this is a passing good cook.

Manes, It is well done, Granichus; for give me pleasure that goes in at the mouth, not the ear; I had rather fill my guts than my brains.

Psyllus. I serve Apelles, who feedeth me, as Diogenes did Manes; for at dinner the one preacheth abstinence, the other commendeth counterfeiting: When I would eat meat, he paints a spit; and when I thirst, O, saith he, is not this a fair pot? and points to a table, which contains the banquet of the gods, where are many dishes to feed the eye, but not to fill the gut.

Granichus. What dost thou then?

Psyllus. This doth he then, bring in many examples that some have lived by savours, and proveth that much easier it is to grow fat by colours, and tells of birds that have been fatted by painted grapes in winter; and how many have so fed their eyes with their mistress's picture, that they never desir'd to take food, being glutted with the delight in their favours. [13] Then

[13] *Then doth he shew me counterfeits,*] Counterfeit was a term formerly used for any kind of painting, but more especially for a portrait. Psyllus says above, " for a dinner the one preacheth " abstinence, the other commendeth *counterfeiting.*"

doth he shew me counterfeits, such as have surfeited with their filthy and loathsome vomits, and with the riotous bacchanals of the god Bacchus, and his disorderly crew, which are painted all to the life in his shop. To conclude, I fare hardly, tho' I go richly, which maketh me when I should begin to shadow a lady's face, to draw a lamb's head, and sometime to set to the body of a maid, a shoulder of mutton ; for *Semper animus meus est in patinis.*

   Manes. Thou art a god to me : for could I see but a

And, in Dekker's *Strange Horserace,* 16—. B. 2 : " — and more " to dignifie the conquerour, pictures, and *counterfets* of all.the " citties, mountaines, rivers, and battailes, from whence they came " victors, were drawn in ensignes to the liveliest portrature, all " supported before the triumpher."

Again, *Arden of Feversham,* 1592 ;
   " I happen'd on painter yesternight,
   " The onely cunning man of Christendoome :
   " For he can temper poyson with his oyle,
   " That who so lookes upon the worke he drawes,
   " Shall with the beames that issue from his sight,
   " Suck vennome to his breast and slay himselfe,
   " Sweet Ales he shall draw thy *counterfet,*
   " That Arden may by gaizing on it perish."

Green's *Historie of Fryer Bacon and Fryer Bungay,* 1630 :
   " After that English Henry by his Lords,
   " Had sent Prince Edward's lovely *counterfeit,*
   " A present to the Castile Elinor,
   " The comly portrait of so brave a man, &c."

Ibid. Sig. G 2 :
   " Seeing my Lord his lovely *counterfeit,*
   " And hearing how his mind and shape agreed,
   " I come not troopt with all this warlike train, &c."

Lyly's *Euphues and his England,* 1582, Dedication to the Ladies ; " Therefore in my mind, you are more beholding to gentlemen that " make the colours than to the painters that draw your *counter-* "*faite,* &c."

Ibid. p. 67 : " At last it came to this passe, that hee in paint- " ing deserved most praise that could set down most colours : " wherby ther was more contention kindled about the colour than " the *counterfait,* and greater emulation for varietie in shew than " workemanship in substance.

Euphues, 1581, p. 55 : " A certaine painter brought Appelles " the *counterfaite* of a face in a table, &c."

   * An expression in one of the plays of Terence.   S.

cook's shop painted, I would make mine eyes fat as butter. For I have nought but sentences to fill my maw.; as, *plures occidit crapula quam gladius : musa jejunantibus amica*: repletion killeth delicately. And an old saw of abstinence by Socrates : *the belly is the head's grave.* Thus with sayings, not with meat, he maketh [14] a gallimafrey.

Granichus. But how do'st thou then live?

Manes. With fine jests, sweet air, and the dogs alms.

Granichus. Well, for this time, I will staunch thy gut; and, among pots and platters, thou shalt see what it is to serve Plato.

Psyllus. For joy of Granicus, let's sing.

Manes. My voice is as clear in the evening as in the morning.

Granichus. Another commodity of emptiness.

SONG.[15]

Gran. O for a bowl of fat canary,
    Rich Palermo, sparkling sherry;
    Some Nectar else from Juno's darry,*
    O these draughts would make us merry.

Psil. O for a wench (I deal in faces,
    And in other daintier things,)
    Tickled am I with her embraces,
    Fine dancing in such fairy rings.

Ma. O for a plump fat leg of mutton,
    Veal, lamb, capon, pig, and coney,
    None is happy but a glutton,
    None an ass but who wants money.

[14] — *a gallimafrey.*] i. e. a medley. So, in *Pierce Penilesse Supplication to the Divell*, 1592, p. 27. " — they mingled them all in " one *gallimafry* of glory."

Prologue to *Wily beguiled*, 1606: " Why noble Cerberus, " nothing but patch pannel stuff, old *gallymawfries* and cotton " candle eloquence.

Gallimaufrey. Ap. Herod. 235.

[15] This Song is restored from Blount's Edition of " Sixe Court " Comedies," 1632. It is omitted in all the 4to Editions.

* I suppose Granichus means Juno's dairy. S.

Cho.   Wines (indeed) and girls are good,
But brave victuals feast the blood,
For wenches, wine, and lusty cheer,
Jove would leap down to surfeit here.

ACT I. SCEN. III.

MELIPPUS, PLATO, ARISTOTLE, CRISIPPUS, CRATES,
CLEANTHES, ANAXARCHUS, ALEXANDER, HE-
PHESTION, PARMENIO, CLYTUS, DIOGENES.

Melippus. I had never such ado to warn scholars to
come before a king: First I came to Crisippus, a tall
lean old mad man, willing him presently to appear before Alexander: he stood staring on my face, neither
moving his eyes nor his body: I urging him to give
some answer, he took up a book, sat down, and said
nothing.   Melissa, his maid, told me it was his manner, and that oftentimes she was fain to thrust meat
into his mouth; for that he would rather starve than
cease study.   Well, thought I, seeing bookish men are
so blockish, and so great clerks such simple courtiers,
I will neither be partaker of their commons nor their
commendations.   From thence I came to Plato, and
to Aristotle, and to divers others, none refusing ro
come, saving an old obscure fellow, who, sitting in a
tub turn'd towards the sun, read Greek to a young
boy; him when I will'd to appear before Alexander,
he answer'd, If Alexander would fain see me, let him
come to me; if learn of me, let him come to me; whatsoever it be, let him come to me.   Why, said I, he is
a king; he answer'd, Why I am a philosopher.   Why,
but he is Alexander; ay, but I am Diogenes.   I was
half angry to see one so crooked in his shape, to be so
crabbed in his sayings.   So, going my way, I said,
Thou shalt repent it, if thou comest not to Alexander:
nay, smiling, answer'd he, Alexander may repent it, if

he come not to Diogenes ; virtue must be sought, not
offered : and so turning himself to his cell, he grunted
I know not what, like a pig under a tub.—But I must
be gone, the philosophers are coming.   [*Exit.*

Plato. It is a difficult controversy, Aristotle, and
rather to be wonder'd at than believed, how natural
causes should work supernatural effects.

Aristotle. I do not so much stand upon the appari-
tion seen in the moon, neither the Dæmonium of Socrates, as that I cannot, by natural reason, give any
reason of. the ebbing and flowing of the sea, which
makes me, in the depth of my studies, to cry out, *O
ens entium miserere mei !*

Plato. Cleanthes and you attribute so much to nature, by searching for things which are not to be
found, that whilst you study a cause of your own, you
omit the occasion itself.   There is no man so savage in
whom resteth not this divine particle, that there is an
omnipotent, eternal, and divine mover, which may be
call'd God.

Cleanthes. I am of this mind, that the first mover,
which you term God, is the instrument of all the mov-
ings which we attribute to nature. The earth, which is
mass, swimmeth on the sea, seasons divided in themselves, fruits growing in themselves, the majesty of the
sky, the whole firmament of the world, and whatever
else appeareth miraculous, what man almost of mean
capacity but can prove it natural.

Anaxarchus. These causes shall be debated at our
philosophers feast, in which controversy I will take
part with Aristotle, that there is *natura naturans,* and
yet not God.

Crates. And I with Plato, that there is D*eus optimus
maximus,* and not nature.

Aristotle. Here cometh Alexander.

Alexander. I see, Hephestion, that these philosophers are here attending for us.

Hephestion. They [16] were not philosophers, if they
knew not their duties.

[16] *These were not,* &c.] The third and Blount's editions read,
These are not.

Alexander. But I much marvel Diogenes should be so dogged.

Hephestion. I do not think but his excuse will be better than Melippus' message.

Alexander. I will go see him, Hephestion, because I long to see him that would command Alexander to come, to whom all the world is like to come,—Aristotle and the rest, sithence my coming from Thebes to Athens, from a place of conquest to a palace of quiet, I have resolved with myself in my court to have as many philosophers as I had in my camp soldiers. My court shall be a school, wherein I will have used as great doctrine in peace, as I did in war discipline.

Aristotle We are all here ready to be commanded, and glad we are that we are commanded; for that nothing better becometh kings than literature, which maketh them come as near to the gods in wisdom, as they do in dignity.

Alexander It is so, Aristotle; but yet there is among you, yea, and of your bringing up, that sought to destroy Alexander: Calistenes, Aristotle, whose treasons against his prince shall not be borne out with the reasons of his philosophy.

Aristotle. If ever mischief entered into the heart of Calistenes, let Calistenes suffer for it; but that Aristotle ever imagined any such thing of Calistenes, Aristotle doth deny.

Alexander. Well, Aristotle, kindred may blind thee, and affection me; but, in kings causes I will not stand to scholars arguments. This meeting shall be for a commandment, that you all frequent my court, instruct the young with rules, confirm the old with reasons: let your lives be answerable to your learnings, lest my proceedings be contrary to my promises.

Hephestion. You said you would ask every one of them a question, which yesternight none of us could answer.

Alexander. I will.—Plato, of all beasts which is the subtilest?

Plato. That which man hitherto never knew.

Alexander. Aristotle, how should a man be thought
a God?

Aristotle. In doing a thing impossible for a man.

Alexander. Crisippus, which was first, the day, or
the night?

Crisippus. The day, by a day.

Alexander. Indeed. strange questions must have
strange answers. Cleanthes, what say you, is life or
death the stronger?

Cleanthes. Life, that suffereth so many troubles.

Alexander. Crates, how long should a man live?

Crates. Till he think it better to die than to live.

Alexander. Anaxarchus, whether doth the sea or the
earth bring forth most creatures?

Anaxarchus. The earth; for the sea is but a part of
the earth.

Alexander. Hephestion, methinks they have answer'd all well; and in such questions I mean often to
try them.

Hephestion. It is better to have in your court a wise
man, than in your ground a golden mine. Therefore
would I leave war to study wisdom, were I Alexander.

Alexander. So would I, were I Hephestion. But
come, let us go and give release, as I promised, to our
Theban thralls.   [*Exeunt.*

Plato. Thou art fortunate, Aristotle, that Alexander
is thy scholar.

Aristotle. And all you happy, that he is your sovereign.

Crisippus. I could like the man well, if he could be
contented to be but a man.

Aristotle. He seeketh to draw near to the Gods in
knowledge, not to be a God.

Enter DIOGENES.

Plato. Let us question a little with Diogenes, why
he went not with us to Alexander.—Diogenes, thou
did'st forget thy duty, that thou went'st not with us to
the king.

Diogenes. And you your profession, that you went to the king.

Plato. Thou tak'st as great pride to be peevish, as others do glory to be virtuous.

Diogenes. And thou as great honour, being a philosopher, to be thought court-like, as others shame, that be courtiers, to be accounted philosophers.

Aristotle. These austere manners set aside, it is well known that thou didst counterfeit money.

Diogenes. And thou thy manners, in that thou didst not counterfeit money.

Aristotle. Thou hast reason to contemn the court, being, both in body and mind, too crooked for a courtier.

Diogenes. As good be crooked, and endeavour to make myself straight from the court, as to be straight, and learn to be crooked at the court.

Crates. Thou think'st it a grace to be opposite against Alexander.

Diogenes. [17] And thou to be jump with Alexander.

Anaxarchus. Let us go ; for in contemning him, we shall better please him, than in wondering at him.

Aristotle. Plato, what do'st thou think of Diogenes?

Plato. To be Socrates, furious.   Let us go.

[*Exeunt Philosoph.*

---

[17] *And thou to be jump with Alexander.*]   *To be jump*, is to agree. So, in *Pierce Penilesse his Supplication to the Divell*, p. 29   " Not " two of them *jump* in one tale."

Shakspeare's *Richard* III. A. 3. S. 1 :
" No more can you distinguish of a man,
" Than of his outward shew ; which, God he knows,
" Seldom, or never, *jumpeth* with the heart."

Tarlton's *Newes of Purgatory*, 1630, p. 31 : " Masse Vickar " assoone as hee saw these had a reach in his head and *jumpt* with " the travailler to buie one ; a price was pitcht, &c."

It is a common phrase even at present to say, *Great wits jump*, when two persons concur in the same thought without any communication with each other.

ACT. II. SCEN. I.

DIOGENES, PSYLLUS, MANES, GRANICHUS.

Psyllus. Behold, Manes, where thy master is, seeking either for bones for his dinner, or pins for his sleeves. I will go salute him.

Manes. Do so; but mum, not a word that you saw Manes.

Granichus. Then stay thou behind, and I will go with Psyllus.

Psyllus. All hail, Diogenes, to your proper person.

Diogenes. All hate to thy peevish conditions.

Granichus. O dog!

Psyllus. What do'st thou seek for here?

Diogenes. For a man, and a beast.

Granichus. That is easy, without thy light, to be found—be not all these men?

Diogenes. Call'd men.

Granichus. What beast is it thou look'st for?

Diogenes. The beast my man, Manes.

Psyllus. He is a beast, indeed, that will serve thee.

Diogenes. So is he that begat thee.

Granichus. What would'st thou do, if thou should'st find Manes?

Diogenes. Give him leave to do as he hath done before.

Granichus. What's that?

Diogenes. To run away.

Psyllus. Why, hast thou no need of Manes?

Diogenes. It were a shame for Diogenes to have need of Manes, and for Manes to have no need of Diogenes.

Granichus. But put the case he were gone, would'st thou entertain any of us two?

Diogenes. Upon condition.

Psyllus. What?

Diogenes. That you should tell me wherefore any of you both were good.

Granichus. Why, I am a scholar, and well seen in philosophy.

Psyllus. And I a 'prentice, and well seen in painting.

Diogenes. Well then, Granichus, be thou a painter to amend thine ill face; and thou, Psyllus, a philosopher, to correct thine evil manners.—But who is that, Manes?

Manes. I care not who I were, so I were not Manes.

Manes. You are taken tardy.

Psyllus. Let us slip aside, Granichus, to see the salution between Manes and his master.

Diogenes. Manes, thou know'st the last day I threw away my dish, to drink in my hand, because it was superfluous; now I am determined to put away my man, and serve myself: *quia non egeo tui vel te.*

Manes. Master, you know a while ago I ran away; so do I mean to do again: *quia scio tibi non esse argentum.*

Diogenes. I know I have no money, neither will I have ever a man; for I was resolv'd long since to put away both my slaves, money and Manes.

Manes. So was I determin'd to shake off both my dogs, hunger and Diogenes.

Psyllus. [18] O sweet consent between a crowd and a Jew's harp!

Granichus. Come, let us reconcile them.

Psyllus. It shall not need, for this is their use: now do they dine one upon another.   [*Exit Diogenes.*

---

[18] *O sweet consent between a crowd and a Jew's harp!*] The word *crowd* is an antient word for a fiddle, and a crowder a player on that instrument. It appears from Junius's *Etymologicon,* in voce, and from Spelman's *Glossary,* v. *crotta,* that it is a term of considerable antiquity, but it is very doubtful whether it had originally the same meaning we now assign to it. Probably it might mean a musical instrument, very different from the violin. See *Gent. Mag.* 1757, p. 561.

Ben Jonson's *Cynthia's Revels,* A. 1. S. 1: " — a laquey that " runs on errands for him, and can whisper a light message to " a loose wench with some round volubility, wait mannerly at a " table with a trencher, and warble upon *a crowd* a little, fill out " Nectar when Ganymede's away, &c.

Granichus. How now, Manes, art thou gone from
　　thy master ?

Manes. No, I did but now bind myself to him.

Psyllus. Why, you were at mortal jars.

Manes. In faith, no ; we brake a bitter jest one upon
　　another.

Granichus. Why, thou art as dogged as he.

Psyllus. My father knew them both little whelps.

Manes. Well, I will hie me after my master.

Granichus. Why, is it supper-time with Diogenes ?

Manes. Ay, with him at all times when he hath
　　meat.

Psyllus. Why then, every man to his home ; and let
us steal out again anon.

Granichus. Where shall we meet ?

Psyllus. Why, at *Ala vendibili suspensa hædera non
est opus.*

Manes. O Psyllus, *habeo te loco parentis,* thou
　　blessest me.　　　　　　　　　　　　　　[*Exeunt.*

ACT. II. SCEN. II.

ALEXANDER, HEPHESTION, PAGE, DIOGENES, APELLES.

Alexander. Stand aside, sir boy, till you be call'd.—
Hephestion, how do you like the sweet face of Campaspe?

Hephestion. I cannot but commend the stout courage of Timoclea.

Alexander. Without doubt, Campaspe had some
great man to her father.

Hephestion You know Timoclea had Theagines to
her brother.

Alexander. Timoclea still in thy mouth! art thou
not in love?

Hephestion. Not I.

Alexander. Not with Timoclea you mean; [19] wherein you resemble the lapwing, who crieth most where her nest is not. And so, you lead me from espying your love with Campaspe, you cry Timoclea.

Hephestion. Could I as well subdue kingdoms, as I can my thoughts, or where I as far from ambition as I am from love, all the world would account me as valiant in arms, as I know myself moderate in affection.

Alexander. Is love a vice?

Hephestion. It is no virtue.

Alexander. Well, now shalt thou see what small difference I make between Alexander and Hephestion. And since thou hast been always partaker of my triumphs, thou shalt be partaker of my torments: I love, Hephestion, I love Campaspe; a thing far unfit for a Macedonian, for a king, for Alexander. Why hangest thou down thy head, Hephestion, blushing to hear that which I am not asham'd to tell?

Hephestion. Might my words crave pardon, and my counsel credit, I would both discharge the duty of a

---

[19] — *wherein you resemble the lapwing, who crieth most where her nest is not.*] This simile occurs in our ancient writers perhaps more frequently than any other which can be pointed out.

In the *Old Law*, by Massinger, Middleton, and Rowley, A. 4. S. 2:

> " H'as the lapwing's cunning, I am afraid my lord,
> " That cries most when she's farthest from the nest."

The Witch of Edmonton, 1638, by Rowley, Dekker, and Ford, A. 2. S. 2 : " Like to the lapwing have you all this while deluded " me? pretending counterfeit senses for your discontent, and now " at last it is by chance stole from you."

Rowley's *Search for Money*, 1609, p. 22 : " — yet it may be this " sir, dealt like a lapwing with us, and cryed furthest of the nest."

The Bel-man's night walkes, by Dekker : " It hath the head of a " man (the face well bearded), the eyes of a hawke, the tongue " of a lapwing which saies heere it is, when the nest is a good " way off."

Lylie himself also uses it in the *Epistle Dedicatorie to Euphues and his England*, 1582 : " And in this I resemble the lapwing, who " fearing her young ones to be destroyed by passengers, flieth with " a false crie farre from the neasts, making those that look for " them seeke where they are not."

See other examples in the Notes of Mr. Steevens, Mr. Smith, and Dr. Grey, to Shakspeare, vol. II. p. 28 and 215.

subject or so I am, and the office of a friend, for so I will.

Alexander. Speak, Hephestion; for whatsoever is spoken, Hephestion speaketh to Alexander.

Hephestion. I cannot tell, Alexander, whether the report be more shameful to be heard, or the cause sorrowful to be believed? What, is the son of Philip, king of Macedon, become the subject of Campaspe, the captive of Thebes? Is that mind, whose greatness the world could not contain, drawn within the compass of an idle alluring eye? Will you handle the spindle with Hercules, when you should shake the spear with Achilles? [20] Is the warlike sound of drum and trump turned to the soft noise of lyre and lute? the neighing of barbed steeds *, whose loudness filled the air with terror, and whose breaths dimned the sun with smoak, converted to delicate tunes and amorous glances? O Alexander, that soft and yielding mind should not be in him, whose hard and unconquered heart hath made so many yield. But you love: ah grief! but whom? Campaspe? ah shame! a maid forsooth unknown, un-noble, and who can tell whether immodest? whose eyes are framed by art to enamour, and whose heart was made by nature to enchant. Ay, but she is beautiful; yea, but not therefore chaste. Ay, but she is comely in all parts of the body; yea, but she may be crooked in some part of the mind: ay, but she is wise: yea, but she is a woman. Beauty is like the blackberry, which seemeth red when it is not ripe, resembling precious stones that are polished with honey, which the smoother they look, the sooner they break. It is thought won-

---

[20] *Is the warlike sound,* &c.] So, in Shakspeare's *Richard* III. A. 1. S. 1:

> " Grim visag'd war hath smooth'd his wrinkled front;
> " And now,—instead of mounting barbed steeds,
> " To fright the souls of fearful adversaries,—
> " He capers nimbly in a lady's chamber,
> " To the lascivious pleasing of a lute."

* *barbed steeds.*] See Note 41 to *The Four Prentices of London*, vol. VI. p. 514.   S.

derful among the seamen, that mugil*, of all fishes the
swiftest, is found in the belly of the Bret, of all the
slowest: and shall it not seem monstrous to wise men,
that the heart of the greatest conqueror of the world
should be found in the hands of the weakest creature
of nature? of a woman? of a captive? Ermins have
fair skins, but foul livers; sepulchres fresh colours but
rotten bones; women fair faces, but false hearts. Remember, Alexander, thou hast a camp to govern, not
a chamber; fall not from the armour of Mars to the
arms of Venus; from the fiery assaults of war, to the
maidenly skirmishes of love; from displaying the eagle
in thine ensign, to set down the sparrow. I sigh,
Alexander, that where fortune could not conquer, folly
should overcome. But behold all the perfection that
may be in Campaspe; a hair curling by nature, not
art; sweet alluring eyes; a fair face made in despite
of Venus, and a stately port in disdain of Juno; a wit
apt to conceive, and quick to answer; a skin as soft as
silk, and as smooth as jet; a long white hand, a fine
little foot; to conclude, all parts answerable to the best
part: what of this? though she have heavenly gifts,
virtue and beauty, is she not of earthly metal, flesh and
blood? You, Alexander, that would be a god, shew
yourself in this worse than a man, so soon to be both
overseen and overtaken in a woman, whose false tears
know their true times, whose smooth words wound
deeper than sharp swords. There is no surfeit so dangerous, as that of honey, nor any poison so deadly, as
that of love; in the one physick cannot prevail, nor in
the other counsel.

Alexander. My case were light, Hephestion, and not
worthy to be called love, if reason were a remedy, or
sentences could salve that sense cannot conceive.
Little do you know, and therefore slightly do you regard, the dead embers in a private person, or live coals
in a great prince, whose passions and thoughts do as
far exceed others in extremity, as their callings do in

---

* *the mugil.*] The mugil is the mullet.
 " Quosdam mæchos et mujilis intrat."—Juo. Sat. 10. S.

majesty. An eclipse in the sun is more than the falling of a star; none can conceive the torments of a
king, unless he be a king, whose desires are not infe-
riour to their dignities.   And then judge, Hephestion,
if the agonies of love be dangerous in a subject, whether
they be not more than deadly unto Alexander, whose
deep and not to be conceived sighs cleave the heart in
shivers; whose wounded thoughts can neither be expressed nor endured.   [21] Cease then, Hephestion, with
arguments to seek to refell that which with their deity
the gods cannot resist; and let this suffice to answer
thee, that it is a king that loveth, and Alexander, whose
affections are not to be measured by reason, being immortal, nor I fear me to be born, being intolerable.

Hephestion. I must needs yield, when neither reason
nor counsel can be heard.

Alexander. Yield, Hephestion, for Alexander doth
love, and therefore must obtain.

Hephestion. Suppose she loves not you: affection
cometh not by appointment or birth; and then as
good hated as enforced.

Alexander. I am king, and will command.

Hephestion. You may, to yield to lust by force; but
to consent to love by fear, you cannot.

Alexander Why, what is that which Alexander may
not conquer as he list?

Hephestion. Why, that which you say the gods cannot
resist, love.

Alexander. I am a conqueror, she a captive; I as
fortunate, as she fair: my greatness may answer her
wants, and the gifts of my mind, the modesty of hers:

---

[21] *Cease then, Hephestion, with arguments to seek to refell*] i. e. to
refute. So, in Erasmus's *Praise of Folie*, by Chaloner, Sig, L 1:
" Yea, so muche dooe rhetoriciens attribute to foolishenes, as
" oftentimes what abjection by no arguments *mai be refelled*, the
" same yet with some laughing and scoffynge conceits thei wolde
" have shifted of."
Euphues and his England, p. 60: " But I will not *refell* that
" heere, which shall be confuted hereafter."
Ibid. p. 98: " —and though I doubt not but that Martius is
" sufficiently armed to aunswere you, yet would I not have those
" reasons *refelled*, which I loath to have repeated."

Is it not likely then that she should love? is it not reasonable?

Hephestion. You say that in love there is no reason, and therefore there can be no likelihood.

Alexander. No more, Hephestion; in this case I will use mine own counsel, and in all other thine advice : thou may'st be a good soldier, but never a good lover. Call my page. [*Enter Page.*] Sirrah, go presently to Apelles, and will him to come to me, without either delay or excuse.

Page. I go.

Alexander. In the mean season, to recreate my spirits, being so near, we will go see Diogenes. And see where his tub is—Diogenes!

Diogenes Who calleth?

Alexander. Alexander—how happen'd it that you would not come out of your tub to my palace?

Diogenes. Because it was as far from my tub to your palace, as from your palace to my tub.

Alexander. Why then, do'st thou owe no reverence to kings?

Diogenes. No.

Alexander. Why so?

Diogenes. Because they be no Gods.

Alexander. They be Gods of the earth.

Diogenes. Yea, Gods of earth.

Alexander. Plato is not of thy mind.

Diogenes. I am glad of it.

Alexander. Why?

Diogenes. Because I would have none of Diogenes's mind, but Diogenes.

Alexander. If Alexander have any thing that may pleasure Diogenes, let me know, and take it.

Diogenes. Then take not from me that you cannot give me, the light of the world.

Alexander. What do'st thou want?

Diogenes. Nothing that you have.

Alexander. I have the world at command.

Diogenes. And I in contempt.

Alexander. Thou shalt live no longer than I will.

Diogenes. But I shall die whether you will or no.

Alexander. How should one learn to be content?

Diogenes. Unlearn to covet.

Alexander. Hephestion, were I not Alexander, I would wish to be Diogenes.

Hephestion. He is dogged, but discreet; I cannot tell how: sharp with a kind of sweetness, full of wit, yet too too wayward.

Alexander. Diogenes, when I come this way again, I will both see thee and confer with thee.

Diogenes. Do.

Alexander. But here cometh Apelles. [*Enter Apelles.*] How now, Apelles, is Venus's face yet finish'd?

Apelles. Not yet: beauty is not so soon shadow'd, whose perfection cometh not within the compass either of cunning or of colour.

Alexander. Well, let it rest unperfect; and come you with me, where I will shew you that finish'd by nature, that you have been trifling about by art.

[*Exeunt.*

ACT. III. SCEN. I.

APELLES, CAMPASPE.

Apelles. Lady, I doubt whether there be any colour so fresh, that may shadow a countenance so fair.

Campaspe. Sir, I thought you had been commanded to paint with your hand, not to glose with your tongue [22]. But, as I have heard, it is the hardest thing in painting to set down a hard favour, which maketh you to despair of my face; and then shall you have as great thanks to spare your labour, as to discredit your art.

---

[22] —*not to glose with your tongue.*] *To glose* is to flatter. So, in *Euphues and his England*, p. 75: " --but wil beleeve but what they " list, and in extolling their beauties, they give more credite to " their owne glasses, than mens *gloses*."

Apelles. Mistress, you neither differ from yourself, nor your sex; for, knowing your own perfection, you seem to dispraise that which men most commend, drawing them by that mean into an admiration, where feeding themselves, they fall into an extasy; your modesty being the cause of the one, and of the other your perfections.

Campaspe. I am too young to understand your speech, tho' old enough to withstand your device; you have been so long used to colours, you can do nothing but colour.

Apelles. Indeed the colours I see, I fear, will alter the colour I have. But come, madam, will you draw near? for Alexander will be here anon.—Psyllus, stay you here at the window: if any inquire for me, answer *Non lubet esse domi.*   [*Exeunt.*

ACT. III. SCEN. II.

PSYLLUS, MANES.

Psyllus. It is always my master's fashion, when any fair gentlewoman is to be drawn within, to make me stay without. But if he should paint Jupiter like a bull, like a swan, like an eagle, then must Psyllus with one hand grind colours, and with the other hold the candle. But let him alone, the better he shadows her face, the more will he burn his own heart. And now, if any man could meet with Manes, who, I dare say, looks as lean as if Diogenes dropt out of his nose—

Manes. And here comes Manes, who hath as much meat in his maw, as thou hast honesty in thy head.

Psyllus. Then I hope thou art very hungry.

Manes. They that know thee, know that.

Psyllus. But do'st thou not remember, that we have certain liquor to confer withal?

Manes. Ay, but I have business; I must go cry a thing.

Psyllus. Why, what hast thou lost?

Manes. That which I never had, my dinner.

Psyllus. Foul lubber, wilt thou *cry for thy dinner?

Manes. I mean I must cry, not as one would say cry, but cry, that is, make a noise.

Psyllus. Why, fool, that is all one; for if thou cry, thou must needs make a noise.

Manes. Boy, thou art deceived. Cry hath divers significations, and may be alluded to many things; Knave but one, and can be apply'd but to thee.

Psyllus. Profound Manes!

Manes. We Cynicks are mad fellows; did'st thou not find I did quip thee?

Psyllus. No verily; why, what's a quip?

Manes. †We great girders call it a short saying of a sharp wit, with a bitter sense in a sweet word.

Psyllus. How canst thou thus divine, divide, define, dispute, and all on the sudden?

Manes. Wit will have his swing: I am bewitch'd, inspir'd, inflam'd, infected.

Psyllus. Well, then will not I tempt thy gibing spirit.

Manes. Do not, Psyllus; for thy dull head will be but a grind-stone for my quick wit, which if thou whet with over-thwarts, *periisti, actum est de te.* I have drawn blood at one's brains with a bitter bob.

Psyllus. Let me cross myself; for I die, if I cross thee.

Manes. Let me do my business; I myself am afraid, lest my wit should wax warm, and then must it needs

---

* In old copy thus.

Foul lubber, wilt thou *crie* for thy dinner?

I mean I must *crie*, not as one would say cry, but *crie*, that is make a noyse. O. G.

† *We great girders.*] *i. e.* We who are much addicted to satirical reflections. Falstaff complains of being *girded* at; and Lucentio, in the Taming of the Shrew, last scene, says,

" I thank thee for that *gird*, good Tranio." S.

consume some hard head with fine and pretty jests.   I
am sometimes in such a vein, that for want of some dull
pate to work on, I begin to gird myself.

Psyllus. The Gods shield me from such a fine fellow,
whose words melt wits like wax.

Manes. Well then, let us to the matter.   In faith,
my master meaneth to-morrow to fly.

Psyllus. It is a jest.

Manes. Is it a jest to fly? should'st thou fly so soon,
thou should'st repent it in earnest.

Psyllus. Well, I will be the crier.

Manes and Psyllus (one after another). Oyez, Oyez,
Oyez, All manner of men, women, or children, that
will come to-morrow into the market-place, between
the hours of nine and ten, shall see Diogenes, the
Cynick, fly.

Psyllus.   I do not think he will fly.

Manes. Tush, say fly.

Psyllus. Fly.

Manes. Now let us go; for I will not see him again
till midnight.   I have a back-way into his tub.

. *Psyllus.* Which way call'st thou the back-way, when
every way is open?

Manes. I mean to come in at his back.

Psyllus. Well, let us go away, that we may return
speedily.   [*Exeunt.*

ACT. III. SCEN. III.

APELLES, CAMPASPE.

Apelles. I shall never draw your eyes well, because
they blind mine.

Campaspe. Why then paint me without eyes, for I
am blind.

Apelles. Were you ever shadow'd before of any?

Campaspe. No: and would you could so now shadow me, that I might not be perceived of any.

Apelles. It were pity, but that so absolute a face should furnish Venus's temple amongst these pictures.

Campaspe. What are these pictures?

Apelles. This is Læda, whom Jove deceived in likeness of a swan.

Campaspe. A fair woman; but a foul deceit.

Apelles. This is Alcmena, unto whom Jupiter came in shape of Amphitrion her husband, and begat Hercules.

Campaspe. A famous son, but an infamous fact.

Apelles. He might do it, because he was a God.

Campaspe. Nay, therefore it was evil done, because he was a God.

Apelles. This is Danae, into whose prison Jupiter drizled a golden shower, and obtained his desire.

Campaspe. What! gold can make one yield to desire.

Apelles. This is Europa, whom Jupiter ravish'd— This Antiopa.

Campaspe. Were all the Gods like this Jupiter?

Apelles. There were many Gods, in this, like Jupiter.

Campaspé. I think, in those days, love was well ratified among men on earth, when lust was so fully authorized by the Gods in heaven.

Apelles. Nay, you may imagine there were women passing amiable, when there were gods exceeding amorous.

Campaspe. Were women never so fair, men would be false.

Apelles. Were women never so false, men would be fond.

Campaspe. What counterfeit is this, Apelles?

Apelles. This is Venus, the goddess of love.

Campaspe. What, be there also loving goddesses?

Apelles. This is she that hath power to command the very affections of the heart.

Campaspe. How is she hired, by prayer, by sacrifice, or bribes?

Apelles. By prayer, sacrifice, and bribes.

Campaspe. What prayer?

Apelles. Vows irrevocable.

Campaspe What sacrifice?

Apelles. Hearts ever sighing, never dissembling.

Campaspe. What bribes?

Apelles. Roses and kisses.   But were you never in love?

Campaspe. No, nor love in me.

Apelles. Then have you injured many.

Campaspe. How so?

Apelles. Because you have been loved of many.

Campaspe. Flattered perchance of some.

Apelles. It is not possible that a face so fair, and a wit so sharp, both without comparison, should not be apt to love.

Campaspe. If you begin to tip your tongue with cunning, I pray dip your pencil in colours, and fall to that you must do, not that you would do.

ACT. III. SCEN. IV.

CLYTUS, PARMENIO, ALEXANDER, HEPHESTION,
CRYSUS, DIOGENES, APELLES, CAMPASPE.

Clytus. Parmenio, I cannot tell how it cometh to pass, that in Alexander now a days there groweth an unpatient kind of life: in the morning he is melancholy, at noon solemn; at all times either more sour or severe than he was accustomed.

Parmenio. In king's causes I rather love to doubt than conjecture, and think it better to be ignorant than inquisitive : [23] they have long ears and stretched arms,

---

[23] — *they have long ears and stretched arms,*] So, in *Euphues,* 1581, p. 23: " Knowest thou not Euphues, that kings have long " armes, and rulers large reaches ?"

Again, in *Damon and Pithias,* vol. I.

" What then ? *An nescis longas regibus esse manus?*"

in whose heads suspicion is a proof, and to be accused is to be condemn'd.

Clytus. Yet between us there can be no danger to find out the cause : for that there is no malice to with-stand it. It may be an unquenchable thirst of con-quering maketh him unquiet : it is not unlikely his long ease hath altered his humour : that he should be in love, it is not impossible.

Parmenio. In love, Clytus ? no, no, it is as far from his thought, as treason from ours : he, whose ever-waking eye, whose never-tired heart, whose body patient of labour, whose mind unsatiable of victory hath always been noted, cannot so soon be melted into the weak conceits of love : Aristotle told him there were many worlds, and that he hath not conquered one that gapeth for all galleth Alexander. But here he cometh.

Alexander. Parmenio and Clytus, I would have you both ready to go into Persia about an ambassage no less profitable to me, than to yourselves honourable.

Clytus. We are ready at all commands, wishing nothing else, but continually to be commanded.

Alexander. Well, then withdraw yourselves, till I have father considered of this matter. [*Exeunt Clytus and Parmenio.*] Now we will see how Apelles goeth for-ward : I doubt me that nature hath overcome art, and her countenance his cunning.

Hephestion. You love, and therefore think any thing.

Alexander. But not so far in love with Campaspe, as with Bucephalus, if occasion serve either of conflict or of conquest.

Hephestion. Occasion cannot want, if Will do not. Behold all Persia swelling in the pride of their own power, the Scythians careless what courage or fortune can do : the Egyptians dreaming in sooth-sayings of their augures, and gaping over the smoak of their beasts intrails. All these, Alexander, are to be sub-dued, if that world be not slipped out of your head which you have sworn to conquer with that hand.

Alexander. I confess the labour's fit for Alexander,

and yet recreation necessary among so many assaults, bloody wounds, intollerable troubles : give me leave a little, if not to sit, yet to breathe. And doubt not but Alexander can, when he will, throw affections as far from him, as he can cowardise. But behold Diogenes talking with one at his tub.

Crysus. One penny Diogenes, I am a Cynick.

Diogenes. He made thee a begger, that first gave thee any thing.

Crysus. Why, if thou wilt give nothing, no body will give thee.

Diogenes. I want nothing, till the springs dry, and the earth perish.

Crysus. I gather for the gods.

Diogenes. And I care not for those gods, which want money.

Crysus. Thou art a right Cynick, that wilt give nothing.

Diogenes. Thou art not, that wilt beg any thing.

Crysus. Alexander, king Alexander, give a poor Cynick a groat.

Alexander. It is not for a king to give a groat.

Crysus. Then give me a talent.

Alexander. It is not for a beggar to ask a talent. Away. Apelles!

Apelles. Here.

Alexander. Now gentlewoman, doth not your beauty put the painter to his trump ?

Campaspe. Yes, my lord, seeing so disordered a countenance, he feareth he shall shadow a deformed counterfeit.

Alexander. Would he could colour the life with the feature. And me thinketh, Apelles, were you as cunning as report saith you are, you may paint flowers as well with sweet smells as fresh colours, observing in your mixturesuch things as should draw near to their favours.

Apelles. Your majesty must know, it is no less hard to paint savours than virtues ; colours can neither speak, nor think.

Alexander. Where do you first begin, when ye draw any picture?

Apelles. The proportion of the face in as just compass as I can.

Alexander. I would begin with the eye, as a light to the rest.

Apelles. If you will paint as you are a king, your majesty may begin where you please; but as you would be a painter, you must begin with the face.

Alexander. Aurelius would in one hour colour four faces.

Apelles. I marvel in half an hour he did not four.

Alexander. Why, is it so easy?

Apelles. No, but he doth it so homely.

Alexander. When will you finish Campaspe?

Apelles. Never finish: for always in absolute beauty there is somewhat above art.

Alexander. Why should not I [24] be as cunning as Apelles?

Apelles. God shield you should have cause to be so cunning as Apelles!

Alexander. Me thinketh four colours are sufficient to shadow any countenance, and so it was in the time of Phydias.

Apelles. Then had men fewer fancies, and woman not so many favours. For now if the hair of her eyebrows be black, yet must the hair of her head be yellow: the attire of her head must be different from

---

[24] — *be as cunning as Apelles?*]   The word *cunning*, at the time this play was written, had not acquired its present bad signification. It was generally as here used synonymously with *skilful*. So, in Lyly's *Epistle Dedicatorie to Euphues and his England*, 1582: "So " that whereas I had thought to shewe *the cunning* of a chyrurgian " by mine anatomie with a knife, I must plaie the tailour on the " shoppe board with a paire of sheeres."

Again, in his *Epistle to the Ladies:* " — it was objected unto her " by a Ladie more captious than *cunning*, that in her worke there wanted some coulours."

And in the same sense it is frequently used throughout the English translation of the Bible.

the habit of her body, else would the picture seem like the blazon of ancient armory, not like the sweet delight of new-sound amiableness. For as in garden knots, diversity of odours make a more sweet favour, or as in musick divers strings cause a more delicate consent ;* so in painting, the more colours, the better counterfeit, observing black for a ground, and the rest for grace.

Alexander. Lend me thy pencil, Apelles; I will paint, and thou shalt judge.

Apelles. Here.

Alexander. The coal breaks.

Apelles. You lean too hard.

Alexander. Now it blacks not.

Apelles. You lean too soft.

Alexander. This is awry.

Apelles. Your eye goeth not with your hand.

Alexander. Now it is worse.

Apelles. Your hand goeth not with your mind.

Alexander. Nay, if all be too hard or soft, so many rules and regards, that one's hand, one's eye, one's mind, must all draw together, I had rather be setting of a battle, than blotting of a board. But how have I done here?

Apelles. Like a king.

Alexander. I think so: but nothing more unlike a painter. Well, Apelles, Campaspe is finished as I wish, dismiss her, and bring presently her counterfeit after me.

Apelles. I will.

Alexander. Now, Hephestion, [25] doth not this matter

---

* — *delicate consent*] *i. e.* union of sounds. See note on King Henry VI. p. 1. Shaksp. 1778. Vol. VI. p. 176. S.

[25] — *doth not this matter cotton as I would* ?] The Glossary to the *Praise of Yorkshire Ale*, 1697, explains the phrase *Naught cottons weell*, to be *Nothing goes right*. Alexander therefore means, *doth not this matter go as I would* ? So, in *Mons. Thomas*, by Beaumont and Fletcher, A. 4. S. 8 :

" Still mistress Dorothy ? *this geer will cotton.*"

cotton as I would? Campaspe looketh pleasantly;
liberty will encrease her beauty, and my love shall advance her honour.

  Hephestion. [26] I will not contrary your majesty; for
time must wear out that love hath wrought, and reason
wean what appetite nursed.

  Alexander. How stately she passeth by, yet how
soberly! a sweet consent in her countenanee, with
a chaste disdain! desire mingled with coyness! and I
cannot tell how to term it, a curst yielding modesty!

  Hephestion. Let her pass.

  Alexander. So she shall for the fairest on the earth.

                                        [*Exeunt.*

ACT. III.   SCENE. V.

PSYLLUS, MANES, APELLES.

  Psyllus. I shall be hang'd for tarrying so long.

  Manes. I pray God, my master be not flown before
I come.

  Psyllus. Away, Manes, my master doth come.

  Apelles. Where have you been all this while?

  Psyllus. No where but here.

  Apelles. Who was here sithence my coming?

  Psyllus. No body.

  Apelles. Ungracious wag, I perceive you have been
a loitering; was Alexander no body?

  Psyllus. He was a king, I meant no mean body.

Again, in Middleton's *Inner Temple Masque*, 1619:
    " To shew you good, bad, and indifferent dayes,
    " And all have their inscriptions, here's cock a hoop,
    " This the *geere cotton,* and this faint heart."
  [26] *I will not contrary your majesty;*] 1 will not *contradict* your
majesty. So, in the *Fable of Ferdinando Jeronimi.* Gascoigne's
Works, 1587, p. 273: " The Lady Fraunces did not seeme to
" *contrary* him, but rather smiled, &c."

Apelles. I will cudgel your body for it, and then will I say it was no body, because it was no honest body. Away, in. [*Exit Psyllus*]. Unfortunate Apelles, and therefore unfortunate because Apelles! Hast thou by drawing her beauty brought to pass, that thou canst scarce draw thine own breath? And by so much the more hast thou increased thy care, by how much the more thou hast shewed thy cunning : was it not sufficient to behold the fire and warm thee, but with Satyrus thou must kiss the fire and burn thee ? O Campaspe, Campaspe, art must yield to nature, reason to appetite, wisdom to affection! Could Pygmalion entreat by prayer to have his ivory turned into flesh ? And cannot Apelles obtain by plaints to have the picture of his love changed to life? Is painting so far inferior to carving? or do'st thou, Venus, more delight to be hewed with chissels, than shadowed with colours? What Pygmalion, or [27] what Pyrgoteles, or what Lysippus, is he, that ever made thy face so fair, or spread thy fame so far as I; unless, Venus, in this thou enviest mine art, that in colouring my sweet Campaspe, I have left no place by cunning to make thee so amiable? But, alas! she is the paramour to a prince, Alexander the monarch of the earth hath both her body and affection. For what is it that kings cannot obtain by prayers, threats and promises? Will not she think it bettter to sit under a cloth of estate like a queen, than in a poor shop like a housewife? and esteem it sweeter to be the concubine of the lord of the world, than spouse to a painter in Athens? Yes, yes, Apelles, thou may'st swim against the stream with the crab, and feed against the wind with the deer, and peck against the steel with the cockatrice: Stars are to be look'd at, not reach'd at; princes to be yielded unto, not contended with ; Campaspe to be

---

[27] — *what Pyrgoteles,* &c.]   " Idem hic imperator [Alexander] " edixit, ne quis ipsum alius, quam Apelles pingeret : quam Pyr- " goteles, sculperet : quam Lysippus, ex ære duceret : quæ artes " pluribus inclaruere exemplis." Plinii *Nat. Hist.* lib. vii. c. 37.

honóur'd, not obtain'd ; to be painted, not possessed of
thee.   O fair face! O unhappy hand ! and why didst
thou draw it so fair a face ? O beautiful countenance !
the express image of Venus, but somewhat fresher : the
only pattern of that eternity which Jupiter dreaming
asleep, could not conceive again waking.   Blush,
Venus, for I am asham'd to end thee.   Now must
I paint things unpossible for mine art, but agreeable'
with my affections : deep and hollow sighs, sad and
melancholy thoughts, wounds and slaughters of conceits, a life posting to death, a death galloping from
life, a wavering constancy, an unsettled resolution, and
what not, Apelles? and what but Apelles? but as
they that are shaken with a fever are to be warm'd with
cloaths, not groans, and as he that melteth in a con-
sumption is to be recur'd by [28] cullises, not conceits ;
so the feeding canker of my care, the never-dying
worm of my heart, is to be killed by counsel, not cries ;
by applying remedies, not by replying of reasons.   And
sith in cases desperate there must be used medicines
that are extream, I will hazard that little life that is left
to restore the grater part that is lost; and this shall be
my first practice; for wit must work where authority
is not.   As soon as Alexander hath view'd this por-
traiture, I will by device give it a blemish, that by that
means she may come again to my shop, and then
as good it were to utter my love, and die with denial,
as conceal it, and live in despair.

SONG BY APELLES[29].

Cupid and my Campaspe play'd
   At cards for kisses, Cupid paid ;

[28] — cullises] Cullises were compositions calculated to restore
worn-out constitutions, and invigorate feeble ones.   They were of
the same kind as jellies.   See Marston's Fawne, A. 2. S. 1. Massinger's Bondman, A. 4. S. 4.   The Picture, A. 1. S. 2.   The Emperor of the East, A. 1. S. 2. and in most of the Plays of the times.
   — coulis Fr. strained gravy or strong broth. S.
[29] This elegant little Sonnet is restored from Blount's Edition. It
is also printed in the third volume of Dr. Percy's Reliques of Ancient
Poetry, p. 83. A Translation of it into French, by an unknown
hand, is likewise published in the same volume, p. 348.

He stakes his quiver, bow and arrows,
His mother's doves, and team of sparrows;
Loses them too; then down he throws
The coral of his lip, the rose
Growing on's cheek, (but none knows how)
With these, the crystal of his brow,
And then the dimple of his chin;
All these did my Campaspe win.
At last he set her both his eyes,
She won, and Cupid blind did rise.
O Love! has she done this to thee?
What shall, alas! become of me?

ACT IV. SCEN. I.

SOLINUS, PSYLLUS, GRANICHUS, MANES, DIOGENES,
POPULUS.

Solinus. This is the place, the day, the time, that
Diogenes hath appointed to fly.

Psyllus. I will not lose the flight of so fair a fowl as
Diogenes is, though my master cudgel my nobody, as
he threaten'd.

Granichus. What, Psyllus, will the beast wag his
wings to-day?

Psyllus. We shall hear, for here cometh Manes—
Manes, will it be?

Manes. Be! he were best be as cunning as a bee, or
else shortly he will not be at all.

Granichus. How is he furnish'd to fly, hath he
feathers?

Manes. Thou art an ass; capons, geese, and owls, have
feathers. He hath found Dedalus' old waxen wings,
and hath been piecing them this month, he is so broad
in the shoulders; O you shall see him cut the air even
like a tortoise.

VOL. II.

Solinus. Methinks so wise a man should not be so mad, his body must needs be too heavy.

Manes. Why, he hath eaten nothing this seven-night but cork and feathers.

Psyllus. Touch him, Manes.

Granichus. He is so light that he can scarce keep him from flying at midnight.

Populus intrat.

Manes. See, they begin to flock, and behold my master bustles himself to fly.

Diogenes. Ye wicked and bewitch'd Athenians, whose bodies make the earth to groan, and whose breaths infect the air with stench. Come ye to see Diogenes fly? Diogenes cometh to see you sink: you call me dog, so I am, for I long to gnaw the bones in your skins. Yet term me an hater of men; no, I am a hater of your manners. Your lives dissolute, not fearing death, will prove your deaths desperate, not hoping for life. What do you else in Athens but sleep in the day, and surfeit in the night? Back-gods in the morning with pride, in the evening belly-gods with gluttony. You flatter kings, and call them gods; speak truth of yourselves, and confess you are devils. From the bee you have taken not the honey, but the wax to make your religion, framing it to the time, not to the truth. Your filthy lust you cover under a courtly colour of love; injuries abroad under the title of policies at home; and secret malice creepeth under the name of publick justice. You have caused Alexander to dry up springs, and plant vines; to sow rocket, and weed endive; to shear sheep, and shrine foxes. All conscience is [30] seared at Athens. Swearing cometh of a hot metal; lying of a quick wit, flattery of a flowing tongue, undecent talk of a merry disposition; all things are lawful at Athens. Either you think there are

---

[30] *seared*] All the editions read *sealed*, except the last by Mr. Dodsley. I have retained his alteration; although *sealed* may probably be right, being a term in falconry, signifying *blinded*.

no gods, or I must think ye are no men. You build
as though you should live for ever, and surfeit as
though you should die to morrow. None teacheth
true philosophy but Aristotle, because he was the king
of schoolmasters. O times! O men! O corruption in
manners! Remember that green grass must turn to
dry hay. When you sleep, you are not sure to wake;
and when you rise, not certain to lie down. Look you
never so high, your heads must lie level with your feet.
Thus have I flown over your disorder'd lives, and
if you will not amend your manners, I will study to fly
farther from you, that I may be nearer to honesty.

Solinus. Thou ravest Diogenes, for thy life is different from thy words. Did I not see thee come out of
a brothel-house? was it not a shame?

Diogenes. It was no shame to go out, but a shame to
go in.

Granichus. It were a good deed, Manes, to beat thy
master.

Manes. You were as good eat my master.

One of the people. Hast thou made us all fools, and
wilt thou not fly?

Diogenes. I tell thee, unless thou be honest, I will fly.

People. Dog, dog, take a bone.

Diogenes. Thy father need fear no dogs, but dogs
thy father.

People. We will tell Alexander, that thou reprovest
him behind his back.

Diogenes. And I will tell him, that you flatter him
before his face.

People. We will cause all the boys in the street to
hiss at thee.

Diogenes. Indeed I think the Athenians have their
children ready for any vice, because they be Athenians.

Manes. Why, master, mean you not to fly?

Diogenes. No, Manes, not without wings.

Manes. Every body will account you a liar.

Diogenes. No, I warrant you; for I always say the
Athenians are mischievous.

Psyllus. I care not, it was sport enough for me to see these [31] old huddles hit home.

Granichus. Nor I.

Psyllus. Come, let us go, and hereafter when I mean to rail upon any body openly, it shall be given out I will fly.   [*Exeunt.*

ACT. IV. SCEN. II.

CAMPASPE, APELLES.

Campaspe sola. Campaspe, it is hard to judge whether thy choice be more unwise, or thy chance unfortunate. Dost thou prefer—but stay, utter not that in words, which maketh thine ears to glow with thoughts.— Tush, better thy tongue wag, than thy heart break. Hath a painter crept farther into thy mind than a prince? Apelles, than Alexander? [32] fond wench! the baseness of thy mind bewrays the meanness of thy birth.   But alas, affection is a fire, which kindleth as well in the bramble, as in the oak, and catcheth hold where it first lighteth, not where it may best

[31] — *old huddles*] This contemptuous term is frequently used by our ancient writers, and is always applied to old people who are either covetous or subject to any other vice peculiar to old age.

As in *Euphues*, 1581, p. 7 : " But as to the stomacke quarted " with deinties, all delicates seeme queasie, and as he that sur- " fetteth with wine, useth afterwards to allay with water : so these " *olde huddles* having overcharged their corges with fancie, ac- " compt all honest recreation mere follye, &c."

Ibid. p. 54 : " — this olde miser asking of Aristippus what " he woulde take to teach and bring up his sonne, he answered " a thousande groates: a thousand groates God shield answered " this *olde huddle*, 1 can have two servants of that price."   See also " *Tom Tyler and his Wife*, 1661, p. 4.

[32] *fond wench*] It is observed by Mr. Steevens (Notes to Shakspeare, vol. X. p. 619.) that *wench* originally signified a young woman.   The truth of this observation will appear from many instances in the court of these volumes.   The word in the common acceptation of it is hardly yet disused.

burn.   Larks that mount aloft in the air, build their nests below in the earth ; and women that cast their eyes upon kings, may place their hearts upon vassals. A needle will become thy fingers better than a lute, and a distaff is fitter for thy hand than a scepter. Ants live safely till they have gotten wings ; and Juniper is not blown up, till it hath gotten an high top. The mean estate is without care as long as it continueth without pride.   But here cometh Apelles, in whom I would there were the like affection.

Enter APELLES.

Apelles. Gentlewoman, the misfortune I had with your picture will put you to some pains to sit again to be painted.

Campaspe. It is small pains for me to sit still, but infinite for you to draw still.

Apelles. No, madam, to paint Venus was a pleasure ; but to shadow the sweet face of Campaspe, it is a heaven

Campaspe. If your tongue were made of the same flesh that your heart is, your words would be as your thoughts are ; but such a common thing it is amongst you to commend, that oftentimes for fashion sake you call them beautiful whom you know black.

Apelles. What might men do to be believ'd ?

Campasp. Whet their tongues on their hearts.

Apelles. So they do, and speak as they think.

Campaspe. I would they did.

Apelles. I would they did not.

Campaspe. Why, would you have them dissemble ?

Apelles. Not in love, but their love.   But will you give me leave to ask you a question without offence ?

Campaspe. So that you will answer me another without excuse.

Apelles. Whom do you love best in the world ?

Campaspe. He that made me last in the world.

Apelles. That was a god.

Campaspe. I had thought it had been a man : but whom do you honour most, Apelles ?

Apelles. The thing that is likest you, Campaspe.

Campaspe My picture?

Apelles. I dare not venture upon your person. But come, let us go in: for Alexander will think it long till we return.   [*Exeunt.*

ACT. IV. SCEN. III.

CLYTUS, PARMENIO.

Clytus. We hear nothing of our embassage; a colour belike to blear our eyes, or tickle our ears, or inflame our hearts. But what doth Alexander in the mean season, but use for tantara, sol, fa, la; for his hard couch, down beds; for his handful of water, his standing cup of wine?

Parmenio. Clytus, I mislike this new delicacy and pleasing peace; for what' else do we see now than a kind of softness in every man's mind? Bees to make their hives in soldiers helmets, our steeds are furnish'd with foot-cloths* of gold instead of saddles of steel: More time is required to scower the rust off our weapons, than there was wont to be in subduing the countries of our enemies. Sithence Alexander fell from his hard armour to his soft robes, behold the face of his court; youths that were wont to carry devices of victory in their shields, engrave now posies of love in their rings; they that were accustom'd on trotting horses to charge the enemy with a launce, now in easy coaches ride up and down to court ladies; instead of sword and target to hazard their lives, use pen and paper to paint their loves: Yea, such a fear and faintness is grown in court, that they wish rather to hear the blowing of a

---

*— *foot cloths*] Housings of horses, such as were worn in times of peace, but not adopted to purposes of war. Lord Hastings, in King Richard III., observes that his *foot-cloth* horse did stumble. S.

horn to hunt, than the sound of a trumpet to fight.
O Philip, wert thou alive to see this alteration, thy
men turn'd to women, thy soldiers to lovers, [33] gloves
worn in velvet caps, instead of plumes in graven helmets, thou wouldst either die among them for sorrow,
or confound them for anger.

Clytus. Cease, Parmenio, lest in speaking what be
cometh thee not, thou feel what [34] liketh thee not:
truth is never without a scratch'd face, whose tongue,
although it cannot be cut out, yet must it be tied up.

Parmenio. It grieveth me not a little fos Hephestion,
who thirsteth for honour, not ease; but such is his
fortune and nearness in friendship to Alexander, that
he must lay a pillow under his head, when he would
put a target in his hand.

[33] — *gloves worn in velvet caps, instead of plumes in graven helmets,*]
It is observed by Mr. Steevens (Notes on Shakspeare, vol. IX.
p. 467.) that it was " anciently the custom to wear gloves in the
" hat on three distinct occasions, viz. as the favour of a mistress,
" the memorial of a friend, and as a mark to be challenged by an
" enemy.   Prince Henry boasts that he *will pluck a glove from the*
" *commonest creature*, and fix it in his helmet;" and Tucca says to
Sir Quintilian, in Decker's *Satiromastrix :* " — thou shalt wear
her *glove* in thy worshipful *hat*, like to a leather brooch;" and
Pandora, in Lyly's *Woman in the Moon*, 1597:
             " — he that first presents me with his head,
             " Shall wear my *glove* in favour of the deed."
" Portia, in her assumed character, asks Bassanio for his *gloves*,
" which she says *she will wear for his sake :* and King Henry V.
" gives the pretended *glove* of Alencon to Fluellin, which after-
" wards occasions the quarrel with the English soldier."   See also
Note to vol. V. p. 234.
    Again, in Hall's *Chronicle*, 1550, Henry IV. fol. 12 : " One part
" had their plumes at whyt, another hadde them at redde, and the
" thyrde had them of severall colours.   One ware on his head-
" piece his ladies sleve, and another bare on hys helme *the glove* of
" his dearlynge."
And *The Battle of Agincourt*, by Drayton, vol. I. p 16 :
             " The nobler youth, the common rank above,
             " On their courvetting coursers mounted fair,
            -" One wore his mistress garter, *one her glove;*
             " And he a lock of his dear lady's hair;
             " And he her colours whom he most did love.
             " There was not one but did some favour wear."
[34] — *liketh thee*] See Note on *Cornelia*, Act I.

But let us draw in, to see how well it becomes them to [35] tread the measures in a dance, that were wont to set the order for a march.   [*Exeunt.*

ACT. IV. SCEN. IV.

APELLES. CAMPASPE.

Apelles. I have now, Campaspe, almost made an end.
Campaspe. You told me, Apelles, you would never end.
Apelles. Never end my love; for it shall be eternal.
Campaspe. That is, neither to have beginning nor ending.
Apelles. You are disposed to mistake, I hope you do not mistrust.
Campaspe. What will you say, if Alexander perceive your love?

[35] — *tread the measures in a dance,*] The measures were dances solemn and slow. They were performed at court and at public entertainments of the societies of Law and Equity at their halls on particular occasions. It was formerly not deemed inconsistent with propriety even for the gravest characters to join in them, and accordingly at the revels which were celebrated at the Inns of Court, it has not been unusual for the first characters in the law to become performers in *treading the measures.* See Dugdale's *Origines Juridiciales.* Sir John Davies, in his Poem called *Orchestra,* 1622, describes them in this manner, S. 65:

" But after these as men more civil grew,
  " He did more *grave and solemn measures frame,*
  " With such fair order and proportion true,
  " And correspondence ev'ry way the same,
  " That no fault finding eye did ever blame,
  " For ev'ry eye was moved at the sight,
  " With sober wond'ring, and with sweet delight."
Not those young students of the heav'nly book,
  Atlas the great, Prometheus the wise,
Which on the stars did all their life-time look,
  Could ever find such measure in the skies,
  So full of change and rare varieties;
    Yet all the feet whereon these measures go,
    Are only spondees, solemn, grave, and slow.

Apelles. I will say, it is no treason to love.

Campaspe. But how, if he will not suffer thee to see my person.

Apelles. Then will I gaze continually on thy picture.

Campaspe. That will not feed thy heart.

Apelles. Yet shall it fill mine eye: besides the sweet thoughts, the sure hopes, thy protested faith, will cause me to embrace thy shadow continually in mine arms, of the which by strong imagination I will make a substance.

Campaspe. Well, I must be gone: but this assure yourself, that I had rather be in thy shop grinding colours, than in Alexander's court, following higher fortunes.   [*Exit Apelles.*

Campaspe alone. Foolish wench, what hast thou done? that, alas! which cannot be undone, and therefore I fear me undone. O Apelles, thy love cometh from the heart, but Alexander's from the mouth. *The love of kings is like the blowing of winds, which whistle sometimes gently among the leaves, and straightways turn the trees up by the roots; or fire, which warmeth afar off, and burneth near hand; or the sea, which makes men hoise their sails in a flattering calm, and to cut their masts in a rough storm. They place affection by times, by policy, by appointment; if they frown, who dares call them unconstant? if bewray secrets, who will term them untrue? if fall to other loves, who trembles not, if he call them unfaithful? In kings there can be no love, but to queens: for as near must they meet in majesty, as they do in affection. It is requisite to stand aloof from king's love, Jove and lightning.   [*Exit.*

* *The love of kings, &c.*] The author, whether accidentally or on purpose, has given no faint portrait of the conduct of King Henry VIII. in this speech. S.

ACT. IV. SCEN. V.

APELLES, PAGE.

Apelles. Now, Apelles, gather thy wits together: Campaspe is no less wise than fair, thyself must be no less cunning than faithful. It is no small matter to be rival with Alexander.

Page. Apelles, you must come away quickly with the picture; the king thinketh that now you have painted it, you play with it.

Apelles. If I would play with pictures, I have enough at home.

Page. None perhaps you like so well.

Apelles. It may be I have painted none so well.

Page. I have known many fairer faces.

Apelles. And I many better boys*.   [*Exeunt.*

ACT. V. SCEN. I.

DIOGENES, SYLVIUS, PERIM, MILO, TRICO, MANES.

Sylvius. I have brought my sons, Diogenes, to be taught of thee.

Diogenes. What can thy sons do?

Sylvius. You shall see their qualities: dance, sirrah.
                         [*Then Perim danceth.*
How like you this? doth he well?

Diogenes. The better, the worser.

Sylvius. The musick very good.

Diogenes. The musicians very bad, who only study to have their strings in tune, never framing their manners to order.

Sylvius. Now shall you see the other—tumble, sirrah.
                         [*Milo tumbleth.*
How like you this? why do you laugh?

Diogenes. To see a wag that was born to break his neck by destiny, to practise it by art.

* *Qu:* Toys—*i. e.* to play with. O. G.

Milo. This dog will bite me, I will not be with him.

Diogenes. Fear not, boys, dogs eat no thistles.

Perim. I marvel what dog thou art, if thou be a dog.

Diogenes. When I am hungry, a mastiff; and when my belly is full, a spaniel.

Sylvius. Dost thou believe that there are any gods, that thou art so dogged?

Diogenes. I must needs believe there are gods: for I think thee an enemy to them.

Sylvius. Why so?

Diogenes. Because thou hast taught one of thy sons to rule his legs, and not to follow learning; the other to bend his body every way, and his mind no way.

Perim. Thou doest nothing but snarl, and bark like a dog.

Diogenes. It is the next way to drive away a thief.

Sylvius. Now shall you hear the third, who sings like a nightingale.

Diogenes. I care not: for I have heard a nightingale sing herself.

Sylvius. Sing, sirrah.　　　　　　　　[*Tryco singeth.*

SONG [36].

What bird so sings, yet so does wail?
O'tis the ravish'd nightingale.
Jug, jug, jug, jug, tereu she crys,
And still her woes at midnight rise.
Brave prick song! who is't now we hear?
[37] None but the lark so shril and clear;

[36] *Song.*] This Song, as the two former, is omitted in all the quarto editions. It is here restored from Blount's edition, where it first appeared.

[37] *None but the lark,* &c.] Milton seems to have had this passage in his mind when he wrote the following lines in his *L'Allegro:*
　　" To hear the lark begin his flight,
　　" And singing startle the dull night;
　　" From his watch tow'r in the skies,
　　" Till the dappled dawn doth rise;
And a late elegant writer, Mr. F. Coventry, appears also to have been indebted to our Author in the last of the following lines
　　" When morn returns with doubtful light,
　　" And Phebe pales her lamp of night.

Now at heavens gates she claps her wings,
The morn not waking till she sings.
Hark, hark, with what a pretty throat,
Poor robin red breast tunes his note;
Hark how the jolly cuckoes sing,
Cuckoe to welcome in the spring.
Cuckoe to welcome in the spring.

Sylvius. Lo, Diogenes, I am sure thou canst not do so much.

Diogenes. But there is never a thrush but can.

Sylvius. What hast thou taught Manes thy man?

Diogenes. To be as unlike as may be thy sons.

Manes. He hath taught me to fast, lye hard, and run away.

Sylvius. How sayest thou, Perim, wilt thou be with him?

Perim. Ay, so he will teach me first to run away.

Diogenes. Thou needest not be taught, thy legs are so nimble.

Sylvius. How sayest thou, Milo, wilt thou be with him?

Diogenes. Nay, hold your peace, he shall not.

> " Still let me wander forth anew,
> " And print my footsteps on the dew;
> " What time the swain with ruddy cheek,
> " Prepares to yoke his oxen meet,
> " And early drest in neat array,
> " To milk maid chanting shrill her lay,
> " Comes abroad with milking pail,
> " And the sound of distant flail;
> " Gives the ear a rough good morrow,
> " And the lark from out the furrow;
> " *Soars upright on matin wings,*
> " *And at the gate of heaven sings.*"

Penshurst, a Poem.   Dodsley's *Collection of Poems,* vol. IV.
Mr. Coventry might have been indebted either to a song in Shakspeare's *Cymbeline,* or to a passage in his 29 sonnet.

> " Hark! hark! the *lark* at *heaven's gate sings.*"

Again,

> " Like to the *lark* at *break of day arising*
> " From sullen earth, *sings hims at heaven's gate.*"

Again, to *Milton's Paradise Lost.*   B. 5.

> " —————— ye birds,
> " That singing up *to heaven's gate ascend.*"   S.

Sylvius. Why?

Diogenes. There is not room enough for him and me to tumble both in one tub.

Sylvius. Well, Diogenes, I perceive my sons brook not thy manners.

Diogenes. I thought no less, when they knew my virtues.

Sylvius. Farewell, Diogenes, thou needest not have scraped roots, if thou wouldst have followest Alexander.

Diogenes. Nor thou have followed Alexander, if thou hadst scraped roots.

ACT. V. SCEN. II.

APELLES ALONE.

I fear me, Apelles, that thine eyes have blabbed that which thy tongue durst not. What little regard hadst thou, whilst Alexander viewed the counterfeit of Campaspe! thou stoodst gazing on her countenance. If he espy or but suspect, thou must needs twice perish, with his hate, and thine own love. Thy pale looks, when he blushed, thy sad countenance, when he smiled, thy sighs, when he questioned, may breed in him a jealousy, perchance a frenzy. O love, I never before knew what thou wert, and now hast thou made me that I know not what myself am! only this I know, that I must endure intolerable passions, for unknown pleasures. Dispute not the cause, wretch, but yield to it: for better it is to melt with desire, than wrestle with love. Cast thyself on thy careful bed, be content to live unknown, and die unfound. O Campaspe, I have painted thee in my heart! painted? nay, contrary to mine art, imprinted, and that in such deep characters, that nothing can rase it out, unless it rub my heart out. [*Exit.*

ACT. V. SCEN. III.

MILECTUS, PHRYGIUS, LAYIS, DIOGENES.

Milectus. It shall go hard, but this peace shall bring us some pleasure.

Phrygius. Down with arms, and up with legs, [38] this is a world for the nonce.

Layis. Sweet youths, if you knew what it were to save your sweet blood, you would not so foolishly go about to spend it. What delight can there be in gashing, to make foul scars in fair faces, and crooked maims in strait legs? as though men being

---

[38] — *this is a world for the nonce.*] " That is" (says Mr. Tyrwitt, in his Notes on Chaucer, vol. IV. 207.) " as I conceive *for the* " *occasion.* This phrase, which was very frequently, though not " always very precisely, used by our old writers, I suppose to " have been originally a corruption of corrupt Latin.   From *pro-* " *nunc*, I suppose came *for the nunc*, and so *for the nonce;* just as' " from *ad-nunc* came *anon.* The Spanish *entonces* has been formed " in the same manner from *in tunc.*"

To confirm this explanation, the following examples may be produced :

Erasmus's *Praise of Folie*, 1549, Sig. K 2 : " This man mourneth, " and lorde, what folies saieth he, and dooeth he, hyrynge also " some plaires (as it were) to wepe and howle *for the nones.*"

Ibid. Sig. L 3 : " — eche of whome; in bablyng maye compare " with ten women chosen *for the nones.*"

Gascoigne's *Supposes*, 1587, A. 3. S. 3 : " — step to him all at " once ; take him ; and with a cord that I have lay'd on the table " *for the nonce*, bind him hand and foot."

Ben Jonson's *Volpone*, A. 2. S. 2 : " Here's a medicine *for the* " *nones.*" Nash's *Lenten Stuff*, 1599 : " Norwich at her majesty's " coming in progress thither, presented her with a shew of knit- " ters, on high stage placed *for the nonce.*"

The wonderfull Years, 1603, by Tho. Dekker : " Oh lamentable ! " never did the olde buskinde tragedy beginne till now : for the " wives of those husbands, with whom she had play'd at fast and " loose, came with their nayles sharpened *for the nonce*, like cattes, " and tongues forkedly cut like the stings of adders, &c."

Gascoigne's Works, 1587, p. 272 : " In the ende she tooke out " a booke (which she had brought *for the nonce*) and bound him by " othe to accomplish it."

born goodly by nature, would of purpose become deformed by folly ; and all forsooth for a new-found
term, call'd valiant, a word which breedeth more
quarrels than the sense can commendation.

Milectus. It is true, Layis, a featherbed hath no
fellow ; good drink makes good blood ; and shall
*pelting words spill it ?

Phrygius. I mean to enjoy the world, and to draw
out my life at the wiredrawers, not to curtail it off
at the cutlers.

Layis You may talk of war, speak big, conquer
worlds with great words ; but stay at home, where instead of alarms you shall have dances, for hot battels
with fierce men, gentle skirmishes with fair women.
These pewter coats can never sit so well as satten
doublets. Believe me, you cannot conceive the pleasure of peace, unless you despise the rudeness of war.

Milectus. It is so. But see Diogenes prying over his
tub ! Diogenes, what sayest thou to such a morsel ?

Diogenes. I say, I would spit it out of my mouth,
because it should not poison my stomach.

Phrygius. Thou speakest as thou art, it is no meat
for dogs.

Diogenes. I am a dog, and philosophy rates me from
carion.

Layis. Uncivil wretch, whose manners are answerable to thy calling ; the time was thou wouldest have
had my company, had it not been, as thou saidst, too
dear.

Diogenes. I remember there was a thing, that I
repented me of, and now thou hast told it : indeed
it was too dear of nothing; and thou dear to nobody.

Layis. Down, villain, or I will have thy head broken.

Milectus. Will you couch ?

Phrygius. Avant, cur. Come, sweet Layis, let us
go to some place, and possess peace. But first let us

— *pelting words]* i. e. paltry. See note on The Midsummer
Night's Dream, Shaks : 1778, vol. II. p. 33. S.

sing ; there is more pleasure in tuning of a voice, than in a vŏlly of shot [38].

Milectus. Now let us make haste, lest Alexander find us here.   [*Exeunt.*

ACT. V. SCEN. IV.

ALEXANDER, HEPHESTION, PAGE, DIOGENES, APELLES, CAMPASPE.

Alexander. Me thinketh, Hephestion, you are more melancholy than you were accustomed ; but I perceive it is all for Alexander. You can neither brook this peace, nor my pleasure ; be of good chear, though I wink, I sleep not.

Hephestion. Melancholy I am not, nor well content : for I know not how, there is such a rust crept into my

---

[38] — *than in a volly of shot.*] The writers of the sixteenth and seventeenth centuries paid very little attention to the manners and customs either of the times or the country in which the scenes of their Dramas were laid. They frequently introduce allusions to facts and circumstances in one age and country peculiar only to another, and perpetually violate every rule of chronology. Beaumont and Fletcher introduce one of the successors of Alexander with a pistol, and Shakspeare is ever at war with propriety and probability. Ben Jonson seems the only poet of the times to whom the charge of uniting dissimilar manners and discordant periods is not to be laid. Later writers have been more careful of falling into these mistakes ; but improvements in these particulars by the directors of our theatres have not kept pace with others which have been with propriety adopted. It may be said, that these gentlemen have rather increased the number of their authors' errors and made them guilty of anachronisms, where their writings do not give the least countenance for them. Absurd as it must appear to every intelligent spectator, and incredible to every informed reader, yet it is certainly true that Hamlet has been lately represented with all the decorations of a modern order, that of the Elephant ; and it is reported a late actor was with difficulty prevailed upon to forbear arming Macbeth with a case of pistols at his girdle.

A volley of shot means only a flight of arrows. S.

bones with this long case, that I fear I shall not scower it out with infinite labours.

Alexander. Yes, yes, if all the travels of conquering the world will set either thy body or mine in tune, we will undertake them. But what think you of Apelles ? did ye ever see any so perplexed ? he neither answered directly to any question, nor looked stedfastly upon any thing. I hold my life the painter is in love.

Hephestion. It may be; for commonly we see it incident in artificers to be enamoured of their own works, as Archidamus of his wooden dove, Pygmalion of his ivory image, Arachne of his wooden swan; especially painters, who playing with their own conceits, now coveting to draw a glancing eye, then a rolling, now a winking, still mending it, never ending it, till they be caught with it ; and then (poor souls) they kiss the colours with their lips, with which before they were loth to taint their fingers.

Alexander. I will find it out. Page, go speedily for Apelles, will him to come hither, and when you see us earnestly in talk, suddenly cry out, Apelles's shop is on fire.

Page. It shall be done.

Alexander. Forget not your lesson.

Hephestion. I marvel what your device shall be.

Alexander. The event shall prove.

Hephestion. I pity the poor painter, if he be in love.

Alexander. Pity him not, I pray thee ; that severe gravity set aside, what do you think of love ?

Hephestion. As the Macedonians do of their herb beet, which looking yellow in the ground, and black in the hand, think it better seen than touch'd.

Alexander. But what do you imagine it to be?

Hephestion. A word by superstition thought a god, by use turn'd to an humour, by self-will made a flatering madness.

Alexander. You are too hard-hearted to think so of love. Let us go to Diogenes—Diogenes, thou may'st think it somewhat, that Alexander cometh to thee again so soon.

Diogenes. If you come to learn, you could not come soon enough; if to laugh, you be come too soon.

Hephestion. It would better become thee to be more courteous, and frame thyself to please.

Diogenes. And you better to be less, if you durst displease.

Alexander. What dost thou think of the time we have here?

Diogenes. That we have little, and lose much.

Alexander. If one be sick, what wouldst thou have him do?

Diogenes. Be sure that he make not his physician his heir.

Alexander. If thou mightest have thy will, how much ground would content thee?

Diogenes. As much as you in the end must be contented withal.

Alexander. What, a world?

Diogenes. No, the length of my body.

Alexander. Hephestion, shall I be a little pleasant with him?

Hephestion. You may; but he will be very perverse with you.

Alexander. [40] It skilleth not, I cannot be angry with him. Diogenes, I pray thee what dost thou think of love?

Diogenes. A little worser than I can of hate.

Alexander. And why?

Diogenes. Because it is better to hate the things which make to love, than to love the things which give occasion of hate.

Alexander. Why, be not women the best creatures in the world?

[40] *It skilleth not,*] i. e. it matters not; it is of no importance. So, in Lyly's *Euphues and his England,* 1582, p. 82: " Whether it be " an inchaunted leafe, a vearse of Pythia, a figure of Amphion, a " character of Aschanes, an image of Venus, or a braunch of " Sybilla, *it skilleth not.*"

Again, p. 85: " — saying that it *skilleth not,* how long things " were a doing, but how well they were done."

Diogenes. Next men and bees.

Alexander. What dost thou dislike chiefly in a woman?

Diogenes. One thing.

Alexander. What?

Diogenes. That she is a woman.

Alexander. In mine opinion thou wert never born of a woman, that thou thinkest so hardly of women. But now cometh Apelles, who I am sure is as far from thy thoughts, as thou art from his cunning. Diogenes, I will have thy cabin removed nearer to my court, because I will be a philosopher.

Diogenes. And when you have done so, I pray you remove your court farther from my cabin, because I will not be a courtier.

Enter APELLES.

Alexander. But here cometh Apelles. Apelles, what piece of work have you now in hand?

Apelles. None in hand, if it like your majesty; but I am devising a platform in my head.

Alexander. I think your hand put it into your head. Is it nothing about Venus?

Apelles. No, but something [41] above Venus.

Page. Apelles! Apelles! look about you, your shop is on fire.

Apelles. Ay me! if the picture of Campaspe be burnt, I am undone.

Alexander. Stay, Apelles, no haste, it is your heart is on fire, not your shop; and if Campaspe hang there, I would she were burnt. But have you the picture of Campaspe? belike you love her well, that you care not though all be lost, so she be safe.

Apelles. Not love her: but your majesty knows that painters in their last works are said to excel themselves; and in this I have so much pleased myself, that the shadow as much delighteth me, being an artificer, as the substance doth others that are amorous.

Alexander. You lay your colours grosly;   though

---

[41] *above*] Former editions read *about.*

I could not paint in your shop, I can spy into your excuse. Be not ashamed, Apelles, it is a gentleman's sport to be in love. Call hither Campaspe. Methinks I might have been made privy to your affection; though my counsel had not been necessary, yet my countenance might have been thought requisite. But Apelles, forsooth, lov'd under hand, yea and under Alexander's nose, and—but I say no more.

Apelles. Apelles loveth not so; but he liveth to do as Alexander will.

Enter CAMPASPE.

Alexander. Campaspe, here is news; Apelles is in love with you.

Campaspe. It pleaseth your majesty to say so.

Alexander. Hephestion, I will try her too.—Campaspe, for the good qualities I know in Apelles, and the virtue I see in you, I am determin'd you shall enjoy one another. How say you, Campaspe, would you say ay?

Campaspe. Your handmaid must obey, if you command.

Alexander. Think you not, Hephestion, that she would fain be commanded?

Hephestion. I am no thought-catcher, but *I guess unhappily.

Alexander. I will not enforce marriage, where I cannot compel love.

Campaspe. But your majesty may move a question, where you be willing to have a match.

Alexander. Believe me, Hephestion, these parties are agreed; they would have me both priest and witness. Apelles, take Campaspe. Why move ye not?—Campaspe, take Apelles. Will it not be? If you be asham'd one of the other, by my consent you shall never come together. But dissemble not, Campaspe, do you love Apelles?

---

* *I guess unhappily*] i. e. mischievously. We still call a mischievous boy an *unlucky* rogue. See note on Hamlet, Shaksp: 1778, vol. X. p. 344.

Campaspe. Pardon, my lord, I love Apelles.

Alexander. Apelles, it were a shame for you, being lov'd so openly of so fair a virgin, to say the contrary. Do you love Campaspe?

Apelles. Only Campaspe.

Alexander. Two loving worms, Hephestion! I perceive Alexander cannot subdue the affections of men, though he conquer their countries. Love falleth like a dew, as well upon the low grass, as upon the high cedar. Sparks have their heat, ants their gall, flies their spleen. Well, enjoy one another, I give her to thee frankly, Apelles. Thou shalt see that Alexander maketh but a toy of love, and leadeth affection in fetters; using fancy as a fool to make him sport, or a minstrel to make him merry. It is not the amorous glance of an eye can settle an idle thought in the heart; * no, no, it is children's game, a life for sempsters and scholars: the one pricking † in clouts, have nothing else to think on: the other picking fancies out of books, have little else to marvel at. Go, Apelles, take with you your Campaspe; Alexander is cloy'd with looking on that, which thou wond'rest at.

Apelles. Thanks to your majesty on bended knee, you have honour'd Apelles.

Campaspe. Thanks with bow'd heart, you have blest Campaspe.   [*Exeunt.*

Alexander. Page, go warn Clytus and Parmenio, and the other lords, to be in readiness; let the trumpet sound, strike up the drum, and I will presently into Persia. How now, Hephestion, is Alexander able to resist love as he list?

Hephestion. The conquering of Thebes was not so honourable as the subduing of these thoughts.

* See Nugæ Antiquæ, vol. II. p. 14.   I. R.

† *pricking in clouts,* &c.]   *Pricking in clouts* was a term formerly used for *sewing.* So in *Sir John Harrington's Treatise on Playe.* " For it is (be yt spoken under correction) an unfittynge syght to " see a presence chamber empty more that haulfe the day, and " men cannot bee always discowrsing, nor women always " *pricking in clowts;* and therefore I say, it is not amisse to play " at some sociable game," &c.

Alexander. It were a shame Alexander should desire to command the world, if he could not command himself. But come, let us go, I will try whether I can better my hand with my heart, than I could with mine eye. And, good Hephestion, when all the world is won, and every country is thine and mine, either find me out another to subdue, or on my word I will fall in love.   [*Exeunt.*

FINIS.

EPILOGUE AT THE BLACK FRIERS.

WHERE the rainbow toucheth the tree, no caterpillers will hang on the leaves; where the glow-worm creepeth in the night, no adder will go in the day: We hope, in the ears where our travails be lodged, no carping shall harbour in those tongues. Our exercises must be as your judgment is, resembling water, which is always of the same colour into what it runneth. In the *Trojan* horse lay couch'd soldiers, with children; and in heaps of many words we fear divers unfit, among some allowable.* But as *D*emosthenes, with often breathing up the hill, amended his stammering; so we hope, with sundry labours [42] against the hair, to correct our studies. If the tree be blasted that blossoms, the fault is in the wind, and not in the root; and if our pastimes be mis-liked, that have been allow'd, you must impute it to the malice of others, and not our endeavour.—And so we rest in good case, if you rest well content.

* *allowable, allow'd*] i. e. praise-worthy, praised. See note on King Lear, Shaksp: 1778, vol. IX. p. 441. S.

[42] — *against the hair,*] This phrase occurs in the *Merry Wives of Windsor*, A. 2. S. 3. and Mr. Steevens observes, that it is "'pro-" verbial, and is taken from stroking the hair of animals a " contrary way to that in which it grows. We now say against " the grain."

So, in Dekker's *Satiromastrix*: " — go, let them lift up baldness " to the sky; and thou shalt see twill turn MineVer's heart " *quite against the hair.*"

Middleton's *Mayor of Quinborough*, A. 3. S. 2:

" Books in women's hands are as much *against*
" *The hair* methinks, as to see men wear stomachers."

EPILOGUE AT THE COURT.

WE cannot tell whether we are fallen among Diomedes's birds or his horses; the one receiv'd some men with sweet notes, the other bit all men with sharp teeth. But as Homer's gods convey'd them into clouds, whom they would have kept from curses; and as Venus, lest Adonis should be prick'd with the stings of adders, cover'd his face with the wings of swans; so we hope, being shielded with your highness's countenance, we shall, though we hear the neighing, yet not feel the kicking, of those jades; and receive, tho' no praise (which we cannot deserve) yet a pardon, which in all humility we desire. As yet we cannot tell what we should term our labours, iron, or bullion; only it belongeth to your majesty to make them fit either for the forge or the mint; current by the stamp, or counterfeit by the anvil. For as nothing is to be called white, unless it had been named white by the first creator, so can there be nothing thought good in the opinion of others, unless it be christen'd good by the judgment of yourself. For ourselves again, we are like these torches, wax, of which, being in your highness's hands, you may make doves or vultures, roses or nettles, laurel for a garland, or * elder for a disgrace.

* *elder for a disgrace.*] Because Judas is said to have hung himself on an *elder*-tree

EDITIONS.

(1.) " A most excellent Comedie of Alexander, Cam-
" paspe, and Diogenes, played beefore the Queenes
" Majestie on Twelfe-day at night, by her Majesties
" Children, and the Children of Paules. Imprinted at
" London for Thomas Cadman, 1584, 4to."

(2.) " Campaspe, played beefore the Queenes Ma-
" jestie on New-yeares-day at night, by her Majesties
" Children, and the Children of Paules. Imprinted
" at London for Thomas Cadman, 1584, 4to."

(3.) " Campaspe, played beefore the Queenes Ma-
" jestie on Twelfe-day at night, by her Majesties Chil-
" dren, and the Children of Paules. Imprinted at
" London by Thomas Orwin, for William Broome,
" 1591, 4to."

(4.) " Campaspe, played before the Queenes Ma-
" jestie on Twelfe-day at night, by her Majesties Chil-
" dren, and the Children of Paules. London, Printed
" by William Stansby, for Edward Blount, 1632,
" 12mo."

TANCRED AND GISMUNDA.

THIS Play was originally acted before Queen Elizabeth, at the Inner Temple, in the year 1568. It was
the production of five Gentlemen, who were probably
Students of that Society; and by one of them, Mr.
Robert Wilmot, afterwards much altered and published
in the year 1592. Of the Editor Mr. Wilmot[1] no further account can be obtained*. From a passage in
his Dedication to the Societies of the Inner and Middle
Temples, in which he speaks of the censure which
might be cast upon him from the indecorum of publishing a Dramatick Work arising from his calling, it
may be conjectured that he had diverted his studies
from Law to Divinity, and had then taken orders. He
was certainly then resident in the County of Essex;
but when he died, or whether he left any other works,
I have not been able to discover.

[1] He is mentioned by Webbe, in his *Discourse of English Poetrie*,
1586, Sign. C 4, with other Poets of that time, as Whetstone,
Munday, John Graunge Knight. *Wylmot*, Darrell, FC, FK, GB,
and others whose names he could not remember.

* Robert Wilmot, A. M. was presented to the rectory of North
Okenham in Essex, the 28th of Nov. 1582, by Gabriel Poyntz:
and to the vicarage of Horndon on the Hill, in the same county,
the 2d Dec. 1585, by the Dean and Chapter of St. Paul's.—New-
court's Repertorium. S.

To the Right Worshipful and Virtuous Ladies, the Lady MARY PETER, and the Lady ANNE GRAY, long health of body, with quiet of mind, in the favour of God and Men for ever.

IT is most certain (right virtuous and worshipful) that of all human learning, Poetry (how contemptible so ever it is in these days) is the most ancient; and in Poetry, there is no argument of more antiquity and elegancy than is the matter of Love; for it seems to be as old as the world, and to bear date from the first time that man and woman was: therefore in this, as in the finest metal, the freshest wits have in all ages shown their best workmanship. So amongst others these Gentlemen, which with what sweetness of voice and liveliness of action they then expressed it, they which were of her Majesty's right Honourable Maidens can testify.

Which being a discourse of two lovers, perhaps it may seem a thing neither 'fit to be offered unto your Ladyships, nor worthy me to busy myself withall : yet can I tell you, Madams, it differeth so far from the ordinary amorous discourses of our days, as the manners of our time do from the modesty and innocency of that age.

And now for that weary winter is come upon us, which bringeth with him drooping days and tedious nights, if it be true, that the motions of our minds follow the temperature of the air wherein we live, then I think, the perusing of some mournful matter, tending to the view of a notable example, will refresh your wits in a gloomy day, and ease your weariness of the louring night. Which if it please you, may serve ye also for a solemn revel against this Festival time, for *Gismunds* bloody shadow, with a little cost, may be intreated in her self-like person to speak to ye.

Having therefore a desire to be known to your W. I devised this way with myself to procure the same, persuading myself, there is nothing more welcome to your wisdoms, then the knowledge of wise, grave, and worthy matters, tending to the good instructions of youths, of whom you are mothers.

In this respect therefore, I shall humbly desire ye to bestow a favourable countenance upon this little labour, which when ye have graced it withall, I must and will acknowledge myself greatly indebted unto your Ladyships in this behalf: neither shall I amongst the rest, that admire your rare virtues (which are not a few in Essex), cease to commend this undeserved gentleness.

Thus desiring the king of heaven to increase his graces in ye both, granting that your ends may be as honourable, as your lives are virtuous, I leave with a vain babble of many needless words to trouble you longer.

Your Worships most dutiful

and humble Orator,

ROBERT WILMOT.

TO HIS FRIEND R. W.

MASTER R. W. look not now for the terms of an intreator, I will beg no longer; and for your promises, I will refuse them as bad Payment: neither can I be satisfied with any thing, but a peremptory performance of an old intention of yours, the publishing I mean of those waste papers (as it pleaseth you to call them, but, as I esteem them, a most exquisite invention) of Gismund's tragedy*. Think not to shift me off with longer delays, nor alledge more excuses to get further

---

* It appears from William Webbe's Epistle prefixed to the Tragedy of Gismond, that after its first exhibition it was laid aside, and at some distance of time was new-written by W. Wilmot. The reader, therefore, may not be displeased with a specimen of it in its original dress. It is here given from the fragment of an ancient MS. taken out of a chest of papers formerly belonging to Mr. Powell, father-in-law to the author of Paradise Lost, at Forest-Hill, about four miles from Oxford, where in all probability some curiosities of the same kind may remain, the contents of these chests (for I think there are more than one) having never yet been properly examined. The following extract is from the conclusion of the piece:—REED.

> But in thie brest if eny sparke remaine
> Of thie dere love. If ever yet I coulde
> So moche of the deserve, or at the least
> If with my last desire I may obtaine
> This at thie handes give me this one request
> And lett me not spend my last breath in vaine.
> My lief desire I not, which neither is
> In the to geave nor in my self to save
> Allthoughe I wolde. Nor yet I aske not this
> As mercye for myne Erle in ought to crave
> Whom I to well do knowe howe thou hast slaine.
> No no father thy hande and cruell wronge
> With pacience as I may I will sustaine
> In woefull lief which nowe shall not be longe.
> But this one suite, father, if unto me
> Thou graunte, thoughe I cannot the same requite
> Th' immortall godds shall render unto the
> Thie due rewarde and largely guerdon it,
> That since it pleasde the not thus secretly
> I might enjoye my love, his corps and myne
> May natheles together graved be
> And in one tombe our bodies both to shrine

respite, lest I arrest you with my *actum est*, and com-
mence such a suit of unkindness against you, as when

> With which this small request eke do I pràie
> That on the same graven in bras thou place
> This woefull epitaphe which I shall saye,·
> That all lovers may rewe this moornful case.
> Loe here within one tombe where harbor twaine
> Gismonda Quene and Countie Pallurine!
> She loved him, he for her love was slaine,
> For whoes revenge eke lyes she here in shrine.　　118
> 　　　　　　　　　　　　　　　 [*Gismonda dieth.*
> 　*Tancred.* O me alas, nowe do the cruell paines
> Of cursed death my dere daughter bereave.
> Alas whie bide I here? the sight constraines
> Me woefull man, this woefull place to leave.

SCENE III.

Tancred cometh out of Gismonds Chamber:

> *Tancred.* O dolorous happe, rufull and all of woe
> Alas I caitif wretche what resteth me
> Shall I now live that with these eyes did soe
> Beholde my daughter die, what shall I see
> Her death before my face that was my lyfe
> And I to live that was her lives decaie?
> Shall not this hande reach to this harte the knyf
> That maye bereve both sight and lief awaye,
> And in the shadowes darke to seke her ghoste
> And wander there with her? shall not alas
> This speedie death be wrought, sith I have loste
> My dearest joie of all? what shall I pas
> My latter daies in paine, and spende myne age
> In teares and plainte! shall I nowe leade my lief
> All solitaire as doth the birde in cage,
> And feede my woefull yeres with waillfull grief?
> No no, so will I not my dayes prolonge
> To seke to live one hower sith she is gone:
> This brest so can not bende to suche a wronge,
> That she shulde die and I to live alone.
> No, this will I: she shall have her request
> And in most royall sorte her funerall
> Will I performe.　Within one tombe shall rest
> Her Erle and she, her epitaphe withall
> Gravde thereon shal be.　This will I doe
> And when these eyes some aged teares have shedd
> The tombe my self then will I creepe into
> And with my blood all bayne their bodies dedd.

the case shall be scan'd before the judges of courtesy,
the court will cry out of your immoderate modesty.

This harte there will I place, and reave this brest
The irksome lyf, and wreake my wrathful yre
Upon my self. She shall have her request,
And I by death will purchase my desire.   47

FINIS.

EPILOGUS.

If nowe perhapps ye either looke to see
Th' unhappie lovers, or the cruell sire
Here to be buried as fittes their degree
Or as the dying lady did require
Or as the ruthfull kinge in deepe despaire
Behight of late (who nowe himself hath slaine)
Or if perchance ye stande in dowtfull feare
Sith madd Megera is not returnde againe
Least wandring in the world she so bestowe
The snakes that crall about her furious face
As they maye raise newe ruthes new kinds of woe
Both so and there, and suche as you percase
Wold be full loth so great so neare to see
I am come forthe to do you all to wete
Through griefe wherein the lords of Salerne be
The buriall pomp is not prepared yet:
And for the furie you shall understande
That neither doth the little greatest god
Find such rebelling here in Britayne lande
Against his royall power as asketh rodd
Of ruth from hell to wreake his names decaie
Nor Pluto hereth englishe ghostes complaine
Or dames disteyned lives. Therfore you maye
Be free from feare, sufficeth to maintaine
The virtues which we honour in you all,
So as our Britayne ghostes when life is past
Maie praise in heaven, not plaine in Pluto's hall
Our dames, but holde them virtuous and chaste,
Worthie to live where furie never came,
Where love can see, and beres no dedly bowe,
Whoes lives th' eternall trompe of glorious fame
With joiefull sounde to honest cares shall blowe.   60

FINIS.

The Tragedie of Gismonde of Salerne.

Here follow in the MS. Three " Sonetts on the Quenes Maides"
The Argument, and Personæ Dramatis, which it were useless to
transcribe.

And thus much I tell you before, you shall not be able
to wage against me in the charges growing upon this
action, especially if the worshipful company of the
Inner-Temple gentlemen patronize my cause, as un-
doubtedly they will, yea, and rather plead partially for
me, than let my cause miscarry, because themselves are
parties. The tragedy was by them most pithily framed,
and no less curiously acted in view of her Majesty, by
whom it was then as princely accepted, as of the whole
honourable audience notably applauded: yea, and of
all men generally desired, as a work, either in stateli-
ness of shew, depth of conceit, or true ornaments of
poetical art, inferior to none of the best in that kind:
no, were the Roman Seneca the censurer. The brave
youths that then (to their high praises) so feelingly performed the same in action, did shortly after lay up the
book unregarded, or perhaps let it run abroad (as
many parents do their children once past dandling)
not respecting so much what hard fortune might befall
it being out of their fingers, as how their heroical wits
might again be quickly conceived with new inventions
of like worthiness, whereof they have been ever since
wonderful fertile. But this orphan of theirs (for he
wand'reth as it were fatherless) hath notwithstanding,
by the rare and beautiful perfections appearing in him,
hitherto never wanted great favourers and loving pre-
servers. Among whom I cannot sufficiently commend
your charitable zeal, and scholarly compassion towards
him, that have not only rescued and defended him
from the devouring jaws of oblivion, but vouchsafed
also to apparel him in a new suit at your own charges,
wherein he may again more boldly come abroad, and
by your permission return to his old parents, cloathed
perhaps not in richer or more costly furniture than it
went from them, but in handsomeness and fashion
more answerable to these times, wherein fashions are
so often altered. Let one word suffice for your en-
couragement herein; namely, that your commendable
pains in disrobing him of his antique curiosity, and
adorning him with the approved guise of our stateliest

English terms (not diminishing, but more augmenting his artificial colours of absolute poesy, derived from his first parents) cannot but be grateful to most men's appetites, who upon our experience we know highly to esteem such lofty measures of sententiously composed tragedies.

How much you shall make me, and the rest of your private friends beholden to you, I list not to discourse: and therefore grounding upon these alledged reasons, that the suppressing of this tragedy, so worthy for the press, were no other thing than wilfully to defraud yourself of an universal thank, your friends of their expectations, and sweet *Gismund* of a famous eternity. I will cease to doubt of any other pretence to cloak your bashfulness, hoping to read it in print (which lately lay neglected amongst your papers) at our next appointed meeting.

I bid you heartily farewel. From *Pyrgo* in *Essex*, *August* the eighth, 1591.

Tuus fide & facultate

GUIL. WEBBE[2].

[2] William Webbe was the Author of " A Discourse of English " Poetrie : together with the Authors Judgment, touching the " reformation of our English Verse." B. L. 4to. 1586.

To the Worshipful and Learned Society, the GENTLE-
MEN STUDENTS of the Inner Temple, with the rest
of his good Friends, the GENTLEMEN of the Middle
Temple, and to all other courteous Readers, R. W.
wisheth increase of all health, worship, and learning,
with the immortal glory of the graces adorning the
same.

YE may perceive (right Worshipful) in perusing the
former Epistle, sent to me, how sore I am beset with
the importunities of my friends, to publish this Pam-
phlet: truly I am and have been (if there be in me any
soundness of judgement) of this opinion, that whatsoever is committed to the press is commended to eternity, and it shall stand a lively witness with our conscience, to our comfort or confusion, in the reckoning
of that great day.

Advisedly therefore was that Proverb used of our
elder Philosophers, *Manum a Tabula:* with-hold thy
hand from the paper, and thy papers from the print or
light of the world: for a lewd word escaped is irrevocable, but a bad or base discourse published in print is
intolerable.

Hereupon I have indured some conflicts between
reason and judgement, whether it were convenient for
the commonwealth, with the *indecorum* of my calling
(as some think it) that the memory of *Tancred's* Tragedy
should be again by my means revived, which the oftner
I read over, and the more I considered thereon, the
sooner I was won to consent thereunto: calling to mind
that neither the thrice reverend and learned father, M.
Beza, was ashamed in his younger years to send abroad,
in his own name, his Tragedy of *Abraham*, nor that
rare Scot (the scholar of our age) *Buchanan*, his most
pathetical *Jephtha*.

Indeed I must willingly confess this work simple,
and not worth comparison to any of theirs: for the
writers of them were grave men; of this, young heads:
In them is shewn the perfection of their studies; in
this, the imperfection of their wits.   Nevertheless

herein they all agree, commending virtue, detesting vice, and lively deciphering their overthrow that suppress not their unruly affections. These things noted herein, how simple soever the verse be, I hope the matter will be acceptable to the wise.

Wherefore I am now bold to present *Gismund* to your sights, and unto yours only, for therefore have I conjured her, by the love that hath been these twenty-four years betwixt us, that she wax not so proud of her fresh painting, to straggle in her plumes abroad, but to contain herself within the walls of your house; so am I sure she shall be safe from the *Tragedian Tyrants* of our time, who are not ashamed to affirm that there can no amorous poem savour of any sharpness of wit, unless it be seasoned with scurrilous words.

But leaving them to their lewdness, I hope you, and all discreet readers will thankfully receive my pains, the fruits of my first harvest: the rather, perceiving that my purpose in this Tragedy tendeth only to the exaltation of virtue, and suppression of vice, with pleasure to profit and help all men, but to offend or hurt no man. As for such as have neither the grace, nor the good gift, to do well themselves, nor the common honesty to speak well of others, I must (as I may) hear and bear their baitings with patience.

Yours devoted in his ability,

R. WILMOT.

A PREFACE

TO

THE QUEEN'S MAIDS OF HONOUR.

FLOWERS of prime, pearls couched all in gold,
Light of our days, that glads the fainting hearts
Of them that shall your shinning gleams behold,
Salve of each sore, recure of inward smarts,
In whom virtue and beauty striveth so
As neither yields : behold here, for your gain,
Gismund's unlucky love, her fault, her woe,
And death ; at last her cruel father slain
Through his mishap ; and though you do not see,
Yet read and rue their woful tragedy.
So Jove, as your high virtues done deserve,
Grant you such [3] pheers as may your virtues serve
With like virtues ; and blissful Venus send
Unto your happy loves an happy end.

ANOTHER TO THE SAME.

GISMUND, that whilome liv'd her father's joy
And died his death, now dead, doth (as she may)
By us pray you to pity her annoy.
And, to requite the same, doth humbly pray,
Heavens to [4] forefend your loves from like decay.

---

[3] *pheers,*] *Pheers* signifies a husband, a friend, or a companion,
and in all these senses it is used in our ancient writers. It here
means *a husband.* So, in Lyly's *Euphues,* 1581, p. 29 : " If he be
" young, he is the more fitter to be thy *pheere.* If he bee olde, the
" lyker to thine aged father."
  Again, A. 2. S. 3. and A. 4. S. 3.
[4] *forefend*] Prevent, or *forbid.* So, in *Euphues and his England,*
1582, p. 40 " For never shall it be said that Iffida was false to
Thirsus, " though Thirsus be faithlesse (which the Gods *forefend*)
" unto Iffida."

The faithful Earl doth also make request,
Wishing those worthy knights whom ye embrace,
The constant truth that lodged in his breast.
His hearty love, not his unhappy case,
Befall to such as triumph in your grace.
The King prays pardon of his cruel hest [5],
And for amends desires it may suffice,
That by his blood he warneth all the rest
Of fond fathers, that they in kinder wise
Intreat the jewels where their comfort lies.
We, as their messengers beseech ye all
On their behalfs to pity all their smarts.
And for ourselves (although the worth be small)
We pray ye to accept our humble hearts,
Avow'd to serve with prayer and with praise
Your honours, all unworthy other ways.

[5] *hest*,] Command. So, in Lyly's *Euphues and his England*, p. 78:
" For this I sweare by her whose lightes canne never die Vesta,
" and by her *whose heasts* are not to be broken Diana, &c."
Again, Shakspeare's *Tempest*, A. 3. S. 1:
" —— O my father,
" I have broke *your hest* to say so!"
Prologue to *Araygnement of Paris*, 1584:
" Done by the pleasure of the powers above,
" Whose *hestes* men must obey:"
The word occurs again in A. 4. S. 2. A. 4. S. 4. and A. 5. S. 1.

DRAMATIS PERSONÆ.

TANCRED, *the King.*
GUISZARD, *Count* Palurin.
JULIO, *Lord Chamberlain.*
RENUCHIO, *Captain of the Guard.*
CUPID.

GISMUNDA, *the King's Daughter.*
LUCRECE, *her Aunt.*
MEGÆRA.

CHORUSSES.

ARGUMENT OF THE TRAGEDY.

TANCRED, the Prince of Salerne, over loves
His only daughter (wonder of that age)
Gismund, who loves the County [6] Palurin
Guishard, who quits their likings with his love :
A letter in a cane describes the means
Of their two meetings in a secret cave.
Unconstant fortune leadeth forth the king
To this unhappy sight, wherewith in rage
The gentle Earl he doometh to his death,
And greets his daughter with her lover's heart.
Gismunda fills the goblet with her tears,
And drinks a poison which she had distill'd,
Whereof she dies, whose deadly countenance
So grieves her father, that he slew himself.

ANOTHER OF THE SAME, MORE AT LARGE, IN PROSE.

Tancred, King of Naples and Prince of Salerne,
gave his only daughter Gismund (whom he most dearly
loved) in marriage to a foreign prince, after whose death
she returned home to her father, who having felt great
grief of her absence whilst her husband lived, immea-
surably esteeming her, determined never to suffer any
second marriage to bereave him of her. She, on the
other side, waxing weary of that her father's purpose,
bent her mind to the secret love of the County Palurin:
to whom (he being likewise inflamed with love of her)
by a letter subtilly enclosed in a cloven cane, she gave
to understand a convenient way for their desired meetings, through an old ruinous vault, whose mouth opened

---

[6] *County*] The County *Palurin*, a few lines lower is called Earl.
Mr. Tyrwhitt says, that *County* signified *Noblemen* in general ; and
the examples which might be quoted from this Play would sufficiently prove the truth of the observation. See Shakspeare, vol. X.
p. 39.

directly under her chamber floor. Into this vault when
she was one day descended (for the conveyance of her
lover), her father in the mean season (whose only joy
was in his daughter) came to her chamber, and not
finding her there, supposing her to have been walked
abroad for disport, he threw him down on her bed, and
covered his head with a curtain, minding to abide and
rest there till her return. She nothing suspecting this
her father's unseasonable coming, brought up her lover
out of the cave into her chamber, where her father
espied their secret love : and he (not espied of them)
was upon this sight stricken with marvellous grief ; but
either for that the sudden despight had amazed him,
and taken from him all use of speech or for that he resolved himself to a more convenient revenge, he then
spake nothing, but noted their return into the vault,
and secretly departed. Afterward, bewailing his mishap,
he commanded the Earl to be attached, imprisoned,
strangled, unbowelled, and his heart in a cup of gold to
be presented to his daughter : she thankfully receiveth
the present, filling the cup (wherein the heart was) with
her tears, with a venomous potion (by her distilled for
that purpose) she drank to her Earl. Which her father
hearing of, came too late to comfort his dying daughter,
who for her last request besought him, that her lover
and herself might in one tomb be together buried for a
perpetual memory of their faithful loves ; which request
he granted, adding to the burial, himself slain with his
own hands, to his own reproach, and the terror of
all other hard-hearted fathers.

TANCRED AND GISMUNDA[7].

ACT. I. SCEN. I.

CUPID *cometh out of the heavens in a cradle of flowers, drawing forth upon the stage, in a blue twist of silk, from his left hand, Vain Hope, Brittle Joy: And with a carnation twist of silk from his right hand, Fair Resemblauce, Late Repentance.*

Cupid. There rest my chariot, on the mountain tops.
I, that in shape appear unto your sight
A naked boy, not cloath'd but with my wings,
Am that great God of Love, who with his might
Ruleth the vast wide world, and living things.
This left hand bears vain Hope, short joyful state,
With fair Resemblance, lovers to allure:
This right hand holds Repentance all too late,

---

[7] The story of this Tragedy is taken from Boccace's *Decameron*, Day 4th, Novel first. It hath also been versified according to Mr. Warton (*History of English Poetry*, vol. II. p. 238.) by William Walter, a retainer to Sir Henry Marney, Chancellor of the Duchy of Lancaster. This versification he supposes to have been printed by Wynkyn de Worde. It was afterwards reprinted in the year 1597, under the title of " *The Statelie Tragedy of Guisthard and Sismond, in two Bookes.*" Amongst other Poems in a Volume, entitled " *Certaine Worthye Manuscript Poems of great Antiquitie re-*" *served long in the Studye of a Northfolke Gent. and now first published* " *by J. S.*" Mr. Dryden also versified it a second time. See his Works, vol. III. 8vo. Edition, p. 245. Oldys, in his MS. Notes on Langbaine, says the same story is in Painter's *Palace of Pleasure*, vol. I. and a French Novel called Guichard and Sigismonde fils de Tancredies Prince de Salerne mis en Latin, par Leon Arretin, et traduit in vers François, par Jean Fleury, 4to. Paris, Let. Gothiques.

War, [8] fire, blood, and pains without recure.
On sweet Ambrosia is not my food,
Nectar is not my drink : as to the rest,
" Of all the gods, I drink the lover's blood, '
" And feed upon the heart within his breast."
Well hath my power in heaven and earth been try'd,
And deepest hell my piercing force hath known.
The marble seas * my wonders hath descry'd,
Which elder age throughout the world hath blown.
To me, the king of gods and men doth yield,
As witness can the Greekish maid [9], whom I
Made like a cow go glowing through the field,
Lest jealous Juno should the 'scape espy.
The doubled night, the sun's restrained course,
His secret stealths, the slander to eschew,
In shape transform'd [10], we list not to discourse.
All that and more we forced him to do.
The warlike Mars hath not subdu'd our might,
We fear'd him not, his fury nor disdain,
That can the gods record, before whose sight
He lay fast wrapt in Vulcan's subtle chain.
He that on earth yet hath not felt our power,
Let him behold the fall and cruel spoil
Of thee, fair Troy, of Asia the flower,
So foul defac'd, and level'd with the soil.
Who forc'd Leander with his naked breast
So many nights to cut the frothy waves,
But Hero's love, that lay inclos'd in Sest ?
The stoutest hearts to me shall yield them slaves.
Who could have match'd the huge [11] Alcides' strength ?

[8] *fire*] This word seems anciently to have been pronounced as two syllables. See *Cornelia,* A. 4. Chorus.

* *The marble seas.*] An epithet adopted from Virgil's Æneid, lib. 6. v. 729.

    Et quæ *marmoreo* fert monstra sub æquore pontus.
      Ibid. lib. 7. v. 28.

       ——— lento luctantur *marmore* tonsæ.
    Again, Georg. 1. v. 254.

       ——— infidum remis impellere *marmor.* S.

[9] Io.

[10] Like to Amphitrio to Alcmena.

[11] Hercules.

Great [12] Macedon, what force might have subdu'd?
Wise Scipio, who overcame at length,
But we, that are with greater force endu'd?
Who could have conquered the golden fleece
But Jason, aided by Medea's art?
Who durst have stoln fair Helen out of Greece
But I, with love that boldned Paris' heart?
What bond of nature, what restraint avails
Against our power? I vouch to witness truth.
The myrrh tree [13], that with shamefac'd tears bewails
Her father's love, still weepeth yet for ruth [14],
But now, this world not seeing in these days
Such present proofs of our all daring power,
Disdains our name, and seeketh sundry ways
To scorn and scoff, and shame us every hour.
A brat, a bastard, and an idle boy,
A rod, a staff, a whip to beat him out,
And to be sick of love, a childish toy:
These are mine honours now the world about,
My name disgrac'd.   To raise again therefore,
And in this age, mine ancient renown
By mighty acts intending to restore,
Down to the earth in wrath now am I come;
And in this place such wonders shall ye hear,
As these your stubborn and disdainful hearts,
In melting tears, and humble yielding fear,
Shall soon relent by sight of others smarts.
This princely palace will I enter in,

[12] Alexander.
[13] Myrrha.
[14] — *still weepeth yet for ruth.*] i. e. for pity. So, A. 2. S. 2:
   " As easily befalls that age which asketh *ruth.*"
A. 5. S. 1:
             " — that hath the tyrant king
   " Withouten *ruth* commanded us to do."
Milton's *Lycidas*, l. 163:
   " Look homeward angel now and melt with *ruth;*
   " And, O ye Dolphins, waft the hapless youth."
Churchyard's *Worthiness of Wales*, 1587:
   " Great *ruth*, to let so trim a seate goe downe,
   " The countries strength, and beautie of the towne."

And there inflame the fair Gismunda so,
Inraging all her secret veins within,
Through fiery Love, that she shall feel much woe.
Too late Repentance, thou shalt bend my bow ;
Vain Hope, take out my pale dead heavy shaft,
Thou fair resemblance, foremost forth shalt go,
With Brittle Joy : myself will not be least,
But after me comes Death, and deadly Pain.
Thus shall ye march, till we return again.
Mean while, sit still, and here I shall you shew
Such wonders, that at last with one accord
Ye shall relent, and say, that now you know
Love rules the world, Love is a mighty lord.   [*Exit.*
    [*Cupid with his train entereth into king Tancred's*
    palace.

ACT I. SCEN. II.

GISMUNDA *in purple cometh out of her chamber, at-*
tended by four maids that are the Chorus.

    " *Gismund.* O vain, unstedfast state of mortal things!
" Who trust this world, leans to a brittle stay :
" Such fickle fruit his flattering bloom forth brings,
" Ere it be ripe, it falleth to decay."
The joy and bliss that late I did possess,
In weal at will, with one I loved best,
Is turned now into so deep distress,
As teacheth me to know the world's unrest.
For neither wit nor princely stomachs serve
Against his force, that slays without respect
The noble and the wretch : ne doth reserve
So much as one for worthiness elect.
Ah me, dear lord ! what well of tears may serve
To feed the streams of my foredulled eyes,
To weep thy death, as thy death doth deserve,
And wail thy want in full sufficing wise ?

Ye lamps of heaven, and all ye heavenly powers,
Wherein did he procure your high disdain?
He never sought with vast huge mounting towers
To reach aloft, and over-view your reign :
Or what offence of mine was it unwares,
That thus your fury should on me be thrown,
To plague a woman with such endless cares?
I fear that envy hath the heavens this shown :
The sun his glorious virtues did disdain ;
Mars at his manhood mightily repin'd ;
Yea, all the gods no longer could sustain,
Each one to be excelled in his kind.
For he my lord surpass'd them every one ;
Such was his honour all the world throughout.
But now, my love, oh! whither art thou gone?
I know thy ghost doth hover hereabout,
Expecting me (thy heart) to follow thee :
And I (dear love) would fain dissolve this strife.
But stay a while, I may perhaps foresee
Some means to be disburden'd of this life,
" And to discharge the duty of a wife,
" Which is, not only in this life to love,
" But after death her fancy not remove."
Mean while accept of these our daily rites,
Which with my maidens I shall do to thee,
Which is, in songs to chear our dying spirits
With hymns of praises of thy memory.
    Cantant. Quæ mihi cantio nondum occurrit *.

---

* *Quæ mihi cantio nondum occurrit.*] These omissions are frequent in our old Plays. See note on *Love's Labour Lost*, edit. of
Shakspeare, 1778, vol. II. p. 410. S.

ACT I. SCEN. III.

The song ended, TANCRED *the king cometh out of his palace with his guard.*

Tancred. Fair daughter, I have sought thee out with
        grief,
To ease the sorrows of thy vexed heart.
How long wilt thou torment thy father thus,
Who daily dies to see thy needless tears?
Such bootless plaints, that know nor mean nor end,
Do but increase the floods of thy lament;
And since the world knows well there was no want
In thee, of aught that did to him belong,
Yet all, thou seest, could not his life prolong :
Why then dost thou provoke the heavens to wrath?
His doom of death was dated by his stars,
" And who is he that may withstand his fate?"
By these complaints, small good to him thou dost,
Much grief to me, more hurt unto thyself,
And unto nature greatest wrong of all.
    Gismunda. Tell me not of the date of nature's days,
Then in the April of her springing age :
No, no, it was my cruel destiny,
That spited at the pleasance of my life.
    Tancred. My daughter knows the proof of nature's
        course.
" For as the heavens do guide the lamp of life,
" So can they reach no farther forth the flame,
" Than whilst with oil they do maintain the same."
    Gismunda. Curst be the stars, and vanish may they
        curst,
Or fall from heaven, that in their dire aspèct[15]
Abridg'd the health and welfare of my love.
    Tancred. Gismund, my joy, set all these griefs apart;
" The more thou art with hard mishap beset,

---

[15] — *aspèct*] In this manner the word was formerly accented.
See Dr. Farmer's *Essay on the Learning of Shakspeare.*

" The more thy patience should procure thine ease."
> *Gismund.* What hope of hap may chear my hapless
>> chance ?·

What sighs, what tears may countervail my cares ?
What should I do, but still his death bewail,
That was the solace of my life and soul?
Now, now, I want the wonted guide and stay
Of my desires, and of my wreckless thoughts.
My lord, my love, my life, my liking gone,
In whom as all the fulness of my joy,
To whom I gave the first-fruits of my love,
Who with the comfort of his only sight,
All care and sorrows could from me remove.
But, father, now my joys forepast to tell,
Do but revive the horrors of my hell.
As she that seems in darkness to behold
The gladsome pleasures of the chearful light.

> *Tancred.* What then avails thee fruitless thus to rue

His absence, whom the heavens cannot return ?
Impartial death thy husband did subdue,
Yet hath he spar'd thy kingly father's life :
Who during life, to thee a double stay,
As father and as husband will remain,
With double love to ease thy widow's want,
Of him whose want is cause of thy complaint.
Forbear thou therefore all these needless tears,
That nip the blossoms of thy beauty's pride.

> *Gismund.* Father, these tears love challengeth of due.
> *Tancred.* But, reason saith thou shouldst the same
>> subdue.
> *Gismund.* His funerals are yet before my sight.
> *Tancred.* In endless moans princes should not delight.
> *Gismund.* The turtle pines in loss of her true mate.
> *Tancred.* And so continues poor and desolate.
> *Gismund.* Who can forget a jewel of such price ?
> *Tancred.* She that hath learn'd to master her desires.

" Let reason work, what time doth easily frame
" In meanest wits, to bear the greatest ills."

> *Gismund.* So plenteous are the springs

Of sorrows that increase my passions,

As neither reason can recure my smart,
Nor can your care, nor fatherly comfort,
Appease the stormy combats of my thoughts;
Such is the sweet remembrance of his life.
Then give me leave, of pity, pity me,
And as I can I shall allay these griefs.

    Tancred. These solitary walks thou dost frequent,
Yield fresh occasions to thy secret moans:
We will therefore thou keep us company,
Leaving thy maidens with their harmony.
[16] Wend thou with us.   Virgins, withdraw yourselves.

> [*Tancred and Gismund, with the guard, depart into
> the palace; the four maidens stay behind, as
> Chorus to the Tragedy.*

    Chorus 1. The diverse haps which always work our
      care,
Our joys so far, our woes so near at hand,
Have long ere this, and daily do declare
The fickle foot on which our state doth stand.
" Who plants his pleasures here to gather root,
" And hopes his happy life will still endure,
" Let him behold how death with stealing foot
" Steps in when he shall think his joys most sure."
No ransom serveth to redeem our days
If prowess could preserve, or worthy deeds,
He had yet liv'd, whose twelve labours displays
His endless fame, and yet his honour spreads.

---

[16] *Wend thou with us.*]   *Wend,* i. e. go.   So, in Epilogue:
    " With violent hands he that his life doth end,"
    " His damned soul to endless night doth *wend.*"
Again, *Return from Parnassus,* 1606, A. 5. S. 4:
    " These my companions still with me must *wend.*"
George a Green Pinner of Wakefield, vol. III.
    " Wilt thou leave Wakefield and *wend* with me,
    " So will I *wend* with Robin all along,
    " For you are wrong, and may not *wend* this way."
Chaucer's *Canterbury Tales,* Prologue, l. 19:
    " Befelle, that, in a seson on a day,
    " In Southwerk at the Tabard as I lay,
    " Redy to *wenden* on my pilgrimage,
    " To Canterbury with devout corage."

And that great king [17], that with so small a power
Bereft the mighty Persian of his crown,
Doth witness well our life is but a flower,
Though it be deck'd with honour and renown.

    Chorus 2. " What grows to day in favour of the
        heaven,
" Nurst with the sun, and with the showers sweet,
" Pluck'd with the hand, it withereth ere even.
" So pass our days even as the rivers fleet."
The valiant Greeks that unto Troia gave
The ten years siege, left but their names behind.
And that he did so long and only save
His father's walls [18], found there at last his end.
Proud Rome herself, that whilome laid her yoke
On the wide world, and vanquish'd all with war,
Yet could she not remove the fatal stroke
Of death, from them that stretcht her pow'r so far.

    Chorus 3. Look what the cruel sisters once de-
        creed,
The Thunderer himself cannot remove:
They are the ladies of our destiny,
To work beneath, what is conspir'd above.
But happy he that ends this mortal life
By speedy death, who is not forc'd to see
The many cares, nor feel the sundry griefs
Which we sustain in woe and misery.
Here fortune rules, who when she list to play,
Whirleth her wheel, and brings the high full low:
To-morrow takes, what she hath given to-day,
To show she can advance and overthrow.
[19] Not Euripus' unquiet flood so oft

---

[17] Alexander.
[18] Hector.
[19] *Not* Euripus' *unquiet flood so oft*] *Euripus Euboicus*, or *Chalci-
dicus*, is a narrow passage of sea dividing *Attica* and the Island of
Euboea, now called *Golph de Negroponte.* It ebbs and flows seven
times every day: the reason of which, it is said, when Aristotle
could not find, he threw himself into the sea with these words:
Quia ego non capio te, tu capias me. Sir Thomas Brown, in his *En-
quiries into Vulgar Errors*, b. 7. c. 14. appears to have been not
satisfied with this account of Aristotle's death, which he has taken
some pains to render doubtful.

Ebbs in a day, and floweth to and fro,
As fortune's change plucks down that was aloft,
And mingleth joy with interchange of woe.
 Chorus 4. " Who lives below, and feeleth not the
  strokes,
" Which often times on highest towers do fall,
" Nor blustering winds, wherewith the strongest oaks
" Are rent and torn, his life is sur'st of all:"
For he may fortune scorn, that hath no power
On him, that is well pleas'd with his estate:
He seeketh not her sweets, nor fears her sower,
But lives contented in his quiet rate,
And marking how these worldly things do wade,
Rejoiceth to himself, and laughs to see
The folly of men, that in their wits have made
Fortune a goddess, placed in the sky.
    Finis Actus I. *Exegit Rod. Staf.*

ACT II. SCEN. I.

GISMUNDA AND LUCRECE.

Gismunda. Dear aunt, my sole companion in distress,
And true copartner of my thoughtful cares:
When with myself I weigh my present state,
Comparing it with my forepassed days,
New heaps of cares afresh begin t' assay
My pensive heart, as when the glittering rays
Of bright Phœbus are suddenly o'erspread
With dusky clouds, that dim his golden light:
Namely, when I, laid in my widow's bed,
Amid the silence of the quiet night,
With curious thought the fleeting course observe
Of gladsome youth, how soon his flower decays,
" How time once past, may never have recourse,
" No more than may the running streams revert
" To climb the hills, when they been rolled dow

" The hollow vales.   There is no curious art,
" Nor worldly power, no, not the gods can hold
" The sway of flying time, nor him return
" When he is past : all things unto his might
" Must bend, and yield unto the iron teeth
" Of eating time."   This in the shady night;
'When I record, how soon my youth withdraws
Itself away ! how swift my pleasant spring
Runs out his race ! This, this (aunt) is the cause
[20] When I advise me sadly on this thing,
That makes my heart in pensive dumps dismay'd.
For if I should my springing years neglect,
And suffer youth fruitless to fade away;
Whereto live I ? or whereto was I born ?
Wherefore hath nature deck'd me with her grace ?
Why have I tasted these delights of love,
And felt the sweets of Hymeneus' bed?
But to say sooth (dear aunt) it is not I
Sole and alone, can thus content to spend
My cheerful years : my father will not still
Prolong my mournings, which have griev'd him,
And pleased me too long.   Then this I crave,
To be resolved of his princely mind.
For, stood it with the pleasure of his will
To marry me, my fortune is not such,
So hard, that I so long should still persist
Mateless alone in woful widowhood.

[20] *When I advise me sadly on this thing*,] *Sadly*, in most of our
ancient writers, is used as here for *seriously*. So, in Nash's *Lenten
Stuff*, 1599 : " Nay, I will lay no wagers, for, now I perponder
" more *sadly* upon it, I think I am out indeed."
Hall's *Chronicle*, 1550, *Henry* IV. fo. 2 : " — his cosyn ger-
" maine was nowe brought to that trade of livynge, that he litle or
" nothynge regarded the counsaill of his uncles, nor of other grave
" and *sadde* persones, but did all thynge at his pleasure."
Ascham's *Toxophilus*, 1571 : " — and when I sawe not you
" amonges them, but at the last espyed you lookinge on your
" booke here so *sadlye*, I thought to come and hold you with some
" communication."
Warton's *Life of Sir Thomas Pope*, p. 30 : " Wherein is an abbes
" namyd Dame Alice Fitzherbert, of the age LX yeares, a very
" *sadde*, discreate, and relegyous woman."

And shall I tell mine aunt? come hither then,.
Give me that hand : By thine own right hand,
I charge thy heart my councils to conceal.
Late have I seen, and seeing took delight,
And with delight, I will not say, I love
A prince, an earl, a countie in the court.
But love and duty force me to refrain,
And drive away these fond affections,
Submitting them unto my father's hest.
But this (good aunt) this is my chiefest pain,
Because I stand at such uncertain stay,
For, if my kingly father would decree
His final doom, that I must lead my life
Such as I do, I would content me then
To frame my fancies to his princely hest,
And as I might endure the grief thereof.
But now his silence doubleth all my doubts,
Whilst my suspicious thoughts 'twixt hope and fear
Distract me into sundry passions :
Therefore (good aunt) this labour must be yours,
To understand my father's will herein,
For well I know your wisdom knows the means,
So shall you both allay my stormy thoughts,
And bring to quiet my unquiet mind.
    Lucrece. Sufficeth this (good niece) that you have
        said ;
For I perceive what sundry passions
Strive in your breast, which oftentimes ere this
Your countenance confused did bewray.
The ground whereof since I perceive to grow
On just respect of this your sole estate,
And skilful care of fleeting youth's decay,
Your wise foresight such sorrowing to eschew
I much commend, and promise as I may
To break this matter, and impart your mind
Unto your father, and to work it so,
As both your honour shall not be impeach'd,
Nor he unsatisfied of your desire.
Be you no farther grieved, but return
Into your chamber. I shall take this charge,

And you shall shortly truly understand
What I have wrought, and what the king affirms.
   Gismunda. I leave you to the fortune of my stars.
      [*Gismunda departeth into her chamber, Lucrece*
      abiding on the stage.
   Lucrece. The heavens, I hope, will favour your re-
quest.
My niece shall not impute the cause to be
In my default, her will should want effect:
But in the king is all my doubt, lest he
My suit for her new marriage should reject.
Yet shall I prove him : and I heard it said,
[21] He means this evening in the park to hunt.
Here will I wait attending his approach.

ACT II.   SCEN. II.

TANCRED *cometh out of his palace with* GUISZARD,
the Countie PALURIN, JULIO, *the Lord Chamberlain,*
RENUCHIO, *captain of his guard, all ready to hunt.*

   Tancred. Uncouple all our hounds; Lords, to the
      chace—
Fair sister * Lucre, what's the news with you?
   Lucrece. Sir, as I always have employ'd my power,
And faithful service, such as lay in me,
In my best wise to honour you and yours:

---

[21] *He means,* &c.] Formerly this diversion was as much followed
in the evening, as it was at an earlier hour in the day. In *Lane-
ham's Account of the Entertainment at Kenelworth Castle,* we find that
Queen Elizabeth always, while there, hunted in the afternoon.
" Monday was hot, and therefore her highness kept in till *five*
" *a clok in the eeveing ;* what time it pleaz'd to ryde forth into the
" chase too hunt the hart of fors : which found anon, and after
" sore chased," &c. Again, " Munday the 18 of this July, the
" weather being hot, her highness kept the castle for coolness, till
" about *five a clok,* her majesty in the chase, hunted the hart (as
before) of forz," &c.
   * Lucrece. O. G.

So now my bounden duty moveth me
Your majesty most humbly to intreat,
With patient ears, to understand the state
Of my poor niece, your daughter.
    Tancred.   What of her?
Is she not well? Enjoys she not her health?
Say, sister, ease me of this jealous fear?
    Lucrece. She lives, my lord, and hath her outward
        health;
But all the danger of her sickness lies
In the disquiet of her princely mind.
    Tancred. Resolve me; what afflicts my daughter so?
    Lucrece. Since when the princess hath intomb'd her
        lord,
Her late deceased husband of renown;
Brother, I see, and very well perceive,
She hath not clos'd together in his grave
All sparks of nature, kindness, nor of love:
But as she lives, so living may she feel
Such passions as our tender hearts oppress,
Subject unto th' impressions of desire:
For well I wot my niece was never wrought
Of steel, nor carved from the stony rock:
Such stern hardness we ought not to expect
In her, whose princely heart and springing years
Yet flow'ring in the chiefest heat of youth,
Is led of force to feed on such conceits,
As easily befalls that age, which asketh ruth
Of them, whom nature bindeth by foresight
Of their grave years, and careful love, to reach
The things that are above their feeble force:
And for that cause, dread lord, although—
    Tancred. Sister, I say,
If you esteem, or aught respect my life,
Her honour, and the welfare of our house,
[22] Forbear, and wade no farther in this speech.

---

[22] *Forbear, and* wade *no farther,* &c.] That is, *proceed no further.*
So, A. 2. S. 3:
      " Therefore my counsel is you shall not stir,
      " Nor farther *wade* in such a case as this:"

Your words are wounds.   I very well perceive
The purpose of this smooth oration:
This I suspected, when you first began
This fair discourse with us: Is this the end
Of all our hopes, that we have promised
Unto ourself by this her widowhood?
Would our dear daughter, would our only joy,
Would she forsake us ?. would she leave us now
Before, she hath clos'd up our dying eyes,·
And with her tears bewail'd our funeral?
No other solace doth her father crave;
But, whilst the fates maintain his dying life,
Her healthful presence, gladsome, to his soul,·
Which rather than he willing would forego,
His heart desires the bitter tase of death.
Her late marriage hath taught us to our grief,
That in the fruits of her perpetual sight
Consists the only comfort and relief
Of our unweildy age: for what delight,
What joy, what comfort, have we in this world;
Now grown in years, and overworn with cares,
Subject unto the sudden stroke of death,·
Already falling like the mellowed fruit,
And dropping by degrees into our grave?·
But what revives us, what maintains our soul
Within the prison of our wither'd breast,
But our Gismunda, and her chearful sight?
O daughter, daughter! what desert of mine,
Wherein have I been so unkind to thee,
Thou should'st desire to make my naked house
Yet once again stand desolate by thee?
O let such fancies vanish with their thoughts.
Tell her, I am her father, whose estate,
Wealth, honour, life, and all that we possess,
Wholly relies upon her presence here.

Turberville's *Tragical Tales*, 1587 :
  " Eare thou 'doe *wade* so farre, revoke
   " to minde to bedlam boy,
   " That in his forged wings of waxe
   " reposed too great a joy ."

Tell her, I must account her all my joy,
Work as she will : But yet she were unjust,
To haste his death that liveth by her sight.

    Lucrece. Her gentle heart abhors such ruthless
      thoughts.

    Tancred. Then let her not give place to these desires.

    Lucrece. She craves the right that nature challengeth.

    Tancred. Tell her, the king commandeth otherwise.

    Lucrece. The king's commandment always should
      be just.

    Tancred. Whate'er it be, the king's command is just.

    Lucrece. Just to command: but justly must he charge.

    Tancred. He chargeth justly that commands as king.

    Lucrece. The king's command concerns the body best.

    Tancred. The king commands obedience of the mind.

    Lucrece. That is exempted by the law of kind.

    Tancred. That law of kind* to children doth belong.

    Lucrece. In due obedience to their open wrong?

    Tancred. I then, as king and father, will command.

    Lucrece. No more than may with right of reason
      stand.

    Tancred. Thou knowest our mind, [23] resolve her, de-
      part—

Return the chace, we have been chas'd enough.

    [*Tancred returneth into his palace, and leaveth
    the hunt.*

    Lucrece. He cannot hear, anger hath stopp'd his ears,
And over-love his judgment hath decay'd.
Ah, my poor neice! I shrewdly fear thy cause,
Thy just complaint, shall never be reliev'd.

---

    * — *that law of kind.*] *i. e* of nature.

    [23] — *resolve her.*] Acquaint her with my resolution. *To resolve,*
however, was sometimes used for *convince,* or *satisfy.* It may
therefore mean, *convince her of the propriety of my command.* So,
in Middleton's *More Dissemblers besides Women,* A. 1. S. 3 :

      " The blessing of perfection to your thoughts lady,
      " For I'm *resolv'd* they are good ones."

    Read is right in his first explanation, it is so used in Chapman's
May Day, Act 1. S. 1.

    Tell her such a man will *resolve* her naming me. Anc. Dram.
vol. 6. p. 6. O. G.

ACT II. SCEN. III.

GISMUNDA *cometh alone out of her chamber.*

Gismunda. By this I hope my aunt hath mov'd the
    king,
And knows his mind, and makes return to me
To end at once all this perplexity.
Lo, where she stands.   Oh! how my trembling heart
In doubtful thoughts panteth within my breast.
For in her message doth rely my smart,
Or the sweet quiet of my troubled mind.

Lucrece. Niece, on the point you lately willed me
To treat of with the king in your behalf,
I brake even now with him so far, till he
In sudden rage of grief, ere I scarce had
My tale out told, pray'd me to stint my suit,
As that from which his mind abhorred most.
And well I see, his fancy to refute
Is but displeasure gain'd, and labour lost.
So firmly fixed stands his kingly will,
That till his body shall be laid in grave,
He will not part from the desired sight
Of your presence, which silder he should have,
If he had once allied you again
In marriage to any prince or peer.
This is his final resolution.

Gismunda. [24] A resolution that resolves my blood
Into the icy drops of Lethe's flood.

---

[24] *A resolution that resolves my blood*] *Resolve* has the same meaning as *dissolve*. So, in Lyly's *Euphues and his England*, p. 38 : " I
" could be content to *resolve* myselfe into teares to rid thee of
" trouble."

Christopher Marlow, as quoted in *England's Parnassus*, 1600,
p. 480 :

    " No molten Christall but a richer mine,
    " Even natures rarest alchumie ran there,
    " Diamonds *resolv'd*, and substance more divine,
    " Through whose bright gliding current might appeare
    " A thousand naked Nymphes, whose yvorie shine,
    " Enameling the bankes, made them more deare

Lucrece. Therefore my counsel is, you shall not stir,
Nor farther wade in such a case as this:
But since his will is grounded on your love,
And that it lies in you to save or spill
His old fore-wasted age ; you ought t' eschew
The thing that grieves so much his crazed heart,
And, in the state you stand, content yourself :
And let this thought appease your troubled mind,
That in your hands relies your father's death,
Or blissful life ; and since without your sight
He cannot live, nor can his thoughts endure
Your hope of marriage, you must then relent,
And over-rule these fond affections ;
Lest it be said, you wrought your father's end.

 Gismunda. Dear aunt, I have with patient ears in-
  dur'd
The hearing of my father's hard behest ;
And since I see, that neither I myself,
Nor your request, can so prevail with him,
Nor any sage advice persuade his mind
To grant me my desire, in willing wise
I must submit me unto his command,
And frame my heart to serve his majesty.
And (as I may) to drive away the thoughts
That diversly distract my passions,
Which as I can, I'll labour to subdue,
But sore I fear, I shall but toil in vain ;
Wherein (good aunt) I must desire your pain.

 Lucrece. What lies in me by comfort or advice,
I shall discharge with all humility.

  [*Gismunda and Lucrece depart into Gismunda's
   chamber.*

 Chorus 1. Who marks our former times and present
  years,
What we are now, and looks what we have been,
He cannot but lament with bitter tears

  " Then ever was that glorious Pallas gate,
  " Where the day shining sunne in triumph sate."
 See also Shakspeare's *Hamlet,* A. 1. S. 2. and Mr. Steevens's
Note on it.

The great decay and change of all women.
For as the world wore on, and waxed old,
25 So virtue quail'd, and vice began to grow.
So that that age, that whilome was of gold,
Is worse than brass, more vile than iron now.
The times were such (that if we aught believe
Of elder days), women examples were
Of rare virtues: Lucrece disdain'd to live
Longer than chast; and boldly, without fear,
Took sharp revenge on her inforced heart,
With her own hands : for that it not withstood
The wanton will, but yielded to the force
Of proud Tarquin, who bought her fame with blood.
   Chorus 2. Queen Artemissa thought an heap of
      stones,
(Although they were the wonder of that age)
A worthless grave, wherein to rest the bones
Of her dear lord, but with bold courage
She drank his heart, and made her lovely breast
His tomb, and failed not of wifely faith,
Of promis'd love, and of her bound behest,
Until she ended had her days by death.
Ulysses' wife (such was her stedfastness)
Abode his slow return whole twenty years :
And spent her youthful days in pensiveness,
Bathing her widow's bed with brinish tears.
     Portia,
   Chorus 3. The stout daughter of Cato, Brutus' wife,
When she had heard his death, did not desire
Longer to live : and lacking use of knife,
(A most strange thing) ended her life by fire,
And eat hot burning coals.   O worthy dame !
O virtues worthy of eternal praise !

   25 *So virtue quail'd*]   *To quail, is to* languish, *to sink into* dejection.
So, in Churchyard's *Challenge*, 24 :
      " Where malice sowes, the seedes of wicked waies,
      " Both honor *quailes*, and credit crackes with all :
      " Of noblest men, and such as fears no fall."
   See also Mr. Steevens's Notes on the First Part of *Henry* IV.
A. 4. S. 2. and *Cymbeline*, A. 5. S. 5.

The flood of Lethe cannot wash out thy fame,
To others great reproach, shame, and dispraise.

    Chorus 4. Rare are those virtues now in women's
        mind!
Where shall we seek such jewels passing strange?
Scarce can you now among a thousand find
One woman stedfast: all delight in change.
Mark but this princess, that lamented here
Of late so sore her noble husband's death,
And thought to live alone without a pheer;
Behold how soon she changed hath that breath!
I think those ladies that have liv'd tofore,
A mirror and a glass to womenkind;
By those their virtues they did set such store,
That unto us they none bequeath'd behind;
Else in so many years we might have seen
As virtuous as ever they have been.

    Chorus 1. Yet let not us maidens condemn our
        kind,
Because our virtues are not all so rare:
For we may freshly yet record in mind,
[26] There lives a virgin, one without compare,
Who of all graces hath her heavenly share;
In whose renown, and for whose happy days,
Let us record this Pæan of her praise.
           Cantant.
      Finis Actus 2.   *Per Hen. No.*[27]

---

   [26] *There lives a virgin,*] A complement to Queen Elizabeth.
S. P.

   It was, as Mr. Steevens observes, no uncommon thing to intro-
duce a compliment to Queen Elizabeth in the body of a play.
See *Midsummer's Night's Dream,* A. 2. S. 2. See also *Locrine,*
A. 5. S. last.

   [27] *Per Hen. No.*] Probably Henry Noel, younger brother to Sir
Andrew Noel, and one of the gentlemen pensioners to Queen Elizabeth, a man, says Wood, of excellent parts, and well skilled in
musick. See *Fasti,* p. 145. A Poem, entitled, *Of disdainful
Daphne,* by M. H. Nowell, is printed in *England's Helicon,* 1600·
4to. The name of *Mr. Henry Nowell* also appears in the list of
those lords and gentlemen that ran at a tilting before Queen Elizabeth. See " *Polyhymnia describing the honourably Triumph at*
" *Tylt before her Majestie, on the* 17 *of November last past, being the*

ACT III. SCEN. I.

Cupid. So, now they feel what lordly Love can do,
  That proudly practise to deface his name;
In vain they wrestle with so fierce a foe;
  Of little sparks arise a blazing flame.
" By small occasions Love can kindle heat,
  " And waste the oaken breast to cinder dust."
Gismund I have enticed to forget
  Her widow's weeds, and burn in raging lust:

" *first day of the three and thirtieth yeare of her Highnesse raigne. With*
" *Sir Henrie Lea, his resignation of honour at Tylt, to her Majestie,*
" *and received by the right honorable, the Earl of Cumberland.*" By
George Peele, 4to. 1590.

I cannot here let pass unremembered a worthy gentleman,
master Henry Noel, brother to the said sir Andrew Noel, one of the
gentlemen pensioners * to Queen Elizabeth; a man for personage,
parentage, grace, gesture, valour, and many excellent parts, inferior to none of his rank in the court; who, though his lands and
livelihoods were but small, having nothing known certain but his
annuity and his pension, yet in state, pomp, magnificence and ex-
pences, did equalize barons of great worth. If any shall demand
whence this proceeded, I must make answer with that Spanish
proverb—

  Aquello qual viénne de arriba ninguno lo pregunta.
  That which cometh from above let no one question.

This is the man of whom Queen Elizabeth made this enigmatical
distich :—

  The word of denial, and letter of fifty,
  Is that gentleman's name that will never be thrifty.

He, being challenged (as I have heard) by an Italian gentleman
at the *baloune* (a kind of play with a great ball tossed with wooden
braces upon the arm) used therein such violent motion, and did so
overheat his blood, that he fell into a calenture, or burning fever;
and thereof died, Feb. 26, 1596, and was, by her majesty's appointment, buried ni the abbey church of Westminster, in the chapel
of St. Andrew.

  Benton in Nicholas's Leicestershire, vol. III. p. 249.

Henry Noel was the second son of Sir Edward Noel, of Dalby,
by his second wife, Elizabeth, daughter and heir of William Hop-
ton, of ———, Shropshire, relict of Sir John Peryent, Knt.

  Ibid. 254.   O. G.

* See Peck's Life of Milton, p. 225, for the Gentleman Pensioners.

'Twas I enforc'd her father to deny
  Her second marriage to any peer;
'Twas I allur'd her once again to try
  The sower sweets that lovers buy too dear.
The County Palurin, a man right wise,
  A man of exquisite perfections,
I have like wounded with her piercing eyes,
  And burnt her heart with his reflections.
These two shall joy in tasting of my sweet,
  To make them prove more feelingly the grief
That bitter brings : for when their joys shall fleet,
  Their dole shall be increas'd without relief.
Thus Love shall make worldlings to know his might;
  Thus Love shall force great princes to obey;
Thus Love shall daunt each proud rebelling sprite;
  Thus Love shall wreck his wrath on their decay.
Their ghosts shall give black hell to understand,
  How great and wonderful a god is Love :
And this shall learn the ladies of this land
  With patient minds his mighty power to prove.
From whence I did descend, now will I mount
  To Jove, and all the gods in their delights :
In throne of triumph there will I recount,
  How I by sharp revenge on mortal wights,
Have taught the earth, and learned hellish sprites,
To yield with fear their stubborn hearts to Love,
Lest their disdain his plagues and vengeance prove.
                    [*Cupid remounteth into the heavens.*

ACT III. SCEN. II.

LUCRECE *cometh out of* GISMUNDA'S *chamber solitary.*

  Lucrece. Pity, that moveth every gentle heart
To rue their griefs, that be distrest in pain,
Inforceth me to wail my niece's smart,
Whose tender breast no long time may sustain

The restless toil, that her unquiet mind
Hath caus'd her feeble body to endure;
But why it is (alack!) I must not find,
Nor know the man, by whom I might procure
Her remedy, as I of duty ought,
As to the law of kinship doth belong.
With careful heart the secret means I sought,
Though small effect is of my travel sprung:
Full often as I durst, I have assay'd,
With humble words, the princess to require
[28] To name the man which she hath so denay'd,
That it abash'd me further to desire,
Or ask from whence those cloudy thoughts proceed,
Whose stony force, that smoaky sighs forth send,
Is lively witness how that careful dread
And hot desire within her do contend:
Yet she denies what she confess'd of yore,
And then conjoin'd me to conceal the same;
She loved once (she saith) but never more,
Nor ever will her fancy thereto frame.
Though daily I observed in my breast
What sharp conflicts disquiet her so sore,
That heavy sleep cannot procure her rest,
But fearful dreams present her evermore
Most hideous sights, her quiet to molest;
That starting oft therewith she doth awake,
To muse upon those fancies which torment
Her thoughtful heart with horror, that doth make
Her cold chill sweat break forth incontinent
From her weak limbs.   And while the quiet night
Gives others rest, she, turning to and fro,
Doth wish for day: But when the day brings light,
She keeps her bed, there to record her woe.

[28] *To name the man, which she hath so* denay'd,] In the former
edition, the word *denay'd* was altered to the more modern one of
deny'd. *Denay'd*, however, was the ancient manner of spelling it.
So, in the Second Part of *Henry* VI. A. 1. S. 3:
    " Then let him be *denay'd* the regentship."
Again, First Part of *Jeronimo*, 1605:
    " And let not wonted fealty be *denayed*."
Gammer Gurton's Needle, p. 80:
    " Loke as I have promised, I will not *denay it*."

As soon as when she riseth, flowing tears
Stream down her cheeks, immixed with deadly groans,
Whereby her inward sorrow so appears,
That as salt tears the cruel cause bemoans.
In case she be constrained to abide
[29] In prease of company, she scarcely may
Her trembling voice restrain it be not spy'd,
From careful plaints her sorrows to bewray.
By which restraint the force doth so increase,
When time and place give liberty to plain,
That as small streams from running never cease,
Till they return into the seas again ;
So her laments, we fear, will not amend,
Before they bring her princely life to end.
To others talk when as she should attend,
Her heaped cares her senses so oppress,
That what they speak, or whereto their words tend,
She knows not, as her answers do express.
Her chief delight is still to be alone,
Her pensive thoughts within themselves debate :
But whereupon this restless life is grown,
Since I know not, nor how the same t' abate ;
I can no more but wish it as I may,
That he which knows it would the same allay,
For which the muses with my song shall pray.

[29] *In prease of company,*] *Prease* signifies a *crowd* or *multitude,* or *any assemblage of a number of persons.* So, in *Damon and Pithias,* vol. I.

" The Kyng is at hande, stande close in *the prease,* beware," &c. Ibid.

" Away from the prisoner, what *a prease* have we here ?"

History of Euordanus Prince of Denmark, 1605, Sign. H : " — the " Prince passing forwards sorely shaken, having lost both his stir- " rups : at length recovering himselfe, entred *the prease,* where on " all sides he beate downe knights, and unbarred helms."

ACT III. SCEN. III.

After the song, which was by report very sweetly re-
peated by the Chorus, LUCRECE departeth into GIS-
MUNDA'S chamber; and GUISZARD cometh out of
the palace with JULIO and RENUCHIO, gentlemen, to
whom he turneth, and saith,

Guiszard. Leave me, my friends; this solitary walk
Inticeth me to break your company.
Leave me, my friends, I can endure no talk.
Let me intreat this common courtesy.
                              [*The Gentlemen depart.*
What grievous pain they dure, which neither may
Forget their loves, ne yet enjoy their love,
I know by proof, and daily make assay.
Though Love hath brought my lady's heart to love,
My faithful love with like love to requite;
This doth not quench, but rather cause to flame
The creeping fire, which spreading in my breast
With raging heat, grants me no time of rest.
If they bewail their cruel destiny,
Which spend their love where they no love can find,
Well may I plain, since fortune haleth me
To this torment of far more grievous kind;
Wherein I feel as mcuh extremity
As may be felt in body or in mind.
For by that sight which should recure my pain,
My sorrows are redoubled all in vain.
Now I perceive that only I alone
Am her belov'd, her looks allure me so :
The thought thereof provokes me to bemoan
Her heavy plight that grieveth at my woe.
This intercourse of our affections,
I her to serve, she thus to honour me,
Bewrays the truth of our elections,
Delighting in this mutual sympathy.
Thus love, for love intreats the queen of love,
That with her help Love's solace we may prove.

I see my mistress seeks as well as I
To stay the strife of her perplexed mind :
Full fain she would our secret company,
If she the wished way thereof might find.
Heavens, have ye seen, or hath the age of man
Recorded such a miracle as this ?
In equal love two noble hearts to frame,
That never spake one with another's bliss.
I am assured that she doth assent
To my relief, that I should reap the same,
If she could frame the means of my content,
Keeping herself from danger of defame.
In happy hour right now I did receive
This cane from her ; which gift, though it be small,
Receiving it, what joys I did conceive
Within my fainting spirits therewithall !
Who knoweth love aright, may well conceive,
By like adventures that to them befall.
" For needs the lover must esteem that well,
" Which comes from her with whom his heart doth
        " dwell."
Assuredly it is not without cause
She gave me this ; something she meant thereby :
For therewithall I might perceive her pause
A while, as though some weighty thing did lie
Upon her heart, which she concealed, because
The standers-by should not our loves descry :
This cleft bewrays that it hath been disclos'd ;
Perhaps herein she hath something inclos'd.
                                    [*He breaks it.*
O thou great Thunderer ! who would not serve,
Where wit with beauty chosen have their place ?
Who could devise more wisely to conserve
Things from suspect ? O Venus, for this grace
That deigns me, all unworthy, to deserve
So rare a love, in heaven I should thee place.
This sweet letter some joyful news contains,
I hope it brings recure to both our pains. [*He reads it.*

Mine own, as I am yours, whose heart (I know)
No less than mine, for lingering help of woe

Doth long too long : love tendering your case
And mine, hath taught recure of both our pain.
My chamber floor doth hide a cave, where was
An old vault's mouth : the other in the plain
Doth rise southward, a furlong from the wall.
Descend you there.   This shall suffice.   And so
I yield myself, mine honour, life and all,
To you.   Use you the same as there may grow
Your bliss and mine (mine Earl) and that the same
Free may abide from danger of defame.
Farewell ; and fare so well, as that your joy,
Which only can, may comfort mine annoy.

> *Yours more than her own.*
> GISMUND.

O blissful chance my sorrows to asswage !
Wonder of nature, marvel of our age !
Comes this from Gusmund ? did she thus infold
This letter in the cane? may it be so ?
It were too sweet a joy, I am deceiv'd.
Why shall I doubt, did she not give it me ?
Therewith she smil'd, she joy'd, [30] she raught the cane,
And with her own sweet hand she gave it me :
And as we danc'd, she dallied with the cane,
And sweetly whisper'd I should be her king,
And with this cane, the scepter of our rule,
Command the sweets of her surprized heart.
Therewith she raught from her alluring locks
This golden tress, the favour of her grace,
And with her own sweet hand she gave it me.
O peerless queen, my joy, my heart's decree !
And thou fair letter, how shall I welcome thee ?
Both hand and pen wherewith thou written wer't,
Blest may ye be, such solace that impart ;
And blessed be this cane, and he that taught
Thee to descry the hidden entry thus :
Not only through a dark and dreadful vault,

---

[30] — *she* raught *the cane,*] *Raught* is the ancient preterite of the word *reach.* It is frequently used by Spenser, Shakspeare, and other ancient writers.

But fire and sword, and through whatever be,
Mistress of my desires, I come to thee.
>   [*Guiszard departeth in haste unto the palace.*
Chorus 1.   Right mighty is thy power, O cruel
>   Love,
High Jove himself cannot resist thy bow;
Thou sent'st him down, e'en from the heavens above,
In sundry shapes here to the earth below:
Then how shall mortal men escape thy dart,
The fervent flame, and burning of thy fire;
Since that thy might is such, and since thou art
Both of the seas and land the lord and sire?
>   *Chorus* 2.   But why doth he that sprung from Jove's
>   high head,
And Phœbus's sister shene, despise thy power,
Ne fears thy bow? Why have they always led
A maiden life, and kept untouch'd the flower?
Why doth Ægistus love, and to obtain
His wicked will, conspire his uncle's death?
Or why doth Phædra burn, from whom is slain
Theseus' chaste son, or Helen false of faith?
" For love assaults not but the idle heart,
" And such as live in pleasure and delight;
" He turneth oft their gladsome joys to smart,
" Their play to plaint, their sport into despite."
>   *Chorus* 3. 'Tis true, that Dian chaseth with her bow
The flying hart, the goat, and foamy boar;
By hill, by dale, in heat, in frost, in snow,
She recketh not, but laboureth evermore;
Love seeks not her, ne knoweth where her to find.
Whilst Paris kept his herd on Ida down,
Cupid ne'er sought him out; for he is blind:
But when he left the field to live in town,
He fell into his snare, and brought that brand
From Greece to Troy, which after set on fire
Strong Ilium, and all the Phyrges land:
" Such are the fruits of love, such is his hire."
>   *Chorus* 4. Who yieldeth unto him his captive heart,
Ere he resist, and holds his open breast

Withouten war to take his bloody dart,
Let him not think to shake off when him list
His heavy yoke.   " Resist his first assault ;
" Weak is his bow, his quenched brand is cold ;
" Cupid is but a child, and cannot daunt
" The mind that bears him, or his virtues bold."
But he gives poison so to drink in gold,
And hideth under pleasant baits his hook ;
But ye beware, it will be hard to hold
Your greedy minds, if ye but wisely look
What sly snake lurks under those flowers gay.
But ye mistrust some cloudy smoaks, and fear
A stormy shower after so fair a day :
Ye may repent, and buy your pleasure dear ;
For seldom times is Cupid wont to send
" Unto an idle love a joyful end."

Finis Actus 3.   G. *All.*

ACT IV. SCEN. I.

Before this act MEGÆRA *riseth out of hell, with the
other furies,* ALECTO *and* TYSIPHONE *dancing an
hellish round ; which done she saith.*

Megæra. Sisters, begone, bequeath the rest to me,
That yet belongs unto this tragedy.
                    [*The two furies depart down.*
Vengeance and death from forth the deepest hell,
I bring the cursed house where Gismund dwells.
Sent from the grisly god that holds his reign
In Tartar's ugly realm, where Pelop's sire
(Who with his own son's flesh whom he had slain
Did feast the gods) with famine hath his hire ;
To gape and catch at flying fruits in vain,
And yielding waters to his gasping throat ;

Where stormy Æol's son, with endless pain,
Rolls up the rock ; where Titius hath his lot
[31] To feed the gripe that gnaws his growing heart ;
Where proud Ixion, whirled on the wheel,
Pursues himself; where due-deserved smart
The damned ghosts in burning flame do feel,
From thence I mount : Thither the winged god,
Nephew to Atlas, that upholds the sky,
Of late down from the earth, with golden rod,
To Stygian ferry Salerne souls did guide,
And made report, how Love, that lordly boy,
Highly disdaining his renown's decay,
Slipt down from heaven, and fill'd with fickle joy
Gismund's heart, and made her throw away
Chastness of life, to her immortal shame;
Minding to shew, by proof of her foul end,
Some terror unto those that scorn his name.
Black Pluto (that once found Cupid his friend
In winning Ceres' daughter, queen of hells ;)
And Parthie, moved by the grieved ghost
Of her late husband, that in Tartar dwells,
Who pray'd due pains for her, that thus hath lost
All care of him, and of her chastity.
The senate then of hell, by grave advice
Of Minos, Æac, and of Radamant,
Commands me draw this hateful air, and rise
Above the earth, with dole and death to daunt
The pride and present joys, wherewith these two
Feed their disdained hearts; which now to do,
Behold I come with instruments of death.
This stinging snake, which is of hate and wrath,
I'll fix upon her father's heart full fast,
And into her's this other will I cast,

[31] *To feed the gripe that gnaws his growing heart ;*] Alluding to the
Vulture that gnawed the liver of Titius. In *Ferrex and Porrex*,
A. 2 : S. 1. is this line :
    " Or cruell gripe to gnaw my groaning hart."
  For Titius read Tytius. The allusion is rather to the Vulture of
Prometheus. S.

Whose rankling venom shall infect them so
With envious wrath, and with recureless woe,
Each shall be other's plague and overthrow.
" Furies must aid, when men surcease to know
" Their gods : and hell sends forth revenging pain
" On those, whom shame from sin cannot restrain."

ACT IV.   SCEN. II.

MEGÆRA *entereth into the palace, and meeteth with*
TANCRED *coming out of* GISMUND'S *chamber with*
RENUCHIO *and* JULIO, *upon whom she throweth her*
snake*.

Tancred. Gods! are ye guides of justice and revenge?
O thou great Thunderer! dost thou behold
With watchful eyes the subtile 'scapes of men
Harden'd in shame, sear'd up in the desire
Of their own lusts ? why then dost thou withhold
The blast of thy revenge ? why dost thou grant
Such liberty, such lewd occasion
To execute their shameless villainy?
Thou, thou art cause of all this open wrong,
Thou that forbear'st thy vengeance all too long.
If thou spare them, rain then upon my head
The fulness of thy plagues with deadly ire,
To reave this ruthful soul, who all too sore
Burns in the wrathful torments of revenge.
O earth, the mother of each living wight,
Open thy womb, devour this wither'd corps.
And thou, O hell (if other hell there be
Than that I feel) receive my soul to thee.
O daughter, daughter, (wherefore do I grace

---

* *she throweth her snake.*] *Viper, inspirans animam.* The image
is from Virgil. Rowe likewise adopts it in his *Ambitious Step-*
mother.
     " And sends a *snake* to every vulgar breast."   S.

Her with so kind a name?) O thou fond girl,
The shameful ruin of thy father's house,
Is this my hoped joy? Is this the stay
Must glad my grief-full years that waste away?
For life which first thou didst receive from me,
Ten thousand deaths shall I receive by thee.
For all the joys I did repose in thee,
Which I (fond man) did settle in thy sight,
Is this thy recompence; that I must see
The thing so shameful, and so villanous;
That would to God this earth had swallowed
This worthless burthen into lowest deeps,
Rather than I (accursed) had beheld
The sight that hourly massacres my life?
O whither, whither fly'st thou forth, my soul?
O whither wand'reth my tormented mind?
Those pains that make the miser glad of death*
Have seiz'd on me, and yet I cannot have
What villains may command, a speedy death.
Whom shall I first accuse for this outrage?
That god that guideth all, and guideth so
This damned deed? Shall I blaspheme their names,
The gods, the authors of this spectacle?
Or shall I justly curse that cruel star
Whose influence assign'd this destiny?
But may that traytor, shall that vile wretch live,
By whom I have receiv'd this injury?
Or shall I longer make account of her,
That fondly prostitutes her widow's shame?—
I have bethought me what I shall request. [*He kneels.*
On bended knees, with hands heav'd up to heaven,
This (sacred senate of the gods) I crave:
First on the traytor your consuming ire;
Next, on the cursed strumpet, dire revenge;
Last, on myself, the wretched father, shame. [*He riseth.*
Oh! could I stamp, and therewithall command

---

* *— the miser glad of death.*] i. e. the wretch. The word *miser*
was antiently used without comprehending any idea of avarice.
See note on *King Henry VI*. p. 1, edit. of Shakspeare, 1778, vol. 6.
p. 279.   S.

Armies of furies to assist my heart,
To prosecute due vengeance on their souls.—
Hear me, my friends ; but as ye love your lives,
Reply not to me ; hearken and stand amaz'd.
When I, as is my wont, (oh fond delight!)
Went forth to seek my daughter, now my death,
Within her chamber (as I thought) she was ;
But there I found her not : I deemed then
For her disport she and her maidens were
Down to the garden walk'd to comfort them ;
And thinking thus, it came into my mind
There all alone to tarry her return :
And thereupon I (weary) threw myself
Upon her widow's bed (for so I thought)
And in the curtain wrapt my cursed head.
Thus as I lay, anon I might behold
Out of the vault, up through her chamber floor,
My daughter Gismund bringing hand in hand
The County Palurin.   Alas! it is too true ;
At her bed's feet this traytor made me see
Her shame, his treason, and my deadly grief.
Her princely body yielded to this thief ;
The high despite whereof so wounded me,
That, trans-like, as a senseless stone I lay ;
For neither wit, nor tongue could use the mean
T' express the passions of my pained heart.
Forceless, perforce, I sunk down to this pain,
As greedy famine doth constrain the hawk
Piece meal to rend and tear the yielding prey :
So far'd it with me in that heavy stound.
But now what shall I do ? how may I seek
To ease my mind, that burneth with desire
Of dire revenge ? For never shall my thoughts
Grant ease unto my heart, till I have found
A mean of vengeance to requite his pains,
That first convey'd this sight unto my soul.—
Renuchio!
    Renuchio. What is your highness' will ?
    Tancred. Call my daughter : my heart boils till I see
Her in my sight, to whom I may discharge

All the unrest that thus distempereth me.
Should I destroy them both? O gods, ye know
How near and dear our daughter is to us.
And yet my rage persuades me to imbrue
My thirsty hands in both their trembling bloods,
Therewith to cool my wrathful fury's heat.
But, Nature, why repin'st thou at this thought?
Why should I think upon a father's debt
To her that thought not on a daughter's due?
But still, methinks, if I should see her die,
And therewithall reflex her dying eyes
Upon mine eyes, that sight would slit my heart:
Not much unlike the coackatrice, that slays
The object of his foul infections.
Oh! what a conflict doth my mind endure?
Now fight my thoughts against my passions:
Now strive my passions against my thoughts:
Now sweats my heart, now chill-cold falls it dead.
Help heavens, and succour ye celestial powers.
Infuse your secret virtue on my soul.
Shall nature win? shall justice not prevail?
Shall I (a king) be proved partial?
" How shall our subjects then insult on us,
" When our examples (that are light to them)
" Shall be eclipsed with our proper deeds?"
And may the arms be rented from the tree?
The members from the body be dissever'd?
And can the heart endure no violence?
My daughter is to me mine only heart,
My life, my comfort, my continuance;
Shall I be then not only so unkind
To pass all nature's strength, and cut her off?
But therewithall so cruel to myself,
Against all law of kind to shred in twain
The golden thred that doth us both maintain?
But were it that my rage should so command,
And I consent to her untimely death,
Were this an end to all our miseries?
No, no, her ghost will still pursue our life,
And from the deep her bloodless ghastful spirit

Will, as my shadow in the shining day,
Follow my footsteps till she take revenge.
I will do thus: therefore the traytor dies,
Because he scorned the favour of his king,
And our displeasure wilfully incurr'd:
His slaughter, with her sorrow for his blood,
Shall to our rage supply delightful food.—
Julio!

 Julio. What is't your Majesty commands?

 Tancred. Julio, if we have not our hope in vain,
Nor all the trust we do repose in thee,
Now must we try if thou approve the same.
Herein thy force and wisdom we must see,
For our command requires them both of thee.

 Julio. How by your Grace's bounty I am bound,
Beyond the common bond wherein each man
Stands bound unto his king; how I have found
Honour and wealth by favour in your sight,
I do acknowledge with most thankful mind.
My truth (with other means to serve your Grace,
Whatever you in honour shall assign)
Hath sworn her power true vassal to your hest:
For proof, let but your majesty command,
I shall unlock the prison of my soul,
(Although unkindly horror would gainsay)
Yet in obedience to your highness' will,
By whom I hold the tenor of this life,
This hand and blade will be the instruments
To make pale death to grapple with my heart.

 Tancred. Well, to be short (for I am griev'd too long
By wrath without revenge) I think you know
Whilom there was a palace builded strong
For war, within our court, where dreadless peace
Hath planted now a weaker entrance.
But of that palace yet one vault remains
Within our court, the secret way whereof
Is to our daughter Gismund's chamber laid:
There is also another mouth hereof
Without our wall, which now is overgrown;
But you may find it out, for yet it lies

Directly south a furlong from our palace:
It may be known, hard-by an ancient stoop [32],
Where grew an oak in elder days, decay'd;
There will we that you watch, there shall you see
A villain traytor mount out of a vault:
Bring him to us, it is th' earl Palurin.
What is his fault, neither shall you enquire,
Nor list we to disclose; these cursed eyes
Have seen the flame, this heart hath felt the fire
That cannot else be quench'd but with his blood.
This must be done: this will we have you do.
    Julio. Both this, and else whatever you think good.
                     [*Julio departeth into the palace.*

ACT. IV.   SCEN. III.

RENUCHIO *bringeth* GISMUND *out of her chamber, to whom* TANCRED *saith.*

    Tancred. Renuchio, depart, leave us alone.
                     [*Exit Renuchio.*
Gismund, if either I could cast aside
All care of thee! or if thou wouldst have had
Some care of me, it would not now betide,
That either through thy fault my joy should fade,
Or by thy folly I should bear the pain
Thou hast procur'd: but now 'tis neither I
Can shun the grief, whom thou hast more than slain;
Nor may'st thou heal, or ease the grievous wound
Which thou hast given me. That unstained life
Wherein I joy'd, and thought it thy delight,
Why hast thou lost it? Can it be restor'd?
Where is thy widow's bed, there is thy shame.
Gismund, it is no man's, nor men's report,
That have by likely proofs inform'd me thus.

---

[32] — *an ancient stoop.*] " A *stoop,* or *stowp;* a post fastened in the earth, from the Latin *stupa.*" Ray's *North Country Words,* p. 58. Edition 1742.

Thou know'st how hardly I could be induc'd
To vex myself, and be displeas'd with thee,
With flying tales of flattering sycophants.
No, no, there was in us such settled trust
Of thy chaste life and uncorrupted mind
That, if these eyes had not beheld thy shame,
In vain ten thousand censure could have told,
That thou didst once unprincelike make agree
With that vile traytor County Palurin;
Without regard had to thyself or me,
Unshamefac'dly to stain thy state and mine.
But I unhappiest have beheld the same,
And seeing it, yet feel th' exceeding grief
That slays my heart with horror of that thought:
Which grief commands me to obey my rage,
And justice urgeth some extream revenge,
To wreak the wrongs that have been offer'd us.
But nature, that hath lock'd within thy breast
Two lives, the same inclineth me to spare
Thy blood, and so to keep mine own unspilt.
This is that overweening love I bear
To thee undutiful, and undeserved.
But for that traytor, he shall surely die;
For neither right nor nature doth intreat
For him, that wilfully without all awe
Of gods, or men, or of our deadly hate,
Incurr'd the just displeasure of his king,
And to be brief, I am content to know
What for thy self thou canst object to us,
Why thou should'st not together with him die,
So to assuage the griefs that overthrow
Thy father's heart.
    Gismund. O king and father, humbly give her leave
To plead for grace, that stands in your disgrace.
33 Not that she recks this life: for I confess

---

33 *Not that she recks this life:*] Not that she is careful or anxious
about, or regrets the loss of this life. So, in Milton's *Paradise Lost,*
B. 9. l. 171:
              " — Revenge at first though sweet,
       " Bitter ere long back on itself recoils;
       " Let it; *I reck not,* so it light well aim'd."

I have deserv'd, when so it pleaseth you,
[34] To die the death, mine honour and my name
(As you suppose) distained with reproach:
And well contented shall I meet the stroke,
That must dissever this detested head
From these lewd limbs.   But this I wish were known,
That now I live not for myself alone.
For when I saw that neither my request,
Nor the intreaty of my careful aunt,
Could win your highness' pleasure to our will:
" Then love, heat of the heart, life of the soul,
" Fed by desire, increasing by restraint,"
Would not endure controulment any more,
But violently enforc'd my feeble heart
(For who am I, alas! still to resist
Such endless conflicts?) to relent and yield:
Therewith I chose him for my lord and pheer,
Guiszard mine Earl, that holds my love full dear.
Then if it be so settled in your mind,
He shall not live because he dar'd to love
Your daughter; thus I give your grace to know.
Within his heart there is inclos'd my life.
Therefore, O father, if that name may be
Sweet to your ears, and that we may prevail
By name of father, that you favour us:
But otherwise, if now we cannot find
That which our falsed hope did promise us;
Why then proceed, and rid our trembling hearts
Of these suspicions.   Since neither in this case
His good deserts in service to your Grace,
Which always have been just, nor my desires,
May mitigate the cruel rage of grief
That strains your heart, but that mine Earl must die;
Then all in vain you ask what I can say
Why I should live.   Sufficeth for my part
To say I will not live, and so resolve.

History of Sir John Oldcastle, 1600:
    " I *reck* of death, the less in that I die,
    " Not by the sentence of that envious priest."
[34] *To die the death,*] See Note, vol. I.

Tancred. Dar'st thou so desperate decree thy death?
Gismund. A dreadless heart delights in such decrees.
Tancred. Thy kind abhorreth such unkindly thoughts.
Gismund. Unkindly thoughts they are to them that live
In kindly love.
 Tancred. As I do unto thee.
Gismund. To take his life who is my love from me?
Tancred. Have I then lost thy love?
 Gismund.   If he shall lose
His life, that is my love.
 Tancred.   Thy love? Begone.
Return into thy chamber.
 Gismund.   I will go.
   [*Gismunda departeth to her chamber.*

ACT. IV. SCEN. IV.

JULIO *with his guard bringeth in the County* PALURIN
prisoner.

Julio. If it please your highness, hither have we
 brought
This captive Earl, as you commanded us.
Whom (as we were foretold) even there we found
Where by your Majesty we were injoin'd
To watch for him.   What more your highness wills,
This heart and hand shall execute your hest.
 Tancred. Julio, we thank your pains.—Ah, Palurin!
Have we deserved in such traiterous sort
Thou should'st abuse our kingly courtesies,
Which we too long in favour have bestow'd
Upon thy false dissembling heart with us?
What grief thou therewithal hast thrown on us,
What shame upon a house, what dire distress
Our soul endures, cannot be uttered.
And durst thou, villain, dare to undermine
Our daughter's chamber? durst thy shameless face

Be bold to kiss her ? th' rest we will conceal.
Sufficeth that thou knowest I too well know
All thy proceedings in thy private shames.
Herein what has thou won ? thine own content,
With the displeasure of thy lord and king.
The thought whereof, if thou hadst had in mind
The least remorse of love and loyalty,
Might have restrain'd thee from so foul a fact.
But, Palurin, what may I deem of thee,
Whom neither fear of gods, nor love of him
(Whose princely favour hath been thine uprear)
Could quench the fewel of thy lewd desires ?
Wherefore content thee, that we are resolv'd
(And therefore laid to snare thee with this bait)
That thy just death, with thine effused blood,
Shall cool the heat and choler of our mood.
   Guiszard. My lord the king, neither do I mislike
Your sentence, nor do your smoking sighs,
Reach'd from the entrails of your boiling heart,
Disturb the quiet of my calmed thoughts :
For this I feel, and by experience prove,
Such is the force and endless might of love,
As never shall the dread of carrion death,
That hath envy'd our joys, invade my breast.
For if it may be found a fault in me
(That evermore hath lov'd your Majesty)
Likewise to honour and to love your child;
If love unto you both may be a fault,
But unto her my love exceeds compare :
Then this hath been my fault, for which I joy,
That in the greatest lust of all my life,
I shall submit for her sake to endure
The pangs of death.   Oh ! mighty Lord of Love,
Strengthen thy vassal boldly to receive
Large wounds into this body for her sake.
Then use my life or death, my lord and king,
For your relief to ease your grieved soul :
For whether I live, or else that I must die
To end your pains, I am content to bear ;
Knowing by death I shall bewray the truth

Of that sound heart which living was her own,
And died alive for her that lived mine.

    Tancred. Thine Palurin? What! lives my daughter
      thine?

Traytor, thou wrong'st me, for she liveth mine.
Rather I wish ten thousand sundry deaths,
Than I to live, and see my daughter thine.
Thine, that is dearer than my life to me?
Thine, whom I hope to see an empress?
Thine, whom I cannot pardon from my sight?
Thine, unto whom we have bequeath'd our crown?—
Julio, we will that thou inform from us
Renuchio the captain of our guard,
That we command this traytor be convey'd
Into the dungeon underneath our tower;
There let him rest until he be resolv'd
What farther we intend; which to understand,
We will Renuchio repair to us.

    Julio. O that I might your Majesty entreat
With clemency to beautify your seat
Toward this prince, distrest by his desires,
Too many, all too strong to captivate.

    Tancred. " This is the soundest safety for a king,
" To cut them off that vex or hinder him."

    Julio. " This have I found the safety of a king,
" To spare the subjects that do honour him."

    Tancred. Have we been honour'd by this leacher's
      lust?

    Julio. No, but by this devout submission.

    Tancred. Our fortune says we must do what we may.

    Julio. " This is praise-worth, not to do what you may."

    Tancred. And may the subject countermand the king?

    Julio. No, but intreat him.

    Tancred.   What he shall decree?

    Julio. What wisdom shall discern.

    Tancred.   Nay, what our word
Shall best determine. We will not reply.
Thou know'st our mind, our heart cannot be eas'd,
But with the slaughter of this Palurin.

                 [*The king hasteth into his palace.*

Guiszard. O, thou great god! who from thy highest
        throne
Hast stooped down, and felt the force of love,
Bend gentle ears unto the woful moan
Of me poor wretch, to grant that I require:
Help to persuade the same great god, that he
So far remit his might, and slack his fire
From my dear lady's kindled heart, that she
May hear my death without her hurt. Let not
Her face, wherein there is as clear a light
As in the rising moon; let not her cheeks,
As red as is the party-colour'd rose,
Be paled with the news hereof: and so
I yield myself, my silly soul, and all,
To him, for her, for whom my death shall shew
I liv'd; and as I liv'd, I dy'd her thrall.
Grant this, thou Thunderer: this shall suffice,
My breath to vanish in the liquid skies.
                    [*Guiszard is led to prison.*
Chorus 1. Who doth not know the fruits of Paris' love,
Nor understand the end of Helen's joy?
He may behold the fatal overthrow
Of Priam's house, and of the town of Troy;
His death at last, and her eternal shame,
For whom full many noble knights were slain.
So many a duke, so many a prince of fame
Bereft his life, and left there in the plain.
Medea's armed hand, Eliza's sword,
Wretched Leander drenched in the flood.
Phillis, so long that waited for her lord.
All these too dearly bought their loves with blood.
Chorus 2. But he in virtue that his lady serves,
Ne wills but what unto her honour 'longs,
He never from the rule of reason swerves;
He feeleth not the pangs, ne raging throngs,
Of blind Cupid: he lives not in despair,
As done his servants; neither spends his days
In joy and care, vain hope, and throbbing fear;
But seeks alway what may his sovereign please
In honour: he that thus serves, reaps the fruit

Of his sweet service; and no jealous dread,
Nor base suspect of aught to let his suit,
(Which causeth oft the lover's heart to bleed)
Doth fret his mind, or burneth in his breast:
He waileth not by day, nor wakes by night,
When every other living thing doth rest;
Nor finds his life or death within her sight.
    Chorus 3. Remember thou in virtue serve therefore
Thy chaste lady: beware thou do not love,
As whilom Venus did the fair Adone,
But as Diana lov'd th' Amazon's son;
Through whose request the gods to him alone
Restor'd new life.   The twine that was undone,
Was by the sisters twisted up again.
The love of virtue in thy lady's looks,
The love of virtue in her learned talk;
This love yields matter for eternal books.
This love inticeth him abroad to walk,
There to invent and write new rondelays
Of learn'd conceit, her fancies to allure
To vain delights, such humours he allays,
And sings of virtue and her garments pure.
    Chorus 4. Desire not of thy sovereign the thing
Whereof shame may ensue by any mean;
Nor wish thou aught that may dishonour bring.
So whilom did the learned [35]Tuscan serve   ‚
His fair lady; and glory was their end.
Such are the praises lovers done deserve,
Whose service doth to virtue and honour tend.
        Finis Actus 4.   *Composuit Ch. Hat.*[36]

---

    [35] — *learned Tuscan serve*
        His fair lady ;] Petrarch and Laura.
    [36] *Composuit Ch. Hat.*] The initials of these names seem intended
for Christopher Hatton, afterwards knighted and created Chancellor of England and a Peer.   In the fourth year of Queen Elizabeth, 1562, about six years before this Play is supposed to have
been written, we learn from Dugdale's *Origines Juridiciales*, p. 150,
a magnificent Christmas was kept in the Inner Temple, at which
her Majesty was present, and Mr. Hatton was appointed Master
of the Game.   Historians say, he owed his rise, not so much to his
mental abilities, as to the graces of his person, and his excellence

ACT V. SCEN. I.

RENUCHIO *cometh out of the palace.*

Renuchio. Oh cruel fate! oh miserable chance!
Oh dire aspect of hateful destinies!
Oh woe may not be told! Suffic'd it not
That I should see, and with these eyes behold
So foul, so bloody, and so base a deed:
But more to aggravate the heavy cares
Of my perplexed mind, must only I,
Must I alone be made the messenger,
That must deliver to her princely ears
Such dismal news, as when I shall disclose,
I know it cannot but abridge her days?
As when the thunder and three-forked fire,
Rent through the clouds by Jove's almighty power,
Breaks up the bosom of our mother earth,
And burns her heart before the heat be felt.
In this distress whom should I most bewail,
My woe, that must be made the messenger
Of these unworthy and unwelcome news?
Or shall I moan thy death, O noble Earl?
Or shall I still lament the heavy hap,
That yet, O Queen, attends thy funeral?

in dancing; which captivated the Queen to such a degree, that he arose gradually from one of her Gentlemen Pensioners to the highest employment in the Law, which he, however, filled without censure, supplying his own defects by the assistance of the ablest men in the profession. *The grave Lord Keeper,* after his promotion, still retained his fondness for that accomplishment to which he was indebted for his rise, *and led the Brawles,* almost untill his death. In 1589, on the marriage of his heir with Judge Gawdry's daughter, " the Lord Chancellor danced the measures at the solemnity, and left his gown on the chair, saying *Lie there Chancellor.*" His death, which happened two years after, was hastened by an unexpected demand of money from the Queen, urged in so severe a manner, that all the kindness she afterwards shewed to him was insufficient to remove the impression it had made on him. See Birch's *Memoirs of Queen Elizabeth,* vol. I. p. 8. 56.

Chorus 1. What moans be these? Renuchio, is this
        Salerne I see?
Doth here king Tancred hold the awful crown?
Is this the place where civil people be?
Or do the savage Scythians here abound?
    Chorus 2. What mean these questions? whither tend
        these words?
Resolve us maidens, and release our fears.
Whatever news thou bring'st, discover them,
Detain us not in this suspicious dread!
" The thought whereof is greater than the woe."
    Renuchio. O whither may I cast my looks? to heaven?
Black pitchy clouds from thence rain down revenge.
The earth shall I behold, stain'd with the gore
Of his heart-blood, that dy'd most innocent?
Which way soe'er I turn mine eyes, methinks
His butcher'd corps stands staring in my face.
    Chorus 3. We humbly pray thee to forbear these
        words,
So full of terror to our maiden hearts:
" The dread of things unknown breeds the suspect
" Of greater dread, until the worst be known."
Tell therefore what hath chanc'd, and whereunto
This bloody cup thou holdest in thy hand.
    Renuchio. Since so is your request, that I shall do,
Although my mind so sorrowful a thing
Repines to tell; and though my voice eschews
To say what I have seen : yet since your will
So fixed stands, to hear for what I rue,
Your great desires I shall herein fulfill.
First by Salerne city, amids the plain,
There stands a hill, whose bosom huge and round,
Thrown out in breadth, a large space doth contain;
And gathering up in height, small from the ground,
Still less and less it mounts : there sometime was
A goodly tower uprear'd, that flower'd in fame
While fate and fortune serv'd ; but time doth pass,
And with his sway suppresseth all the same :
For now the walls be even'd with the plain,

And all the rest so foully lies defac'd,
As but the only shade doth there remain
Of that, which there was built in time forepass'd :
And yet that shews what worthy work tofore
Hath there been rear'd.   [37] One parcel of that tower
Yet stands, which eating time could not devour :
A strong turret, compact of stone and rock,
Hugy without, but horrible within :
To pass to which by force of handy stroak,
A crooked streight is made, that enters in,
And leads into this ugly loathsome place.
Within the which, carved into the ground,
[38] A dungeon deep there runs of narrow space,
Dreadful and dark, where never light is found :
Into this hollow cave, by cruel hest
Of king Tancred, were divers servants sent
To work the horror of his furious breast,
Erst nourish'd in his rage, and now stern bent
To have the same perform'd.   I, woeful man,
Amongst the rest, was one to do the thing,
That to our charge so straitly did belong,
In sort as was commanded by the king.

[37] *One parcel of that tower*, &c.] Dryden's translation of *Boccace's
Description of the Cave* is as follows :
          " Next the proud palace of Salerno stood
          " A Mount of rough ascent, and thick with wood.
          " Through this a cave was dug with vast expence :
          " The work it seem'd of some suspicious prince,
          " Who, when abusing power with lawless might,
          " From public justice would secure his flight.
          " The passage made by many a winding way,
          " Reach'd ev'n the room in which the tyrant lay.
          " Fit for his purpose on a lower floor,
          " He lodg'd, whose issue was an iron door ;
          " From whence by stairs descending to the ground,
          " In the blind grot a safe retreat he found.
          " Its outlet ended in a brake o'ergrown.
          " With brambles, choak'd by time, and now unknown.
          " A rift there was, which from the mountain's height
          " Convey'd a glimm'ring and malignant light,
          " A breathing place to draw the damps away,
          " A twilight of an intercepted day."
Sigismonda and Guiscardo.   Dryden's Works; vol. III. p. 251.
    [38] *A dungeon*, &c.] See Milton's *Paradise Lost*, B 1. l. 60.

Within which dreadful prison when we came,
The noble county Palurin, that there
[39] Lay chain'd in gives, fast fetter'd in his bolts,
Out of the dark dungeon we did uprear,
And hal'd him thence into a brighter place,
That gave us light to work our tyranny.
But when I once beheld his manly face,
And saw his chear, no more appall'd with fear
Of present death, than he whom never dread
[40] Did once amate; my heart abhorred then
To give consent unto so foul a deed :
That wretched death should reve so worthy a man.
On false fortune I cry'd with loud complaint,
That in such sort o'erwhelms nobility.
But he, whom neither grief ne fear could taint,
With smiling chear himself oft willed me,

[39] *Lay chain'd in gives*, &c.] *Gives*, or, as the word is more frequently spelt, *Gyves*, are *fetters* or *chains*   So, in Beaumont and Fletcher's *Beggars Bush*, A. 3. S. 4 :
   ' *Gyves* I must wear, and cold must be my comfort."
Marston's *What you will*, A. 2. S. 1 :
   ' Think'st thou a libertine, *an ungiv'd* beast,
   " Scornes not the shackles of thy envious clogs ?"
Milton's *Samson Agonistes*, l. 1092 :
   " Dost thou already single me ? I thought
   " *Gyves* and the mill had tam'd thee."
See Dr. Newton's Note on the last passage ; and Mr. Steevens's Note on First Part *Henry* IV. A. 4. S. 3.
[40] *Did once amate*;] *Amate* is to daunt or confound. Skinner, in his *Etymologicon*, explains it thus : " Perterriface, Attonitum reddere, Obstupefacere, consternare, Consilii inopem reddere."
Thule or Verteu's *Historie* by Francis Rous, 4to. 1598, Sign. B :
   " At last with violence and open force,
   " They brake the posternes of the Castle gate,
   " And entred spoyling all without remorce,
   " Nor could old Sobrin now resist his fate,
   " But stiffe with feare ev'n like a senceles corse
   " Whom grisly terror doth so much *amate*,
   " He lyes supine upon his fatall bed,
   " Expecting ev'ry minute to be dead."
Again, Ibid. Sign. D :
   " He would forsake his choyse, and change his fate,
   " And leave her quite, and so procure her woe,
   " Faines that a sudden grief doth her *amate*,
   " Wounded with piercing sicknes Ebon bow."

To leave to plain his case, or sorrow make
For him; for he was far more glad apaid,
Death to embrace thus, for his Lady's sake,
Than life, or all the joys of life, he said.
For loss of life (quoth he) grieves me no more,
Than loss of that which I esteemed least:
My Lady's grief, lest she should rue therefore,
Is all the cause of grief within my breast.
He pray'd therefore, that we would make report
To her, of those his last words he would say:
That though he never could in any sort
Her gentleness requite, nor never lay
Within his power to serve her as he would;
Yet she possess'd his heart with hand and might,
To do her all the honour that he could.
This was to him, of all the joys that might
Revive his heart, the chiefest joy of all,
That, to declare the faithful heart which he
Did bear to her, fortune so well did fall,
That in her love he should both live and die.
After these words he stay'd, and spake no more,
But joyfully beholding us each one,
His words and chear amazed us so sore,
That still we stood; when forthwith thereupon:
But, why slack you (quoth he) to do the thing
For which you come? make speed, and stay no more,
Perform your master's will.   Now tell the king
He hath his life, for which he long'd so sore:
And with those words himself, with his own hand
Fast'ned the bands about his neck.   The rest
[41] Wond'ring at his stout heart, astonied stand
To see him offer thus himself to death.
What stony breast, or what hard heart of flint

---

[41] *Wond'ring at his stout heart,* astonied *stand*] Astonied *is* asto-
nished.   So, in *Euphues and his England,* p. 102:
    " Philanthus *astonied* at this speech, &c."
    Fable of Jeronimi by G. Gascoigne, p. 209: " When Ferdinando
" (somewhat *astonied* with hir strange speech) thus answered:"
    Thieves falling out, by Rob. Green: " — the Gentleman *astonied*
" at this strange Metamorphosis of his mistress."

Would not relent to see this dreary sight?
So goodly a man, whom death nor fortune's dint
Could once disarm, murder'd with such despite;
And in such sort bereft, amidst the flowers
Of his fresh years, that ruthful was to seen:
" For violent is death, when he devours
" Young men, or virgins, while their years be green."
Lo! now our servants seeing him take the bands,
And on his neck himself to make them fast;
Without delay set to their cruel hands,
And sought to work their fierce intent with haste.
They stretch the bloody bands; and when the breath
Began to fail his breast, they slack'd again:
Thrice did they pull, and thrice they loosed him,
So did their hands repine against their hearts:
And oft-times loosed to his greater pain.
" But date of death, that fixed is so fast,
" Beyond his course there may no wight extend;"
For strangled is this noble Earl at last,
Bereft of life; unworthy such an end.
   Chorus. O damned deed!
   Renuchio.   What deem you this to be,
All the sad news that I have to unfold?
Is here (think you) end of the cruelty
That I have seen?
   Chorus.   Could any heavier woe
Be wrought to him, than to destroy him so?
   Renuchio. What, think you this outrage did end so
       well?
The horror of the fact, the greatest grief,
The massacre, the terror is to tell.
   Chorus. Alack! what could be more? they threw
       percase
The dead body to be devour'd and torn
Of the wild beasts.
   Renuchio. Would god it had been cast a savage prey
To beasts and birds: but lo, that dreadful thing
Which e'en the tiger would not work, but to
Suffice his hunger, that hath the tyrant king
Withouten ruth commanded us to do,

Only to please his wrathful heartwithal.
Happy had been his chance, too happy, alas !
If birds, or beasts, had eaten up his corps,
Yea, heart and all, which in this cup I bring,
And am constrained now unto the face
Of his dear lady to present the same.
   Chorus. What kind of cruelty is this you name ?
Declare forthwith, and whereunto doth tend
This farther plaint.
   Renuchio.   After his breath was gone,
Force perforce thus from his panting breast,
Straight they dispoiled him ; and not alone
Contented with his death, on the dead corps,
Which ravenous beasts forbear to lacerate,
Even upon this our villains fresh begun
To show new cruelty: forthwith they pierce
His naked belly, and unrip it so,
That out the bowels gush'd.   Who can rehearse
Their tyranny, wherewith my heart yet bleeds?
The warm intrails were torn out of his breast,
Within their hands trembling, not fully dead ;
His veins smoak'd, his bowels all too reeked,
Ruthless were rent, and thrown about the place :
All clottered lay the blood in lumps of gore,
[42] Sprent on his corps, and on his paled face ;
His trembling heart, yet leaping, out they tore,
And cruelly upon a rapier
They fix'd the same, and in this hateful wise
Unto the king this heart they do present :
A sight long'd for to feed his ireful eyes.
The king perceiving each thing to be wrought
As he had will'd, rejoicing to behold

---

[42] *Sprent on his corpse*] *Sprent* is sprinkled. So, in Spenser's
Shepherds Calendar December:
    " My head *besprent* with hoary frost I find."
Fairfax, Cant. 12. St. 101 :
    " His silver locks with dust he foul *besprent*."
Milton's *Comus,* l. 542 :
    " Of knot grass dew *besprent* :"

Upon the bloody sword the pierced heart,
He calls then for this massy cup of gold,
Into the which the woeful heart he cast;
And reaching me the same, now go, quoth he,
Unto my daughter, and with speedy haste
Present her this, and say to her from me,
Thy father hath here in this cup thee sent
That thing to joy and comfort thee withall,
Which thou lovedst best, even as thou wert content
To comfort him with his chief joy of all.

   Chorus. O hateful fact! O passing cruelty!
O murder wrought with too much hard despite!
O heinous deed, which no posterity
Will once believe!

   Renuchio.   Thus was earl Palurin
Strangled unto the death, yea after death
His heart and blood disbowell'd from his breast.
But what availeth plaint? It is but breath
Forewasted all in vain. Why do I rest
Here in this place? Why go I not, and do
The hateful message to my charge committed?
Oh! were it not that I am forced thereto
By a king's will, here would I stay my feet,
Ne one whit farther wade in this intent:
But I must yield me to my prince's hest;
Yet doth this somewhat comfort mine unrest,
I am resolv'd her grief not to behold,
But get me gone, my message being told.
Where is the princess' chamber?

   Chorus. Lo, where she comes.

ACT. V. SCEN. II.

GISMUNDA *cometh out of her chamber, to whom* RE-
NUCHIO *delivereth his cup, saying,*

Renuchio. Thy father, O queen, here in this cup
    hath sent
The thing to joy and comfort thee withall
Which thou lovedst best, even as thou wast content
To comfort him with his chief joy of all.
    Gismunda. I thank my father, and thee, gentle squire,
For this thy travel; take thou, for thy pains,
This bracelet, and commend me to the king.
                       [*Renuchio departeth.*
So, now is come the long-expected hour,
The fatal hour I have so looked for;
Now hath my father satisfied his thirst
With guiltless blood, which he so coveted.
What brings this cup? (Ah me! I thought no less)
It is mine Earl's my County's pierced heart.
Dear heart, too dearly hast thou bought my love;
Extremely rated at too high a price.
Ah my sweet heart, sweet wast thou in thy life,
But in thy death thou provest passing sweet.
A fitter hearse than this of beaten gold,
Could not be 'lotted to so good an heart:
My father therefore well provided thus,
To close and wrap thee up in massy gold,
And therewithal to send thee unto me,
To whom of duty thou dost best belong.
My father hath in all his life bewray'd
A princely care and tender love to me;
But this surpasseth, in his later days
To send me this, mine own dear heart to me.
Wert thou not mine, dear heart, whil'st that my love
Danced and played upon thy golden strings?
Art thou not mine (dear heart) now that my love
Is fled to heaven, and got him golden wings?

Thou art mine own, and still mine own shalt be,
Therefore my father sendeth thee to me.
Ah, pleasant harborough* of my heart's thought!
Ah, sweet delight, the quick'ner of my soul!
Seven times accursed be the hand that wrought
Thee this despite, to mangle thee so foul:
Yet in this wound I see mine own true love,
And in this wound thy magnanimity,
And in this wound I see thy constancy.
Go, gentle heart, go rest thee in thy tomb,
Receive this token at thy last farewel. [*She kisseth it.*
Thine own true heart anon will follow thee,
Which panting hasteth for thy company.
Thus hast thou run (poor heart!) thy mortal race,
And rid thy life from fickle fortune's snares;
Thus hast thou lost this world, and worldly cares,
And of thy foe, to honour thee withall,
Receiv'd a golden grave, to thy desert.
Nothing doth want to thy just funeral,
But my salt tears to wash thy bloody wound:
Which to the end thou might'st receive, behold
My father sends thee in this cup of gold;
And thou shalt have them, though I was resolv'd
T os hed no tears, but with a chearful face
Once did I think to wet thy funeral
Only with blood, and with no weeping eye.
This done, forthwith my soul shall fly to thee;
For therefore did my father send thee me.
Ah, my pure heart! with sweeter company,
Or more content, how safer may I prove
To pass to places all unknown, with thee!
Why die I not therefore? why do I stay?
Why do I not this woful life forego,
And with these hands enforce this breath away?
What means this gorgeous glittering head attire?
How ill beseem these billaments[43] of gold

---

* *harborough.*] *i. e.* harbour.
[43] *billiaments.*] *i. e.* habillaments.   S. P.

Thy mournful widowhood? away with them—
> [*She undresseth her hair.*

So, let thy tresses flaring in the wind
Untrimmed hang about thy bared neck.
Now, hellish furies, set my heart on fire,
Bolden my courage, strengthen ye my hands
Against their kind, to do a kindly deed.
[44] But shall I then unwreaken down descend?
Shall I not work some just revenge on him
That thus hath slain my love? shall not these hands
Fire his gates, and make the flame to climb
Up to the pinnacles with burning brands,
And on his cinders wreak my cruel [45] teen?
Be still (fond girl) content thee first to die,
This venom'd water shall abridge thy life:
> [*She taketh a vial of poison out of her pocket.*

This for the same intent provided I,
Which can both ease and end this raging strife.

---

[44] *But shall I then* unwreaken *down descend?*] *Unwreaken is* unre-
venged.   So, in Ben Jonson's *Every man out of his humour,* A. 2,
S. 4:
>   " —— Would to heaven
>   " (In *wreak* of my misfortunes) I were turn'd
>   " To some fair water nymph."

Sejanus his fall, A. 4:
>   " —— Made to speak
>   " What they will have to fit their tyrannous *wreak.*"

Massinger's *Fatal Dowry,* A. 4. S. 4:
>   " But there's a Heaven above, from whose just *wreak*
>   " No mists of policy can hide offenders."

Massinger's *Very Woman,* A. 1:
>   " And our just *wreak,* by force or cunning practise
>   " With scorn prevented."

See also Mr. Steevens' Note on *Coriolanus,* A. 4. S. 5.
But shall I then unwreaken, &c.]
> —— moriamur *inultæ?* Virgil's Æn. lib. iv.   S.

[45] —*teen?*] *Sorrow.* Again, A. 5. S. 3:
>   " His death, her woe, and her avenging *teen.*"

Shakspeare's *Venus* and *Adonis.*
>   " More I could tell, but more I dare not say,
>   " The text is old, the orator too green.
>   " Therefore in sadness now I will away,
>   " My face is full of shame, my heart of *teen.*"

Thy father by thy death shall have more woe,
Than fire or flames within his gates can bring :
Content thee then in patience hence to go,
Thy death his blood shall wreak upon the king.
Now not alone (a grief to die alone)
" The only mirror of extreme annoy ;"
But not alone thou diest, my love, for I
Will be copartner of thy destiny.
Be merry then, my soul ; can'st thou refuse
To die with him, that death for thee did chuse?

    Chorus 1. What damned fury hath possess'd our
        Queen ?
Why sit we still beholding her distress?
Madam, forbear, suppress this headstrong rage.

    Gismunda. Maidens, forbear your comfortable words.

    Chorus 2. O worthy Queen, rashness doth overthrow
The author of his resolution.

    Gismunda. Where hope of help is lost, what booteth
        fear ?

    Chorus 3. Fear will avoid the sting of infamy.

    Gismunda. May good or bad reports delight the
        dead?

    Chorus 4. If of the living yet the dead have care.

    Gismunda. An easy grief by counsel may be cur'd.

    Chorus 1. But headstrong mischiefs princes should
        avoid.

    Gismunda. In headlong griefs and cases desperate ?

    Chorus 2. Call to your mind, Gismund, you are the
        Queen.

    Gismunda. Unhappy widow, wife, and paramour.

    Chorus 3. Think on the king.

    Gismunda.   The king, the tyrant king?

    Chorus 4. Your father.

    Gismunda.   Yes, the murderer of my love.

    Chorus 4. His force.

    Gismunda.   The dead fear not the force of men.

    Chorus 1. His care and grief.

    Gismunda.   That neither car'd or me,
Nor grieved at the murder of my love.

My mind is settled; you, with these vain words,
With-hold me but too long from my desire.
Depart ye to my chamber.
  Chorus.   We will haste
To tell the king hereof. [*Chorus depart into the palace.*
  Gismunda.   I will prevent
Both you and him. Lo here, this hearty draught,
The last that in this world I mean to taste,
Dreadless of death, mine Earl, I drink to thee.
So, now work on; now doth my soul begin
To hate this light, wherein there is no love;
No love of parents to their children;
No love of princes to their subjects true;
No love of ladies to their dearest love.
Now pass I to the pleasant land of love,
Where heavenly love immortal flourisheth:
The gods abhor the company of men;
Hell is on earth; yea, hell itself is heaven
Compar'd with earth. I call to witness heaven;
Heaven, said I? No, but hell record I call,
And thou stern goddess of revenging wrongs,
Witness with me, I die for his pure love
That lived mine.
  [*She lieth down and covereth her face with her hair.*

ACT V. SCEN. III.

Tancred *in haste cometh out of his palace with*
Julio.

Tancred. Where is my daughter?
Julio. Behold, here, woeful king!
Tancred. Ah me! break heart; and thou fly forth,
  my soul.
What, doth my daughter Gismund take it so?
What hast thou done? Oh let me see thine eyes!

O let me dress up those [45] untrimmed locks !
Look up, sweet child, look up mine only joy,
'Tis I, thy father, that beseecheth thee :
Rear up thy body, strain thy dying voice
To speak to him; sweet Gismund, speak to me.

    Gismunda. Who stays my soul ? who thus disquiets
        me ?

    Tancred. 'Tis I thy father ; ah ! behold my tears,
Like pearled dew, that trickle down my cheeks,
To wash my silver hairs.

    Gismunda.   Oh, father, king,
Forbear your tears, your plaint will not avail.

    Tancred. Oh, my sweet heart, hast thou receiv'd thy
        life
From me, and wilt thou to requite the same
Yield me my death ? yea, death and greater grief,
To see thee die for him that did defame
Thine honour thus, my kingdom, and thy name?

    Gismunda. Yea, therefore father, gave you life to me,
That I should die, and now my date is done.
As for your kingdom, and mine own renown,
Which you affirm dishonoured to be,
That fault impute it where it is ; for he
That slew mine Earl, and sent his heart to me,
His hands have brought this shame and grief on us.
But, father, yet if any spark remain
Of your dear love; if ever yet I could
So much deserve, or at your hands desire,
Grant that I may obtain this last request.

    Tancred. Say, lovely child, say on, whate'er it be,
Thy father grants it willingly to thee.

    Gismunda. My life I crave not, for it is not now
In you to give, nor in myself to save;

---

[45] *— untrimmed locks !*] *Untrimmed locks* are locks *dishevelled* or
undressed. *Trim,* in the language of the times, was frequently
used for *dress.* Massinger's *Emperor of the East,* A. 2. S. 1 :
    " Our Eastern Queens, at their full height bow to thee,
    " And are, in their best *trim,* thy foils and shadows."
See also Mr. Steevens' Note on *King John,* A. 3. S. 3.

Nor crave I mercy for mine Earl and me,
Who hath been slain with too much cruelty.
With patience I must a while abide
Within this life, which now will not be long.
But this is my request; father, I pray,
That, since it pleased so your majesty,
I should enjoy my love alive no more,
Yet ne'ertheless let us not parted be,
Whom cruel death could never separate:
But as we liv'd and dy'd together here,
So let our bodies be together tomb'd:
Let him with me, and I with him, be laid
Within one shrine, wherever you appoint.
This if you grant me, as I trust you will,
Although I live not to requite this grace,
Th' immortal gods due recompence shall give
To you for this: and so, vain world, farewell—
My speech is painful, and mine eye-sight fails.

    Tancred. My daughter dies—see how the bitter pangs
Of tyrannous death torment her princely heart,
She looks on me, at me she shakes her head;
For me she groans; by me my daughter dies;
I, I the author of this tragedy.—
On me, on me, ye heavens, throw down your ire!
Now dies my daughter!—hence with princely robes.
Oh fair in life! thrice fairer in thy death!
Dear to thy father in thy life thou wert,
But in thy death, dearest unto his heart;
I kiss thy paled cheeks, and close thine eyes.
This duty once I promised to myself
Thou should'st perform to me; but ah! false hope,
Now ruthful wretched king, what resteth thee?
Wilt thou now live wasted with misery?
Wilt thou now live, that with these eyes didst see
Thy daughter dead? wilt thou now live to see
Her funerals, that of thy life was stay?
Wilt thou now live that wast her life's decay?
Shall not this hand reach to this heart the stroke?
Mine arms are not so weak, nor are my limbs
So feebled with mine age, nor is my heart

So daunted with the dread of cowardice,
But I can wreak due vengeance on that head,
That wrought the means these lovers now be dead.
[46] Julio, come near, and lay thine own right hand
Upon my thigh—now take thine oath of me.

 Julio. I swear to thee, my liege lord, to discharge
Whatever thou enjoinest Julio.

 Tancred. First then, I charge thee that my daughter
  have
Her last request: thou shalt within one tomb
Inter her Earl and her, and thereupon
Engrave some royal epitaph of love.
That done, I swear thee thou shalt take my corps,
Which thou shalt find by that time done to death,
And lay my body by my daughter's side—
Swear this, swear this, I say.

 Julio.   I swear.
But will the king do so unkingly now?

 Tancred. A kingly deed the king resolves to do.

 Julio. To kill himself?

 Tancred.   To send his soul to ease.

 Julio. Doth Jove command it?

 Tancred.   Our stars compell it.

 Julio. The wise man over-rules his stars.

 Tancred.   So we.

 Julio. Undaunted should the minds of kings endure.

 Tancred. So shall it in this resolution.
Julio, forbear: and as thou lov'st the king,
When thou shalt see him welt'ring in his gore,
Stretching his limbs, and gasping in his groans,

---

[46] *Julio come near, and lay thine own right* hand
 Upon my thigh:—*now take thine* oath *to me.*] Alluding to a
custom of which mention is made in *Genesis*, chap. xxiv. 9. "And
the servant put his *hand* under the *thigh* of Abraham his master,
and *sware* to him concerning that matter." The same form was
likewise observed by Jacob and Joseph when they were dying.
Some mystery is supposed to be couched under this practice. The
most probable, at least the most decent, supposition is, that it was
a token of subjection or homage from a servant to his lord, when
the former solemnly promised to perform whatever should be commanded by the latter. S.

Then, Julio, set to thy helping hand,
Redouble stroke on stroke, and drive the stab
Down deeper to his heart, to rid his soul.
Now stand aside, stir not a foot, lest thou
Make up the fourth to fill this tragedy.
These eyes that first beheld my daughter's shame;
These eyes that longed for the ruthful sight
Of her Earl's heart; these eyes that now have seen
His death, her woe, and her avenging teen;
Upon these eyes we must be first aveng'd.
Unworthy lamps of this accursed lump,
Out of your dwellings—so, it fits us thus
In blood and blindness to go seek the path
That leadeth down to everlasting night.
Why fright'st thou, dastard? be thou desperate;
One mischief brings another on his neck,
As mighty billows tumble in the seas.
Now, daughter, seest thou not how I amerce
My wrath, that thus bereft thee of thy love,
Upon my head?—Nòw, fathers, learn by me,
Be wise, be warn'd to use more tenderly
The jewels of your joys.—Daughter, I come.

FINIS.

EPILOGUE.

Lo here the sweets of grisly pale despair!
These are the blossoms of this cursed tree,
Such are the fruits of too much love and care,
O'erwhelmed in the sense of misery.
With violent hands he that his life doth end,
His damned soul to endless night doth wend.
Now resteth it that I discharge mine oath,
To see th' unhappy lovers and the king
Laid in one tomb—I would be very loth
You should wait here to see this mournful thing:
For I am sure, and do ye all to wit,
Through grief wherein the lords of Salerne be,
These funerals are not prepared yet:
Nor do they think on that solemnity.
As for the fury, ye must understand,
Now she hath seen th' effect of her desire,
She is departed, and hath left our land,
Granting this end unto her hellish ire.
Now humbly pray we, that our English dames
May never lead their loves into mistrust;
But that their honours may avoid the shames
That follow such as live in wanton lust.
We know they bear them on their virtues bold,
With blissful chastity so well content,
That, when their lives and loves abroad are told,
All men admire their virtuous government;
Worthy to live where fury never came,
Worthy to live where love doth always see,
Worthy to live in golden trump of fame,
Worthy to live, and honoured still to be.
Thus end our sorrows with the setting sun:
Now draw the curtains, for our scene is done.

R. W.

Introductio in Actum secundum.

BEFORE the second act there was heard a sweet noise of still pipes, which sounding, Lucrece entered, attended by a maiden of honour with a covered goddard of gold, and, drawing the curtains, she offereth unto Gismunda to taste thereof; which when she had done, the maid returned, and Lucrece raiseth up Gismunda from her bed, and then it followeth ut in Act 2, Scen. 1.

Introductio in Actum tertium.

Before this act the hautbois sounded a lofty almain, and Cupid ushereth after him Guiszard and Gismunda hand in hand; Julio and Lucrece, Renuchio and another maiden of honour. The measures trode, Gismunda gives a cane into Guiszard's hand, and they are all led forth again by Cupid, et sequitur.

Introductio in Actum quartum.

Before this act there was heard a concert of sweet musick, which playing, Tancred cometh forth, and draweth Gismunda's curtains, and lies down upon her bed; then from under the stage ascendeth Guiszard, and he helpeth up Gismund, they amorously embrace and depart. The king ariseth enraged; then was heard and seen a storm of thunder and lightning, in which the furies rise up, et sequitur.

Introductio in Actum quintum.

Before this act was a dead march play'd, during which entered on the stage Renuchio captain of the guard, attended upon by the guard. They took up Guiszard from under the stage; that, after Guiszard had kindly taken leave of them all, a strangling cord was fastened about his neck, and he haled forth by them. Renuchio bewaileth it; and then, entering in, bringeth forth a standing cup of gold, with a bloody heart reeking hot in it, and then saith, ut sequitur.

EDITION.

The Tragedie of Tancred and Gismund.—Compiled by the Gentlemen of the Inner Temple, and by them presented before her Majestie. Newly revived and polished according to the decorum of these daies. By R. W. London, Printed by Thomas Scarlet, and are to be solde by R. Robinson, 1592, 4to.

CORNELIA.

THOMAS KYD, the translator of the following Play, is better known as the Author of the *Second Part of Jeronimo*, a performance which was ridiculed by almost every contemporary Poet, than by any other of his works. The time and place of his birth and death, the circumstances of his life and his profession, otherwise than as a writer, are all equally unknown. From the Dedication of *Cornelia* to the Countess of Sussex, it may be inferred that, like the generality of the devotees of poetry in his time, he was poor; and from the promise of another Tragedy, called *Portia*, as *his next summer's better travel* which never appeared, it may be conjectured that he was prevented by death. Notwithstanding the ridicule thrown upon him, on account of the Spanish Tragedy, he appears to have been well-esteemed by some of his contemporaries. [1] Francis Meres enumerates him among the best tragic writers of his times; and [2] Ben Jonson ranks him with Lyly and Marlow, calling him Sporting Kyd. Another writer [3] says, " Cornelia's Tragedy, however not re- " spected, was excellently well done by Thomas Kyd." Mr. Hawkins [4] was of opinion, that Kyd was the Author of *Solyman and Perseda*, a Play which certainly in its manner bears a striking resemblance to the Spanish Tragedy.

Robert Garnier, from whom this Play is translated, was a Poet in considerable estimation during the reigns of Charles IX. and Henry III. and IV. He was born in the country of Maine, in 1534, studied the

---

[1] Second Part, Wit's *Commonwealth*, 1598, p. 283.

[2] Verses to the Memory of Shakspeare.

[3] *Polimantcia*, &c. by W. C. 4to. Cambr. 1595.   In the Epistle, &c. (Oldys's MS. Notes on Langbaine).

[4] Origin of the Drama, vol. II.

Law, and obtained some preferment, as well as reputation, in that profession. He was the Author of eight Plays, and died at Paris in the year 1590, at the age of 56 years. See *Recherches sur les Theatres De France*, par *M. De Beuuchamps*, 4to. 1755, p. 39.

To the vertuously Noble, and rightly honoured Lady,
the COUNTESS OF SUSSEX.

HAVING no leisure (most noble Lady) but such as
evermore is traveld with th'afflictions of the mind, than
which the world affords no greater misery, it may be
wondered at by some, how I durst undertake a matter
of this moment: which both requireth cunning, rest and
oportunity; but chiefly, that I would attempt the
Dedication of so rough unpolished a work, to the
survey of your so worthy self.

But being well instructed in your noble and heroick
dispositions, and perfectly assured of your honourable
favours past (though neither making needless glozes
of the one, nor spoiling paper with the other's Phari-
saical embroidery,) I have presumed upon your true
conceit and entertainment of these small endeavours,
that thus I purposed to make known, my memory of
you and them to be immortal.

A fitter present for a patroness so well accomplished,
I could not find, than this fair president of honour,
magnanimity, and love. Wherein, what grace that
excellent GARNIER hath lost by my default, I shall
beseech your Honour to repair, with the regard of
those so bitter times, and privy broken passions that I
endured in the writing it.

And so vouchsafing but the passing of a Winter's
week with desolate *Cornelia*, I will assure your Ladyship my next Summer's better travell, with the Tragedy
of *Portia*. And ever spend one hour of the day in
some kind service to your Honour, and another of the
night in wishing you all happiness. Perpetually thus
devoting my poor self

Your Honour's in all humbleness.

T. K.

THE ARGUMENT.

CORNELIA, the daughter of *Metellus Scipio,* a young Roman Lady, as much accomplish'd with the graces of the body, and the virtues of the mind as ever any was, was first married to young *Crassus,* who died with his father, in the disconfiture of the Romans against the Parthians; afterward she took to second husband *Pompey* the great, who (three years after) upon the first fires of the civil wars betwixt him and *Cæsar,* sent her from thence to *Mitilen,* there to attend the uncertain success of those affairs. And when he saw that he was vanquish'd at *Pharsalia,* returned to find her out, and carry her with him into Egypt, where his purpose was to have re-enforced a new army, and give a second assault to *Cæsar.*

In this voyage, he was murdered by *Achillus* and *Septimius* the Roman before her eyes, and in the presence of his young son *Sextus,* and some other Senators his friends. After which, she retired herself to Rome. But *Scipio* her father (being made general of those that survived after the battle) assembled new forces, and occupied the greater part of Afrique, allying himself to *Juba* king of *Numidia.* Against all whom *Cæsar* (after he had ordered the affairs of Egypt and the state of Rome) in the end of winter marched. And there (after many light encounters) was a fierce and furious battle given amongst them, near the walls of *Tapsus.* Where *Scipio* seeing himself subdued, and his army scattered, he betook himself with some small troop, to certain ships which he caused to stay for him.

Thence he sailed toward *Spain,* where *Pompey's*

faction commanded, and where a sudden tempest took him on the sea, that drave him back to Hippon, a town in Afrique, at the devotion of *Cæsar*, where (lying at anchor) he was assailed, beaten, and assaulted by the adverse fleet; and for he would not fall alive into the hands of his so mighty enemy, he stab'd himself, and suddenly leapt over board into the sea, and there dyed.

Cæsar (having finished these wars, and quietly reduced the towns and places thereabout to his obedience) returned to Rome in triumph for his victories; where this most fair and miserable Lady, having over-mourn'd the death of her dear husband, and understanding of these cross events and hapless news of Afrique, together with the piteous manner of her father's end, she took (as she had cause) occasion to redouble both her tears and lamentations: wherewith she closeth the catastrophe of this their Tragedy.

INTERLOCUTORES.

M. Cicero.
Philip.
Deci Brutus.
M. Antony.
Cornelia.
C. Cassius.
Julius Cæsar.
The Messenger.

CHORUSES.

CORNELIA.

ACT I.

Cicero. VOUCHSAFE, Immortals, and (above the rest)
Great Jupiter, our city's sole protector,
That if (provok'd against us by our evils)
You needs will plague us with your ceaseless wrath,
At least to chuse those forth that are in fault,
And save the rest in these tempestuous broils:
Else let the mischief that should them befall,
Be pour'd on me, that one may die for all.
　　Oft hath such sacrifice appeas'd your ires,
And oft ye have your heavy hands with-held
From this poor people, when (with one man's loss)
Your pity hath preserv'd the rest untouch'd:
But we, disloyal to our own defence,
Faint-hearted, do those liberties enthrall,
Which to preserve (unto our after-good)
Our fathers hazarded their dearest blood.
　　Yet Brutus Manlius, hardy Scevola,
And stout Camillus, are returned from Styx,
Desiring arms to aid our Capitol.
Yea, come they are, and fiery as before,
Under a tyrant see our bastard hearts
Lie idly sighing; while our shameful souls
Endure a million of base controuls.
　　Poison'd ambition (rooted in high minds)
'Tis thou that train'st us into all these errors:

[5] Thy mortal covetice perverts our laws,
And tears our freedom from our franchis'd hearts.
Our fathers found thee at their former walls ;
And humbled to their offspring left thee dying.
Yet thou reviving, [6] soil'dst our infant town,
With guiltless blood by brothers hands out-launch'd ;
And hang'st (O hell) upon a fort half finish'd,
Thy monstrous murder for a thing to mark.
" But faith continues not where men command.
" Equals are ever bandying for the best :
" A state divided cannot firmly stand.
" Two kings within one realm could never rest."
This day, we see, the father and the son
Have fought like foes Pharsalia's misery ;
And with their blood made marsh the parched plains,
While th' earth, that groan'd to bear their carcases,
Bewail'd th' insatiate humours of them both ;
That as much blood in wilful folly spent,
As were to tame the world sufficient.
   ·Now, Parthia, fear no more for Crassus' death,
That we will come thy borders to besiege :
Nor fear the darts of our courageous troops ;
For those brave soldiers, that were sometime wont
To terrify thee with their names, are dead ;
And civil fury, fiercer than thine hosts,
Hath in a manner this great town o'er-turn'd,
That whilom was the terror of the world,
Of whom so many nations stood in fear,
To whom so many nations prostrate stoopt,
O'er whom (save Heaven) nought could signorize,

---

[5] *Thy mortal covetice*] So, in Ben Jonson's *Catiliñe*, A. 2. S. 3 :
            " — But you think, Carius,
      " 'Tis *covetise* hath wrought me : if you love me,
      " Change that unkind conceit "
Alchymist, A. 2. S. 3 :
      " Why, this is *covetise* !
Pierce Penilesse his Supplication to the Divell, p. 29 : " — under
" vellany I comprehend murder, treason, theft, cousnage, cut throat
" *covetise*, and such like."
[6] *— soil'dst*] foyld'st, first and second edition.

And whom (save Heaven) nothing could affright;
Impregnable, immortal, and whose power
Could never have been curb'd, but by itself.
For neither could the flaxen-hair'd High Dutch,
(A martial people, madding after arms)
Nor yet the fierce and fièry-humour'd French,
The Moor that travels to the Libyan sands,
The Greek, th' Arabian, Macedons, or Medes,
Once dare t' assault it, or attempt to lift
Their humbled heads, in presence of proud Rome.
But by our laws from liberty restrain'd,
Like captives liv'd eternally inchain'd.

　　But, Rome, (alas) what helps it that thou ty'dst
The former world to thee in vassalage?
What helps thee now t' have tam'd both land and sea?
What helps it thee, that under thy controul
The morn and mid-day both by east and west,
And that the golden sun, where-e'er he drive
His glitt'ring chariot, finds our ensigns spread;
Sith it contents not thy posterity;
But as a bait for pride (which spoils us all,)
Embarks us in so perilous a way,
As menaceth our death, and thy decay?

　　For, Rome, thou now resemblest a ship
At random wand'ring in a boist'rous sea,
When foaming billows feel the northern blasts:
Thou toil'st in peril, and the windy storm
Doth topside-turvey toss thee as thou float'st.
Thy mast is shiver'd, and thy main-sail torn,
Thy sides sore beaten, and thy hatches broke.
Thou want'st thy tackling, and a ship unrigg'd
Can make no shift to combat with the sea.
See how the rocks do heave their heads at thee!
Which if thou shouldst but touch, thou strait becom'st
A spoil to Neptune, and a sportful prey
To th' Glaucs and Tritons, pleas'd with thy decay.

　　Thou vaunt'st not of thine ancestors in vain,
But vainly count'st thine own victorious deeds.
What helpeth us the things that they did then,
Now we are hated both of gods and men?

" Hatred accompanies prosperity,
" For one man grieveth at another's good,
" And so much more we think our misery,
" The more that fortune hath with others stood :
" So that we 7 sild are seen as wisdom would,
" To bridle time with reason as we should.
     " For we are proud when Fortune favours us,
" As if inconstant chance were always one,
" Or standing now, we should continue thus.
" O fools, look back, and see the rolling stone,
" Whereon she blindly lighting sets her foot,
" And slightly sows that seldom taketh root.'
Heaven heretofore (inclin'd to do us good)
Did favour us with conquering our foes,
When jealous Italy (exasperate
With our uprising) sought our city's fall.
But we, soon tickled with such flatt'ring hope,
Wag'd farther war with an insatiate heart,
And tir'd our neighbour countries so with charge,
And with their loss we did our bounds enlarge.
     Carthage and Sicily we have subdued,
And almost yoked all the world beside :
And solely through desire of public rule,
Rome and the earth are waxen all as one :
Yet now we live despoil'd and robb'd by one,
Of th' ancient freedom wherein we were born.
And e'en that yoke, that wont to tame all others,
Is heavily return'd upon ourselves.
" A note of Chance that may the proud controul,
" And shew God's wrath against a cruel soul.
" For heaven delights not in us when we do
" That to another, which ourselves disdain.
" Judge others as thou would'st be judg'd again ;
" And do but as thou would'st be done unto.
" For sooth to say (in reason) we deserve
" To have the self-same measure that we serve."
     What right had our ambitious ancestors

---

7 — *sild*] i. e. *seldom*. It is a word often used by ancient writers.
See Mr. Steevens's Note on *Coriolanus*, A. 2. S. 1.
     Again, Churchyard's *Worthiness of Wales :*
          " So many springs that *sield* that soyle is dry."

(Ignobly issued from the cart and plough,)
To enter Asia? What, were they the heirs
To Persia or the Medes, first Monarchies?
What interest had they to Africa?
To Gaul or Spain? Or what did Neptune owe us
Within the bounds of farther Brittany?
Are we not thieves and robbers of those realms,
That ow'd us nothing but revenge for wrongs?
What toucheth us the treasure or the hopes,
The lives or liberties of all those nations,
Whom we by force have held in servitude;
Whose mournful cries and shrieks to heaven ascend,
Importuning both vengeance and defence
Against this city, rich of violence?
   " 'Tis not enough (alas) our power t'extend,
" Or over-run the world from east to west,
" Or that our hands the earth can comprehend,
" [8] Or that we proudly do what like us best.
" He lives more quietly whose rest is made,
" And can with reason chasten his desire,
" Than he that blindly toileth for a shade,
" And is with others' empire set on fire.
" Our bliss consists not in possessions,
" But in commanding our affections;
" In virtue's choice, and vice's needful chace
" Far from our hearts, for staining of our face."

Chorus. Upon thy back, (where Misery doth sit)
   O Rome, the heavens with their wrathful hand
Revenge the crimes thy fathers did commit.
   But if (their farther fury to withstand,

---

  [8] *Or that we proudly do what* like *us best.*] i. e. what please us best. So, in *Ling Lear*, A. 2. S. 2:
    " His face *likes* me not."
Maids Tragedy, A. 2:
    " What look *likes* you best?"
The Woman hater, A. 1. S. 3:
    " If I can find no company that *likes* me."
Euphues and his England, 1582, p. 16: " Enquire no farther
" than beseemeth you, least you heare that which cannot *like you.*"
  Ibid. p. 92: " This *liked* them all exceedingly. And thus
" Surius with a good grace and pleasant speech began to enter into
the lists with Camilla."

Which o'er thy walls thy wrack sits menacing)
  Thou dost not seek to calm heaven's ireful king,
  A farther plague will pester all the land.

" The wrath of heaven (though urg'd) we see, is slow,
  " In punishing the evils we have done :
" For what the father hath deserv'd, we know,
" Is spar'd in him, and punish'd in the son.
" But to forgive the apter that they be,
  " They are the more displeased when they see,
  " That we continue our offence begun."

" Then from her loathsome cave doth Plague repair,
  " That breathes her heavy poisons down to hell;
" Which with their noisome fall corrupt the air,
  " Or meagre Famine which the weak foretell,
" Or bloody War (of other woes the worst)
  " Which where it lights doth show the land accurst,
  " And ne'er did good wherever it befell."

War, that hath sought th' Ausonian fame to rear,
  In warlike Emony[9] (now grown so great
With soldiers' bodies that were buried there,)
  Which yet to sack us toils in bloody sweat:
T'enlarge the bounds of conquering Thessaly,
  Through murder, discord, wrath, and enmity,
  Even to the peaceful Indian's pearled seat.

Whose entrails fir'd with rancour, wrath, and rage,
  The former petty combats did displace,
And camp to camp did endless battles wage,
  Which on the mountain tops of warlike Thrace,
Made thund'ring Mars (Dissension's common friend)
  Amongst the forward soldiers first descend,
  Arm'd with his blood-besmeared keen coutelace.

Who first attempted to excite to arms,
  The troops enraged with the trumpet's sound,
Head-long to run and reck no after-harms ;
  Where in the flow'red meads dead men were found
Falling as thick (through warlike cruelty) .
  As ears of corn for want of husbandry;
  That (wastful) shed their grain upon the ground.

[9] *Emony*] i. e. Æmonia, where Pharsalia was. S. P.

O war, if thou were subject but to death,
　And by desert might'st.fall to Phlegethon,
The torment that Ixion suffereth,
　Or his whose soul the vulture seizeth on,
Were all too little to reward thy wrath :
　Nor all the plagues that fiery Pluto hath
　The most outrageous sinners laid upon.

Accursed caitives! wretches that we are!
　Perceive we not that for the fatal doom
The Fates make haste enough, but we (by War)
　Must seek in hell to have a hapless room?
Or fast enough do foolish men not die,
　But they (by murder of themselves) must hie,
　Hopeless to hide them in a hapless tomb?

All sad and desolate our city lies,
　And for fair corn-ground are our fields surcloy'd
[10] With worthless gorse, that yearly fruitless dies,
　And choaks the good, which else we had enjoy'd.
Death dwells within us, and if gentle Peace
　Descend not soon, our sorrows to surcease,
　Latium (already quail'd) will be destroy'd.

ACT II.

CORNELIA, CICERO.

Cornelia. And will ye needs bedew my dead-grown
　　joys,
And nourish sorrow with eternal tears?
O eyes, and will ye ('cause I cannot dry
Your ceaseless springs) not suffer me to die?
Then make the blood from forth my branch-like veins,
Like weeping rivers trickle by your vaults;
And spunge my body's heat of moisture so,

---

[10] — *worthless gorse*] i. e. *furze.* So, in Shakspeare's *Tempest*, A. 4.
S. 1: " *pricking goss* and thorns." S.

As my displeased soul may shun my heart.
Heavens, let me die, and let the Destinies
Admit me passage to th' infernal lake ;
That my poor ghost may rest where pow'rful fate
In death's sad kingdom hath my husband lodg'd.
Fain would I die, but darksome ugly death
·With-holds his dart, and in disdain doth fly me,
Maliciously knowing, that hell's horror
Is milder than mine endless discontent ;
And that, if death upon my life should seize,
The pain supposed would procure mine ease.
　　But ye sad Powers, that rule the silent deeps
Of dead-sad night, where sins do mask unseen :
You that amongst the darksome mansions
Of pining ghosts, twixt sighs, and sobs, and tears,
[11] Do exercise you mirthless empory :
Ye gods (at whose arbitrament all stand,)
Dislodge my soul, and keep it with yourselves,
For I am more than half your prisoner.
My noble husbands (more than noble souls,
Already wander under your commands.
O then shall wretched I, that am but one,
(Yet once both theirs) survive now they are gone ?
　　Alas ! thou should'st, thou should'st, Cornelia,
Have broke the sacred thread that ty'd thee here,
When as thy husband Crassus (in his flower)
Did first bear arms, and bare away my love.
And not (as thou hast done) go break the bands,
By calling Hymen once more back again.
Less hapless, and more worthiless thou might'st
Have made thine ancestors and thee renown'd :

[11] *Do exercise your mirthless* empory :] i. e. *imperium*, or *command.*
　　" My noble husbands (more than noble souls)
　　" Already wander under *your commands.*"　S. P.
The word also occurs in *Henry* V. A. 1. S. 2 :
　　　　" — Or there we'll sit,
　　" Ruling, in large and ample *empery.*"
　" This word, says Mr. Steevens, which signifies *dominion*, is now
" obsolete, though formerly in general use." So, in *Claudius Tiberius*
" *Nero,* 1607 :
　　" Within the circuit of our *empery.*"

If (like a royal dame) with faith fast kept,
Thou with thy former husband's death had'st slept.
　But partial Fortune, and the powerful Fates,
That at their pleasures wield our purposes,
Bewitch'd my life, and did beguile my love.
Pompey, the fame that ran of thy frail honours
Made me thy wife, thy love, and (like a thief)
From my first husband stole my faithless grief.
　But if (as some believe) in heaven or hell
Be heavenly powers, or infernal spirits,
That care to be aveng'd of lovers oaths;
Oaths made in marriage, and after broke;
Those powers, those spirits, (mov'd with my light faith,)
Are now displeas'd with Pompey and my self,
And do with civil discord (furthering it)
Untie the bands that sacred Hymen knit:
Else only I am cause of both their wraths,
And of the sin that sealeth up thine eyes;
Thine eyes (O deplorable Pompey!) I am she,
I am that plague, that sacks thy house and thee.
For 'tis not heaven, nor Crassus (cause he sees
That I am thine) in jealousy pursues us.
No, 'tis a secret cross, and unknown thing,
That I receiv'd from heaven at my birth,
That I should heap misfortunes on their head,
Whom once I had receiv'd in marriage-bed.
　Then ye, the noble Romulists that rest,
Henceforth forbear to seek my murdering love,
And let their double loss that held me dear,
Bid you beware for fear you be beguil'd.
Ye may be rich and great in Fortune's grace,　·
And all your hopes with hap may be effected:
But if ye once be wedded to my love,
Clouds of adversity will cover you.
So pestilently fraught with change of plagues
Is mine infected bosom from my youth.
Like poison that (once lighting in the body)　ι
No sooner toucheth than it taints the blood;
One while the heart, another while the liver,
(According to th'encountering passages)

Nor spareth it what purely feeds the heart,
More than the most infected filthiest part.

    Pompey, what holpe it thee, (say dearest life)
Tell me what holpe thy warlike valiant mind
T'encounter with the least of my mishaps?
What holpe it thee, that under thy command
Thou saw'st the trembling earth with horror maz'd?
Or where the sun forsakes th' ocean sea,
Or watereth his coursers in the west,
T' have made thy name be far more fam'd and fear'd,
Than summer's thunder to the silly herd?

    What holpe it, that thou saw'st, when thou wert young,
Thy helmer deck'd with coronets of bays?
So many enemies, in battle rang'd,
Beat back like flies before a storm of hail?
T' have look'd askance, and see so many kings
To lay their crowns and scepters at thy feet?
T' embrace thy knees, and, humbled by their fate,
T' attend thy mercy in this mournful state?

    Alas, and here-withal what holpe it thee,
That even in all the corners of the earth,
Thy wand'ring glory was so greatly known,
And that Rome saw thee while thou triumph'dst thrice
O'er three parts of the world that thou hadst yok'd;
That Neptune welt'ring on the windy plains,
Escap'd not free from thy victorious hands;
Since thy hard hap, since thy fierce destiny,
(Envious of all thine honours) gave thee me?

    By whom the former course of thy fair deeds
Might (with a biting bridle) be restrain'd;
By whom the glory of thy conquests got,
Might die disgrac'd with mine unhappiness;
O hapless wife! thus ominous to all,
Worse than Megæra, worse than any plague;
What foul infernal, or what stranger hell
Henceforth wilt thou inhabit, where thy hap
None other's hopes with mischief may entrap?

    Cicero. What end, O race of Scipio, will the Fates
Afford your tears? Will that day never come,
That your disast'rous griefs shall turn to joy,

And we have time to bury our annoy?
　　Cornelia. Ne'er shall I see that day; for heaven and
　　　　time
Have fail'd in power to calm my passion.
Nor can they (should they pity my complaints)
Once ease my life, but with the pangs of death.
Cicero. " The wide world's accidents are apt to change,
　　" [11] And tickle Fortune stays not in a place;
" But (like the clouds) continually doth range,
　　" Or like the sun that hath the night in chace.
" Then as the heavens (by whom our hopes are guided)
　　" Do coast the earth with an eternal course,
" We must not think a misery betided
　　" Will never cease, but still grow worse and worse.
" When icy winter's past, then comes the spring,
　　" Whom summer's pride with sultry heat pursues;
" To whom mild autumn does earth's treasure bring,
　　" The sweetest season that the wise can chuse.
" Heaven's influence was ne'er so constant yet,
　　" In good or bad as to continue it."
When I was young, I saw against poor Sylla,
Proud Cynna, Marius, and Carbo flesh'd
So long, till they 'gan tyrannize the town,
And spilt such store of blood in every street,
As there were none but dead men to be seen.
Within a while, I saw how Fortune play'd,
And wound those tyrants underneath her wheel,
Who lost their lives and power at once by one,
That (to revenge himself) did with his blade
Commit more murder than Rome ever made.
　　Yet Sylla, shaking tyranny aside,

---

[11] *And* tickle *Fortune,* &c.] *Tickle* here means *uncertain,* or *inconstant.* We still use the word *ticklish*; and a *ticklish situation* is understood for that state in which we can have no sure dependance. So, in Churchyard's *Challenge,* p. 28 :
　　" Yet climbing up, the tree of *tickle* trust
　　" Wee streache the arme, as farre as reach may goe,
　　" Disguis'd with pompe, and pampred up with lust;
　　" We gase alof, and never looke belowe,
　　" Till hatchet comes, and gives the fauling bloe."
See also Mr. Steevens's Note on *Measure for Measure,* A. 1. S. 3.

Return'd due honours to our commonwealth,
Which peaceably retain'd her ancient state,
Grown great without the strife of citizens;
Till this ambitious tyrant's time, that toil'd
To stoop the world and Rome to his desires.
But flatt'ring Chance, that train'd his first designs,
May change her looks, and give the tyrant over,
Leaving our city, where so long ago
Heavens did their favours lavishly bestow.

    Cornelia. 'Tis true, the heavens (at least-wise if they
        please)
May give poor Rome her former liberty.
But though they would, 1 know they cannot give
A second life to Pompey that is slain.

    Cicero. Mourn not for Pompey; Pompey could not
        die
A better death, than for his country's weal.
For oft he search'd amongst the fierce alarms,
But (wishing) could not find so fair an end;
Till, fraught with years and honour both at once,
He gave his body (as a barricade)
For Rome's defence, by tyrants overlaid.
Bravely he dy'd, and (haplie) takes it ill,
That (envious) we repine at heaven's will.

    Cornelia. Alas, my sorrow would be so much less,
If he had dy'd, his faulchion in his fist.
Had he amidst huge troops of armed men
Been wounded by another any way,
It would have calmed many of my sighs.
For why, t'have seen his noble Roman blood
Mixt with his enemies, had done him good.

    But he is dead, (O heavens!) not dead in fight,
With pike in hand upon a fort besieg'd,
Defending of a breach: but basely slain;
Slain traiterously, without assault in war.
Yea, slain he is, and bitter Chance decreed
To have me there, to see this bloody deed.
I saw him, I was there, and in mine arms
He almost felt the poignard when he fell.
Whereat my blood stopt in my straggling veins;

Mine hair grew bristled, like a thorny grove;
My voice lay hid, half dead within my throat;
My frightful heart (stunn'd in my stone-cold breast)
Faintly redoubled ev'ry feeble stroke;
My spirit, chained with impatient rage,
Did raving strive to break the prison ope,
(Enlarg'd) to drown the pain it did abide
In solitary Lethe's sleepy tide.
　　Thrice (to absent me from this hated light)
I would have plung'd my body in the sea;
And thrice detain'd, with doleful shrieks and cries,
(With arms to heaven uprear'd) I 'gan exclaim
And bellow forth against the Gods themselves
[12] A bed-roll of outrageous blasphemies;
Till (grief to hear, and hell for me to speak,)
My woes wax'd stronger, and my self grew weak.
　　Thus day and night I toil in discontent,
And sleeping wake, when sleep itself, that rides
Upon the mists, scarce moisteneth mine eyes.
Sorrow consumes me, and instead of rest,
With folded arms I sadly sit and weep.
And, if I wink, it is for fear to see
The fearful dreams effects that trouble me
　　O heavens! what shall I do? alas, must I,
Must I myself be murderer of myself?
Must I myself be forc'd to ope the way,
Whereat my soul in wounds may sally forth?
　　Cicero. Madam, you must not thus transport your-
　　　self.
We see your sorrow; but who sorrows not?
The grief is common. And I muse, besides
The servitude that causeth all our cares,
Besides the baseness wherein we are yok'd,
Besides the loss of good men dead and gone,
What one he is that in this broil hath been,
And mourneth not for some man of his kin?

----

[12] *A bed-roll*] *A bed-roll*, or *bede-roll*, says Blount, in his *Glos-
sographia*, "is a roll or list of such as Priests were wont to pray
for in churches."

Cornelia. If all the world were in the like distress,
My sorrow yet would never seem the less.

    Cicero. " O, but men bear misfortunes with more
         " ease,
" The more indifferently that they fall ;
" And nothing more (in uproars) men can please,
" Than when they see their woes not worst of all."

    Cornelia. " Our friend's misfortune doth increase our
         " own."

    Cicero. But ours of others will not be acknown."

    Cornelia. " Yet one man's sorrow will another
         " touch."

    Cicero. Ay, when himself will entertain none such."

    Cornelia. " Another's tears draw tears from forth
         " our eyes."

    Cicero. " And choice of streams the greatest river
         " dries."

    Cornelia. When sand within a whirlpool lies unwet,
My tears shall dry, and I my grief forget.

    Cicero. [13] What boot your tears, or what avails your
         sorrow,
Against th' inevitable dart of death?
Think you to move with lamentable plaints
Persiphone, or Pluto's ghastly spirits,
To make him live that's locked in his tomb,
And wand'reth in the centre of the earth?
" No, no, Cornelia, Charon takes not pain
" To ferry those that must be fetch'd again."

    Cornelia. Proserpina indeed neglects my plaints,
And hell itself is deaf to my laments.
Unprofitably should I waste my tears,
If over Pompey I should weep to death,
With hope to have him be reviv'd by them.
Weeping avails not, therefore do I weep.
Great losses greatly are to be deplor'd,
The loss is great that cannot be restor'd.

    Cicero. " Nought is immortal underneath the sun,
" All things are subject to death's tyranny:

---

[13] *What boot, &c.*]   *What avail* your tears.

" Both clowns and kings one self-same course must
          " run,
" And whatsoever lives, is sure to die."
Then wherefore mourn you for your husband's death,
Sith being a man, he was ordain'd to die?
Since Jove's own sons, retaining human shape,
No more than wretched we, their death could 'scape.
    Brave Scipio, your famous ancestor,
That Rome's high worth to Africk did extend;
And those two Scipios (that in person fought
Before the fearful Carthaginian walls)
Both brothers, and both war's fierce lightning fires,
Are they not dead? Yes, and their death (our dearth)
Hath hid them both embowel'd in the earth.
    And those great cities, whose foundations reach'd
From deepest hell, and with their tops touch'd heaven;
Whose lofty towers like thorny-pointed spears,
Whose temples, palaces, and walls embost,
In power and force, and fierceness, seem'd to threat
The tired world, that trembled with their weight;
In one day's space (to our eternal moans)
Have we not seen them turn'd to heaps of stones?
    Carthage can witness; and thou, heaven's hand-
          work,
Fair Ilium, razed by the conquering Greeks;
Whose ancient beauty, worth and weapons, seem'd
Sufficient t' have tam'd the Myrmidons.
" But whatsoe'er hath been begun, must end.
" Death (haply that our willingness doth see)
" With brandish'd dart doth make the passage free;
" And timeless doth our souls to Pluto send."
    Cornelia. Would death had steep'd his dart in
          Lerna's blood!
That I were drown'd in the Tartarian deeps!
I am an offering fit for Acheron.
A match more equal never could be made,
Than I, and Pompey, in th' Elysian shade.
    Cicero. " Death's always ready, and our time is
          " known
" To be at heaven's dispose, and not our own."

Cornelia. Can we be over-hasty to good hap?

Cicero. What good expect we in a fiery gap?

Cornelia. To 'scape the fears that follow Fortune's
     glances.

Cicero. " A noble mind doth never fear mischances."

Cornelia. " A noble mind disdaineth servitude."

Cicero. Can bondage true nobility exclude?

Cornelia. How if I do, or suffer that I would not?

Cicero. " True nobless never doth the thing it should
     " not."

Cornelia. Then must I die.

Cicero.   Yet dying think this still :
" No fear of death should force us to do ill,"

Cornelia. If death be such, why is your fear so rife?

Cicero. My works will shew I never fear'd my life.

Cornelia. And yet you will not that (in our distress,)
We ask death's aid to end life's wretchedness.

Cicero. " We neither ought to urge, nor ask a thing,
" Wherein we see so much assurance lies.
" But if perhaps some fierce offended king,
" (To fright us) set pale death before our eyes,
" To force us do that goes against our heart ;
" 'Twere more than base in us to dread his dart.
" But when, for fear of an ensuing ill,
" We seek to shorten our appointed race,
" Then 'tis (for fear) that we ourselves do kill,
" So fond we are to fear the world's disgrace."

Cornelia. 'Tis not for frailty, or faint cowardice,
That men (to shun mischances) seek for death;
But rather he that seeks it, shows himself
Of certain courage 'gainst uncertain chance.
" He that retires not at the threats of death,
" Is not, as are the vulgar, slightly [14] frayed.

---

[14] — *frayed.*] i. e. affrighted. So, *Wily beguiled*, 1606: " I'll
" attire myself fit for the same purpose like to some hellish hag, or
" damned fiend, and meet with Sophos wand'ring in the woods:
" O, I shall *fray* him terribly."

Ibid.   " — he'll make himself like a devil, and *fray* the
     scholar."

Ibid.   " Why, didst thou *fray* him ?"

" For heaven itself, nor hell's infectious breath,
" The resolute at any time have stayed.
" And (sooth to say) why fear we, when we see,
" The thing we fear, less than the fear to be ?"
Then let me die, my liberty to save,
For 'tis a death to live a tyrant's slave.
 Cicero. Daughter, beware how you provok the
  heavens,
Which in our bodies (as a tower of strength)
Have plac'd our souls, and fortify'd the same ;
As discreet princes set their garrisons,
In strongest places of their provinces.
" Now, as it is not lawful for a man,
" At such a king's departure or decease,
" To leave the place, and falsify his faith;
" So in this case , we ought not to surrender
" That dearer part, till heaven itself command it :
" For as they lent us life to do us pleasure,
" So look they for return of such a treasure."
 Chorus. " Whate'er the massie earth hath fraight,
  " Or on her nurse-like back sustains,
" Upon the will of heaven doth wait,
 " And doth no more than it ordains.
" All fortunes, all felicities,
 " Upon their motion do depend :
" And from the stars doth still arise
 " Both their beginning and their end.
" The monaichies, that cover all
 " This earthly round with majesty,
" Have both their rising and their fall
 " From heaven and heaven's variety.
" Frail men, or man's more frail defence,
 " Had never power to practise stays
" Of this celestial influence,
 " That governeth and guides our days.
" No cloud but will be over-cast;
 " And what now flourisheth, must fade ;
" And that that fades, revive at last,
 " To flourish as it first was made.

" The forms of things do never die,
    " Because the matter that remains
" Reforms another thing thereby,
    " That still the former shape retains.
" The roundness of two bowls cross-cast,
    " (So they with equal pace be aim'd),
" Shows their beginning by their last,
    " Which by old nature is new-fram'd.
" So peopled cities, that of yore
    " Were desert field where none would bide,
" Become forsaken as before,
    " Yet after are re-edify'd."
Perceive we not a petty vein,
    Cut from a spring by chance or art,
Engendereth fountains, whence again
    Those fountains do to floods convert?
Those floods to waves, those waves to seas,
    That oft exceed their wonted bounds:
And yet those seas (as heavens please)
    Return to springs by under-grounds.
E'en so our city (in her prime)
    Prescribing princes every thing,
Is now subdu'd by conquering time,
    And liveth subject to a king,
And yet perhaps the sun-bright crown,
    That now the tyrant's head doth deck,
May turn to Rome with true renown,
    If fortune chance but once to check.
The stately walls that once were rear'd,
    And by a shepherd's hands erect,
(With hapless brothers blood besmear'd)
    Shall show by whom they were infect.
And once more unjust Tarquin's frown
    (With arrogance and rage inflam'd)
Shall keep the Roman valour down,
    And Rome itself a while be tam'd.
And chastest Lucrece once again
    (Because her name dishonour'd stood)
Shall by herself be careless slain,
    And make a river of her blood;

Scorning her soul a seat should build
  Within a body basely seen,
By shameless rape to be defil'd,
  That erst was clear as heaven's queen.
But heavens, as tyranny shall yoke
  Our bastard hearts with servile thrall;
So grant your plagues (which they provoke)
  May light upon them once for all.
And let another Brutus rise,
  Bravely to fight in Rome's defence,
To free our town from tyranny,
  And tyrannous proud insolence.

ACT III.

CORNELIA, CHORUS.

The chearful cock (the sad night's comforter)
Waiting upon the rising of the sun,
Doth sing to see how Cynthia shrinks her horn,
While Clytie takes her progress to the east;
  Where wringing wet with drops of silver dew,
  Her wonted tears of love she doth renew.
The wand'ring swallow, with her broken song,
The country-wench unto her work awakes;
While Cytherea sighing walks to seek
Her murder'd love transform'd into a rose;
  Whom (though she see) to crop she kindly fears;
  But (kissing) sighs, and dews him with her tears;
Sweet tears of love, remembrancers to time,
Time past with me, that am to tears converted;
Whose mournful passions dull the morning's joys,
Whose sweeter sleeps are turn'd to fearful dreams;
  And whose first fortunes (fill'd with all distress)
  Afford no hope of future happiness.
But what disastrous or hard accident
Hath bath'd your blubber'd eyes in bitter tears,

That thus consort me in my misery?
Why do you beat your breasts? why mourn you so?
  Say, gentle sisters, tell me, and believe
  It grieves me that I know not why you grieve.
    Chorus. O poor Cornelia, have not we good cause,
For former wrongs to furnish us with tears?
    Cornelia. O, but I fear that Fortune seeks new flaws,
And still (unsatisfy'd) more hatred bears.
    Chorus. Wherein can Fortune farther injure us,
Now we have lost our conquer'd liberty,
Our common-wealth, our empire, and our honours,
Under this cruel Tarquin's tyranny?
Under this outrage now are all our goods,
Where scattered they run by land and sea
(Like exil'd us) from fertile Italy,
To proudest Spain, or poorest Getuly.
    Cornelia. And will the heavens, that have so oft de-
      fended
Our Roman wars from fury of fierce kings,
Not once again return our senators,
That from the Libyck plains and Spanish fields,
With fearless hearts do guard our Roman hopes?
Will they not once again encourage them
To fill our fields with blood of enemies,
And bring from Africk to our Capitol,
Upon their helms, the empire that is stole?
  Then home-born houshold gods, and ye good spirits,
To whom in doubtful things we seek access,
By whom our family had been adorn'd,
And graced with the name of African;
Do ye vouchsafe that this victorious title
Be not expired in Cornelia's blood;
And that my father now (in th' Africk wars)
The self-same stile by conquest may continue!
But, wretched that I am, alas, I fear—
    Chorus. What fear you, Madam?
    Cornelia. That the frowning heavens
Oppose themselves against us in their wrath.
    Chorus. Our loss (I hope) hath satisfy'd their ire.
    Cornelia. O no, our loss lifts Cæsar's fortunes higher.

Chorus. Fortune is fickle.
Cornelia.   But hath fail'd him never.
Chorus. The more unlike she should continue ever.
Cornelia. My fearful dreams do my despairs re-
    double.
Chorus. Why suffer you vain dreams your head to
    trouble?
Cornelia. Who is not troubled with strange visions?
Chorus. That of our spirit are but illusions.
Cornelia. God grant these dreams to good effect be
    brought!
Chorus. We dream by night what we by day have
    thought.
Cornelia. The silent night, that long had sojourned,
Now 'gan to cast her sable mantle off,
And now the sleepy wain-man softly drove
His slow-pac'd team, that long had travelled;
When (like a slumber, if you term it so)
A dulness, that disposeth us to rest,
'Gan close the windows of my watchful eyes,
Already tir'd and loaden with my tears;
And lo (methought) came gliding by my bed,
The ghost of Pompey, with a ghastly look;
All pale and [15] brawn-fall'n*, not in triumph borne
Amongst the conquering Romans, as we us'd,
When he (enthroniz'd) at his feet beheld
Great emperors, fast bound in chains of brass.
But all amaz'd, with fearful hollow eyes,
His hair and beard deform'd with blood and sweat,
Casting a thin coarse linsel o'er his shoulders,
That torn in pieces trail'd upon the ground,
And, gnashing of his teeth, unlock'd his jaws,

[15] — *brawn-fall'n.*] Similar to this expression is *chap fallen*, still used by the vulgar. In Beaumont and Fletcher's *Mad Lover*, A. 2. Calis says, *his palate's down*, which seems to have the same signification.

* *All pale and brawn-fall'n.*] It will be seen by the following quotation from Webster's Appius and Virginia, 4to. 1654, that brawn-fall'n is something different from what Reed has described it:

                              " —Let
    " Th' enemies stript arm have his crimson'd *brawns*
    " Up to the elbowes in your traiterous bloud."—Page 9.

Which slightly cover'd with a scarce-seen skin,
This solemn tale he sadly did begin :
   Sleep'st thou, Cornelia? sleep'st thou, gentle wife,
And seest thy father's misery and mine?
Wake, dearest sweet, and o'er our sepulchres
In pity show thy latest love to us.
Such hap as ours attendeth on my sons,
The self same foe and fortune following them.
Send Sextus over to some foreign nation,
Far from the common hazard of the wars;
That (being yet sav'd) he may attempt no more
To 'venge the valour that is try'd before.
   He said; and suddenly a trembling horror,
A chill cold shivering (settled in my veins)
Brake up my slumber; when I ope'd my lips
Three times to cry, but could nor cry, nor speak.
I mov'd mine head, and flung abroad mine arms,
To entertain him, but his airy spirit
Beguiled mine embracements, and (unkind)
Left me embracing nothing but the wind.
   O valiant soul, when shall this soul of mine
Come visit thee in the Elysian shades?
O dearest life, or when shall sweetest death
Dissolve the fatal trouble of my days,
And bless me with my Pompey's company?
But may my father, (O extreme mishap!)
And such a number of brave regiments,
Made of so many expert soldiers,
That lov'd our liberty, and follow'd him,
Be so discomfited? O would it were but an illusion!
   Chorus. Madam, never fear.
Nor let a senseless idol of the night
Encrease a more than needful fear in you.
   Cornelia. My fear proceeds not of an idle dream,
For 'tis a truth that hath astonish'd me.
I saw great Pompey, and I heard him speak;
And, thinking to embrace him, ope'd mine arms,
When drowsy sleep, that wak'd me at unwares,
Did with his flight unclose my fearful eyes
So suddenly, that yet methinks I see him.

Howbeit I cannot touch him, for he slides
More swiftly from me than the ocean glides.

 Chorus. " [16] These are vain thoughts, or melancholy
  shews,
" That wont to haunt and trace by cloister'd tombs :
" [17] Which eath's appear in sad and strange disguises
" To pensive minds, deceived with their shadows ;
" They counterfeit the dead in voice and figure,
" Divining of our future miseries.
" For when our soul the body hath disgag'd,
" It seeks the common passage of the dead,
" Down by the fearful gates of Acheron ;
" Where when it is by Æacus adjudg'd,
" It either turneth to the Stygian lake,
" Or stays for ever in th' Elysian fields,
" And ne'er returneth to the corse interr'd,
" To walk by night, or make the wise afraid.
" None but inevitable conquering death
" Descends to hell, with hope to rise again ;
" For ghosts of men are lock'd in fiery gates,
" Fast guarded by a fell remorseless monster,

[16] *These are vain thoughts,*] Dryden and Lee, in their Tragedy of
Oedipus, A. 4, S. 1. have the following beautiful passage, which
may be compared with the present :
  " When the sun sets, shadows, that shew'd at noon
  " But small, appear most long and terrible ;
  " So when we think fate hovers o'er our heads,
  " Our apprehensions shoot beyond all bounds,
  " Owls, ravens, crickets seem the watch of death,
  " Nature's worst vermin scare her god-like sons.
  " Echoes, the very leavings of a voice,
  " Grow babling ghosts, and call us to our graves :
  " Each mole-hill thought swells to a huge Olympus,
  " While we fantastick dreamers heave and puff,
  " And sweat with an imagination's weight ;
  " As if, like Atlas, with these mortal shoulders
  " We could sustain the burden of the world."
[17] *Which* eath's *appear,* &c.] i. e. *easy, easily.* Eath is an old
Saxon word, signifying *ease.* Hence *uneath* for *uneasily.* So, in the
Second Part of *Henry VI.* A. 2. S. 4 :
  " *Uneath* may she endure the flinty streets." S.
Again, Spenser's *Fairy Queen,* B. 4. c. 12. § 1 :
  " For much more *eath* to tell the starres on hy,
  " Albe they endlesse seeme in estimation."

" And therefore think not it was Pompey's sprite,
" But some false Dæmon that beguil'd your sight.

[Exit.

Enter CICERO.

    Cicero. Then, O world's queen! O town that did
    extend
Thy conquering arms beyond the ocean,
And throng'dst thy conquests from the Libyan shores,
Down to the Scythian swift-foot fearless porters[18],
[19] Thou art embas'd; and at this instant yield'st
Thy proud neck to a miserable yoke.
Rome, thou art tam'd, and th' earth, dew'd with thy
    blood,
Doth laugh to see how thou art signioriz'd.
The force of heaven exceeds thy former strength:
For thou that wont'st to tame and conquer all,
Art conquer'd now with an eternal fall.
    [20] Now shalt thou march (thy hands fast bound be-
    hind thee)
Thy head hung down, thy cheeks with tears besprent,

---

[18] — *porters.*] Probably *booters.* S. P.
    S. P. would read *booters;* but he ought to have known that the
Scythians were contemptuously styled *porters,* because they *carried*
their huts and families about with them in wans ; omnia sua secum
portantes.
    So Lucan, lib. ii. v. 641.
        Pigra palus *Scythici* patiens Mæotica *plaustri.*
    Again, Horace Carm. lib. iii. Od. 24.
        Campestres melius *Scythæ,*
        Quorum *plaustra* vagas rite trahunt domos.
    After all, what could *booters* mean ? unless S. P. designed to cha-
racterize the *Scythians,* as Homer does his countrymen, εϋκνήμιδες
'Αχαιοὶ, the well-*booted* Greeks. [Il. a. 17.] Free-*booters,* indeed,
is used for plunderers ; but I know not that *booters* is ever employed,
unless in conjunction with some epithet that fixes its meaning. S.
[19] — *embas'd.*] Dishonour'd. So, in Spenser's *Fairy Queen,* B. 3.
c. 1. § 12 :
    " Thus reconcilement was betweene them knitt,
    " Through goodly temp'rance and affection chaste ;
    " And either vow'd with all their power and witt,
    " To let not other's honour be defaste,
    " Of friend or foe, who ever it *embaste.*"
[20] *Now shalt thou march,* &c.] Mr. Steevens observes, that this

Before the victor ; while thy rebel son,
With crowned front triumphing follows thee.
Thy bravest captains, whose courageous hearts
(Join'd with the right) did reinforce our hopes,
Now murder'd lie for fowl to feed upon.
Petreus, Cato, and Scipio, are slain,
And Juba, that amongst the Moors did reign.

　Now you, whom both the gods and fortune's grace
Hath sav'd from danger in these furious broils,
Forbear to tempt the enemy again,
For fear you feel a third calamity.
Cæsar is like a brightly-flaming blaze,
That fiercely burns a house already fir'd ;
And, ceaseless launching out on every side,
Consumes the more, the more you seek to quench it,
Still darting sparkles, till it find a train
To seize upon, and then it flames amain.
　　[21] The men, the ships, wherewith poor Rome affronts
　　　　him,
All powerless, give proud Cæsar's wrath free passage.
Nought can resist him, all the power we raise,
Turns but to our misfortune, and his praise.
　'Tis thou, O Rome, that nurs'd his insolence ;
'Tis thou, O Rome, that gav'st him first the sword,

passage is very like the following in Shakspeare's *Anthony and
Cleopatra*, A. 4. S. 12 :
　　　　" Would'st thou be windowed in great Rome, and see
　　　　" Thy master thus with pleach'd arms bending down
　　　　" His corrigible neck, his face subdu'd
　　　　" To penetrative shame, whilst the wheel'd seat
　　　　" Of fortunate Cæsar drawn before him branded
　　　　" His baseness that ensued ?"
　[21] *The men, the ships, wherewith poor Rome* affronts *him.*] *To affront,*
is to *meet directly.*　As in *Fumus Troes*, A. 2. S. 1. vol. VII.
　　　　" Lets then dismiss the legate with a frown ;
　　　　" And draw our forces toward the sea, to join
　　　　" With the four kings of *Kent,* and so *affront*
　　　　" His first arrival."
　Hamlet, A. 3. S. 1 :
　　　　" That he, as 'twere by accident, may here
　　　　" *Affront* Ophelia."
　　　　　　See Mr. Steevens's Note on the last passage.

Which murd'rer-like against thyself he draws,
And violates both God and Nature's laws.

    Like moral Esop's misled country swain,
That found a serpent pining in the snow,
And full of foolish pity took it up,
And kindly laid it by his houshold fire,
Till (waxen warm) it nimbly 'gan to stir,
And stung to death the fool that foster'd her.

    O gods! that once had care of these our walls,
And fearless kept us from th' assault of foes;
Great Jupiter, to whom our Capitol
So many oxen yearly sacrific'd;
Minerva, Stator, and stout Thracian Mars,
Father to good Quirinus our first founder;
To what intent have ye preserv'd our town,
This stately town, so often hazarded
Against the Samnites, Sabins, and fierce Latins?
Why, from once footing in our fortresses,
Have ye repell'd the lusty warlike Gauls?
Why from Molossus and false Hanibal,
Have ye reserv'd the noble Romulists?
Or why from Cat'line's lewd conspiracies
Preserv'd by Rome by my prevention?
To cast so soon a state, so long defended,
Into the bondage where (enthral'd) we pine?
To serve (no stranger, but amongst us) one
That with blind frenzy buildeth up his throne?

    But if in us be any vigour resting,
If yet our hearts retain one drop of blood,
Cæsar, thou shalt not vaunt thy conquest long,
Nor longer hold us in this servitude.
Nor shalt thou bathe thee longer in our blood:
For I divine, that thou must vomit it,
Like to a cur that carrion hath devour'd,
And cannot rest until his maw be scour'd.

    Think'st thou to signiorize, or be the king
Of such a number, nobler than thyself?
Or think'st thou Romans bear such bastard hearts,
To let thy tyranny be unreveng'd?
No; for methinks I see the shame, the grief,

The rage, the hatred, that they have conceiv'd,
And many a Roman sword already drawn,
T'enlarge the liberty that thou usurp'st.
And thy dismember'd body (stabb'd and torn),
Dragg'd through the streets, disdained to be borne.

[*Exit.*

Enter PHILIP *and* CORNELIA.

Philip. Amongst the rest of mine extreme mishaps,
I find my fortune not the least in this,
That I have kept my master company,
Both in his life, and at his latest hour,
Pompey the great, whom I have honoured
With true devotion, both alive and dead.
    One self-same ship contain'd us, when I saw
The murd'ring Egyptians bereave his life;
And when the man that had afright the earth,
Did homage to it with his dearest blood;
O'er whom I shed full many a bitter tear,
And did perform his exequies with sighs:
And on the strand upon the river side
(Where to my sighs the waters seem'd to turn)
I wove a coffin for his corse, of seggs [22],
That with the wind did wave like bannerets,
And laid his body to be burn'd thereon;
Which, when it was consum'd, I kindly took,
And sadly clos'd within an earthen urn
The ashy reliques of his hapless bones;
Which having 'scap'd the rage of wind and sea,
I bring to fair Cornelia, to interr
Within his elders tomb that honour'd her.
    Cornelia. Ah me! what see I?
    Philip.   Pompey's tender bones,
Which (in extremes) an earthen urn containeth.
    Cornelia. O sweet, dear, deplorable cinders?
O miserable woman, living, dying!
O poor Cornelia! born to be distress'd,
Why liv'st thou toil'd, that (dead) might'st lie at rest?
O faithless hands, that under cloak of love

---

[22] *seggs.*] i. e. sedges. S.

Did entertain him, to torment him so!
O barbarous, inhuman, hateful traitors!
This your disloyal dealing hath defam'd
Your king, and his inhospitable seat,
Of the.extreamest and most odious crime,
That 'gainst the heavens might be imagined.
For ye have basely broke the law of arms,
And out-rag'd over an afflicted soul;
Murder'd a man that did submit himself,
And injur'd him that ever us'd you kindly.
For which misdeed, be Egypt pestered
With battle, famine, and perpetual plagues!
Let aspics, serpents, snakes, and Libyan bears,
Tigers, and lions, breed with you for ever!
And let fair Nilus (wont to nurse your corn)
Cover your land with toads and crocodiles,
That may infect, devour, and murder you!
Else earth make way, and hell receive them quick,
A hateful race, 'mongst whom there doth abide
All treason, luxury, and homicide.

 Philip. Cease these laments.
 Cornelia.   I do but what I ought
To mourn his death.
 Philip.   Alas! that profits nought.
 Cornelia. Will heaven let treason be unpunished?
 Philip. Heavens will perform what they have promised.
 Cornelia. I fear the heavens will not hear our prayer.
 Philip. The plaints of men oppress'd do pierce the
  air.
 Cornelia. Yet Cæsar liveth still.
 Philip.   " Due punishment
" Succeeds not always after an offence:
" For oftentimes 'tis for our chastisement
" That heaven doth with wicked men dispense,
" That, when they list, they may with usury,
" For all misdeeds pay home the penalty."
 Cornelia. This is the hope that feeds my hapless days,
Else had my life been long ago expired.
I trust the gods, that see our hourly wrongs,

Will fire his shameful body with their flames;
Except some man (resolved) shall conclude,
With Cæsar's death to end our servitude.
    Else (god to fore) my self may live to see
His tired corse lie toiling in his blood:
Gor'd with a thousand stabs, and round about
The wronged people leap for inward joy.
And then come Murder; then come ugly Death;
Then, Lethe, open thine infernal lake,
I'll down with joy: because before I dy'd,
Mine eyes have seen what I in heart desir'd.
Pompey may not revive, and (Pompey dead)
Let me but see the murd'rer murdered.
    Philip. Cæsar bewail'd his death.
    Cornelia. His death he mourn'd,
Whom while he liv'd, to live like him he scorn'd.
    Philip. He punished his murd'rers.
    Cornelia. Who murder'd him,
But he that followed Pompey with the sword?
He murder'd Pompey that pursu'd his death,
And cast the plot to catch him in the trap.
He that of his departure took the spoil,
Whose fell ambition (founded first in blood)
By nought but Pompey's life could be withstood.
    Philip. Photin and false Achillas he beheaded.
    Cornelia. That was, because that Pompey being their
        friend,
They had determin'd once of Cæsar's end.
    Philip. What got he by his death?
    Cornelia. Supremacy.
    Philip. Yet Cæsar speaks of Pompey honourably.
    Cornelia. Words are but wind, nor meant he what he
        spoke.
    Philip. He will not let his [23] statues to be broke.
    Cornelia. By which disguise (whate'er he doth pre-
        tend)
His own from being broke he doth defend:

[23] — *statues.*] See Suetonius Jul. c. 75. S. P.

And by the trains wherewith he us allures,
His own estate more firmly he assures.

   Philip. He took no pleasure in his death, you see.
   Cornelia. Because himself of life did not bereave him.
   Philip. Nay, he was mov'd with former amity.
   Cornelia. He never trusted him but to deceive him.
But, had he lov'd him with a love unfeign'd,
Yet had it been a vain and trustless league:
" For there is nothing in the soul of man
" So firmly grounded, as can qualify
" Th' inextinguishable thirst of signiory.
" Not heaven's fear, nor country's sacred love,
" Not ancient laws, nor nuptial chaste desire,
" Respect of blood, or (that which most should move,)
" The inward zeal that nature doth require:
" All these, nor any thing we can devise,
" Can stop the heart resolv'd to tyrannize.

   Philip. I fear your griefs increase with this discourse.
   Cornelia. My griefs are such, as hardly can be worse.
   Philip. " Time calmeth all things."
   Cornelia. No time qualifies
My doleful spirit's endless miseries.
My grief is like a rock, whence ceaseless strain
Fresh springs of water at my weeping eyes,
Still fed by thoughts, like floods with winter's rain :
For when, to ease th' oppression of my heart,
I breathe an autumn forth of fiery sighs,
Yet herewithall my passion neither dies,
Nor drys the heat the moisture of mine eyes.

   Philip. Can nothing then recure these endless tears?
   Cornelia. Yes, news of Cæsar's death that med'cine
      bears.
   Philip. Madam, beware; for, should he hear of this,
His wrath against you 'twill exasperate.
   Cornelia. I neither stand in fear of him nor his.
   Philip. 'Tis policy to fear a powerful hate.
   Cornelia. What can he do?
   Philip.   Madam, what cannot men
That have the power to do what pleaseth them?

Cornelia. He can do me no mischief that I dread.
Philip. Yes, cause your death.
Cornelia.   Thrice happy were I dead.
Philip. With rigorous torments—
Cornelia.   Let him ture me,
Pull me in pieces, famish, fire me up,
Fling me alive into a lion's den;
There is no death so hard torments me so,
As his extreme triumphing in our woe.
   But if he will torment me, let him then
Deprive me wholly of the hope of death;
For I had died before the fall of Rome,
And slept with Pompey in the peaceful deeps,
Save that I live in hope to see ere long
That Cæsar's death shall satisfy his wrong.
   Chorus. Fortune in power imperious,
Us'd o'er the world and worldlings thus
                              to tyrannize,
When she hath heap'd her gifts on us,
                              away she flies.
Her feet more swift than is the wind,
Are more inconstant in their kind
                         than autumn's blasts;
A woman's shape, a woman's mind,
                         that seldom lasts.
One while she bends her angry brow,
And of no labour will allow:
                              Another while
She fleers again, I know not how,
                              still to beguile.
Fickle in our adversities,
And fickle when our fortunes rise,
                         she scoffs at us;
That (blind herself) can blear our eyes,
                         to trust her thus.
The sun that lends the earth his light,
Beheld her never over-night
                              lie calmly down,
But in the morning following, might
                              perceive her frown.

She hath not only power and will,
T' abuse the vulgar wanting skill;

                        but when she list,

To kings and clowns doth equal ill,
    N a

                        without resist.

Mischance, that every man abhors,
And cares for crowned emperors

                        she doth reserve,

As for the poorest labourers,

                        that work or starve.

The merchant, that for private gain
Doth send his ships to pass the main,

                        upon the shore,

In hope he shall his wish obtain,

                        doth thee adore.

Upon the sea, or on the land,
Where health or wealth, or vines do stand,

                        thou canst do much,

And often help'st the helpless band;

                        thy power is such.

And many times (dispos'd to jest)
'Gainst one whose power and cause is best,

                        (thy power to try,)

To him that ne'er put spear in rest,

                        giv'st victory.

For so the Libyan monarchy,
That with Ausonian blood did dye

                        our warlike field,

To one that ne'er got victory,

                        was urg'd to yield.

So noble Marius, Arpin's friend,
That did the Latin state defend

                        from Cymbrian rage,

Did prove thy fury in the end,

                        which nought could swage.

And Pompey, whose days haply led,
So long thou seem'dst t' have favoured

                        in vain, 'tis said,

When the Pharsalian field he led,

                        implor'd thine aid.

Now Cæsar, swoln with honour's heat,
Sits signiorizing in her seat,
                                    and will not see
That Fortune can her hopes defeat,
                                    whate'er they be.

From chance is nothing franchised;
And till the time that they are dead,
                                    is no man blest;

He only, that no death doth dread,
                                    doth live at rest.

ACT IV.

Cassius, Decim Brutus.

Cassius. Accursed Rome, that arm'st against thy self
A tyrant's rage, and mak'st a wretch thy king.
For one man's pleasure (O injurious Rome)
Thy children 'gainst thy children thou hast arm'd;
And think'st not of the rivers of their blood,
That erst were shed to save thy liberty,
Because thou ever hatedst monarchy.
　　Now o'er our bodies (tumbled up on heaps,
Like cocks of hay when July shears the field)
Thou build'st thy kingdom, and thou seat'st thy king.
And to be servile (which torments me most)
Employest our lives, and lavishest our blood.
O Rome, accursed Rome, thou murd'rest us,
And massacrest thyself in yielding thus.
　　Yet are there gods, yet is there heaven and earth,
That seem to fear a certain Thunderer?
No no, there are no gods; or if there be,
They leave to see into the world's affairs;
They care not for us, nor account of men,
For what we see is done, is done by Chance.
'Tis Fortune rules, for equity and right
Have neither help nor grace in heaven's sight.
　　Scipio hath wrench'd a sword into his breast,
And launch'd his bleeding wound into the sea.

Undaunted Cato tore his intrails out.
Affranius and Faustus murder'd dy'd.
Juba and Petreus, fiercely combating,
Have each done other equal violence.
Our army's broken, and the Libyan bears
Devour the bodies of our citizens.
The conquering tyrant, high in Fortune's grace,
Doth ride triumphing o'er our common-wealth ;
And mournful we behold him bravely mounted
(With stern looks) in his chariot, where he leads
The conquer'd honour of the people yok'd.
So Rome to Cæsar yields both power and pelf,
And o'er Rome Cæsar reigns in Rome itself.
    But, Brutus, shall we dissolutely sit,
And see the tyrant live to tyrannize ?
Or shall their ghosts that dy'd to do us good,
'Plain in their tombs of our base cowardice ?
Shall lamed soldiers, and grave grey-hair'd men,
Point at us in their bitter tears, and say,
See where they go that have their race forgot !
And rather chuse (unarm'd) to serve with shame,
Than (arm'd) to save their freedom and their fame?
    Brutus. I swear by heaven, the Immortals highest.
        throne,
Their temples, altars, and their images,
To see (for one) that Brutus suffer not
His ancient liberty to be repress'd.
I freely march'd with Cæsar in his wars,
Not to be subject, but to aid his right.
But if (envenom'd with ambitious thoughts)
He lift his hand imperiously o'er us ;
If he determine but to reign in Rome,
Or follow'd Pompey but to this effect:
Or if (these civil discords now dissolv'd)
He render not the empire back to Rome ;
Then shall he see, that Brutus this day bears
The self-same arms to be aveng'd on him ;
And that this hand (though Cæsar blood abhor)
Shall toil in his, which I am sorry for.
    I love, I love him dearly. '' But the love

" That men their country and their birth-right bear,
" Exceeds all loves ; and dearer is by far
" Our country's love, than friends or children are."
　　Cassius. If this brave care be nourish'd in your blood,
Or if so frank a will your soul possess,
Why haste we not, even while these words are utter'd,
To sheathe our new-ground swords in Cæsar's throat ?
Why spend we day-light, and why dies he not,
That, by his death, we wretches may revive ?
We stay too long, I burn till I be there
To see this massacre, and send his ghost
To theirs, whom (subtilly) he for monarchy
Made fight to death with show of liberty.
　　Brutus. Yet haply he (as Sylla whilom did)
When he hath rooted civil war from Rome,
Will therewithall discharge the power he hath.
　　Cassius. Cæsar and Sylla, Brutus, be not like.
Sylla (assaulted by the enemy)
Did arm himself (but in his own defence)
Against both Cinna's host and Marius ;
Whom when he had discomfited and chas'd,
And of his safety throughly was assur'd,
He laid apart the power that he had got,
And gave up rule, for he desir'd it not.
　　Where Cæsar, that in silence might have slept,
Nor urg'd by aught but his ambition,
Did break into the heart of Italy ;
And like rude Brennus brought his men to field,
Travers'd the seas, and shortly after (back'd
With winter'd soldiers us'd to conquering,)
He aim'd at us, bent to exterminate
Who ever sought to intercept his state :
Now, having got what he hath gaped for,
(Dear Brutus) think you Cæsar such a child,
Slightly to part with so great signiory ?
Believe it not, he bought it dear, you know,
And travelled too far to leave it so.
　　Brutus. But, Cassius, Cæsar is not yet a king.
　　Cassius. No, but dictator, in effect as much.
He doth what pleaseth him, a princely thing.

And wherein differ they whose power is such?
   Brutus. He is not bloody.
   Cassius. But by bloody jars
He hath unpeopled most part of the earth.
Both Gaul and Africk perish'd by his wars;
Egypt, Emathia, Italy and Spain,
Are full of dead mens bones by Cæsar slain.
Th'infectious plague, and famine's bitterness,
Or th' ocean (whom no pity can asswage)
Though they contain dead bodies numberless,
Are yet inferior to Cæsar's rage;
Who (monster-like) with his ambition,
Hath left more tombs than ground to lay them on.
   Brutus. Soldiers with such reproach should not be
      blam'd.
   Cassius. He with his soldiers hath himself defam'd.
   Brutus. Why then you think there is no praise in
      war.
   Cassius. Yes, where the causes reasonable are.
   Brutus. He hath enrich'd the empire with new states.
   Cassius. Which with ambition now he ruinates.
   Brutus. He hath reveng'd the Gauls old injury,
And made them subject to our Roman laws.
   Cassius. The restfull Almains, with his cruelty,
He rashly stirr'd against us without cause;
And hazarded our city and ourselves
Against a harmless nation, kindly given;
To whom we should do well (for some amends)
To render him, and reconcile old friends.
These nations did he purposely provoke,
To make an army for his after-aid
Against the Romans, whom in policy
He train'd in war to steal their signiory.
" Like them that (striving at th' Olympian sports,
" To grace themselves with honour of the game)
" Anoint their sinews fit for wrestling,
" And (ere they enter) use some exercise."
   The Gauls were but a fore-game fetch'd about
For civil discord, wrought by Cæsar's sleights;
Whom (to be king himself) he soon remov'd;

Teaching a people hating servitude,
To fight for that that did their deaths conclude.

Brutus. The wars once ended, we shall quickly know,
Whether he will restore the state or no.

Cassius. No, Brutus, never look to see that day,
For Cæsar holdeth signiory too dear.
But know, while Cassius hath one drop of blood,
To feed this worthless body that you see,
What reck I death to do so many good?
In spite of Cæsar, Cassius will be free.

Brutus. A generous, or true ennobled spirit
Detests to learn what tastes of servitude.

Cassius. Brutus, I cannot serve, nor see Rome yok'd;
No, let me rather die a thousand deaths.
" The stiff-neck'd horses champ not on the bit,
" Nor meekly bear the rider but by force:
" The sturdy oxen toil not at the plough,
" Nor yield unto the yoke, but by constraint."
Shall we then, that are men, and Romans born,
Submit us to unurged slavery?
Shall Rome, that hath so many over-thrown,
Now make herself a subject to her own?

O base indignity! A beardless youth,
Whom king Nicomedes could over-reach,
Commands the world, and bridleth all the earth,
And like a prince controuls the Romulists;
Brave Roman soldiers, stern-born sons of Mars,
And none, not one, that dares to undertake
The intercepting of his tyranny.
O Brutus speak! O say, Servilius!
[23] Why cry you, ayme! and see us used thus?

---

[23] *Why cry you, ayme !*] In the former edition, Mr. Dodsley had
substituted, instead of the words in the text, *cry you ah me!* the
alteration was, however, intirely unnecessary. *To cry ayme,* signified, as Dr. Warburton observes, *to consent to,* or *approve of any
thing.* " The phrase was taken originally from archery. When
" any one had challenged another to shoot at the butts (the per-
" petual diversion, as well as exercise of that time), the standers-
" by used to say one to the other, *cry aim,* i. e. accept the chal-
" lenge." See Dr. Warburton's Note on *Merry Wives of Windsor,*

But Brutus lives, and sees, and knows, and feels,
That there is one that curbs their country's weal.
Yet (as he were the semblance, not the son
Of noble Brutus, his great grandfather)
As if he wanted hands, sense, sight, or heart,
He doth, deviseth, sees, nor dareth aught,
That may extirp or raze these tyrannies.
Nor aught doth Brutus that to Brute belongs,
But still increaseth by his negligence,
His own disgrace, and Cæsar's violence.
   The wrong is great, and over-long endur'd ;
We should have practis'd, conspired, conjured
A thousand ways and weapons to repress
Or kill out-right this cause of our distress.
   Chorus. Who prodigally spends his blood
Bravely to do his country good,
And liveth to no other end,
But resolutely to attempt
What may the innocent defend,
And bloody tyrants rage prevent :

A. 2. S. 3. where he has produced several examples of the use of
the phrase. Dr. Johnson says, " I once thought that it was bor-
" rowed from archery ; and that *aim!* having been the word of
" command, as we now say, *present!* to cry *aim*, had been *to in-*
" *cite notice*, or raise attention. But I rather think, that the old
" word of applause was J' *aime, I love it*, and that to applaud was
" to cry J' *aime*, which the English, not easily pronouncing *je*,
" sunk into *aime* or *aim.*" Mr. Steevens is of opinion, that Dr.
Johnson's first thought is best. See Notes on *King John*, A. 2.
S. 1. To the several instances produced by these gentlemen, the
following may be added :
   Middleton and Rowley's *Fair Quarrel*, A. 1. S. 1 :
         " How now, Gallants ?
         " Beleeve me then, I must *give aime* no longer."
   Beaumont and Fletcher's *False One*, A. 5. S. 4. Edit. 1778 :
         " By Venus, not a kiss
         " 'Till our work be done ! The traitors once dispatch'd,
         " To it, and we'll *cry aim.*"
   It is remarkable, that Mr Seward had made the same alteration
in the last passage, and consequently fallen into the same mistake
as Mr. Dodsley had in the text.

And he that, in his soul assur'd,
Hath water's force and fire endur'd,
And past the pikes of thousand hosts,
To free the earth from tyranny,
And fearless scours on dang'rous coasts,
T' enlarge his country's liberty :

Were all the world his foes before,
Now shall they love him evermore.
His glory spread abroad by Fame,
On wings of his posterity,
From obscure death shall free his name,
To live in endless memory.

All after-ages shall adore,
And honour him with hymns therefore.
Yearly the youth for joy shall bring
The fairest flowers that grow in Rome ;
And yearly in the summer sing,
O'er his heroic kingly tomb.

For so the two Athenians,
That from their fellow-citizens
Did freely chase vile servitude,
Shall live for valiant prowess blest ;
No sepulchre shall e'er exclude
Their glory, equal with the best.

But when the vulgar, mad and rude,
Repay good with ingratitude,
Hardly then they them reward,
That to free them from the hands
Of a tyrant, ne'er regard
In what plight their person stands.

For high Jove, that guideth all,
When he lets his just wrath fall,
To revenge proud diadems,
With huge cares did cross kings lives,
Raising treasons in their realms,
By their children, friends, or wives.

Therefore he whom all men fear,
Feareth all men every where.
Fear, that doth engender hate,
(Hate enforcing them thereto)
Maketh many undertake,
Many things they would not do.

O how many mighty kings
Live in fear of petty things!
For when kings have sought by wars
Stranger towns to have o'erthrown,
They have caught deserved scars,
Seeking that was not their own.

For no tyrant commonly,
Living ill, can kindly die;
But either traiterously surpriz'd
Doth coward poison [24] quail their breath,
Or their people have devis'd,
Or their guard to seek their death.

He only lives most happily,
That, free and far from majesty,
Can live content, although unknown;
He fearing none, none fearing him,
Meddling with nothing but his own,
While gazing eyes at crowns grow dim.

Enter CÆSAR *and* MARK ANTONY.

Cæsar. O Rome, that with thy pride dost over-peer
The worthiest cities of the conquer'd world;
Whose honour got by famous victories,
Hath fill'd heaven's fiery vaults with frightful horror!
O lofty towers! O stately battlements!
O glorious temples! O proud palaces!
And you brave walls, bright heaven's masonry,
Grac'd with a thousand kingly diadems!
Are ye not stirred with a strange delight,
To see your Cæsar's matchless victories?

[24] — *quail*] See Note on *Tancred and Gismund*, p. 190. The
word here has a different sense from the former. It signifies *to
quell* or *overcome.*

And how your empire and your praise begins
Through fame, which he of stranger nations wins?
　O beauteous Tiber, with thine easy streams,
That glide as smoothly as a Parthian shaft!
25 Turn not thy crispy tides like silver curl,
Back to thy grass-green banks to welcome us;
And with a gentle murmur haste to tell
The foaming seas the honour of our fight?
Trudge not thy streams to Triton's mariners,
To bruit the praises of our conquests past?
And make their vaunts to old Oceanus,
That henceforth Tiber shall salute the seas,
More fam'd than Tiger or fair Euphrates?
　Now all the world (well-nigh) doth stoop to Rome.
The sea, the earth, and all is almost ours.
Be't where the bright sun with his neighbour beams
Doth early light the pearled Indians,
Or where his chariot stays to stop the day,
Till heaven unlock the darkness of the night.
Be't where the sea is wrapt in crystal ice,
Or where the summer doth but warm the earth.
Or here, or there, where is not Rome renown'd?
There lives no king (how great soe'er he be)
But trembleth if he once but hear of me.
　Cæsar is now earth's fame, and Fortune's terror,
And Cæsar's worth hath stain'd old soldiers praises.
Rome, speak no more of either Scipio,
Nor of the Fabii, or Fabritians;
Here let the Decii and their glory die.
Cæsar hath tam'd more nations, ta'en more towns,
And fought more battles than the best of them.
Cæsar doth triumph over all the world,

25 *Turn not thy* crispy *tides*] *Crispy* is *curling*, So, in Shak-
speare's *Henry IV.* A. 1. S. 3:
　　　" Three times they breath'd, and three times did they drink,
　　　" Upon agreement, of swift Severn's flood;
　　　" Who then, affrighted with their bloody looks,
　　　" Ran fearfully among the trembling reeds,
　　　" And hid his *crisp* head in the hollow bank,
　　　" Blood stained with these valiant combatants."
　　　　　　　　　See Mr. Steevens's Note on this passage.

And all they scarcely conquered a nook.
The Gauls, that came to Tiber to carouse,
Did live to see my soldiers drink at Loire ;
And those brave Germans, true-born martialists,
Beheld the swift Rhine under-run mine ensigns.
The Britains (lock'd within a wat'ry realm,
And wall'd by Neptune) stoopt to me at last.
The faithless Moor, the fierce Numidian,
Th' earth that the Euxine sea makes sometimes marsh,
The stony-hearted people that inhabit
Where sevenfold Nilus doth disgorge itself,
Have all been urg'd to yield to my command ;
Yea, even this city, that hath almost made
An universal conquest of the world ;
And that brave warrior, my brother-in-law,
That, ill-advis'd, repined at my glory ;
Pompey, that second Mars, whose [26] haught' renown,
And noble deeds, were greater than his fortunes,
Prov'd to his loss but even in one assault,
My hand, my hap, my heart exceeded his,
When the Thessalian fields were purpled o'er
With either army's murder'd soldiers gore ;
When he (to conquering accustomed)
Did (conquered) fly, his troops discomfited.
    Now. Scipio, that long'd to shew himself
Descent-of African (so fam'd for arms),
He durst affront me and my warlike bands
Upon the coasts of Lybia, till he lost
His scatter'd army : and to shun the scorn
Of being taken captive, kill'd himself.
    Now, therefore, let us triumph, Antony ;
And rend'ring thanks to heaven as we go,
For bridling those that did malign our glory,
Let's to the Capitol.
    Antony. Come on, brave Cæsar,

<hr>

[20] — *haught*] This word is common to many writers. As Shakspeare's Third Part of *Henry VI.* A. 2. S. 1 :
        "— The proud insulting queen,
        " With Clifford, and the *haught* Northumberland."
    See several examples in Mr. Steevens's Note on the last passage.

And crown thy head, and mount thy chariot.
Th' impatient people run along the streets,
And in a rout against thy gates they rush,
To see their Cæsar, after dangers past,
Made conqueror and emperor at last.

　　Cæsar. I call to witness heaven's great Thunderer,
That 'gainst my will I have maintain'd this war,
Nor thirsted I for conquests bought with blood.
I joy not in the death of citizens;
But through my self-will'd enemies despite,
And Romans wrong, was I constrain'd to fight.

　　Antony. They sought t' eclipse thy fame, but destiny
Revers'd th' effect of their ambition;
And Cæsar's praise, increas'd by their disgrace.
That reck'd not of his virtuous deeds.　But thus
We see it fareth with the envious.

　　Cæsar. I never had the thought to injure them.
Howbeit I never meant my greatness should
By any other's greatness be o'er-rul'd.
For as I am inferior to none,
So can I suffer no superiors.

　　Antony. Well, Cæsar, now they are discomfited.
And crows are feasted with their carcases;
And yet I fear you have too kindly sav'd
Those, that your kindness hardly will requite.

　　Cæsar. Why Antony, what would you wish me do?
Now shall you see that they will pack to Spain,
And (joined with the exiles there encamp)
Until th' ill spirit that doth them defend,
Do bring their treasons to a bloody end.

　　Antony. I fear not those that to their weapons fly,
And keep their state in Spain, in Spain to die.

　　Cæsar. Whom fear'st thou then, Mark Antony?
　　Antony.　　　　　　　　　　The hateful crew,
That, wanting power in field to conquer you,
Have in their coward souls devised snares
To murder thee, and take thee at unwares.

　　Cæsar. Will those conspire my death that live by
　　　me?
　　Antony. In conquer'd foes what credit can there be?

Cæsar. Besides their lives, I did their goods restore.

Antony. O but their country's good concerns them
    more.

Cæsar. What think they me to be their country's
    foe ?

Antony. [27] No, but that thou usurp'st the right they
    owe.

Cæsar. To Rome have I submitted mighty things.

Antony. Yet Rome endures not the command of
    kings.

Cæsar. Who dares to contradict our [28] empory?

Antony. Those whom thy rule hath robb'd of liberty.

Cæsar. I fear them not whose death is but deferr'd.

Antony. I fear my foe until he be interr'd.

Cæsar. A man may make his foe his friend, you know.

Antony. A man may easier make his friend his foe.

Cæsar. Good deeds the cruel'st heart to kindness
    bring.

Antony. But resolution is a deadly thing.

Cæsar. If citizens my kindness have forgot,
Whom shall I then not fear?

Antony.   Those that are not.

Cæsar. What, shall I slay then all that I suspect?

Antony. Else cannot Cæsar's [28] empory endure.

Cæsar. Rather I will my life and all neglect.
Nor labour I my vain life to assure;
But so to die, as dying I may live,
And leaving off this earthly tomb of mine,
Ascend to heaven upon my winged deeds.
And shall I not have lived long enough,

---

[27] *No, but that thou usurp'st the right they owe.*] That is, *the right
they own or possess.* So, in the *Virgin Martyr,* by Massinger and
Dekker, A. 2. S. 2 :
         " Sir ; he is more indebted
         " To you for praise, than you to him that *owes it.*"
Othello, A. 3. S. 3 :
         " — Not poppy nor mandragora,
         " Nor all the drowsy syrups of the world,
         " Shall ever med'cine thee to that sweet sleep
         " Which thou *ow'dst* yesterday."

[28] — *empory*] See Note 11. A. 2. p. 248.

That in so short a time am so much fam'd?
Can I too soon go taste Cocytus' flood?
No, Antony, death cannot injure us,
" For he lives long, that dies victorious."
   Antony. Thy praises show thy life is long enough,
But for thy friends and country all too short.
Should Cæsar live as long as Nestor did,
Yet Rome may wish his life eternized.
   Cæsar. Heaven sets our time, with heaven may
      nought dispense.
   Antony. But we may shorten time with negligence.
   Cæsar. But Fortune and the heavens have care of us.
   Antony. Fortune is fickle, heaven imperious.
   Cæsar. What shall I then do?
   Antony.   As befits your state,
Maintain a watchful guard about your gate.
   Cæsar. What more assurance may our state defend,
Than love of those that do on us attend?
   Antony. There is no hatred more, if it be mov'd,
Than theirs whom we offend, and once belov'd.
   Cæsar. Better it is to die than be suspicious.
   Antony. 'Tis wisdom yet not to be credulous.
   Cæsar. The quiet life that carelesly is led,
Is not alonely happy in this world,
But death itself doth sometime pleasure us.
That death that comes unsent for or unseen,
And suddenly doth take us at unware,
Methinks is sweetest; and, if heaven were pleas'd,
I could desire that I might die so well.
The fear of evil doth afflict us more,
Than th' evil itself, though it be ne'er so sore.

     A Chorus of CÆSAR's *Friends.*

O fair sun, that gently smiles
From the orient-pearled isles,
Gilding these our gladsome days
With the beauty of thy rays:

Free fro' rage of civil strife,
Long preserve our Cæsar's life,

That from sable Africk brings
Conquests, whereof Europe rings.

And fair Venus, thou of whom
The Æneades are come,
Henceforth vary not thy grace,
From Iulus' happy race.

Rather cause thy dearest son,
By his triumphs new begun,
To expel fro' forth the land
Fierce war's quenchless fire-brand.

That of care acquitting us,
(Who at last adore him thus)
He a peaceful star appear,
From our walls all woes to clear.

And so let his warlike brows
Still be deck'd with laurel boughs,
And his statues newly set
With many a fresh-flower'd coronet.

So in every place let be
Feasts, and masks, and mirful glee,
Strewing roses in the street,
When their emperor they meet.

He his foes. hath conquered,
Never leaving till they fled,
And (abhorring blood) at last
Pardon'd all offences past.

" For high Jove the heavens among,
" (Their support that suffer wrong)
" Doth oppose himself again
" Bloody-minded cruel men.

" For he shorteneth their days,
" Or prolongs them with dispraise :
" Or (his greater wrath to show)
" Gives them over to their foe."

Cæsar, a citizen so wrong'd
Of the honour him belong'd,

To defend himself from harms,
Was enforc'd to take up arms.

For he saw that envy's dart,
(Pricking still their poisoned heart,
For his sudden glory got)
Made his envious foe so hot.

Wicked envy feeding still,
Foolish those that do thy will ;;
For thy poisons in them pour
Sundry passions every hour.

And to choler doth convert,
Purest blood about the heart,
Which (o'er-flowing of their breast)
Suff'reth nothing to digest.

" Other mens prosperity,
" Is their infelicity ;
" And their choler then is rais'd
" When they hear another prais'd.

" Neither Phœbus' fairest eye,
" Feasts, nor friendly company,
" Mirth, or whatsoe'er it be,
" With their humour can agree.

" Day or night they never rest
" Spiteful hate so pecks their breast.
" Pinching their perplexed lungs,
" With her fiery poisoned tongues.

" Fire-brands in their breasts they bear,
" As if Tisiphon were there.
" And their souls are pierc'd as sore
" As Prometheus' ghost, and more.

" Wretches, they are woe-begone [29],
" For their wound is always one.
" Nor hath Charon power or skill
" To recure them of their ill."

[29] —woe-begone] *Far gone in woe.* Dr. Warburton observes,
" This word was common enough amongst the old Scottish and
" English poets, as G. Douglas, Chaucer, Lord Buckhurst, Fairfax."

ACT V.

MESSENGER, CORNELIA, CHORUS.

Messenger. Unhappy man! amongst so many wracks
As I have suffer'd both by land and sea,
That scornful destiny denies my death.
Oft have I seen the ends of mightier men,
Whose coats of steel base death hath stoln into;
And in this direful war before mine eyes,
Beheld their corses scatter'd on the plains,
And endless numbers falling by my side;
Nor those ignoble, but the noblest lords.
'Mongst whom above the rest that moves me most,
Scipio (my dearest master) is deceas'd;
And death, that sees the nobles blood so rife,
Full gorged triumphs, and disdains my life.
  Cornelia. We are undone.
  Chorus. Scipio hath lost the day;
But hope the best, and hearken to his news.
  Cornelia. O cruel fortune!
  Messenger. These misfortunes yet
Must I report to sad Cornelia;
Whose ceaseless grief (which I am sorry for)
Will aggravate my former misery.
  Cornelia. Wretch that I am, why leave I not the
          world?
Or wherefore am I not already dead?
O world! O wretch!
  Chorus. Is this th' undaunted heart
That is required in extremities?
Be more confirmed. And, madam, let not grief
Abuse your wisdom like a vulgar wit.
Haply the news is better than the noise;

See Notes on Second Part *Henry* IV. A. 1. S. 1. by him and Mr.
Steevens.
  Again, Erasmus's *Praise of Folie*, Sign. E 3: —" as who before
" represented a Kinge, being clothed all in purpre havynge no
" more but shifted hymselfe a litle, shoulde shew hymselfe agayne .
" lyke *a woo begon* myser."

Let's hear him speak.

Cornelia. O no, for all is lost!
Farewell, dear father.

Chorus. He is sav'd perhaps.

Messenger. Methinks I hear my master's daughter
    speak.
What sighs, what sobs, what plaints, what passions
Have we endur'd, Cornelia, for your sake?

Cornelia. Where is thine emperor?

Messenger. Where our captains are.
Where are our legions? where our men at arms?
Or where so many of our Roman souls?
The earth, the sea, the vultures, and the crows,
Lions and bears are their best sepulchres.

Cornelia. O miserable!

Chorus. Now I see the heavens
Are heap'd with rage and horror 'gainst this house.

Cornelia. O earth! why ope'st thou not?

Chorus. Why wail you so?
Assure your self that Scipio bravely dy'd;
And such a death excels a servile life.
Say, messenger; the manner of his end
Will haply comfort this your discontent.

Cornelia. Discourse the manner of his hard mishap,
And what disast'rous accident did break
So many people, bent so much to fight.

Messenger. Cæsar, that wisely knew his soldiers
    hearts,
And their desire to be approv'd in arms,
Sought nothing more than to encounter us.
And therefore (faintly skirmishing) in craft,
Lamely they fought, to draw us further on.
Oft (to provoke our wary well-taught troops)
He would attempt the entrance on our bars:
Nay, even our trenches, to our great disgrace,
And call our soldiers cowards to their face.

But when he saw his wiles nor bitter words
Could draw our captains to endanger us,
Coasting along and following by the foot,

He thought to tire and weary us fro' thence;
And got his willing hosts to march by night,
With heavy armour on their hard'ned backs,
Down to the sea side; where, [30] before fair Thapsus,
He made his pioneers, poor weary souls,
The self-same day to dig and cast new trenches,
And plant strong barricades; where he encamp'd,
Resolv'd by force to hold us hard at work,
Scipio, no sooner heard of his designs,
But, being afraid to lose so fit a place,
March'd on the sudden to the self-same city;
Where few men might do much, which made him see
Of what importance such a town would be.
    The fields are spread, and as a houshold camp
Of creeping emmets in a country farm,
That come to forage when the cold begins,
Leaving their crannies to go search about,
Cover the earth so thick, as scarce we tread,
But we shall see a thousand of them dead.
    Even so our battles scatter'd on the sands,
Did scour the plains in pursuit of the foe.
One while at Thapsus we begin t' entrench,
To ease our army if it should retire;
Another while we softly sally forth.
And wakeful Cæsar, that doth watch our being,
(When he perceives us marching o'er the plain)
Doth leap for gladness; and (to murder vow'd)
Runs to the tent, for fear we should be gone,
And quickly claps his rusty armour on.
    For true it is, that Cæsar brought at first
An host of men to Africk, meanly arm'd;
But such as had brave spirits (and combating)
Had power and wit to make a wretch a king.
    Well, forth to field they marched all at once,
Except some few that staid to guard the trench.
Them Cæsar soon and subt'ly sets in rank,

---

[30] — *before fair* Thapsus,] *Thapsus*, a maritime town in Africa,
where Cæsar defeated the remains of Pompey's army. S.

And every regiment warned with a word,
Bravely to fight for honour of the day.
He shows, that ancient soldiers need not fear
Them that they had so oft disordered;
Them that already dream'd of death or flight;
That, tir'd, would ne'er hold out, if once they see
That they o'erlaid them in the first assault.

Meanwhile our emperor, at all points arm'd,
Whose silver hairs and honourable front
Were (warlike) lock'd within a plumed cask,
In one hand held his targe of steel embost,
And in the other grasp'd his coutelas [31],
And with a chearful look survey'd the camp ;
Exhorting them to charge, and fight like men,
And to endure what e'er betided them.

For now, quoth he, is come that happy day
Wherein our country shall approve our love.
Brave Romans know, this is the day and hour,
That we must all live free, or friendly die :
For my part (being an ancient senator)
An emperor and consul, I disdain
The world should see me to become a slave.
I'll either conquer, or this sword you see
(Which brightly shone) shall make an end of me.

We fight not, we, like thieves, for others wealth ;
We fight not, we t'enlarge our scant confines ;
To purchase fame to our posterities,
By stuffing of our trophies in their houses :
But 'tis for publick freedom that we fight,
For Rome we fight, and those that fled for fear.
Nay more, we fight for safety of our lives,
Our goods, our honours, and our ancient laws.
As for the empire, and the Roman state,
(Due to the victor) thereon ruminate.

Think how this day the honourable dames,
With blubber'd eyes, and hands to heaven uprear'd,
Sit invocating for us to the gods,

[31] —coutelas,] A cuttelas, courtelas, or short sword for a man at
armes.   Cotgrave's *Dictionary*, voce *coutelas*.

That they will bless our holy purposes.
Methinks I see poor Rome in horror clad,
And aged senators in sad discourse,
Mourn for our sorrows and their servitude.
Methinks I see them (while lamenting thus),
Their hearts and eyes lie hovering over us.
  On then, brave men, my fellows and Rome's friends,
To shew us worthy of our ancestors :
And let us fight with courage, and conceit
That we may rest the masters of the field ;
That this brave tyrant, valiantly beset,
May perish in the press before our faces ;
And that his troops (as touch'd with lightning flames)
May by our horse in heaps be overthrown,
And he (blood-thirsting) wallow in his own.
  This said : His army crying all at once,
With joyful tokens did applaud his speech;
Whose swift shrill noise did pierce into the clouds,
Like northern winds that beat the horned Alps.
The clatt'ring armour, buskling as they pac'd,
Rung through the forests with a frightful noise,
And every echo took the trumpet's clang.
When (like a tempest rais'd with whirl-wind's rage)
They ran at ever-each other hand and foot ;
Wherewith the dust, as with a darksome cloud,
Arose, and over-shadow'd horse and man.
The darts and arrows on their armour glanc'd,
And with their fall the trembling earth was shaken.
The air (that thick'ned with their thund'ring cries)
With pale wan clouds discoloured the sun.
The fire in sparks fro' forth their armour flew,
And, with a duskish yellow, choak'd the heavens.
The battles lock'd (with bristle pointed spears)
Do at the half pike freely charge each other,
And dash together like two lusty bulls,
That (jealous of some heifer in the herd)
Run head to head, and (sullen) will not yield,
Till, dead or fled, the one forsake the field.
  The shivered launces (rattling in the air)
Fly forth as thick as motes about the sun :

When with their swords (flesh'd with the former fight)
They hew their armour, and they cleave their[32] casks,
Till streams of blood like rivers fill the downs ;
That being infected with the stench thereof,
Surcloys the ground, and of a champant land
Makes it a quagmire, where (knee-deep) they stand.

   Blood-thirsty Discord, with her snaky hair,
A fearful hag, with her fire-darting eyes,
Runs cross the squadrons with a smoaky brand,
And with her murd'ring whip encourageth
The over-forward hands to blood and death.

   Bellona, fired with a quenchless rage,
Runs up and down, and in the thickest throng
Cuts, casts the ground, and madding makes a pool,
Which in her rage free passage doth afford,
That with our blood she may annoint her sword.

   Now we of our side urge them to retreat,
And now before them we retire as fast,
As on the Alps the sharp nor northeast wind,
Shaking a pine-tree with her greatest power,
One while the top doth almost touch the earth,
And then it riseth with a counterbuff.
So did the armies press and charge each other,
With self-same courage, worth, and weapons too :
And, prodigal of life for liberty,
With burning hate let each at other fly.

   Thrice did the cornets of the soldiers clear'd,
Turn to the standard to be new supply'd ;
And thrice the best of both was fain to breathe ;
And thrice recomforted they bravely ran,
And fought as freshly as they first began.
  [33] Like two fierce lions fighting in a desert,

---

[32] —*casks*,] *Head-pieces* or *helmets*.
Marston's *Sophonisba*, A. 1. S. 2 :
    " —— and while our ore-toyl'd foe
    " Snores on his unlac'd *cask*, all faint, though proud
    " Through his successful fight."
  Ibid. S. 2 : " Enter Massinissa in his gorget and shirt, shield,
" sword, his arme transfixt with a dart ; Jugurth followes with his
" cures and *caske*."
  The word is generally spelt *casques*.
[33] *two fierce lions*—passant—regardant.] Terms of heraldry. S.

To win the love of some fair lioness,
When they have vomited their long-grown rage,
And prov'd each other's force sufficient,
Passant regardant softly they retire;
Their jaw-bones dy'd with foaming froth and blood;
Their lungs like spunges ramm'd within their sides;
Their tongues discover'd, and their tails long-trailing;
Till jealous rage (engendered with rest)
Returns them sharper set than at the first;
And makes them couple when they see their prize,
With bristled backs, and fire-sparkling eyes,
Till tir'd or conquer'd, one submits or flies.
    [34] Cæsar, whose king-like looks, like day-bright stars,
Both comfort and encourage his to fight,
March'd through the battle (laying still about him)
And subt'ly mark'd whose hand was happiest;
Who nicely did but dip his spear in blood,
And who more roughly smear'd it to his fist;
Who staggering fell with every feeble wound,
And who (more strongly) pac'd it through the thickest;
Him he enflam'd, and spur'd, and fill'd with horror.
As when Alecto in the lowest hell,
Doth breathe new heat within Orestes' breast,
Till outward rage with inward grief begins
A fresh remembrance of our former sins.
    For then (as if provok'd with pricking goads)
Their warlike armies (fast lock'd foot to foot)
Stooping their heads low bent to toss their staves,
They fiercely open both battalions,

---

[34] *Cæsar, whose king-like looks, &c.*
    March'd thro' the battle—
    And subt'ly mark'd whose hand was happiest;
    Who nicely did but dip his spear in blood,
    And who more roughly smear'd it to his fist, &c.]
This speech is in great measure translated from the 7th Book of
Lucan. l. 560, &c.
            Hic Cæsar, rabies populi, stimulasque furoris
            Ne qua parte sui pereat scelus, agmina circum
            It vagus, atque ignes animis flagrantibus addit.
            Inspicit et gladios, qui toti sanguine manent,
            Qui niteant primo tantum mucrone cruenti,
            Quæ presso tremat ense manus, &c.   S.

Cleave, break, and raging tempest-like o'er turn
What e'er makes head to meet them in this humour.
Our men at arms (in brief) begin to fly,
And neither prayers, intreaty, nor example
Of any of their leaders left alive,
Had power to stay them in this strange career;
Straggling, as in the fair Calabrian fields,
When, wolves for hunger ranging fro' the wood,
Make forth amongst the flock, that scattered flies
Before the shepherd, that resistless lies.

   Cornelia. O cruel fortune!

   Messenger. None resisting now,
The field was fill'd with all confusion,
Of murder, death, and direful massacres.
The feeble bands that yet were left entire
Had more desire to sleep than seek for spoil.
No place was free from sorrow, every where
Lay armed men, o'ertroden with their horses;
Dismember'd bodies drowning in their blood,
And wretched heaps lie mourning of their maims,
Whose blood, as from a spunge, or bunch of grapes,
Crush'd in a wine-press, gusheth out so fast,
As with the sight doth make the sound aghast.

   Some should you see that had their heads half cloven,
And on the earth their brains lie trembling.
Here one new wounded helps another dying.
Here lay an arm, and there a leg lay shiver'd.
Here horse and man (o'erturn'd) for mercy cry'd,
With hands extended to the merciless,
That stopp'd their ears, and would not hear a word,
But put them all (remorseless) to the sword.

   He that had hap to 'scape, doth help afresh
To reinforce the side whereon he serv'd.
But seeing that there the murd'ring enemy,
[35] Pesle-mesle pursued them like a storm of hail,

---

[35] *Pesle-mesle*] " Pell-Pell.   Confusedly, hand over head, all in a
" heape one with another."   Cotgrave, *voce Pesle-mesle.*   So, in
" Marston's *Sophonisba,* A. 1. S. 2:
    " We gave the signe of battaile : shouts are rais'd
    " That shook the heavens : *Pell-mell* our armies joyn
    " Horse, targets, pikes, all against each oppos'd."

They 'gan retire where Juba was encamp'd;
But there had Cæsar eftsoons tyranniz'd:
So that despairing to defend themselves,
They laid aside their armour, and at last
Offer'd to yield unto the enemy;
Whose stony heart, that ne'er did Roman good,
Would melt with nothing but their dearest blood.

    And Scipio, thy father, when he beheld
His people so discomfited and scorn'd;
When he perceiv'd the labour profitless,
To seek by new encouraging his men
To come upon them with a fresh alarm;
And when he saw the enemies pursuit,
To beat them down as fierce as thund'ring flints,
And lay them level with the charged earth,
Like ears of corn with rage of windy show'rs,
Their battles scatter'd, and their ensigns taken;
And, to conclude, his men dismay'd to see
The passage choak'd with bodies of the dead,
(Incessantly lamenting th' extreme loss,
And suspirable death of so brave soldiers:)
He spurs his horse, and (breaking through the press:)
Trots to the haven, where his ships he finds,
And hopeless trusteth to the trustless winds.

    Now had he thought to have arriv'd in Spain,
To raise new forces, and return to field;
But as one mischief draws another on,
A sudden tempest takes him by the way,
And casts him up near to the coasts of Hyppon,
Where th' adverse navy, sent to scour the seas,
Did hourly keep their ordinary course;
Where seeing himself at anchor slightly shipp'd,
Besieg'd, betray'd by wind, by land, by sea,
(All raging mad to rig his better vessels,
The little while this naval conflict lasted)
Behold, his own was fiercely set upon;
Which being sore beaten, till it brake again,
Ended the lives of his best fighting men.

    There did the remnant of our Roman nobles,
Before the foe, and in their captain's presence,

Die bravely, with their faulchions in their fists.
Then Scipio (that saw his ships through-gall'd,
And by the foe fulfill'd with fire and blood,
His people put to sword, sea, earth, and hell,
And heaven itself conjur'd to injure him)
Steps to the poop, and with a princely visage
Looking upon his weapon dy'd with blood,
Sighing he sets it to his breast, and said :
Since all our hopes are by the gods beguil'd,
What refuge now remains for my distress,
But thee, my dearest ne'er-deceiving sword?
Yea, thee, my latest fortune's firmest hope :
By whom I am assur'd this hap to have,
That, being free-born, I shall not die a slave.
   Scarce had he said, but cruelly resolv'd,
He drench'd it to the pommel through his sides,
That fro' the wound the smoaky blood ran bubbling,
Wherewith he stagger'd ; and I stepp'd to him
To have embrac'd him : But he (being afraid
T' attend the mercy of his murd'ring foe,
That still pursued him, and opprest his ships)
Crawl'd to the deck, and, life with death to ease,
Headlong he threw himself into the seas.
   Cornelia. O cruel gods ! O heaven ! O direful Fates !
O radiant sun, that slightly gild'st our days !
O night-stars, full of infelicities !
O triple-titled Hecate, queen and goddess,
Bereave my life, or living strangle me !
Confound me quick, or let me sink to hell !
Thrust me fro' forth the world, that 'mongst the spirits
Th' infernal lakes may ring with my laments !
O miserable, desolate, distressful wretch,
Worn with mishaps, yet in mishaps abounding !
What shall I do, or whither shall I fly,
To venge this outrage, or revenge my wrongs?
   Come, wrathful furies, with your ebon locks,
And feed yourselves with mine enflamed blood !
Ixion's torment, Sysiph's rolling stone,
And th' eagle [36] tyering on Prometheus,

[36] — *tyering*] So both the antient editions. Mr. Dodsley altered

Be my eternal tasks; that th' extream fire
Within my heart may from my heart retire.
   I suffer more, more sorrows I endure,
Than all the captives in th' infernal court.
O troubled fate! O fatal misery!
That unprovoked deal'st so partially.
   Say, fretful heavens, what fault have I committed,
Or wherein could mine innocence offend you,
When (being but young) I lost my first love Crassus?
Or wherein did I merit so much wrong,
To see my second husband Pompey slain?
But 'mongst the rest, what horrible offence,
What hateful thing, unthought of, have I done,
That, in the midst of this my mournful state,
Nought but my father's death could expiate?
   Thy death, dear Scipio, Rome's eternal loss,
Whose hopeful life preserv'd our happiness;
Whose silver hairs encouraged the weak;
Whose resolutions did confirm the rest:
Whose end, sith it hath ended all my joys,
O heavens, at least permit, of all these plagues,
That I may finish the catastrophe;
Sith in this widowhood of all my hopes,
I cannot look for further happiness.
For both my husbands and my father gone,
What have I else to wreck your wrath upon?
   Now as for happy thee, to whom sweet death
Hath given blessed rest for life's bereaving;
O envious Julia, in thy jealous heart
Venge not thy wrong upon Cornelia.

it to *tearing*, unnecessarily and improperly. *To tire* is a term in
falconry, and signifies *to prey on*, or *tear in pieces*.
   So, in Ben Jonson's *Poetaster*, A. 4. S. 3:
      " What, and be *tir'd* on by yond' vulture?"
   The Honest Man's Fortune, by Beaumont and Fletcher, vol. X.
p. 426. Edit. 1778:
      " Ye dregs of baseness, vultures amongst men,
      " That *tire* upon the hearts of generous spirits."
   Dekkar's *Match me in London:*
      " —— the vulture *tires*
      " Upon the Eagle's heart."

But sacred ghost, appease thine ire, and see
My hard mishap in marrying after thee.
  O see mine anguish! haply seeing it,
'Twill move compassion in thee of my pains,
And urge thee (if thy heart be not of flint,
Or drunk with rigour) to repent thy self,
That thou enflam'dst so cruel a revenge
In Cæsar's heart, upon so slight a cause;
And mad'st him raise so many mournful tombs,
Because thy husband did revive the lights
Of thy forsaken bed; (unworthily)
Opposing of thy fretful jealousy
'Gainst his mishap, as it my help had been,
Or as if second marriage were a sin.
  Was never city where calamity
Hath sojourn'd with such sorrow as in this?
Was never state wherein the people stood
So careless of their conquered liberty,
And careful of another's tyranny?
  O gods, that erst of Carthage took some care,
Which by our fathers pityless was spoil'd;
When thwarting destiny at Africk walls
Did topside-turvey turn their common-wealth;
When forceful weapons fiercely took away
Their soldiers (sent to nourish up those wars;)
When (fir'd) their golden palaces fell down;
When through the slaughter th' Africk seas were dy'd,
And sacred temples quenchlessly enflam'd:
Now is our hapless time of hopes expir'd.
Then satisfy yourselves with this revenge:
Content to count the ghosts of those great captains,
Which (conquer'd) perish'd by the Roman swords.
The Hannons, the Amilcars, Asdrubals,
Especially that proudest Hannibal,
Who made the fair Thrasymene so desert:
For even those fields that mourn'd to bear their bodies,
Now (loaden) groan to feel the Roman corses.
Their earth we purple o'er, and on their tombs
We heap our bodies, equalling their ruin.
And as a Scipio did reverse their power,

They have a Scipio to revenge them on.
　　Weep therefore, Roman dames, and from henceforth
Vailing your chrystal eyes to your fair bosoms,
Rain showers of grief upon your rose-like cheeks,
And dew yourselves with spring-tides of your tears.
Weep, ladies, weep, and with your reeking sighs,
Thicken the passage of the purest clouds,
And press the air with your continual plaints.
Beat at your ivory breasts, and let your robes
(Defac'd and rent) be witness of your sorrows.
And let your hair, that wont be wreath'd in tresses,
Now hang neglectly, dangling down your shoulders,
Careless of art, or rich accoutrements.
That with the gold and pearl we us'd before,
Our mournful habits may be deck'd no more.
　　Alas! what shall I do? O dear companions,
Shall I, O shall I live in these laments?
Widow'd of all my hopes, my haps, my husbands,
And last, not least, bereft of my best father;
And of the joys mine ancestors enjoy'd,
When they enjoy'd their lives and liberty?
And must I live to see great Pompey's house,
(A house of honour and antiquity)
Usurp'd in wrong by lawless Antony?
　　Shall I behold the sumptuous ornaments,
(Which both the world and Fortune heap'd on him)
Adorn and grace his graceless enemy?
Or see the wealth that Pompey gain'd in war,
[37] Sold at a pike, and borne away by strangers?
Die, rather die, Cornelia; and (to spare
Thy worthless life, that yet must one day perish)
Let not these captains vainly lie interr'd,
Or Cæsar triumph in thine infamy,
That wert the wife to th' one, and th' other's daughter.
　　But if I die before I have entomb'd
My drowned father in some sepulchre,
Who will perform that care in kindness for me?
Shall his poor wand'ring limbs lie still tormented,

---

[37] *Sold at a pike.*] i. e. venalis sub hasta.　S.
See also Note on *The Parson's Wedding*, vol. XI. A. 2. S. 7.

Tost with the salt waves of the wasteful seas?
No, lovely father, and my dearest husband,
Cornelia must live (though life she hateth)
To make your tombs, and mourn upon your hearses;
Where, languishing, my famous faithful tears
May trickling bathe your generous sweet cinders;
And afterward (both wanting strength and moisture,
Fulfilling with my latest sighs and gasps,
The happy vessels that enclose your bones)
I will surrender my surcharged life;
And (when my soul earth's prison shall forego)
Encrease the number of the ghosts below.

Non prosunt domino, quæ prosunt omnibus, artes.

THO. KYD.

FINIS.

EDITIONS.

1. Cornelia.   At London, Printed by James Roberts, for N. L. and John Busbie, 1594, 4to.

2. Pompey the Great, his faire Cornelia's Tragedie ⁚ Effected by her Father and Husbandes downe-cast, death, and fortune.   Written in French by that excellent Poet Ro. Garnier, and translated into English by Thomas Kid.   At London, Printed for Nicholas Ling, 1595, 4to.

EDWARD II.

CHRISTOPHER MARLOW, a writer of considerable eminence in his time, was, according to Oldys [1], born in the former part of the reign of Edward the Sixth, and received his education at Cambridge. The place of his birth is unknown, as are the circumstances of his parents, and the reason which induced him to quit the destination for which by the nature of his education he seemed to be intended. After leaving the university, he appeared upon the stage with applause as an actor, and then commenced dramatick writer with no inconsiderable degree of reputation. His character as a man does not appear in a favourable light. He is represented by an author [2] quoted in Wood's Athenæ, p. 338, as " giving too large a swing to his own wit, " and suffering his lust to have the full reins, by which " means he fell to that outrage and extremity as " Jodelle, a French tragical poet, did (being an Epicure " and Atheist), that he denied God and his Son Christ, " and not only in word blasphemed the Trinity, but " also, as was credibly reported, wrote divers discourses " against it, affirming our Saviour to be a deceiver, and " Moses to be a conjuror; the holy Bible also to contain " only vain and idle sories, and all religion but a device " of policy [3]." A late writer [4] is willing to believe,

[1] MS. Additions of Langbaine.
[2] Beard's Theatre of God's Judgments.
[3] Among the papers of Lord Keeper Puckering, in the British Museum, are some which give an account of Marlow's principles and tenets.

Since the account of Marlow was written I, have seen the information of Richard Baine against him, now in the British Museum, Harl. MSS. No. 6853, in which he is charged with the offences mentioned by Beard and many others. In a marginal note it is said to have been delivered on Whitson-eve, and that in three days after Marlow came to a sudden and fearful end of his

that the whole of Marlow's offence was daring to reason
on matters of religion ; than which nothing could be a
greater crime, in the opinion of those who did not
dare to think for themselves. But the opinion of this
Gentleman will have less weight, when the violence of
his prejudices against every kind of religious establish-
ment are considered. Marlow was most probably a
dissipated, abandoned man ; and the circumstances of
his death, as related by Wood, sufficiently prove it :
" being deeply in love with a certain woman, he had for
" his rival a bawdy serving-man, one rather fit to be a
" pimp than an ingenious amoretto, as Marlow con-
" ceived himself to be. Whereupon Marlow, taking it
" to be a high affront, rushed in upon, to stab him with
" his dagger : but the serving-man, being very quick,
" so avoided the stroke, that withal catching hold of
" Marlow's wrist, he stabbed his own dagger into his
" own head, in such sort that, notwithstanding all the
" means of surgery that could be wrought, he shortly
" after died of his wound before the year 1593." *

As a writer, Marlow's character stands in a much
fairer light. Langbaine[5] observes, that he was accounted an excellent poet by Jonson ;[6] and Heywood,
his fellow-actor, stiles him the best of poets. Meres[7]
names him with Sydney, Spenser, Shakspeare, Daniel,

life. This event probably occasioned there being no proceedings
carried on in consequence of the application. S.

[4] Berkenhout's Historia Literaria, vol. I. p. 358.

* Sir W. Vaughan who wrote it in 1599, though his Golden
Grove was not printed till 1608, repeats Beard's story of Marlow's
blasphemies, but he had been previously charged with being an
Atheist and an upholder of the religion of the Heathen, by T. B.
who translated the French Academie in 1594. Marlow was then
recently dead, and the precise period of this event has been ascer-
tained very lately by consulting the Burial Registers of St.Nicholas,
Deptford, where the following entry is made :—

" June 1st. 1593, Christopher Marlow, slain by Francis
Archer." C.

[5] P. 342.

[6] Verses to the Memory of Shakspeare.

[7] Second Part of Wit's Commonwealth, p. 280.

&c. for having mightily enriched and gorgeously invested in rare ornaments, and resplendent habiliments the English tongue. Carew[8], the Cornish Antiquary, places him along with Shakspeare, where he says, " Would you read Catullus, take Shakspeare and " Marlow's fragments." Nash[9], speaking of Hero and Leander, says, " Of whom divine Musæus sung, and a " diviner Muse than he, Kit Marlow." The author of *The Return from* [10] *Parnassus* characterizes him thus :

" Marlowe was happy in his buskin'd Muse,
" Alas! unhappy in his life and end ::
" Pity it is that wit so ill should dwell,
" Wit lent from heav'n, but vices sent from hell."

Drayton[11] in these terms :

"Next Marlow, bathed in the Thespian springs,
" Had in him those brave translunary things,
" That your first poets had; his raptures were
" All air and fire, which made his verses clear:
" For that fine madness still he did retain,
" Which rightly should possess a poet's brain."

And George Peele, in *The Honour of the Garter*, 4to. 1593, or 99, mentions him in this manner :

" ⸺ unhappy in thy end
" Marlow, the Muses darling for thy verse,
" Fit to write passions for the souls below
" If any wretched souls in passions speak." *

---

[8] Excellencies of the English Tongue, p. 13.
[9] Lenten Stuff, 4to. 1599, p. 42.
[10] 1606, A. 1. S. 2 :
[11] Epistle to Mr. Henry Reynolds.
* Mr. Reed omits part of what Peele says, and spells the name differently.

And after thee
Why hie they not, unhappy in thine end
Marley, the Muses' darling for thy Verse,
Fit to write passions for the soules below,
If any wretched soules in passion speake.

Peele's expressions are the more interesting, because the ceremony commemorated took place only 26 days after the funeral of Marlow, and Peele published his poem very soon afterwards, and not in 1599, as Mr. Reed thinks possible. This production is in-

His Dramatick Works are as follow :

1. " The Tragedie of Dido Queene of Carthage.
" Played by the Children of her Majesties Chappel.
" Written by Christopher Marlowe and Thomas Nash,
" Gent," 1594, 4to.

2. " The troublesome Raigne and lamentable Death
of Edward the Second," &c. See the end of this
Volume.

3. " Tamberlaine the Greate. Who, from the state
" of a Shepherd in Scythia, by his rare and wonderful
" Conquests, became a most puissant and mighty
" Monarque," 1605, 4to. 1st Part, B. L. It was first
printed in 1590.

4. " Tamberlaine the Greate. With his impas-
" sionate furie, for the death of his Lady and Love
" faire Zenocrate : his forme of exhortation and dis-
" cipline to his three sonnes, and the manner of his
" owne death. The second Part," 4to. 1606, 4to.
" B. L.

5. " The Massacre of' Paris, with the Death of the
" Duke of Guise. A Tragedy play'd by the Right
" Honourable the Lord Admiral's Servants." 8vo. N. D.

6. " The Famous Tragedy of the rich Jew of Malta."
See vol. VIII.

7. " The Tragicall Historie of the Life and Death of
" Doctor Faustus," 1604, 4to. 1616, 4to. 1624, 4to.
with new Additions, 1631, 4to. B. L. 1663, 4to.
B. L.†

---

teresting as a very early specimen of undramatic blank verse, and
because in an address intitled, *Ad Mæcenatem Prologus,* the author
notices the following Poets :—Sir P. Sidney, E. Spenser, Sir I.
Harrington, S. Daniel, T. Campion, A. Fraunce, T. Phaer and
T. Watson. C.

† It seems doubtful whether there was not an English prose tract
on the subject of Doctor Faustus, previous to the appearance of
Marlow's Play. O. G.

In the Blacke Booke 1604, the same year as the first known
edition of Marlow's Tragedy is the following allusion to it :—" He
had a head of hayre like one of my Divells in Doctor Faustus,
when the olde Theatre crackt and frighted the audience." C.

8. " Lust's Dominion; or, The Lascivious Queen. " A Tragedy," 12mo. 1657 and 1661.*

Besides these, he was the Author of

1. Hero and Leander, translated from Musæus, with the first Book of Lucan, 4to. 1600.

This translation, or at least Marlow's part of it, must

---

* " The true Tragedie of Richard, Duke of York, and the death of good King Henrie the Sixt, with the whole contention betweene the two houses, Lancaster and Yorke." 1595, 12mo.

From this Drama (says Chalmers, Sup.Apol, p. 293) Shakespeare literally copied in many scenes the third part of Henry VI.

In Warbuton's list was a play assigned to Marlow, called the Maydens Holiday. O. G.

This play, *Lust's Dominion*, though hitherto supposed to have been written by Marlow is unquestionably not his. Some confusion is occasioned in the plot by the insertion of characters unknown to history; but the King Philip who expires in the first act is Philip II. of Spain, who did not die [Vide Watson's Philip II. vol. III. p. 332] until 1598. Marlow was killed by Archer, in 1593. If this be not sufficient, or if it should be supposed for a moment that Philip I. might be intended, there is still further and conclusive evidence to shew that Marlow could not be the author of Lust's Dominion. A tract was printed in London in 1599, [Vide Lord Somers' collection II. 505] called " A briefe and true Declaration of the Sicknesse, last words and Death of the King of Spain, Philip Second," from which various passages in the play were clearly borrowed. We will compare a few quotations from both relating to the death of the King.

" Dry your wet eyes, for sorrow wanteth force
T'inspire a breathing soul in a dead corse."   *Lust's Dom.*

" My friends and subjects your sorrowes are of no force to recover my health."—*Tract.*

——— when I am embalm'd
Apparel me in a rich royal robe ....
Then place my bones within that brazen shrine."
                                        Lust's Dominion.

" Commanding that this my bodie .... be embalm'd; then apparelled with a royal robe and so placed within this brazen shrine."—*Tract.*

——— Have care to Isabel:
Her virtue was King Philip's looking glass.
                                        Lust's Dominion.

" I pray you have a great care and regard to your sister, because she was my looking glasse."—*Tract.*

This is not similarity but identity. Whatever author may justly claim Lust's Dominion, it cannot hereafter be truly assigned to Marlow. C.

have been published before 1599, being mentioned by
several writers earlier than that year. It was entered at
Stationers Hall in 1593 and 1597; and [12] Henry
Petowe's Second Part of it appeared in 1598. Marlow's part was left unfinished, and was completed by
Chapman. Although the first Book of Lucan is mentioned in the Title-page, not a line of that author is to
be found with Marlow's Work. †

2. Certaine of Ovid's Elegies. By C. Marlow,
12mo. at Middleburgh, no date. Afterwards published, with Additions, under the title of All Ovid's
Elegies three Bookes. By C. M. at Middleburgh,
no date.

Mr. Steevens says (first volume of Shakspeare, p.
94.) that, in the forty-first of Queen Elizabeth, these
translations from Ovid were commanded by the Arch-

[12] This Author exceeds all the Panegyrists of Marlow in the ex-
travagance of his Eulogium. The following lines are taken from
his Poem :

" Marlo admir'd whose honney flowing vaine,
" No English writer can as yet attaine.
" Whose name in Fame's immortall treasurie,
" Truth shall record to endles memorie,
" Marlo late mortall, now fram'd all divine,
" What soule more happy, than that soule of thine ?
" Live still in heaven thy soule, thy fame on earth
" (Thou dead) of Marlo's Hero findes a dearth."
Again,
" What mortall soule with Marlo might contend,
" That could against reason force him stoope or bend ?
" Whose silver charming toung mov'd such delight,
" That men would shun their sleepe in still darke night,
" To meditate upon his goulden lynes,
" His rare conceyts and sweete according rimes.
" But Marlo, still admired Marlo's gon,
" To live with beautie in Elyzium,
" Immortal beautie who desires to heare,
" His sacred Poesies sweete in every eare :
" Marlo must frame to Orpheus melodie,
" Himnes all divine to make heaven harmonie,
" There ever live the Prince of Poetrie,
" Live with the living in eternitie."
† Mr. Malone had a copy of " Lucan's First Booke translated
line for line by Chr. Marlow."—Printed by P. Short, 1600.

bishop of Canterbury and the Bishop of London to be burnt at Stationers Hall.

He was also the Author of that beautiful Sonnet quoted in *The Merry Wives of Windsor*, A. 3. S. 1. called *The Passionate Shepherd to his Love ;* to which Sir Walter Raleigh wrote a Reply. Both these pieces are printed in Dr. Percy's *Reliques of Antient Poetry*, vol. I. p. 218*.

* Several particulars regarding Marlow, and among them the register of his burial, are to be found in the ingenious preface to the late reprint of Marlow's and Chapman's " Hero and Leander," 1606. His birth is conjectured to have occurred about the year 1562, and it is stated that he took his degree of B.A. of Benet College, Cambridge, in 1583, and of M. A in 1587. The writer of this preface doubts whether Marlow was the author of " Tamberlaine the Greate," and analyses " Lust's Dominion" at some length, remarking that the reader " can hardly fail to observe in it the variety and melody of Marlow's versification." What would have been said of it had he known, as is unquestionably the fact, that Marlow did not write a single line of that tragedy? C.

DRAMATIS PERSONÆ.

EDWARD II.
EDWARD III.
GAVESTON.
SPENCER, sen.
SPENCER, jun.
Earl MORTIMER, sen.
MORTIMER, jun.
LANCASTER.
LEICESTER.
KENT.
ARUNDEL.
WARWICK.
PEMBROKE.
Archbishop of CANTERBURY.
Bishop of WINCHESTER.
Bishop of COVENTRY.
Lord MATREVIS.
Sir JOHN of HAINAULT.
LEVUNE.
BALDOCK.
BEAMONT.
GURNIE, RICE AP HOWEL, LIGHTBORNE, ABBOT,
    MESSENGERS, &c.
Queen ISABELLA.
The LADY.

The Scene lies in England and France.

EDWARD II.*

Enter GAVESTON, *reading in a letter that was brought
him from the king.*

(E d I)

GAVESTON. *My father is deceas'd!* come, Gaveston,
And share the kingdom with thy dearest friend.
Ah! words that make me surfeit with delight!
What greater bliss can hap to Gaveston,
Than live and be the favourite of a king!
Sweet prince, I come; these, these thy amorous lines
Might have enforc'd me to have swum from France,
And, like Leander, gasp'd upon the sand,
So thou wouldst smile, and take me in thine arms.
The sight of London to mine exil'd eyes
Is as Elysium to a new-come soul;
Not that I love the city, or the men,
But that it harbours him I hold so dear,
The king, upon whose bosom let me die, (...)
And with the world be still at enmity.
What need the artick people love star-light,
To whom the sun shines both by day and night?
Farewell base stooping to the lordly peers;
My knee shall bow to none but to the king.
As for the multitude, they are but sparks,
Rak'd up in embers of their poverty,
Tanti :† I'll fan first on the wind,
That glanceth at my lips, and flieth away.
But how now, what are these?

---

* The action of this play includes the whole of the reign of Edward II., commencing with the recal of Gaveston, which happened before the funeral of Edward I. C.
† There is probably some misprint or omission here.

Enter three poor men.

Poor men. Such as desire your worship's service.

Gaveston. What canst thou do ?

1 *Poor.* I can ride.

Gaveston. But I have no horse. What art thou ?

2 *Poor.* A traveller.

Gaveston. Let me see—thou wouldst do well
To wait at my trencher, and tell me lies at dinner-
    time ;
And as I like your discoursing, I'll have you.
And what art thou ?

3 *Poor.* A soldier, that hath serv'd against the Scot.

Gaveston. Why there are hospitals for such as you ;
I have no war, and therefore, sir, be gone.

Soldier. Farewell, and perish by a soldier's hand,
That would'st reward them with an hospital.

Gaveston. Ay, ay, these words of his move me as
    much
As if a goose should play the porcupine,
And dart her plumes, thinking to pierce my breast.
But yet it is no pain to speak men fair ;
I'll flatter these, and make them live in hope.   [*Aside.*
You know that I came lately out of France,
And yet I have not view'd my lord the king ;
If I speed well, I'll entertain you all.

Omnes. We thank your worship.

Gaveston. I have some business. Leave me to my-
    self.

Omnes. We will wait here about the court. [*Exeunt.*

Gaveston. Do :—these are not men for me ;
I must have wanton poets, pleasant wits,
Musicians, that with touching of a string
May draw the pliant king which way I please :
[13] Musick and poetry are his delight ;

---

[13] *Musick and Poetry,* &c.] How exactly the Author, as the
learned Dr. Hurd observes, has painted the humour of the times
which esteemed masks and shews as the highest indulgence that
could be provided for a luxurious and happy monarch, we may see
from the entertainment provided, not many years after, for the re-

Therefore I'll have Italian masks by night,
Sweet speeches, comedies, and pleasing shows;
And in the day, when he shall walk abroad,
Like Sylvan nymphs my pages shall be clad;
My men, like satyrs grazing on the lawns,
Shall with their goat-feet dance the antick hay.
Sometimes a lovely boy in Dian's shape,
With hair that gilds the water as it glides,
Crownets of pearl about his naked arms,
And in his sportful hands an olive-tree,
To hide those parts which men delight to see,
Shall bathe him in a spring; and there hard-by,
[14] One like Acteon peeping thro' the grove
Shall by the angry goddess be transform'd,
And running in the likeness of an hart,
By yelping hounds pull'd down, shall seem to die;
Such things as these best please his majesty.
My Lord here comes; the king and the nobles,
From the parliament.   I'll stand aside.
Enter the King, LANCASTER, MORTIMER *senior,*
   MORTIMER *junior,* EDMUND *earl of* KENT, GUY
   earl of WARWICK, *&c.*
   Edward. Lancaster.
   Lancaster. My lord.
   Gaveston. That earl of Lancaster do I abhor. [*Aside.*
   Edward. Will you not grant me this? In spite of
      them
I'll have my will; and these two Mortimers,
That cross me thus, shall know I am displeas'd.
   Mortimer senior. If you love us, my lord, hate Gave-
      ston.
   Gaveston. That villain Mortimer, I'll be his death.
                                          [*Aside.*
   Mortimer junior. Mine uncle here, this earl, and I
      myself,
Were sworn unto your father at his death,

ception of King James at Althorp, in Northamptonshire; where
this very design of *Sylvan Nymphs, Satyrs,* and *Acteon,* was executed in a Masque by *Ben Jonson.*
                  Moral and Political Dialogues, vol. I. p. 194.
[14] *One like Acteon,* &c.] See *Grim the Collier of Croydon,* vol. XI.

That he should ne'er return into the realm :
And know, my lord, ere I will break my oath,
This sword of mine, that should offend your foes,
Shall sleep within the scabbard at thy need,
And underneath thy banners march who will,
For Mortimer will hang his armour up.

    Gaveston. Mort dieu.   [*Aside.*

    Edward. Well, Mortimer, I'll make thee rue these
        words.

Beseems it thee to contradict thy king?
Frown'st thou thereat, aspiring Lancaster?
The sword shall plain the furrows of thy brows,
And hew these knees that now are grown so stiff.
I will have Gaveston; and you shall know
What danger 'tis to stand against your king.

    Gaveston. Well done, Ned.   [*Aside.*

    Lancaster. My lord, why do you thus incense your
        peers,

That naturally would love and honour you?
But for that base and obscure Gaveston,
Four earldoms have I, besides Lancaster,
Derby, Salisbury, Lincoln, Leicester;
These will I sell, to give my soldiers pay,
Ere Gaveston shall stay within the realm.
Therefore, if he be come, expel him straight.

    Edward. Barons and earls, your pride hath made me
        mute;

But now I'll speak, and to the proof, I hope.
I do remember, in my father's days,
Lord Piercy of the North, being highly mov'd,
Brav'd Moubery in presence of the king;
For which, had not his highness lov'd him well,
He should have lost his head; but with his look
Th' undaunted spirit of Piercy was appeas'd,
And Moubery and he were reconcil'd.
Yet dare you brave the king unto his face :
Brother, revenge it, and let these their heads,
Preach upon poles, for trespass of their tongues.*

---

    * I rather think we should read — *Perch* upon poles, &c.; but see
the same expression afterwards.

Warwick. ·O, our heads!

Edward. Ay, yours; and therefore I would wish you
    grant—

Warwick. Bridle thy anger, gentle Mortimer.

Mortimer junior. I cannot, nor I will not; I must
    speak.

Cousin, our hands I hope shall fence our heads,

And strike off his that makes you threaten us.

Come, uncle, let us leave the brainsick king,

And henceforth parly with our naked swords.

Mortimer senior. Wiltshire hath men enough to save
    our heads.

Warwick. All Warwickshire will love him for my
    sake.

Lancaster. And northward Gaveston hath many
    friends.

Adieu, my lord, and either change your mind,

Or look to see the throne, where you should sit,

To float in blood; and at thy wanton head,

The glozing[15] head of thy base minion thrown.

                              [*Exeunt nobles.*

Edward. I cannot brook these haughty menaces:

And I a king, and must be over-rul'd?

Brother, display my ensigns in the field;

I'll bandy[16] with the barons and the earls,

And either die or live with Gaveston.

Gaveston. I can no longer keep me from my lord.

Edward. What, Gaveston! welcome—Kiss not my
    hand.

Embrace me, Gaveston, as I do thee.

Why should'st thou kneel?

Know'st thou not who I am?

Thy friend, thyself, another Gaveston!

Not Hilas was more mourn'd for Hercules,

Than thou hast been of me since thy exile.

---

15 *glozing*] Flattering. See Note 22 to *Alexander and Campaspe.*

16 *bandy*] Oppose with all my force, *totis viribus se opponere*,
says Skinner, voce *bandy.*

Gaveston. And since I went from hence, no soul in
    hell
Hath felt more torment than poor Gaveston.
    Edward. I know it—Brother, welcome home my
    friend.
Now let the treach'rous Mortimers conspire,
And that high-minded earl of Lancaster:
I have my wish, in that I joy thy sight;
And sooner shall the sea o'erwhelm my land,
Than bear the ship that shall transport thee hence.
I here create thee lord high chamberlain,
Chief secretary to the state and me,
Earl of Cornwall, king and lord of Man.
    Gaveston. My lord, these titles far exceed my worth.
    Kent. Brother, the least of these may well suffice
For one of greater birth than Gaveston.
    Edward. Cease, brother; for I cannot brook these
    words.
Thy worth, sweet friend, is far above my gifts,
Therefore, to equal it, receive my heart;
[17] If for these dignities thou be envy'd,
I'll give thee more; for but to honour thee,
Is Edward pleas'd with kingly regiment [18].

---

[17] *If for these dignities thou be* envy'd,] That is, *hated;* in this
sense the word is frequently used.
    Green's *Thieves falling out:* " The mayd replied, that she spake
" not of *envy* to him, but of meere love she bare unto him."
    Lyly's *Euphues,* p. 47: " although I have bene bolde to invay
" against many, yet am I not so brutish *to envie* them all."
    Ben Jonson's *Devil is an Ass,* A. 2. S. 5:
        " —— And, I am justly pay'd,
        " That might have made my profit of his service,
        " But by mistaking have drawn on *his envy,*
        " And done the worst defeat upon myself."
    See also Mr. Steevens's Note on the *Merchant of Venice,* A. 4.
S. 1.
    [18] —*kingly regiment.*] *Kingly government.*
    Euphues and his England, p. 111: " *The regiment* that they have
" dependeth upon statute law, and that is by parliament, &c."
    Again, *Antony and Cleopatra,* A. 3. S. 6:
        " And gives his potent *regiment* to a trull."
    See Mr. Steevens's Note on the last passage.

Fear'st thou thy person ? thou shalt have a guard.
Want'st thou gold ? go to my treasury.
Would'st thou be lov'd and fear'd ? receive my seal,
Save or condemn, and in our name command
What so thy mind affects, or fancy likes.

    Gaveston. It shall suffice me to enjoy your love,
Which whiles I have, I think myself as great
As Cæsar riding in the Roman street,
With captive kings at his triumphant car.
         Enter the bishop of Coventry.

    Edward. Whither goes my lord of Coventry so fast?
    Bishop. To celebrate your father's exequies.
But is that wicked Gaveston returned ?
    Edward. Ay, priest, and lives to be reveng'd on thee,
That wert the only cause of his exile.
    Gaveston. 'Tis true ? and but for reverence of these
    robes,
Thou should'st not plod one foot beyond this place.
    Bishop. I did no more than I was bound to do ;
And, Gaveston, unless thou be reclaim'd,
As then I did incense the parliament,
So will I now, and thou shalt back to France.
    Gaveston. Saving your reverence, you must pardon
    me*.
    Edward. Throw off his golden mitre, rend his stole,
And in the channel christen him anew.
    Kent. Ah, brother, lay not violent hands on him,
For he'll complain unto the see of Rome.
    Gaveston. Let him complain unto the see of hell,
I'll be reveng'd on him for my exile.
    Edward. No, spare his life, but sieze upon his
    goods ;
Be thou lord bishop, and receive his rents,
And make him serve thee as thy chaplain :
I give him thee—here, use him as thou wilt.
    Gaveston. He shall to prison, and there die in bolts.
    Edward. Ay, to the Tower, the Fleet, or where thou
    wilt.
    Bishop. For this offence, be thou accurst of God.

---

* He "lays violent hands" upon the bishop. See p. 323.

Edward. Who's there? Convey this priest to th'
    tower.

Bishop. Do, do.

Edward. But in the mean time, Gaveston, away,
And take possession of his house and goods.
Come, follow me, and thou shalt have my guard
To see it done, and bring thee safe again.

    Gaveston. What should a priest do with so fair a
    house?

A prison may best beseem his holiness.   [*Exeunt.*

Enter both the MORTIMERS, WARWICK, *and* LAN-
CASTER.

Warwick. 'Tis true! the bishop is in the Tower,
And goods and body given to Gaveston.

    Lancaster. What! will they tyrannize upon the
    church?

Ah, wicked king! accursed Gaveston!
This ground, which is corrupted with their steps,
Shall be their timeless sepulchre, or mine.

    Mortimer junior. Well, let that peevish Frenchman
    guard him sure;

Unless his breast be sword-proof, he shall die.

    Mortimer senior. How now! why droops the earl of
    Lancaster?

    Mortimer junior. Wherefore is Guy of Warwick dis-
    content?

Lancaster. That villain Gaveston is made an earl.

Mortimer senior. An earl!

Warwick. Ay, and besides lord chamberlain of the
    realm,

And secretary too, and lord of Man.

    Mortimer senior. We may not, nor we will not suffer
    this.

    Mortimer junior. Why post we not from hence to
    levy men?

Lancaster. My lord of Cornwall now, at every word!
And happy is the man, whom he vouchsafes,
[19] For vailing of his bonnet, one good look.

---

    [19] *For vailing of his bonnet,*] See Note to *The Pinner of Wakefield,*
vol. III.

Thus, arm in arm, the king and he doth march:
Nay more, the guard upon his lordship waits;
And all the court begins to flatter him.
    Warwick. Thus leaning on the shoulder of the king,
He nods, and scorns, and smiles at those that pass.
    Mortimer senior. Doth no man take exceptions at
      the slave?
    Lancaster. All stomach him, but none dare speak a
      word.
    Mortimer junior. Ah, that bewrays their baseness,
      Lancaster.
Were all the earls and barons of my mind,
We'll hale him from the bosom of the king,
And at the court-gate hang the peasant up;
Who, swoln with venom of ambitious pride,
Will be the ruin of the realm and us.
         Enter the archbishop of Canterbury.
    Warwick. Here comes my lord of Canterbury's grace.
    Lancaster. His countenance bewrays he is displeas'd.
    Archbishop. First were his sacred garments rent and
      torn,
Then laid they violent hands upon him; next
Himself imprison'd, and his goods asseiz'd:
This certify the pope;—away, take horse.
    Lancaster. My lord, will you take arms against the
      king?
    Archbishop. What need I? God himself is up in
      arms,
When violence is offer'd to the church.
    Mortimer junior. Then, will you join with us, that
      be his peers,
To banish or behead that Gaveston?
    Archbishop. What else, my lords? for it concerns
      me near;
The bishoprick of Coventry is his.
         Enter the Queen.
    Mortimer junior. Madam, whither walks your ma-
      jesty so fast?
    Queen. Unto the forest, gentle Mortimer,
To live in grief and baleful discontent;

For now my lord the king regards me not,
But doats upon the love of Gaveston.
He claps his cheeks, and hangs about his neck,
Smiles in his face, and whispers in his ears ;
And when I come he frowns, as who should say,
Go whither thou wilt, seeing I have Gaveston.

 Mortimer senior. Is it not strange, that he is thus
  bewitch'd ?

 Mortimer junior. Madam, return unto the court
  again :
That sly inveigling Frenchman we'll exile,
Or lose our lives : and yet ere that day come
The king shall lose his crown ; for we have power,
And courage too, to be reveng'd at full.

 Archbishop. But yet lift not your swords against the
  king.

 Lancaster. No ; but we'll lift Gaveston from hence.

 Warwick. And war must be the means, or he'll stay
  still.

 Queen. Then let him stay ; for, rather than my lord
Shall be oppress'd with civil mutinies,
I will endure a melancholy life,
And let him frolick with his minion.

 Archbishop. My lords, to ease all this, but hear me
  speak.
We and the rest, that are his counsellors,
Will meet, and with a general consent
Confirm his banishment with our hands and seals.

 Lancaster. What we confirm, the king will frustrate.

 Mortimer junior. Then may we lawfully revolt from
  him.

 Warwick. But say, my lord, where shall this meeting be ?

 Archbishop. At the new Temple.

 Mortimer junior. Content.

 Archbishop. And, in the meantime, I'll intreat you
  all
To cross to Lambeth, and there stay with me.

 Lancaster. Come then, let's away.

 Mortimer junior. Madam, farewell !

Queen. Farewell, sweet Mortimer; and, for my sake,
Forbear to levy arms against the king.

Mortimer junior. Ah, if words will serve; if not, I
must.   [*Exeunt.*

Enter GAVESTON *and the earl of* KENT.

Gaveston. Edmund, the mighty prince of Lancaster,
That hath more earldoms than an ass can bear,
And both the Mortimers, two goodly men,
With Guy of Warwick, that redoubted knight,
Are gone towards Lambeth—there let them remain.
                              [*Exeunt.*

Enter Nobles.

Lancaster. Here is the form of Gaveston's exile:
May it please your lordship to subscribe your name.

Archbishop. Give me the paper.

Lancaster. Quick, quick, my lord;
I long to write my name.

Warwick. But I long more to see him banish'd
hence.

Mortimer junior. The name of Mortimer shall fright
the king,
Unless he be declin'd from that base peasant.

Enter the King *and* GAVESTON.

Edward. What! are you mov'd that Gaveston sits
here?
It is our pleasure, we will have it so.

Lancaster. Your grace doth well to place him by
your side,
For no where else the new earl is so safe.

Mortimer senior. What man of noble birth can brook
this sight!
Quam male conveniunt!
See what a scornful look the peasant casts!

Pembroke. Can kingly lions fawn on creeping ants?

Warwick. Ignoble vassal! that, like Phaeton,
Aspir'st unto the guidance of the sun.

Mortimer junio. Their downfall is at hand, their
forces down:
We will not thus be fac'd and over-peer'd.

Edward. Lay hands on* that traitor Mortimer!

Mortimer senior. Lay hands on that traitor Gaveston!

Kent. Is this the duty that you owe your king?

Warwick. We know our duties,—let him know his
  peers.

Edward. Whither will you bear him? Stay, or ye
  shall die.

Mortimer senior. We are no traitors, therefore
  threaten not.

Gaveston. No! threaten not, my lord, but pay them
  home!

Were I a king—

Mortimer junior. Thou villain! wherefore talk'st thou
  of a king,

That hardly art a gentleman by birth?

Edward. Were he a peasant, being my minion,

I'll make the proudest of you stoop to him.

Lancaster. My lord, you may not thus disparage
  us.—

Away! I say, with hateful Gaveston.

Mortimer senior. And with the earl of Kent that
  favours him.

Edward. Nay, then lay violent hands upon your king.

Here, Mortimer, sit thou in Edward's throne;

Warwick and Lancaster, wear you my crown:

Was ever king thus over-rul'd as I?

Lancaster. Learn then to rule us better, and the
  realm.

Mortimer junior. What we have done,

Our heart-blood shall maintain.

Warwick. Think you that we can brook this upstart
  pride?

Edward. Anger and wrathful fury stops my speech.

Archbishop. Why are you mov'd? be patient, my
  lord,

And see what we your counsellors have done.

---

* Here and elsewhere the measure is defective, often from the
omission of otherwise unimportant syllables. We ought to read
" upon" instead of " on." C.

Mortimer junior. My lords, now let us all be resolute,
And either have our wills, or lose our lives.

Edward. Meet you for this? proud over-daring peers!
Ere my sweet Gaveston shall part from me,
This isle shall [20] fleet upon the ocean,
And wander to the unfrequented Inde!

Archbishop. You know that I am legate to the pope;
On your allegiance to the see of Rome,
Subscribe, as we have done, to his exile.

Mortimer junior. Curse him, if he refuse; and then
may we
Depose him, and elect another king.

Edward. Ay, there it goes—but yet I will not yield:
Curse me, depose me, do the worst you can!

Lancaster. Then linger not, my lord, but do it
straight.

Archbishop. Remember how the bishop was abus'd!
Either banish him that was the cause thereof,
Or I will presently discharge these lords
Of duty and allegiance due to thee.

Edward. It boots me not to threat—I must speak
fair:
The legate of the pope will be obey'd.   [*Aside.*
My lord, you shall be chancellor of the realm;
Thou, Lancaster, high admiral of our fleet;
Young Mortimer and his uncle shall be earls;
And you, lord Warwick, president of the North;
And thou of Wales. If this content you not,
Make several kingdoms of this monarchy,
And share it equally amongst you all;
So I may have some nook or corner left,
To frolick with my dearest Gaveston.

Archbishop. Nothing shall alter us—we are resolv'd.

Lancaster. Come, come, subscribe.

Mortimer junior. Why should you love him,

[20] —*fleet*] *Fleet* is the old word for *float.* See Notes by Mr.
Steevens, Mr. Tollet, and Mr. Tyrwhitt, on *Antony and Cleopatra,*
A. 3. S. II.

Whom the world hates so ?

Edward. Because he loves me more than all the
world.
Ah ! none but rude and savage-minded men,
Would seek the ruin of my Gaveston;
You that be noble born should pity him.

Warwick. You that are princely born should shake
him off ;
For shame, subscribe ! and let the loon depart.

Mortimer senior. Urge him, my lord.

Archbishop. Are you content to banish him the
realm ?

Edward. I see I must, and therefore am content :
Instead of ink, I'll write it with my tears.

Mortimer junior. The king is love-sick for his minion.

Edward. 'Tis done—and now, accursed hand ! fall
off !

Lancaster. Give it me—I'll have it publish'd in the
streets.

Mortimer junior. I'll see him presently dispatch'd
away.

Archbishop. Now is my heart at ease.

Warwick. And so is mine.

Pembroke. This will be good news to the common
sort.

Mortimer senior. Be it or no, he shall not linger here.

[*Exeunt Nobles.*

Edward. How fast they run to banish him I love !
They would not stir, were it to do me good.
Why should a king be subject to a priest ?
Proud Rome ! that hatchest such imperial grooms,
For these thy superstitious taper-lights,
Wherewith thy Antichristian churches blaze,
I'll fire thy crased buildings, and enforce
Thy papal towers to kiss the lowly ground !
With slaughter'd priests may Tyber's channel swell,
And banks raise higher with their sepulchres !
As for the peers, that back the clergy thus,
If I be king, not one of them shall live.

Enter GAVESTON*.

Gaveston. My lord, I hear it whisper'd every-where,
That I am banish'd, and must fly the land.

    Edward. 'Tis true, sweet Gaveston—Oh! were it,
      were it false!
The legate of the pope will have it so,
And thou must hence, or I shall be depos'd.
But I will reign to be reveng'd of them;
And therefore, sweet friend, take it patiently.
Live where thou wilt, I'll send thee gold enough;
And long thou shalt not stay, or, if thou do'st,
I'll come to thee; my love shall ne'er decline.

    Gaveston. Is all my hope turn'd to this hell of grief?

    Edward. Rend not my heart with thy too piercing
      words:
Thou from this land, I from myself am banish'd.

    Gaveston. To go from hence grieves not poor
      Gaveston;
But to forsake you, in whose gracious looks
The blessedness of Gaveston remains;
For no where else seeks he felicity.

    Edward. And only this torments my wretched soul,
That, whether I will or no, thou must depart.
Be governor of Ireland in my stead,
And there abide till fortune call thee home.
Here, take my picture, and let me wear thine.
O, might I keep thee here, as I do this,
Happy were I! but now most miserable!

    Gaveston. 'Tis something to be pitied of a king.

    Edward. Thou shalt not hence—I'll hide thee,
      Gaveston.

    Gaveston. I shall be found, and then 'twill grieve me
      more.

    Edward. Kind words, and mutual talk, makes our
      grief greater:
Therefore, with dumb embracement, let us part—
Stay, Gaveston, I cannot leave thee thus.

---

  * The *exit* of Gaveston is not marked, but it takes place probably shortly before Edward signs his banishment. C.

Gaveston. For every look, my love drops down a tear :
Seeing I must go, do not renew my sorrow.

Edward. The time is little that thou hast to stay,
And therefore give me leave to look my fill :
But come, sweet friend, I'll bear thee on thy way.

Gaveston. The peers will frown.

Edward. I pass not for their anger—Come let's go ;
O that we might as well return as go !

Enter EDMUND* *and* QUEEN ISABEL.

Queen. Whither goes my lord ?

Edward. Fawn not on me, French strumpet ! get
thee gone.

Queen. On whom but on my husband should I fawn ?

Gaveston. On Mortimer ! with whom, ungentle
queen—
I say no more—judge you the rest, my lord.

Queen. In saying this thou wrong'st me, Gaveston :
Is't not enough that thou corrupt'st my lord,
And art a bawd to his affections,
But thou must call mine honour thus in question ?

Gaveston. I mean not so ; your grace must pardon
me.

Edward. Thou art too familiar with that Mortimer,
And by thy means is Gaveston exil'd ;
But I would wish thee reconcile the lords,
Or thou shalt ne'er be reconcil'd to me.

Queen. Your highness knows it lies not in my power.

Edward. Away then! touch me not—Come Gaveston.

Queen. Villain ! 'tis thou that robb'st me of my lord.

Gaveston. Madam ! 'tis you that rob me of my lord.

Edward. Speak not unto her ; let her droop and
pine.

Queen. Wherein, my lord, have I deserv'd these
words ?
Witness the tears that Isabella sheds,

---

* Edmund means Edmund Earl of Kent, but in other parts of
the play he is often called Kent. In this scene he seems merely a
mute.

Witness this heart, that, sighing for thee, breaks,
How dear my lord is to poor Isabel.
    Edward. And witness heaven how dear thou art to
        me!
There weep: for till my Gaveston be repeal'd,
Assure thyself thou com'st not in my sight.
               [*Exeunt Edward and Gaveston.*
    Queen. O miserable and distressed queen!
Would, when I left sweet France, and was embark'd,
That charming Circe, walking on the waves,
Had chang'd my shape, or at the marriage-day
The cup of Hymen had been full of poison,
Or with those arms, that twin'd about my neck,
I had been stifled, and not liv'd to see
The king my lord thus to abandon me!
Like frantick Juno will I fill the earth
With ghastly murmur of my sighs and cries;
For never doated Jove on Ganymede
So much as he on cursed Gaveston.
But that will more exasperate his wrath:
I must intreat him, I must speak him fair,
And be a means to call home Gaveston:
And yet he'll ever doat on Gaveston;
And so am I for ever miserable.
               Enter the Nobles.
    Lancaster. Look where the sister* of the king of
        France
Sits wringing of her hands, and beats her breast!
    Warwick. The king, I fear, hath ill-treated her.
    Pembroke. Hard is the heart that injures such a
        saint.
    Mortimer junior. I know 'tis 'long of Gaveston she
        weeps.
    Mortimer senior. Why, he is gone.
    Mortimer junior. Madam, how fares your grace?
    Queen. Ah, Mortimer! now breaks the king's hate
        forth,
And he confesseth that he loves me not.

            * Qu. Daughter. O. G.

Mortimer junior. Cry quittance, madam, then; and
    love not him.

Queen. No, rather will I die a thousand deaths:
And yet I love in vain—he'll ne'er love me.

Lancaster. Fear ye not, madam: now his minion's
    gone,
His wanton humour will be quickly left.

Queen. Oh never! Lancaster: I am enjoin'd
To sue unto you all for his repeal;
This wills my lord, and this must I perform,
Or else be banish'd from his highness' presence.

Lancaster. For his repeal, madam! he comes not
    back,
Unless the sea cast up his shipwreck'd body.

Warwick. And to behold so sweet a sight as that,
There's none here, but would run his horse to death.

Mortimer junior. But, madam, would you have us
    call him home?

Queen. Ay, Mortimer; for till he be restor'd
The angry king hath banish'd me the court;
And therefore, as thou lov'st and tender'st me,
Be thou my advocate unto these peers.

Mortimer junior. What! would you have me plead
    for Gaveston?

Mortimer senior. Plead for him he that will, I am
    resolv'd.

Lancaster. And so am I, my lord; dissuade the
    queen.

Queen. O Lancaster! let him dissuade the king,
For 'tis against my will he should return.

Warwick. Then speak not for him, let the peasant
    go.

Queen. 'Tis for myself, I speak, and not for him.

Pembroke. No speaking will prevail, and therefore
    cease.

Mortimer junior. Fair queen, forbear to angle for the
    fish,
Which, being caught, strikes him that takes it dead;
I mean that vile Torpedo, Gaveston,
That now I hope floats on the Irish seas.

Queen. Sweet Mortimer, sit down by me awhile,
And I will tell thee reasons of such weight,
As thou wilt soon subscribe to his repeal.
    Mortimer junior. It is impossible; but speak your
      mind.
    Queen. Then thus; but none shall hear it but our-
      selves.
    Lancaster. My lords, albeit the queen win Mortimer,
Will you be resolute, and hold with me?
    Mortimer senior. Not I, against my nephew.
    Pembroke. Fear not, the queen's words cannot alter
      him.
    Warwick. No, do but mark how earnestly she
      pleads.
    Lancaster. And see how coldly his looks make de-
      nial.
    Warwick. She smiles, now for my life his mind is
      chang'd.
    Lancaster. I'll rather lose his friendship I, than
      grant.
    Mortimer junior. Well, of necessity it must be so.
My lords, that I abhor base Gaveston,
I hope your honours make no question,
And therefore, tho' I plead for his repeal,
'Tis not for his sake, but for our avail:
Nay, for the realm's behoof, and for the king's.
    Lancaster. Fie, Mortimer, dishonour not thyself;
Can this be true, 'twas good to banish him?
And is this true to call him home again?
Such reasons make white black, and dark night day.
    Mortimer junior. My lord of Lancaster, mark the re-
      spect.
    Lancaster. In no respect can contraries be true.
    Queen. Yet, good my lord, hear what he can alledge.
    Warwick. All that he speaks is nothing, we are re-
      solv'd.
    Mortimer junior. Do you not wish that Gaveston
      were dead?
    Pembroke. I would he were.

Mortimer junior. Why then, my lord, give me but
    leave to speak.

Mortimer senior. But, nephew, do not play the so-
    phister.

Mortimer junior. This which I urge is of a burning
    zeal,

To mend the king, and do our country good.
Know you not Gaveston hath store of gold,
Which may in Ireland purchase him such friends,
As he will front the mightiest of us all?
And whereas he shall live and be belov'd,
'Tis hard for us to work his overthrow.

Warwick. Mark you but that, my lord of Lancaster.

Mortimer junior. But were he here, detested as he is,
How easily might some base slave be suborn'd,
To greet his lordship with a ponyard,
And none so much as blame the murderer,
But rather praise him for that brave attempt,
And in the chronicle enrol his name,
For purging of the realm of such a plague?

Pembroke. He saith true.

Lancaster. Ay, but how chance this was not done
    before?

Mortimer junior. Because, my lords, it was not
    thought upon:

Nay, more, when he shall know it lies in us
To banish him, and then to call him home;
'Twill make him vail the top-flag of his pride,
And fear to offend the meanest nobleman.

Mortimer senior. But how if he do not, nephew?

Mortimer junior. Then may we with some colour rise
    in arms:

For, howseover we have born it out,
'Tis treason to be up against the king;
So shall we have the people on our side,
Which for his father's sake lean to the king,
But cannot brook a night-grown mushrump,
Such a one as my lord of Cornwal is,
Should bear us down of the nobility.

And when the commons and the nobles join,
'Tis not the king can buckler Gaveston,
We'll pull him from the strongest hold he hath.
My lords if to perform this I be slack,
Think me as base a groom as Gaveston.

Lancaster. On that condition, Lancaster will grant.

Warwick. And so will Pembroke and I.

Mortimer senior. And I.

Mortimer junior. In this I count me highly gratify'd,
And Mortimer will rest at your command.

Queen. And when this favour Isabel forgets,
Then let her live abandon'd and forlorn.
But see in happy time, my lord the king,
Having brought the earl of Cornwal on his way,
Is new return'd: this news will glad him much;
Yet not so much as me; I love him more
Than he can Gaveston; would he lov'd me
But half so much, then were I treble bless'd!

   Enter king EDWARD, *mourning.*

Edward. He's gone, and for his absence thus I
  mourn.
Did never sorrow go so near my heart,
As doth the want of my sweet Gaveston!
And could my crown's revenue bring him back,
I would freely give it to his enemies,
And think I gain'd, having bought so dear a friend.

Queen. Hark! how he harps upon his minion.

Edward. My heart is as an anvil unto sorrow,
Which beats upon it like the Cyclops hammers,
And with the noise turns up my giddy brain,
And makes me frantick for my Gaveston.
Ah! had some bloodless fury rose from hell,
And with my kingly scepter struck me dead,
When I was forc'd to leave my Gaveston.

Lancaster. Diablo, what passions call you these?

Queen. My gracious lord, I come to bring you news.

Edward. That you have parly'd with your Mortimer?

Queen. That Gaveston, my lord, shall be repeal'd.

Edward. Repeal'd! the news is too sweet to be
  true!

Queen. But will you love me, if you find it so?

Edward. If it be so, what will not Edward do?

Queen. For Gaveston, but not for Isabel.

Edward. For thee, fair queen, if thou lov'st Gave-
    ston;
I'll hang a golden tongue about thy neck,
Seeing thou hast pleaded with so good success.

Queen. No other jewels hang about my neck
Than these, my lord; nor let me have more wealth
Than I may fetch from this rich treasure—
O how a kiss revives poor Isabel!

Edward. Once more receive my hand; and let this
    be
A second marriage 'twixt thyself and me.

Queen. And may it prove more happy than the first!
My gentle lord, bespeak these nobles fair,
That wait attendance for a gracious look,
And on their knees salute your majesty.

Edward. Courageous Lancaster, embrace thy king,
And as gross vapours perish by the sun,
Even so let hatred with thy sovereign's smile!
Live thou with me as my companion.

Lancaster. This salutation overjoys my heart.

Edward. Warwick shall be my chiefest counsellor;
These silver hairs will more adorn my court,
Than gaudy silks, or rich embroidery.
Chide me, sweet Warwick, if I go astray.

Warwick. Slay me, my lord, when I offend your grace.

Edward. In solemn triumphs, and in publick shows,
Pembroke shall bear the sword before the king.

Pembroke. And with this sword Pembroke will fight
    for you.

Edward. But wherefore walks young Mortimer aside?
Be thou commander of our royal fleet;
Or, if that lofty office [21] like thee not,
I make thee here lord marshal of the realm.

Mortimer junior. My lord, I'll marshall so your
    enemies,

[21] — *like thee not,*] See the Note to *Cornelia*, p. 247.

As England shall be quiet, and you safe.

Edward. And as for you, lord Mortimer of Chirke*,
Whose great atchievements in our foreign war
Deserve no common place, nor mean reward;
Be you the general of the levied troops,
That now are ready to assail the Scots.

Mortimer senior. In this your grace hath highly honour'd me,
For with my nature war doth best agree.

Queen. Now is the king of England rich and strong,
Having the love of his renowned peers.

Edward. Ay, Isabel, ne'er was my heart so light.
Clerk of the crown, direct our warrant forth,
For Gaveston to Ireland: Beamont, fly,
As fast as Iris, or Jove's Mercury!

Beamont. It shall be done, my gracious lord.

Edward. Lord Mortimer, we leave you to your
charge.
Now let us in, and feast it royally,
Against our friend the earl of Cornwal comes:
We'll have a general tilt and tournament;
And then his marriage shall be solemniz'd.
For wot you not that I have made him sure
Unto our cousin, the earl of Glou'ster's heir?

Lancaster. Such news we hear, my lord.

Edward. That day, if not for him, yet for my sake,
Who in the triumph will be challenger,
Spare for no cost, we will requite your love.

Warwick. In this, or aught your highness shall
command us.

Edward. Thanks, gentle Warwick: come, let's in
and revel.   [*Exeunt.*
Manent MORTIMERS.

Mortimer senior. Nephew, I must to Scotland; thou
stay'st here.
Leave now to oppose thyself against the king,
Thou seest by nature he is mild and calm;
And, seeing his mind so doats on Gaveston,

* or Werke. O. G.

Let him without controlment have his will.
The mightiest kings have had their m'nions:
Great Alexander lov'd Hephestion;
The conquering [22] Herc'les for his Hilas wept;
And for Patroclus stern Achilles droop'd.
And not kings only, but the wisest men;
The Roman Tully lov'd Octavius;
Grave Socrates, wild Alcibiades.
Then let his grace, whose youth is flexible,
And promiseth as much as we can wish,
Freely enjoy that vain light-headed earl;
For riper years will wean him from such toys.
   Mortimer junior. Uncle, his wanton humour grieves
        not me;
But this I scorn, that one so basely born
Should by his sovereign's favour grow so pert,
And riot with the treasure of the realm.
While soldiers mutiny for want of pay,
He wears a lord's revenue on his back,
And, Midas like, [23] he jets it in the court,
With base outlandish [24] cullions at his heels,
Whose proud fantastick liveries make such show,
As if that Proteus, god of shapes, appear'd.
I have not seen a dapper jack so brisk;

[22] *Herc'les*]   All the editions read *Hector*. S. P.
   See the same allusion in the first scene between Edward and
Gaveston.
   [23] — *he jets it in the court,*]   *To jet* is *to strut about, or walk in a
supercilious, affected, or haughty manner.*
   So, in Greene's *Quip for an upstart Courtier,* &c, 1592: " — to
" see in that place such a strange headlesse Courtier *jettinge up*
" and downe like the usher of a fense-schoole about to play his
" prise."
   Ibid. " Was he not caled to be dictator from the plough, and
" after many victories, what, did he *jet* up and down the court, in
" costly garments and velvet breeches?"
   Churchyard's *Challenge,* 1593, p. 228:
      " Some in their ruffe, would *jet* about the hall."
   Dekkar's *Bel-man of London,* B 2: " how villainy *jettes* in silks,
" and like a god adorde!'
   Dekkar's *Bel-man's night-walkes,* H 4: " they *jetted* up and
" downe like proud Tragedians."
   [24] *cullions*]   See Note 87 to *Gammer Gurton's Needle.*

He wears a short Italian hooded cloak,
Larded with pearl, and, in his Tuscan cap,
A jewel of more value than the crown.
Whiles others walk below, the king and he,
From out a window, laugh at such as we,
And flout our train, and jest at our attire.
Uncle, 'tis this that makes me impatient.

 Mortimer senior. But, nephew, now you see the king
  is chang'd.

 Mortimer junior. Then so am I, and live to do him
  service;
But whilst I have a sword, a hand, a heart,
I will not yield to any such upstart.
You know my mind: come, uncle, let's away. [*Exeunt.*

  Enter SPENCER *and* BALDOCK.

 Baldock. Spencer, seeing that our lord the earl of
  Glou'ster's dead,
Which of the nobles dost thou mean to serve?

 Spencer. Not Mortimer, nor any of his side;
Because the king and he are enemies.
Baldock, learn this of me, a factious lord
Shall hardly do himself good, much less us;
But he that hath the favour of a king
May with one word advance us while we live:
The liberal earl of Cornwal is the man,
On whose good fortune Spencer's hope depends.

 Baldock. What! mean you then to be his follower?

 Spencer. No, his companion; for he loves me well,
And would have once preferr'd me to the king.

 Baldock. But he is banish'd, there's small hope of
  him.

 Spencer. Ay, for a while; but, Baldock, mark the
  end.
A friend of mine told me in secresy,
That he's repeal'd, and sent for back again;
And even now a post came from the court
With letters to our lady from the king;
And as she read she smil'd, which makes me think
It is about her lover Gaveston.

 Baldock. 'Tis like enough! for since he was exil'd

She neither walks abroad, nor comes in sight.
But I had thought the match had been broke off,
And that his banishment had chang'd her mind.

    Spencer. Our lady's first love is not wavering:
My life for thine she will have Gaveston.

    Baldock. Then hope I by her means to be preferr'd,
Having read unto her since she was a child.

    Spencer. Then, Baldock, you must cast the scholar
        off,
And learn to court it like a gentleman.
'Tis not a black coat and a little band,
A velvet-cap'd cloak, fac'd before with serge,
And smelling to a nosegay all the day,
Or holding of a napkin in your hand,
Or saying a long grace at a table's end,
[25] Or making low legs to a nobleman,
Or looking downward, with your eye-lids close,
And saying, truly an't may please your honour,
Can get you any favour with great men:
You must be proud, bold, pleasant, resolute,
And now and then stab, as occasion serves.

    Baldock. Spencer, thou know'st I hate such formal
        toys,
And use them but of meer hypocrisy.
Mine old lord while he liv'd was so precise,
That he would take exceptions at my buttons
And, being like pins' heads, blame me for the bigness;
Which made me curate-like in mine attire,
Though inwardly licentious enough,
And apt for any kind of villainy.
[26] I am none of these common pedants, I,
That cannot speak without *propterea quod.*

    Spencer. But one of those that saith, *quandoquidem,*
And hath a special gift to form a verb.

---

[25] *Or making low legs*] See Note 20 to *The Parson's Wedding,*
vol. XI.

[26] *I am none of these common pedants, I,*] Dr. Farmer observes,
that this duplication of the pronoun was formerly very common.
See several instances of it by him, Mr. Steevens, and Mr. Malone,
in Note to Second Part of *King Henry* IV. A. 2. S. 4.

Baldock. Leave off this jesting, here my lady comes.
                Enter the LADY.
 Lady. The grief for his exile was not so much,
As is the joy of his returning home.
This letter came from my sweet Gaveston :
What need'st thou, love, thus to excuse thyself?
I know thou could'st not come and visit me : [*reads.*
I will not long be from thee, tho' I die.
This argues the entire love of my lord : [*reads.*
When I forsake thee, death seize on my heart.
But stay thee here where Gaveston shall sleep.
Now to the letter of my lord the king.
He wills me to repair unto the court,
And meet my Gaveston : why do I stay,
Seeing that he talks thus of my marriage-day?
Who's there, Baldock?
See that my coach * be ready, I must hence.
 Baldock. It shall be done, madam. [*Exit.*
 Lady. And meet me at the park-pail presently.
Spencer, stay you and bear me company,
For I have joyful news to tell thee of;
My lord of Cornwal is a coming over,
And will be at the court as soon as we.
 Spencer. I knew the king would have him home again.
 Lady. If all things [27] sort out, as I hope they will,
Thy service, Spencer, shall be thought upon.
 Spencer. I humbly thank your ladyship.
 Lady. Come, lead the way ; I long till I am there.
            [*Exit.*
Enter EDWARD, *the* QUEEN, LANCASTER, MORTIMER,
 WARWICK, PEMBROKE, KENT, *attendants.*
 Edward. The wind is good, I wonder why he stays;
I fear me he is wreck'd upon the sea.

---

 * " The reign of Elizabeth is generally cited as the period when
coaches were introduced into England, and under that term carriages of every kind have been considered as included ; but long
anterior to that reign vehicles with wheels under the denomination
of chairs, cars, chariots, caroches, and whirlicotes were used in
England." Mr. Markland on Carriages in England See Ar-
chaelogia, vol. XX. C.

 [27] —*sort out,*] Succeed, or take effect. *Sortir effect.* Cotgrave.

Queen. Look, Lancaster, how passionate he is,
And still his mind runs on his minion!
   Lancaster. My lord.
   Edward. How now! what news? is Gaveston arriv'd?
   Mortimer junior. Nothing but Gaveston! what means
      your grace?
You have matters of more weight to think upon;
The king of France sets foot in Normandy.
   Edward. A trifle! we'll expel him when we please.
But tell me, Mortimer, what's thy device,
Against the stately triumph we decreed?
   Mortimer*. A homely one, my lord, not worth the
      telling.
   Edward. Pray thee, let me know it.
   Mortimer junior. But seeing you are so desirous, thus
      it is:
A lofty cedar-tree fair flourishing,
On whose top-branches kingly eagles perch,
And by the bark a canker creeps me up,
And gets unto the highest bough of all:
The motto, *Æque tandem.*
   Edward. And what is yours, my lord of Lancaster?
   Lancaster. My lord, mine's more obscure than Mor-
      timer's.
Pliny reports, there is a [28] flying fish,
Which all the other fishes deadly hate,
And therefore being pursued, it takes the air:
No sooner is it up, but there's a fowl
That seizeth it: this fish, my lord, I bear,
The motto this: *Undique mors est.*
   Edward. Proud Mortimer! ungentle Lancaster!
Is this the love you bear your sovereign?
Is this the fruit your reconcilement bears?
Can you in words make show of amity,
And in your shields display your rancorous minds?
What call you this but private libelling,
Against the earl of Cornwal and my brother?
   Queen. Sweet husband! be content, they all love you.

* *Junior* omitted.
[28] —*a flying fish,*] The *Exocætus.* See Plinii *Nat.* Hist. lib. ix. 19.

Edward. They love me not that hate my Gaveston.
I am that cedar, shake me not too much;
And you the eagles; soar ye ne'er so high,
I have the gresses[29] that will pull you down,
And *Æque tandem* shall that canker cry
Unto the proudest peer of Britainy,
Though thou compar'st him to a flying fish,
And threat'nest death whether he rise or fall;
'Tis not the hugest monster of the sea,
Nor foulest harpy, that shall swallow him.
    Mortimer junior. If in his absence thus he favours
        him,
What will he do when as he shall be present?
    Lancaster. That shall we see; look where his lord-
        ship comes.
              Enter GAVESTON.
    Edward. My Gaveston! welcome to Tinmouth! wel-
        come to thy friend!
Thy absence made me droop, and pine away;
For as the lovers of fair Danaë,
When she was lockt up in a brazen tower,
Desir'd her more, and waxt outrageous,
So did it fare with me: and now thy sight
Is sweeter far, than was thy parting hence
Bitter and irksome to my sobbing heart.
    Gaveston. Sweet lord and king, your speech pre-
        venteth mine.
Yet have I words left to express my joy:
The shepherd, nipt with biting winter's rage,
Frolicks not more to see the painted spring,
Than I do to behold your majesty.
    Edward. Will none of you salute my Gaveston?
    Lancaster. Salute him? yes; welcome, lord cham-
        berlain.
    Mortimer junior. Welcome is the good earl of
        Cornwal.
    Warwick. Welcome, lord governor of the Isle of Man.

---

[29] — *gresses*] Or, as it is more commonly written, *Jesses*, which,
Latham says, are those short straps of leather, which are fastened
" to the hawk's-legges, and so to the lease by varvels, amlets, or
" such like."

Pembroke. Welcome, master secretary.

Edmund. Brother, do you hear them?

Edward. Still will these earls and barons use me
thus?

Gaveston. My lord, I cannot brook these injuries.

Queen. Ah me! poor soul, when these begin to jar.

Edward. Return it to their throats, I'll be thy warrant.

Gaveston. Base, leaden earls, that glory in your birth,
Go sit at home and eat your tenants beef;
And come not here to scoff at Gaveston,
Whose mounting thoughts did never creep so low,
As to bestow a look on such as you.

Lancaster. Yet I disdain not to do this for you.
[*Draws.*

Edward. Treason! treason! where's the traitor?

Pembroke. Here! here! king: convey hence Gaveston, they'll murder him.

Gaveston. The life of thee shall salve this foul disgrace.

Mortimer junior. Villain! thy life, unless I miss
mine aim.

Queen. Ah! furious Mortimer, what hast thou done?

Mortimer. No more than I would answer, were he
slain.

Edward. Yes, more than thou canst answer, though
he live;
Dear shall you both abide this riotous deed.
Out of my presence! come not near the court!

Mortimer junior. I'll not be barr'd the court for Gaveston.

Lancaster. We'll hale him by the ears unto the block.

Edward. Look to your own heads; his is sure enough.

Warwick. Look to your own crown, if you back him
thus.

Edmund. Warwick, these words do ill beseem thy
years.

Edward. Nay all of them conspire to cross me thus;
But, if I live, I'll tread upon their heads,
That think with high looks thus to tread me down.
Come, Edmund, let's away, and levy men,

'Tis war that must abate these barons' pride.

[*Exit the King*.

Warwick. Let's to our castles, for the king is mov'd.

Mortimer Junior. Mov'd may he be, and perish in his wrath!

Lancaster. Cousin, it is no dealing with him now,
He means to make us stoop by force of arms;
And therefore let us jointly here protest,
To prosecute that Gaveston to the death.

Mortimer junior. By heaven! the abject villain shall not live.

Warwick. I'll have his blood, or die in seeking it.

Pembroke. The like oath Pembroke takes.

Lancaster. And so doth Lancaster.
Now send our heralds to defie the king;
And make the people swear to put him down.

Enter a Post.

Mortimer junior. Letters! from whence?

Messenger. From Scotland, my lord.

Lancaster. Why, how now, cousin, how fare all our friends?

Mortimer junior. My uncle's taken prisoner by the Scots.

Lancaster. We'll have him ransom'd, man; be of good cheer.

Mortimer junior. They rate his ransom at five thousand pound.
Who should defray the money but the king,
Seeing he is taken prisoner in his wars?
I'll to the king.

Lancaster. Do, cousin; and I'll bear thee company.

Warwick. Mean time, my lord of Pembroke and myself
Will to Newcastle here, and gather head.

Mortimer junior. About it then, and we will follow you.

Lancaster. Be resolute and full of secresy.

Warwick. I warrant you.

Mortimer Junior. Cousin, and if he will not ransom him,

I'll thunder such a peal into his ears,
As never subject did unto his king.

    Lancaster. Content, I'll bear my part—Holla! who's
        there?

    Mortimer junior. Ay, marry, such a guard as this
        doth well.

    Lancaster. Lead on the way.

    Guard. Whither will your lordships?

    Mortimer junior. Whither else but to the king?

    Guard. His highness is dispos'd to be alone.

    Lancaster. Why, so he may; but we will speak to
        him.

    Guard. You may not in, my lord.

    Mortimer junior. May we not?

               Enter EDWARD.

    Edward. How now! what noise is this!
Who have we there, is't you?

    Mortimer junior. Nay, stay, my lord, I come to bring
        you news;
Mine uncle is taken prisoner by the Scots.

    Edward. Then ransom him.

    Lancaster. 'Twas in your wars, you should ransom
        him.

    Mortimer junior. And you shall ransom him, or
        else—

    Edmund. What! Mortimer, you will not threaten
        him?

    Edward. Quiet yourself, you shall have the broad seal,
To gather for him throughout the realm.

    Lancaster. Your minion Gaveston hath taught you
        this.

    Mortimer junior. My lord, the family of the Mortimers
Are not so poor, but, would they sell their land,
Could levy men enough to anger you.
We never beg, but use such prayers as these.

    Edward. Shall I still be haunted thus?

    Mortimer junior. Nay, now you are here alone, I'll
        speak my mind.

    Lancaster. And so will I; and then, my lord,
        farewell.

Mortimer junior. The idle triumphs, masks, lascivious
   shows,
And prodigal gifts bestow'd on Gaveston,
Have drawn thy treasure dry, and made thee weak ;
The murmuring commons, overstretched, break [30].
   Lancaster. Look for rebellion, look to be depos'd ;
Thy garrisons are beaten out of France,
And, lame and poor, lie groaning, at the gates.
The wild Oneyle, with swarms of [31] Irish kerns,

[30] *break*] All the editions read *hath*.

[31] *Irish kerns,*] " *Kern* in Ireland is a kind of foot souldier lightly
" armed with a dart or skeyn." Blount's *Glossary.* " *The kerne,*"
" says Barnaby Ryche, in his *Description of Ireland.* 1610, p. 37.
" are the very drosse and scum of the countrey, a generation of vil-
" laines not worthy to live : these be they that live by robbing and
" spoiling the poore countreyman, that maketh him many times to
" buy bread to give unto them, though he want for himselfe and his
" poore children. These are they, that are ready to run out with
" everie rebell ; and these are the verie hags of hell, fit for nothing but
" for the gallows." The following description of the Irish in general,
and of the dress of the *Kern* in particular, is extracted from the
Second Part of *The Image of Irelande,* by John Derricke, 4to.
B. L. 1581 :
    " This bride it is the soile,
      " the bridegrome is the *karne,*
    " With writhed glibbes like wicked sprits,
      " with visage rough and stearne.
    " With sculles upon their poules,
      " insteade of civill cappes :
    " With speares in haud, and swordes by sides,
      " to beare of after clappes.
    " With jackettes long and large,
      " whiche shrowde simplicitie:
    " Though spitfull dartes which thei do beare
      " importe iniquitie.
    " Their skirtes be verie strange,
      " not reachyng paste the thie :
    " With pleates on pleates thei pleated are,
      " as thicke as pleates maie lye.
    " Whose sleves hang trailing doune
      " almost unto the shoe :
    " And with a mantell commonlie,
      " the *Irish karne* doe goe.
    " Now some emongst the reste,
      " doe use an other weede :
    " A coate I meane of strange device,
      " which fancie first did breede.

Live uncontrol'd with the [32] English pale.
Unto the walls of York the Scots make road,
And unresisted draw away rich spoils.

    Mortimer junior. The haughty Dane commands the
        narrow seas,
While in the harbor ride thy ships unrigg'd.

    Lancaster. What foreign prince sends thee embas-
        sadors ?

    Mortimer junior. Who loves thee ? but a [33] sort of
        flatterers.

    Lancaster. Thy gentle queen, sole sister to Valoys,
Complains, that thou hast left her all forlorn.

    Mortimer junior. Thy court is naked, being bereft of
        those

        " His skirtes be verie shorte,
         " with pleates set thicke about,
        " And Irish trouzes, &c."

The same writer hath given a long detail of the manners of the
Irish kerns. See also Dr. Warburton's Note on *Macbeth*, A. 1. S. 2.

  [32] *English pale.*] " *The English pale,*" says Boate, in his *Ireland's Natural History,* 1657, p. 7. " comprehendeth onlie four
" counties, one whereof is in Ulster, viz. Louth, and the other three
" in Leinster, to wit, Meath, Dublin, and Kildare : the original of
" which division is this. The English at the first conquest, under
" the reign of Henry the Second, having within a little time con-
" quered great part of Ireland, did afterwards, in the space of not
" very many yeares, make themselves masters of almost all the rest,
" having expelled the natives (called the Wild Irish, because that
" in all manner of wildness they may be compared with the most
" barbarous nations of the earth) into the desart woods and
" mountains. But afterwards being fallen at ods among them-
" selves, and making severall great warres the one upon the other,
" the Irish thereby got the opportunitie to recover now this, and
" then that part of the land ; whereby, and through the degenerat-
" ing of a great many from time to time, who, joining themselves
" with the Irish, took upon them their wild fashions and their
" language, the English in length of time came to be so much
" weakened, that at last nothing remained to them of the whole
" kingdome, worth the speaking of, but the great cities and the
" forenamed four counties ; to whom the name of *Pale* was given,
" because that the authority and government of the kings of Eng-
" land, and the English colonies or plantations, which before had
" been spread over the whole land, now were reduced to so small a
" compass, and as it were *impaled* within the same."

  [33] — *sort*] See Note 4. to *Gammer Gurton's Needle.*

That make a king seem glorious to the world :
I mean the peers, whom thou should'st dearly love :
Libels are cast against thee in the street;
Ballads and rhimes made of thy overthrow.

 Lancaster. The Northern borderers seeing their
  houses burnt,
Their wives and children slain, run up and down,
Cursing the name of thee and Gaveston.

 Mortimer junior. When wert thou in the field with
  banner spread ?
But once : and then thy soldiers march'd like players,
With [34] garish robes, not armor ; and thyself,
Bedaub'd with gold, rode laughing at the rest,
Nodding and shaking of thy spangled crest,
Where women's favors hung like labels down.

 Lancaster. And thereof came it, that the fleering
  Scots,
To England's high disgrace, [25] have made this jig ;
[36] *Maids of England, sore may you moorn,*
For your lemmons you have lost, at Bennocks born,

---

[34] — *garish*] *Splendid, gaudy.* A word used by Shakspeare,
Richard III. A. 4. S. 4 :
  "—— a garish flag."
Romeo and Juliet, A. 3. S. 4 :
  "—— all the world shall be in love with night,
  " And pay no worship to the *garish* sun."
And by Milton, *Il Penseroso,* l. 141 :
  " Hide me from day's *garish* eye."

[35] — *have made this* jig;] A *jig,* in Marlow's time, was not a
dance only, if at all, but a Ballad. In the Harleian Collection of
Old Ballads, now in the possession of Thomas Pearson, Esq. are
several under this title, as, " *A Northerne j ge, called Daintie come*
" *thou to me.*" " *A merry new jigge, or the pleasant wooing betwixt*
" *Kit and Pegge.*" " *The West Country Jigg, or A Trenchmore*
" *Galliard;*" and several others.
 Again, in *The Fatall Contract,* by Hemmings, A. 4. S. 4 :
  " Wee'l hear *jigg,*
  " How is your *ballad* titl'd."
 See also Mr. Steeven's Note on *Hamlet,* A. 3. S. 2 :

[36] *Maids of England,* &c.] In Fabian's Chronicle, p. 155. vol. II.
these verses are given with some variation. " Than the Scottes
" enflamed with pryde in derysyon of the Englishmen, made thys
" ryme as followeth :

With a heave and a ho.
What weeneth the king of England,
So soon to have won Scotland
With a rombelow ?

    Mortimer junior. Wigmore* shall fly, to set my uncle
        free.
    Lancaster. And when 'tis gone, our swords shall
        purchase more.
If ye be mov'd, revenge it as you can ;
Look next to see us with our ensigns spread.
                                [Exeunt nobles.
    Edward. My swelling heart for very anger breaks !
How oft have I been baited by these peers,
And dare not be reveng'd, for their pow'r is great !
Yet, shall the crowing of these cockerels
Affright a lion ? Edward, unfold thy paws,
And let their lives' blood slake thy fury's hunger.
If I be cruel and grow tyrannous,
Now let them thank themselves, and rue too late.
    Kent. My lord, I see your love to Gaveston
Will be the ruin of the realm and you,
For now the wrathful nobles threaten wars ;
And therefore, brother, banish him for ever.
    Edward. Art thou an enemy to my Gaveston?
    Kent. Ay, and it grieves me that I favoured him.
    Edward. Traitor, be gone! whine thou with Mortimer.
    Kent. So will I, rather than with Gaveston.
    Edward. Out of my sight, and trouble me no more !
    Kent. No marvel that thou scorn thy noble peers,
When I thy brother am rejected thus.   *[Exit.*

      " Maydens of Englande sore may ye morne,
      " For your lemmans ye have lost at Banockys borne,
        " Wyth heve a lowe.
      " What weneth the king of England,
      " So soone to have wone Scotlande,
        " Wyth rumbylowe.
    " Thys songe was after many daies song in daunces in the carols
" of the maydens and mynstrelles of Scotland to the reprofe and
" disdayne of Englyshemen, with dyvers other whych I over
" passe."
    * Mortimer junior was of Wigmore.   O. G.

Edward. Away! Poor Gaveston, that hast no friend
    but me;
Do what they can, we'll live in Tinmouth here.
And, so I walk with him about the walls,
What care I though the earls begirt us round!—
Here cometh she that's cause of all these jars.
    Enter the QUEEN, *three* LADIES, BALDOCK, *and*
        SPENCER.
Queen. My lord, 'tis thought the earls are up in arms
Edward. Ay, and 'tis likewise thought you favour them.
Queen. Thus do you still suspect me without cause?
Ladies. Sweet uncle! speak more kindly to the queen.
Gaveston. My lord, dissemble with her, speak her fair.
Edward. Pardon me, sweet! I forgot myself.
Queen. Your pardon is quickly got of Isabell.
Edward. The younger Mortimer is grown so brave,
That to my face he threatens civil wars.
Gaveston. Why do you not commit him to the Tower?·
Edward. I dare not, for the people love him well.
Gaveston. Why then we'll have him privily made
    away.
Edward. Would Lancaster and he had both carous'd
A bowl of poison to each other's health!
But let them go; and tell me what are these.
    1 *Lady.* Two of my father's servants whilst he liv'd:
May't please your grace to entertain them now?
Edward. Tell me, where wast thou born?
What is thine arms?
Baldock. My name is Baldock; and my gentry
I fetch from Oxford, not from heraldry.
Edward. The fitter art thou, Baldock, for my turn.
Wait on me, and I'll see thou shalt not want.
Baldock. I humbly thank your majesty.
Edward. Knowest thou him, Gaveston?
Gaveston. Ay, my lord, his name is Spencer, he is
    well allied;
For my sake, let him wait upon your grace;
Scarce shall you find a man of more desert.
Edward. Then, Spencer, wait upon me; for his sake

I'll grace thee with a higher stile ere long.

Spencer. No greater titles happen unto me,
Than to be favoured of your majesty.

Edward. Cousin, this dayshall be your marriage-feast.
And, Gaveston, think that I love thee well,
To wed thee to our niece, the only heir
Unto the earl of Glo'ster late deceas'd.

Gaveston. I know, my lord, many will stomach me;
But I respect neither their love nor hate.

Edward. The head-strong barons shall not limit me;
He that I list to favour shall be great.
Come, let's away; and, when the marriage ends,
Have at the rebels, and their 'complices! [*Exeunt omnes.*

Enter LANCASTER, MORTIMER *junior*, WARWICK,
PEMBROKE, *and* KENT.

Kent. My lords, of love to this our native land,
I come to join with you, and leave the king;
And in your quarrel and the realm's behoof
Will be the first that shall adventure life.

Lancaster. I fear me, you are sent of policy,
To undermine us with a shew of love.

Warwick. He is your brother, therefore have we cause
To cast the worst, and doubt of your revolt.

Edmund. Mine honour shall be hostage of my truth:
If that will not suffice, farewell, my lords.

Mortimer junior. Stay, Edmund; never was Planta-
genet
False of his word, and therefore trust we thee.

Pembroke. But what's the reason you should leave
him now?

Kent. I have inform'd the earl of Lancaster.

Lancaster. And it sufficeth. Now, my lords, know this,
That Gaveston is secretly arriv'd,
And here in Tinmouth frolicks with the king.
Let us with these our followers scale the walls,
And suddenly surprize them unawares.

Mortimer junior. I'll give the onset.

Warwick. And I'll follow thee.

Mortimer junior. This tottered ensign of my ancestors,

Which swept the desert shore of that dead sea,
Whereof we got the name of Mortimer,
Will I advance upon this castle's walls.
Drums strike alarum, raise them from their sport,
And ring aloud the knell of Gaveston!

Lancaster. None be so hardy as to touch the king;
But neither spare you Gaveston, nor his friends.

[*Exeunt.*

Enter the King *and* SPENCER; *to them* GAVESTON, &c.

Edward. O tell me, Spencer, where is Gaveston?

Spencer. I fear me he is slain, my gracious lord.

Edward. No, here he comes; now let them spoil
    and kill.
Fly, fly, my lords, the earls have got the hold,
Take shipping and away to Scarborough;
Spencer and I will post away by land.

Gaveston. O stay, my lord, they will not injure you.

Edward. I will not trust them; Gaveston, away!

Gaveston. Farewell, my lord.

Edward. Lady, farewell.

Lady .Farewell, sweet uncle, till we meet again.

Edward. Farewell, sweet Gaveston; and farewell,
    niece.

Queen. No farewell to poor Isabell thy queen?

Edward. Yes, yes, for Mortimer, your lover's sake.

[*Exeunt omnes, præter Isabella.*

Queen. Heavens can witness, I love none but you.
From my embracements thus he breaks away.
O that mine arms could close this isle about,
That I might pull him to me where I would!
Or that these tears, that drissel from mine eyes,
Had power to mollify his stony heart,
That when I had him we might never part!

Enter the BARONS. *Alarums.*

Lancaster. I wonder how he 'scap'd!

Mortimer junior. Who's this, the Queen?

Queen. Ay, Mortimer, the miserable Queen,
Whose pining heart her inward sighs have blasted,
And body with continual mourning wasted:
These hands are tir'd with haling of my lord

From Gaveston, from wicked Gaveston,
And all in vain; for, when I speak him fair,
He turns away, and smiles upon his minion.

    Mortimer junior. Cease to lament, and tell us where's
        the king.

    Queen. What would you with the king? is't him
        you seek?

    Lancaster. No, madam, but that cursed Gaveston.
Far be it from the thought of Lancaster,
To offer violence to his sovereign.
We would but rid the realm of Gaveston:
Tell us where he remains, and he shall die.

    Queen. He's gone by water unto Scarborough;
Pursue him quickly, and he cannot 'scape;
The king hath left him, and his train is small.

    Warwick. [37] Forslow no time, sweet Lancaster, let's
        march.

    Mortimer. How comes it that the king and he are
        parted?

    Queen. That thus your army, going several ways,
Might be of lesser force; and with the power
That he intendeth presently to raise,
Be easily suppress'd; therefore be gone.

    Mortimer. Here in the river rides a Flemish hoy;
Let's all aboard, and follow him amain.

    Lancaster. The wind that bears him hence will fill
        our sails:
Come, come aboard, 'tis but an hour's sailing.

    Mortimer. Madam, stay you within this castle here.

    Queen. No, Mortimer, I'll to my lord the king.

[37] *Forslow no time, sweet Lancaster, let's march,*] i. e. *Lose no time, do
not delay.*

    So, in Ben Jonson's *Every Man out of his Humour,* A. 5. S. 8:
" Now therefore, if you can think upon any present means for his
" delivery, do not *foreslow* it."

    Lyly's *Euphues,* p. 52: " Let her *foreslow* no occasion that may
" bring the childe to quyetnesse."

    The Curtain Drawer of the World, by W. Parkes, 1612, p. 8.
" How comes it then that prevention never comes? that men see
" this, yet foresee it not? that men know this, yet *foreslow it not.*"

    See also the Third Part of *King Henry* VI. A. 2. S. 3. and Mr.
Steevens's Note thereon.

Mortimer. Nay, rather sail with us to Scarborough.

Queen. You know the king is so suspicious,
As, if he hear I have but talkt with you,
Mine honour will be call'd in question;
And therefore, gentle Mortimer, be gone.

Mortimer. Madam, I cannot stay to answer you,
But think of Mortimer as he deserves.

Queen. So well hast thou deserv'd, sweet Mortimer,
As Isabell could live with thee for ever.
In vain I look for love at Edward's hand,
Whose eyes are fix'd on none but Gaveston:
Yet once more I'll importune him with prayer;
If he be strange and not regard my words,
My son and I will over into France,
And to the king my brother there complain,
How Gaveston hath robb'd me of his love:
But yet I hope my sorrows will have end,
And Gaveston this blessed day be slain.   [*Exeunt.*

Enter GAVESTON *pursued.*

Gaveston. Yet, lusty lords, I have escap'd your hands,
Your threats, your larums, and your hot pursuits;
And, tho' divorced from king Edward's eyes,
Yet liveth Pierce of Gaveston unsurpriz'd,
Breathing, in hope ([38]malgrado all your beards[39],
That muster rebels thus against your kind)
To see his royal sovereign once again.

Enter the Nobles.

Warwick. Upon him, soldiers, take away his weapons.

Mortimer junior. Thou proud disturber of thy country's peace,
Corrupter of thy king, cause of these broils,
Base flatterer, yield! and were it not for shame,
Shame and dishonour to a soldier's name,

---

[38] — *malgrado*] Ital. *maugre, in despite of* Florio's Dictionary, 1598.

[39] — *all your beards,*] To beard a person is to oppose him to his face.
Again, in this play.
    " These barons thus *to beard* me in my land." S. P.

Upon my weapon's point here should'st thou fall,
And welter in thy gore.

 Lancaster. Monster of men ! that, like the Greekish
  strumpet*,
Train'd to arms and bloody wars
So many valiant knights ;
Look for no other fortune, wretch, than death ;
King Edward is not here to buckler thee.

 Warwick. Lancaster, why talk'st thou to the slave?
Go, soldiers, take him hence ,
For by my sword his head shall off :
Gaveston, short warning shall serve thy turn.
It is our country's cause,
That here severely we will execute
Upon thy person : hang him upon a bough.

 Gaveston. My lords !—

 Warwick. Soldiers, have him away ;
But for thou wert the favourite of a king,
Thou shalt have so much honour at our hands.

 Gaveston. I thank you all, my lords : then I perceive,
That heading is one, and hanging is the other,
And death is all.

   Enter earl of ARUNDEL.

 Lancaster. How now, my lord of Arundel ?

 Arundel. My lords, king Edward greets you all by
  me.

 Warwick. Arundel, say your message.

 Arundel. His majesty, hearing that you had taken
  Gaveston,
Intreateth you by me, but that he may
See him before he dies ; for why he says,
And sends you word, he knows that die he shall ;
And, if you gratify his grace so far,
He will be mindful of the courtesy.

 Warwick. How now?

 Gaveston. Renown'd Edward, how thy name
Revives poor Gaveston !

 Warwick. No, it needeth not :
Arundel, we will gratify the king

   * Helen and the Trojan war.

In other matters, he must pardon us in this.
Soldiers, away with him.

Gaveston. Why, my lord of Warwick,
Will these delays beget me any hopes?
I know it, lords, it is this life you aim at,
Yet grant king Edward this.

Mortimer junior. Shalt thou appoint what we shall
grant?
Soldiers, away with him:
Thus we'll gratify the king,
We'll send his head by thee, let him bestow
His tears on that, for that is all he gets
Of Gaveston, or else his senseless trunk.

Lancaster. Not so, my lords, lest he bestow more
cost
In burying him, than he hath ever earn'd.

Arundel My lords, it is his majesty's request,
And on the honour of a king he swears,
He will but talk with him and send him back.

Warwick. When, can you tell? Arundel, no; we
wot,
He that the care of his realm remits,
And drives his nobles to these exigents
For Gaveston, will, if he seize him once,
Violate any promise to possess him.

Arundel. Then, if you will not trust his grace in
keep,
My lords, I will be pledge for his return.

Mortimer junior. It is honourable in thee to offer
this;
But for we know thou art a noble gentleman,
We will not wrong thee so,
To make away a true man for a thief.

Gaveston. How meanest thou, Mortimer? that is
over base.

Mortimer. Away, base groom, robber of king's renown,
Question with thy companions and thy mates.

Pembroke. My lord Mortimer, and you my lords,
each one,

To gratify the king's request therein,
Touching the sending of this Gaveston,
Because his majesty so earnestly
Desires to see the man before his death,
I will upon mine honour undertake
To carry him, and bring him back again;
Provided this, that you, my lord of Arundel,
Will join with me.

 Warwick. Pembroke, what wilt thou do?
Cause yet more bloodshed: is it not enough
That we have taken him, but must we now
Leave him on had I wist, and let him go?

  Pembroke. My lords, I will not over-woo your ho-
   nours,
But, if you dare trust Pembroke with the prisoner,
Upon my oath I will return him back.

  Arundel. My lord of Lancaster, what say you in
   this?

  Lancaster. Why I say, let him go on Pembroke's
   word.

  Pembroke. And you, lord Mortimer?

  Mortimer junior. How say you, my lord of Warwick?

  Warwick. Nay, do your pleasures,
I know how 'twill prove.

  Pembroke. Then give him me.

  Gaveston. Sweet sovereign, yet I come
To see thee ere I die.

  Warwick. Not yet perhaps,
If Warwick's wit and policy prevail.

  Mortimer junior. My lord of Pembroke, we deliver
   him you,
Return him on your honour, sound away. [*Exeunt.*
Manent PEMBROKE, MATREVIS, GAVESTON, *and*
  PEMBROKE'S *men, four soldiers.*

  Pembroke. My lord, you shall go with me.
My house is not far hence, out of the way
A little; but our men shall go along.
We that have pretty wenches to our wives,
Sir, must not come so near to baulk their lips.

  Matrevis. 'Tis very kindly spoke, my lord of Pembroke;

Your honòur hath an adamant of power
To draw a prince.
 Pembroke. So, my lord; come hither, James;
I do commit this Gaveston to thee,
Be thou this night his keeper, in the morning
We will discharge thee of thy charge; be gone.
 Gaveston. Unhappy Gaveston, whither goest thou
  now ?   [*Exit cum serv.* PEM.
 Horse-boy. My lord, we'll quickly be at Cobham.
         [*Exeunt ambo.*
Enter GAVESTON *mourning, and the earl of* PEM-
   BROKE'S *men.*
 Gaveston. O treacherous Warwick! thus to wrong
  thy friend.
 James. I see it is your life these arms pursue.
 Gaveston. Weaponless must I fall? and die in bands?
O must this day be period of my life!
Center of all my bliss! and ye be men,
Speed to the king.
   Enter WARWICK *and his company.*
 Warwick. My lord of Pembroke's men,
Strive you no more, I will have that Gaveston.
 James. Your Lordship doth dishonour to yourself,
And wrong our lord, your honourable friend.
 Warwick. No, James, it is my country's cause I
  follow.
Go, take the villain; soldiers, come away,
We'll make quick work.   Commend me to your
  master,
My friend, and tell him that I watch'd it well.
Come let thy shadow parley with king Edward.
 Gaveston. Treacherous earl! shall I not see the
  king?
 Warwick. The king of heaven, perhaps, no other
  king.
Away.
  [*Exeunt* WARWICK *and his men, with* GAVESTON.
   Manent JAMES, *cum cæteris.*
 James. Come, fellows, it booteth not for us to strive,
We will in haste go certify our lord. [*Exeunt.*

Enter King EDWARD *and* SPENCER, *with drums and fifes.*

Edward. I long to hear an answer from the barons,
Touching my friend, my dearest Gaveston.
Ah! Spencer, not the riches of my realm
Can ransom him! ah, he is mark'd to die!
I know the malice of the younger Mortimer,
Warwick I know is rough, and Lancaster
Inexorable, and I shall never see
My lovely Pierce of Gaveston again.
The barons overbear me with their pride.

Spencer. Were I king Edward, England's sovereign,
Son to the lovely Eleanor of Spain,
Great Edward Longshank's issue, would I bear
These braves, this rage, and suffer uncontrol'd
These barons thus to beard me in my land,
In mine own realm? my lord, pardon my speech,
Did you retain your father's magnanimity,
Did you regard the honour of your name,
You would not suffer thus your majesty
Be counterbuft of your nobility.
Strike off their heads, and let them preach on poles; *
No doubt, such lessons they will teach the rest,
As by their preachments they will profit much,
And learn obedience to their lawful king.

Edward. Yea, gentle Spencer, we have been too mild,
Too kind to them; but now have drawn our sword,
And, if they send me not my Gaveston,
We'll steel it on their crest, and poll their tops.

Baldock. This haught resolve becomes your majesty;
You ought not to be tied to their affection,
As though your highness were a school-boy still,
And must be aw'd and govern'd like a child.

* This is a repetition of a previous expression in the second scene, and discountenances the conjectural emendations of Mr. Reed.

Enter HUGH SPENCER *an old man, father to the young* SPENCER, *with his trunchion and soldiers.*

Spencer senior. Long live my sovereign, the noble
　　Edward,
In peace.triumphant, fortunate in wars!
　　Edward. Welcome, old man, com'st thou in Ed-
　　ward's aid?
Then tell the prince, of whence, and what thou art.
　　Spencer senior. Lo, with a band of bow-men and of
　　pikes,
40 Brown bills, and targiteers, four hundred strong,
Sworn to defend king Edward's royal right,
I come in person to your majesty,
Spencer, the father of Hugh Spencer there,
Bound to your highness everlastingly,
For favour done in him unto us all.
　　Edward. Thy father, Spencer?
　　Spencer junior. True, and it like your grace,
That pours in lieu of all your goodness shown,
His life, my lord, before your princely feet.
　　Edward. Welcome ten thousand times, old man,
　　again.
Spencer, this love, this kindness to thy king,
Argues thy noble mind and disposition.
Spencer, I here create thee earl of Wiltshire,
And daily will enrich thee with our favour,
That as the sun-shine shall reflect o'er thee.
Besides, the more to manifest our love,
Because we hear lord Bruce doth sell his land,
And that the Mortimers are in hand withal,
Thou shalt have crowns of us t'outbid the barons:
And, Spencer, spare them not, lay it on.
Soldiers, a largess and thrice welcome all.
　　Spencer. My, lord, here comes the queen.

43 *Brown bills,*] The old weapon of the English infantry, which,
" says Temple, *gave the most ghastly and deplorable wounds.* It may
" be called the *falcata securis."* Dr Johnson's Note on *Much ado
about Nothing,* A. 3. S. 3.
　　In the last edition of Shakspeare, the reader will find represen-
tations of the several kinds of *bills* which were formerly in use.

Enter the QUEEN *and her Son, and* LEVUNE *a*
Frenchman.

Edward. Madam, what news?

Queen. News of dishonour, lord, and discontent.
Our friend Levune, faithful and full of trust,
Informeth us, by letters and by words,
That Valois our brother, king of France,
Because your highness hath been slack in homage,
Hath seized Normandy into his hands.
These be the letters, this the messenger.

   Edward. Welcome, Levune. Tush, Sib, if this be
    all,
Valois and I will soon be friends again.
But to my Gaveston: shall I never see,
Never behold thee more? Madam, in this matter
We will employ you and your little son;
You shall go parley with the king of France.
Boy, see you bear you bravely to the king,
And do your message with a majesty.

   Prince. Commit not to my youth things of more
    weight
Than fits a prince so young as I to bear,
And fear not, lord and father, heaven's great beams
On Atlas' shoulder shall not lie more safe,
Than shall your charge committed to my trust.

   Queen. Ah, boy! this towardness makes thy mother
    fear
Thou art not mark'd to many days on earth.

   Edward. Madam, we will that you with speed be
    shipp'd,
And this our son; Levune shall follow you
With all the haste we can dispatch him hence.
Chuse of our lords to bear you company,
And go in peace, leave us in wars at home.

   Queen. Unnatural wars, where subjects brave their
    king;
God end them once. My lord, I take my leave,
To make my preparation for France.

            Enter lord MATREVIS.

   Edward. What, lord Matrevis, dost thou come alone?

Matrevis. Yea, my good lord, for Gaveston is dead.
    Edward. Ah, traitors! have they put my friend to
        death?
Tell me, Matrevis, died he ere thou cam'st,
Or did'st thou see my friend to take his death?
    Matrevis. Neither, my lord; for as he was surpriz'd;
Begirt with weapons, and with enemies round,
I did your highness' message to them all;
Demanding him of them, entreating rather,
And said, upon the honour of my name,
That I would undertake to carry him
Unto your highness, and to bring him back.
    Edward. And tell me, would the rebels deny me
        that?
    Spencer. Proud recreants!
    Edward. Yea, Spencer, traitors all.
    Matrevis. I found them at the first inexorable;
The earl of Warwick would not bide the hearing,
Mortimer hardly, Pembroke and Lancaster
Spake least: and when they flatly had deny'd,
Refusing to receive me pledge for him,
The earl of Pembroke mildly thus bespake;
My lords, because our sovereign sends for him,
And promiseth he shall be safe return'd,
I will this undertake, to have him hence,
And see him redeliver'd to your hands.
    Edward. Well, and how fortunes that he came not?
    Spencer. Some treason, or some villainy, was the
        cause.
    Matrevis. The earl of Warwick seiz'd him on his way.
For being deliver'd unto Pembroke's men,
Their lord rode home, thinking his prisoner safe;
But ere he came, Warwick in ambush lay,
And bare him to his death, and in a trench
Struck off his head, and march'd unto the camp.
    Spencer. A bloody part, flatly 'gainst law of arms.
    Edward. O shall I speak! or shall I sigh and die!
    Spencer. My lord, refer your vengeance to the sword
Upon these barons: hearten up your men;
Let them not unreveng'd murder your friends!

Advance your standard, Edward, in the field,
And march to fire them from their starting holes.

[Edward kneels, and saith :

Edward. By earth, the common mother of us all!
By heaven, and all the moving orbs thereof!
By this right hand! and by my father's sword!
And all the honours 'longing to my crown!
I will have heads, and lives for him, as many
As I have manors, castles, towns, and towers.
Treacherous Warwick! traiterous Mortimer!
If I be England's king, in lakes of gore
Your headless trunks, your bodies will I trail,
That you may drink your fill, and quaff in blood,
And stain my royal standard with the same,
That so my bloody colours may suggest
Remembrance of revenge immortally,
On your accursed traiterous progeny,
You villains that have slain my Gaveston.
And in this place of honour and of trust,
Spencer, sweet Spencer, I adopt thee here;
And merely of our love we do create thee
Earl of Glo'ster, and lord chamberlain,
Despite of times, despite of enemies.

Spencer. My lord, here is a messenger from the
    barons,
Desires access unto your majesty.

Edward. Admit him near.

Enter the herald from the Barons, with his coat of arms.

Messenger. Long live king Edward, England's lawful
    lord!

Edward. So wish not they I [41] wis that sent thee
    hither.
Thou com'st from Mortimer and his accomplices,
A ranker root of rebels never was.
Well, say thy message.

Messenger. The barons up in arms, by me salute
Your highness with long life and happiness;
And bid me say, as plainer to your grace,
That if without effusion of blood,

[41] —*wis*] See Note 89 to *Gammer Gurton's Needle.*

You will, this grief have ease and remedy;
That from your princely person you remove
This Spencer, as a putrifying branch,
That deads the royal vine, whose golden leaves
Empale your princely head, your diadem ;
Whose brightness such pernicious upstarts dim,
Say they, and lovingly advise your grace,
To cherish virtue and nobility,
And have old servitors in high esteem,
And shake off smooth dissembling flatterers :
This granted, they, their honours, and their lives,
Are to your highness vow'd and consecrate.
    Spencer. Ah, traitors! will they still display their
        pride ?
    Edward. Away, tarry no answer, but be gone !
Rebels, will they appoint their sovereign
His sports, his pleasures, and his company?
Yet ere thou go, see how I do divorce
                  [*Embraces Spencer.*
Spencer from me—Now get thee to thy lords,
And tell them I will come to chastise them
For murthering Gaveston : hie thee! get thee gone!
Edward, with fire and sword, follows at thy heels.
My lord, perceive you how these rebels swell?
Soldiers, good hearts, defend your sovereign's right,
For now, even now, we march to make them stoop.
Away !   [*Exeunt.*
    Alarums, excursions, a great fight, and a retreat.

Enter the KING, SPENCER *the father,* SPENCER *the
   son, and the noblemen of the king's side.*
    Edward. Why do we sound retreat? upon them,
        lords!
This day I shall pour vengeance with my sword
On those proud rebels that are up in arms,
And do confront and countermand their king.
    Spencer junior. I doubt it not, my lord, right will
      prevail.
    Spencer senior. 'Tis not amiss, my liege, for either
      part

To breathe a while; our men with sweat and dust
All choak'd well near, begin to faint for heat,
And this retire refresheth horse and man.

    Spencer junior. Here come the rebels.

Enter the barons, MORTIMER, LANCASTER, WAR-
        WICK, PEMBROKE, &c.

    Mortimer. Look, Lancaster, yonder's Edward 'mong
    his flatterers.

    Lancaster. And there let him be, till he pay dearly
    for their company.

    Warwick. And shall, or Warwick's sword shall smite
    in vain.

    Edward. What rebels, do you shrink, and sound
    retreat?

    Mortimer junior. No, Edward, no, thy flatterers faint
    and fly.

    Lancaster. Th'ad best betimes forsake thee, and
    their trains,
For they'll bewray thee, traitors as they are.

    Spencer junior. Traitor on thy face, rebellious Lan-
    caster!

    Pembroke. Away, base upstart! brav'st thou nobles
    thus?

    Spencer senior. A noble attempt! and honourable
    deed!
Is it not, trow ye, to assemble aid,
And levy arms against your lawful king?

    Edward. For which ere long their heads shall satisfy,
To appease the wrath of their offended king.

    Mortimer junior. Then, Edward, thou wilt fight it
    to the last,
And rather bathe thy sword in subjects' blood,
Than banish that pernicious company?

    Edward. Ay, traitors all, rather than thus be brav'd,
Make England's civil towns huge heaps of stones,
And plows to go about our palace-gates.

    Warwick. A desperate and unnatural resolution!
Alarum to the fight, [42] St. George for England,
And the baron's right.

[42] *St. George for England,*] See Note to *The Pinner of Wakefield,*
vol III.

Edward. St. George for England, and king Edward's right.   *[Exeunt.*

Re-enter EDWARD, *with the barons captives.*

Edward. Now, lusty lords, now, not by chance of
    war,
But justice of the quarrel, and the cause,
Vail'd is your pride; methinks you hang the heads,
But we'll advance them, traitors; now 'tis time
To be aveng'd on you for all your braves,
And for the murder of my dearest friend,
To whom right well you knew our soul was knit,
Good Pierce of Gaveston, my sweet favourite.
Ah, rebels! recreants! you made him away.

    Edmund. Brother, in regard of thee, and of thy
    land,
Did they remove that flatterer from thy throne.

    Edward. So, sir, you have spoke; away, avoid our
    presence!
Accurs'd wretches, was't in regard of us,
When we had sent our messengers to request
He might be spar'd to come to speak with us,
And Pembroke undertook for his return,
That thou, proud Warwick, watch'd the prisoner,
Poor Pierce, and headed him 'gainst law of arms;
For which thy head shall overlook the rest,
As much as thou in rage outwent'st the rest.

    Warwick. Tyrant! I scorn thy threats and menaces,
It is but temporal that thou canst inflict.

    Lancaster. The worst is death, and better die than
    live,
To live in infamy under such a king.

    Edward. Away with them! my lord of Winchester
These lusty leaders, Warwick and Lancaster,
I charge you roundly, off with both their heads, away.

    Warwick. Farewell, vain world!

    Lancaster. Sweet Mortimer, farewell.

    Mortimer junior. England, unkind to thy nobility,
Groan for this grief, behold how thou art maim'd!

    Edward. Go, take that haughty Mortimer to the
    Tower,

There see him safe bestow'd ; and for the rest,
Do speedy execution on them all.   Be gone.

 Mortimer junior. What, Mortimer! can ragged stony
   walls
Immure thy virtue that aspires to heaven ?
No, Edward, England's scourge, it may not be,
Mortimer's hopes surmounts his fortune far.

 Edward. Sound drums and trumpets, march with
   me my friends;
Edward this day hath crown'd him king anew.   [*Exit.*
 Manent SPENCER *filius,* LEWEN*, *and* BALDOCK.

 Spencer. Lewen, the trust that we repose in thee,
Begets the quiet of king Edward's land.
Therefore be gone in haste, and with advice
Bestow that treasure on the lords of France,
That therewith all enchanted, like the guard
That suffered Jove to pass in showers of gold
To Dänaë, all aid may be denied
To Isabel the queen, that now in France
Makes friends, to cross the seas with her young son,
And step into his father's regiment.

 Lewen. That's it these barons and the subtle queen
Long levied at†.

 Baldock. Yea ; but Lewen, thou seest,
These barons lay their heads on blocks together;
What they intend, the hangman frustrates clean.

 Lewen. Have you no doubt, my lords, I'll clap so
   close
Among the lords of France with England's gold,
That Isabel shall make her plaints in vain,
And France shall be obdurate with her tears.

 Spencer. Then make for France, amain—Lewen,
   away !
Proclaim King Edward's wars and victories.

          [*Exeunt omnes.*

---

 * This name is misprinted for Levune whom the Queen has previously mentioned. It must be so read for the measure. C.
 † I think we ought to read *leveld at, i.e.* aimed at. So Shakspeare.
  " Ambitious York did *level* at thy crown." S.

Enter EDMUND.

Edmund. Fair blows the wind for France; blow
    gentle gale,
Till Edmund be arriv'd for England's good!
Nature, yield to my country's cause in this.
A brother, no, a butcher of thy friends.
Proud Edward, do'st thou banish me thy presence?
But I'll to France, and chear the wronged queen,
And certify what Edward's loosness is.
Unnatural king! to slaughter noble men
And cherish flatterers! Mortimer, I stay
Thy sweet escape; stand gracious, gloomy night,
To his device.

Enter MORTIMER *junior, disguised.*

Mortimer junior. Holla! who walketh there? is't
    you, my lord?
Edmund. Mortimer, 'tis I; but hath thy potion
    wrought so happily?
Mortimer junior. It hath, my lord, the warders all
    asleep,
I thank them, gave me leave to pass in peace.
But hath your grace got shipping unto France?
Edmund. Fear it not.   [*Exeunt.*

Enter the QUEEN *and her son**.

Queen. Ah, boy, our friends do fail us all in France;
The lords are cruel, and the king unkind†;
What shall we do?
Prince. Madam, return to England,
And please my father well; and then a fig
For all my uncle's friendship here in France.
I warrant you, I'll win his highness quickly;
He loves me better than a thousand Spencers.
Queen. Ah, boy, thou art deceiv'd, at least in this,
To think that we can yet be tun'd together:
No, no, we jar too far. Unkind Valois!
Unhappy Isabel! when France rejects,
Whither, O whither dost thou bend thy steps?

* The scene changes to France. C.
† Charles the 5th her brother. O. G.

Enter Sir JOHN *of* HENAULT.

Sir John. Madam, what cheer?

Queen. Ah, good sir John of Henault,
Never so cheerless, nor so far distrest.

Sir John. I hear, sweet lady, of the king's unkind-
ness;
But droop not, madam, noble minds contemn
Despair: will your grace with me to Henault,
And there stay time's advantage with your son?
How say you, my lord, will you go with your friends,
And shake off all our fortunes equally?

Prince. So pleaseth the queen my mother, me it
likes.
The king of England, not the court of France,
Shall have me from my gracious mother's side,
Till I be strong enough to break a staff;
And then have at the proudest Spencer's head.

Sir John. Well said, my lord.

Queen. Oh, my sweet heart! how do I moan thy
wrong,
Yet triumph in the hope of thee my joy!
Ah, sweet sir John, even to the utmost verge
Of Europe, or the shore of Tanaise,
Will we with thee to Henault, so we will.
The marquess is a noble gentleman,
His grace I dare presume will welcome me.
But who are these?

Enter EDMUND *and* MORTIMER *junior.*

Edmund. Madam, long may you live,
Much happier than your friends in England do!

Queen. Lord Edmund and lord Mortimer alive!
Welcome to France! the news was here, my lord,
That you were dead, or very near your death.

Mortimer junior. Lady, the last was truest of the
twain:
But Mortimer, reserv'd for better hap,
Hath shaken off the thraldom of the Tower,
And lives t'advance your standard, good my lord.

Prince. How mean you, and the king my father
lives?

No, my lord Mortimer, not I, I trow.

Queen. Not son, why not? I would it were no worse.
But, gentle lords, friendless we are in France.

Mortimer junior. Monsieur le Grand, a noble friend
    of yours,
Told us, at our arrival, all the news;
How hard the nobles, how unkind the king
Hath shewed himself: but, madam, right makes room,
Where weapons won't; and though so many friends
Are made away, as Warwick, Lancaster,
And others of our party and faction ;
Yet have we friends, assure your grace, in England,
Would cast up caps, and clap their hands for joy,
To see us there, appointed for our foes.

Edmund. Would all were well, and Edward well re-
    claim'd,
For England's honour, peace, and quietness!

Mortimer junior. But by the sword, my lord, it
    must be deserv'd ;
The king will ne'er forsake his flatterers.

Sir John. My lords of England, sith th' ungentle
    king
Of France refuseth to give aid of arms
To this distressed queen his sister here,
Go you with her to Henault; doubt ye not,
We will find comfort, money, men, and friends
Ere long, to bid the English king abase.
How say, young prince, what think you of the match?

Prince. I think, king Edward will outrun us all.

Queen. Nay son, not so; and you must not discou-
    rage
Your friends, that are so forward in your aid.

Edmund. Sir John of Henault, pardon us, I pray;
These comforts that you give our woeful queen
Bind us in kindness all at your command.

Queen. Yea, gentle brother; and the God of heav'n
Prosper your happy motion, good sir John !

Mortimer junior. This noble gentleman, forward in
    arms,
Was born, I see, to be our anchor-hold.

Sir John of Henault, be it thy renown,
That England's queen, and nobles in distress,
Have been by thee restor'd and comforted.

　　Sir John. Madam, along, and you, my lord, with
　　　　me,
That England's peers may Henault's welcome see.

　　　　　　　　　　　　　　[*Exeunt.*

Enter the KING, MATREVIS, *the two* SPENCERS, *with
　　　　others*.*

　　Edward. Thus after many threats of wrathful war,
Triumpheth England's Edward with his friends,
And triumph Edward with his friends uncontrol'd.
My lord of Glo'ster, do you hear the news?

　　Spencer junior. What news, my lord?

　　Edward. Why man, they say there is great execu-
　　　　tion
Done through the realm; my lord of Arundel,
You have the note, have you not?

　　Matrevis. From the lieutenant of the Tower, my
　　　　lord.

　　Edward. I pray let us see it. What have we there?
Read it Spencer.　　　　　　[*Spencer reads their names.*
Why so; they bark'd apace a month ago,
Now, on my life, they'll neither bark nor bite.
Now, sirs, the news from France? Glo'ster, I trow,
The lords of France love England's gold so well,
As Isabel gets no aid from thence.
What now remains? have you proclaim'd, my lord,
Reward for them can bring in Mortimer?

　　Spencer junior. My lord, we have; and, if he be in
　　　　England,
He will be had ere long, I doubt it not.

　　Edward. If, do'st thou say? Spencer, as true as
　　　　death,
He is in England's ground, our portmasters
Are not so careless of their king's command.

　　　　　　　　　Enter a POST.
How now, what news with thee? from whence come
　　　　these?

　　　　* The scene returns to England. C.

Post. Letters, my lords, and tidings forth of France,
To you, my lord of Gloster, from Lewen.
  Edward. Read.

Spencer reads the letters.

My duty to your honour premised, &c. I have, according to instructions in that behalf, dealt with the king of France his lords, and affected, that the queen, all discontented and discomforted, is gone. Whither, if you ask; with sir John of Henault, brother to the marquess, into Flanders: with them are gone lord Edmund, and the lord Mortimer, having in their company divers of your nation, and others ; and, as constant report goeth, they intend to give king Edward battle in England, sooner than he can look for them: this is all the news of import.

Your honour's in all service,
LEWEN.

Edward. Ah, villains! hath that Mortimer escap'd?
With him is Edmund gone associate?
And will sir John of Henault lead the round?
Welcome a God's name, madam, and your son ;
England shall welcome you, and all your rout.
[43] Gallop a-pace bright Phœbus through the sky,
And dusky night, in rusty iron car,
Between you both, shorten the time, I pray,
That I may see that most desired day,
When we may meet these traitors in the field.
Ah, nothing grieves me, but my little boy
Is thus misled to countenance their ills.
Come, friends, to Bristol, there to make us strong ;
And winds, as equal be to bring them in,
As you injurious were to bear them forth.   [*Exeunt.*

---

[43] *Gallop a-pace,* &c.] Shakspeare has imitated these lines in *Romeo and Juliet,* A. 3. S. 2 :
<blockquote>
" Gallop apace, you fiery-footed steeds,
" Towards Phœbus mansion ; such a waggoner
" As Phaeton would whip you to the west,
" And bring in cloudy night immediately."
</blockquote>

Enter the QUEEN, *her son,* EDMUND, MORTIMER *junior,*
and Sir JOHN.

  Queen. Now, lords, our loving friends and country-
    men,
Welcome to England all, with prosperous winds;
Our kindest friends in Belgia have we left,
To cope with friends at home: a heavy case,
When force to force is knit, and sword and [44] gleave
In civil broils make kin and countrymen
Slaughter themselves in others, and their sides,
With their own weapons gore! But what's the help?
Misgovern'd kings are cause of all this wreck;
And, Edward, thou art one among them all,
Whose looseness hath betray'd thy land to spoil,
And made the channel overflow with blood
Of thine own people; patron should'st thou be,
But thou—
  Mortimer junior. Nay, madam, if you be a warrior,
Ye must not grow so passionate in speeches.
Lords, sith that we are by sufferance of heav'n,
Arriv'd and armed in this prince's right,
Here for our country's cause swear we to him
All homage, fealty, and forwardness;
And for the open wrongs and injuries
Edward hath done to us, his queen, and land,
We come in arms to wreck* it with the sword;
That England's queen in peace may repossess
Her dignities and honours: and withall
We may remove these flatterers from the king,
That havock England's wealth and treasury.

[44] *gleave*] Or *glave*, a weapon like a halberd. It is mentioned
in Churchyard's *Challenge*, p. 44:
    " And wanting wealth to pay this heavy sum,
    " With billes and *glayves* from prison was I led."
Again, *Arden of Faversham:*
    " O mistris, the major, and all the watch,
    " Are coming towards our house with *glaves* and bills."
Edward III. A. 3. S. 5:
    " —— with their pond'rous *glaives.*"
  * Perhaps " wreak:" *i. e.* revenge. O. G.

Sir John. Sound trumpets, my lord, and forward
    let us march.
Edward will think we come to flatter him.
    Edmund. I would he never had been flatter'd more!
                             [*Exeunt.*

Enter the KING, BALDOCK, *and* SPENCER *the son,*
      flying about the stage.

    Spencer. Fly, fly, my lord, the queen is overstrong,
Her friends do multiply, and yours do fail.
Shape we our course to Ireland, there to breathe.
    Edward. What! was I born to fly and run away,
And leave the Mortimers conquerors behind?
Give me my horse, let's reinforce our troops;
And in this bed of honour die with fame.
    Baldock. O no, my lord, this princely resolution
Fits not the time; away, we are pursu'd.   [*Exeunt.*

    EDMUND *alone with a sword and target.*
    Edmund. This way he fled, but I am come too late.
Edward, alas! my heart relents for thee.
Proud traitor, Mortimer, why dost thou chase
Thy lawful king, thy sovereign, with thy sword?
Vile wretch! and why hast thou, of all unkind,
Born arms against thy brother and thy king?
Rain showers of vengeance on my cursed head,
Thou God, to whom in justice it belongs
To punish this unnatural revolt!
Edward, this Mortimer aims at thy life:
O fly him then! but Edmund calm this rage,
Dissemble, or thou diest; for Mortimer
And Isabel do kiss, while they conspire:
And yet she bears a face of love forsooth.
Fie on that love that hatcheth death and hate!
Edmund, away; Bristol to Longshank's blood
Is false, be not found single for suspect*:
Proud Mortimer prys near into thy walks.

Enter the QUEEN, MORTIMER *junior, the young*
    PRINCE, *and Sir* JOHN *of* HENAULT.
    Queen. Successful battle gives the God of kings
To them that fight in right, and fear his wrath.

* See Note 45 to this play.

Since then successfully we have prevail'd,
Thanked be heaven's great architect, and you;
Ere farther we proceed, my noble lords,
We here create our well-beloved son,
Of love and care unto his royal person,
Lord warden of the realm; and, sith the fates
Have made his father so unfortunate,
Deal you, my lords, in this, my loving lords,
As to your wisdoms fittest seems in all.
    Edmund. Madam, without offence, if I may ask,
How will you deal with Edward in his fall?
    Prince. Tell me, good uncle, what Edward do you
        mean?
    Edmund. Nephew, your father; I dare not call him
        king.
    Mortimer junior. My lord of Kent, what needs these
        questions?
'Tis not in her controlment, nor in ours,
But as the realm and parliament shall please,
So shall your brother be disposed of.
I like not this relenting mood in Edmund.
                                [*Aside to the Queen.*
Madam, 'tis good to look to him betimes.
    Queen. My lord, the mayor of Bristol knows our
        mind.
    Mortimer junior. Yea, madam, and they 'scape not
        easily,
That fled the field.
    Queen. Baldock is with the king,
A goodly chancellor, is he not, my lord?
    Sir John. So are the Spencers, the father and the
        son.
    Edmund. This Edward is the ruin of the realm.
Enter RICE AP HOWELL, *and the mayor of* BRISTOL,
        with SPENCER *the father.*
    Rice. God save queen Isabel, and her princely son.
Madam, the mayor and citizens of Bristol,
In sign of love and duty to this presence,
Present by me this traitor to the state,
Spencer, the father to that wanton Spencer,
That, like the lawless Catiline of Rome,

Revel'd in England's wealth and treasury.

Queen. We thank you all.

Mortimer junior. Your loving care in this
Deserveth princely favours and rewards.
But where's the king and the other Spencer fled?

Rice. Spencer the Son, created earl of Glo'ster,
Is with that smooth-tongu'd scholar Baldock gone,
And shipp'd but late for Ireland with the king.

Mortimer junior. Some whirlwind fetch them back,
    or sink them all!
They shall be started thence, I doubt it not.

Prince. Shall I not see the king my father yet?

Edmund. Unhappy Edward! chas'd from England's
    bounds,

Sir John. Madam, what resteth*, why stand ye in
    a muse?

Queen. I rue my lord's ill fortune; but, alas!
Care of my country call'd me to this war.

Mortimer junior. Madam, have done with care and
    sad complaint,
'Your king hath wrong'd your country and himself;
And we must seek to right it as we may.
Mean while, have hence this rebel to the block.

Spencer. Rebel is he that fights against the prince;
So fought not they that fought in Edward's right.

Mortimer junior. Take him away, he prates; you,
    Rice ap Howell,
Shall do good service to her majesty,
Being of countenance in your country here,
To follow these rebellious runnagates.
We in mean while, madam, must take advice,
How Baldock, Spencer, and their complices,
May in their fall be followed to their end.

                [*Exeunt omnes.*

Enter the ABBOT, MONKS, EDWARD, SPENCER, *and*
              BALDOCK.

Abbot. Have you no doubt, my lord; have you no
    fear;
As silent and as careful we will be,

    * *i. e.* remaineth: so Milton P. L. x. 48. C.

To keep your royal person safe with us,
Free from [45] suspect, and fell invasion
Of such as have your majesty in chase,
Yourself, and those your chosen company,
As danger of this stormy time requires.

    Edward. Father, thy face should harbour no deceit.
O! hadst thou ever been a king, thy heart,
Pierc'd deeply with a sense of my distress,
Could not but take compassion of my state.
Stately and proud, in riches and in train,
Whilom 1 was, powerful and full of pomp:
But what is he, whom rule and empiry
Have not in life or death made miserable?
Come, Spencer, come, Baldock, come sit down by me;
Make trial now of that philosophy,
That in our famous nurseries of arts
Thou suck'st from Plato and from Aristotle.
Father, this life contemplative is heaven.
O that I might this life in quiet lead!
But we, alas! are chas'd; and, you my friends,
Your lives and my dishonour they pursue.
Yet, gentle monks, for treasure, gold nor fee,
Do you betray us and our company.

    Monks. Your grace may sit secure, if none but we
        do [46] wot of your abode.

    Spencer. Not one alive, but shrewdly I suspect
A gloomy fellow in a mead below;
He gave a long look after us, my lord,
And all the land I know is up in arms,
Arms that pursue our lives with deadly hate.

    Baldock. We were imbark'd for Ireland, wretched
        we!
With aukward winds and sore tempests driven
To fall on shore, and here to pine in fear

---

    [45] *suspect,*] i. e. *suspicion.* So, in Middleton's *More Dissemblers besides Women,* A. 2. S. 1:
        " — what a fair way
        " Had I made for my love to th' General,
        " And cut of all *suspect,* all reprehension?"
    [46] *wot*] See Note 85 to *Gammer Gurton's Needle,* p. 66.

Of Mortimer and his confederates.

Edward. Mortimer! who talks of Mortimer?
Who wounds me with the name of Mortimer!
That bloody man! Good father, on thy lap
Lay I this head, laden with mickle care.
O might I never ope these eyes again!
Never again lift up this drooping head!
O never more lift up this dying heart!

Spencer. Look up, my lord.—Baldock, this drowsi-
ness
Betides no good; here even we are betray'd.

Enter with [47] *Welch hooks,* RICE AP HOWEL, *a* MOWER,
and the earl of LEICESTER.

Mower. Upon my life these be the men ye seek.

Rice. Fellow, enough. My lord, I pray be short,
A fair commission warrants what we do.

Leicester. The queen's commission, urg'd by Mor-
timer,
What cannot Mortimer with the queen!
Alas! see where he sits, and hopes unseen,
T'escape their hands that seek to reave his life.
Too true it is, *quem dies vidit veniens superbum,*
Hunc dies vidit fugiens jacentem.
But, Leicester, leave to grow so passionate.
Spencer and Baldock, by no other names,
I arrest you of high treason here.
Stand not on titles, but obey th' arrest;
'Tis in the name of Isabel the queen.
My lord, why droop you thus?

Edward. O day! the last of all my bliss on earth!
Center of all misfortune! O my stars!
Why do you low'r unkindly on a king?
Comes Leicester then, in Isabella's name,

[47] *Welch hooks,*] What kind of weapons these were is not precisely known. Mr. Steevens is of opinion, that the *Welch hook* and
the brown bill are no more than varieties of the *securis falcata*, or
probably a weapon of the same kind with the Lockabar axe, which
was used in the late rebellion. Colonel Gardner was attacked with
such a one at the battle of Preston Pans. Mr. Tollett imagines a
weapon, of which a print is given, from the hooked form of it to be
the *Welch hook*. See notes in the First Part of *Henry* IV. A. 2.
S. 4.

To take my life, my company from me?
Here man, rip up this panting breast of mine,
And take my heart, in rescue of my friends.
 Rice. Away with them!
 Spencer junior. It may become thee yet,
To let us take our farewell of his grace.
 Abbot. My heart with pity yearns to see this sight,
A king to bear these words and proud commands.
 Edward. Spencer, ah sweet Spencer, thus then must
  we part?
 Spencer junior. We must, my lord, so will the angry
  heav'ns.
 Edward. Nay so will hell and cruel Mortimer;
The gentle heav'ns have not to do in this.
 Baldock. My lord, it is in vain to grieve or storm.
Here humbly of your grace we take our leaves;
Our lots are cast, I fear me, so is thine.
 Edward. In heav'n we may, in earth ne'er shall we
  meet:
And, Leicester, say, what shall become of us?
 Leicester. Your majesty must go to Killingworth*.
 Edward. Must! 'tis somewhat hard, when kings
  must go.
 Leicester. Here is a litter ready for your grace,
That waits your pleasure, and the day grows old.
 Rice. As good be gone, as stay and be benighted.
 Edward. A litter hast thou? lay me in a hearse,
And to the gates of hell convey me hence;
Let Pluto's bells ring out my fatal knell,
And hags howl for my death at Charon's shore.
For friends hath Edward none, but these; and these
Must die under a tyrant's sword.
 Rice. My lord, be going, care not for these,
For we shall see them shorter by the heads.
 Edward. Well, that shall be, shall be: part we must!
Sweet Spencer, gentle Baldock, part we must!
Hence feigned weeds†! unfeigned are my woes;
Father, farewell! Leicester, thou stay'st for me,

---

 * Or Kenelworth.
 † Hence it appears that the king has put on the disguise of a
monk, and wears it during the scene. C.

And go I must.   Life, farewell, with my friends.
[*Exeunt Edward and Leicester.*

Spencer junior. O is he gone! is noble Edward gone!
Parted from hence! never to see us more!
Rend, sphere of heav'n! and, fire, forsake thy orb!
Earth, melt to air! gone is my sovereign!
Gone, gone, alas; never to make return.

Baldock. Spencer, I see our souls are fleeting hence;
We are depriv'd the sunshine of our life;
Make for a new life, man; throw up thy eyes,
And heart and hand, to heav'n's immortal throne,
Pay nature's debt with cheerful countenance;
Reduce we all our lessons unto this,
To die, sweet Spencer, therefore live we all;
Spencer, all live to die, and rise to fall.

Rice. Come, come, keep these preachments till you
    come
To the place appointed.   You, and such as you are,
Have made wise work in England.
Will your lordships away?

Mower. Your lordship I trust will remember me?

Rice. Remember thee, fellow! what else?
Follow me to the town.   [*Exeunt.*

Enter the KING, LEICESTER, *with the Bishop of* WIN-
CHESTER *for the crown.*

Leicester. Be patient, good my lord, cease to lament,
Imagine Killingworth castle were your court,
And that you lay for pleasure here a space,
Not of compulsion or necessity.

Edward. Leicester, if gentle words might comfort
    me,
Thy speeches long ago had eas'd my sorrows;
For kind and loving hast thou always been.
The griefs of private men are soon allay'd,
But not of kings.   The forest deer, being struck,
Runs to an herb that closeth up the wounds;
But when the imperial lion's flesh is gor'd,
He rends and tears it with his wrathful paw,
And highly scorning, that the lowly earth
Should drink his blood, mounts up to th' air.
And so it fares with me, whose dauntless mind

Th' ambitious Mortimer would seek to curb,
And that unnatural queen, fale Isabel,
That thus hath pent and mu'd me in a prison :
For such outrageous passions cloy my soul,
As with the wings of rancour and disdain,
Full oft am I soaring up to high heav'n,
To plain me to the gods against them both.
But when I call to mind I am a king,
Methinks I should revenge me of the wrongs,
That Mortimer and Isabel have done.
But what are kings, when [48] regiment is gone,
But perfect shadows in a sunshine day?
My nobles rule, I bear the name of king ;
I wear the crown, but am controul'd by them,
By Mortimer, and my unconstant queen,
Who spots my nuptial bed with infamy ;
Whilst I am lodg'd within this cave of care,
Where sorrow at my elbow still attends,
To company my heart with sad laments,
That bleeds within me for this strange exchange.
But tell me, must I now resign my crown,
To make usurping Mortimer a king ?
    Winchester. Your grace mistakes, it is for England's
        good,
And princely Edward's right we crave the crown.
    Edward. No, 'tis. for Mortimer, not Edward's
        head ; (*himself*)
For he's a lamb, encompassed by wolves,
Which in a moment will abridge his life.
But if proud Mortimer do wear this crown,
Heav'ns turn it to a blaze of quenchless fire[*]!
Or, like the snaky wreath of Tisiphon,
Engirt the temples of his hateful head ;
So shall not England's vines be perished,
But Edward's name survive, though Edward dies.
    Leicester. My lord, why waste you thus the time
        away?
They stay your answer, will you yield your crown ?

  [48] *regiment*] See Note 18. P.
   [*] Alluding to the crown presented by Medea to Creusa. See
Euripides Medea, A. 5. S.

Edward. Ah, Leicester, weigh how hardly I can
    brook
To lose my crown and kingdom without cause;
To give ambitious Mortimer my right,
That like a mountain overwhelms my bliss,
In which extreams my mind here murther'd is.
But what the heav'ns appoint, I must obey!
Here, take my crown; the life of Edward too;
Two kings in England cannot reign at once.
But stay a while, let me be king till night,
That I may gaze upon this glittering crown;
So shall my eyes receive their last content,
My head, the latest honour due to it,
And jointly both yield up their wished right.
Continue ever, thou celestial sun;
Let never silent night possess this clime;
Stand still, you watches of the element;
All times and seasons, rest you at a stay,
That Edward may be still fair England's king;
But day's bright beam doth vanish fast away,
And needs I must resign my wished crown.
Inhuman creatures! nurs'd with tiger's milk!
Why gape you for your sovereign's overthrow?
My diadem I mean, and guiltless life.
See, monsters, see, I'll wear my crown again.
What, fear you not the fury of your king?
But hapless Edward, thou art fondly led,
They pass not * for thy frowns as late they did,
But seek to make a new-elected king;
Which fills my mind with strange despairing thoughts,
Which thoughts are martyr'd with endless torments,
And in this torment comfort find I none,
But that I feel the crown upon my head;
And therefore let me wear it yet a while.
    Trusty. My lord, the parliament must have present
        news,

* That is, *care not for:* so in Wilson's *Rhetoric*, 1553: " They
passed little of the churche, that would adventure to robbe the
churche."
    And in *Castilio's Courtier*, by Hobby, 1557: " They *passe not* to
be ill reported of in every other matter, so their honesty be not
touched." **C.**

And therefore say, will you resign or no?

The king rageth.

Edward. I'll not resign! but whilst I live, be king!
Traitors be gone, and join with Mortimer.
Elect, [49] conspire, install, do what you will;
Their blood and yours shall seal these treacheries!

Winchester. This answer we'll return, and so farewell.

Leicester. Call them again, my lord, and speak them fair;
For if they go, the prince shall lose his right.

Edward. Call thou them back, I have no power to speak.

Leicester. My lord, the king is willing to resign

Winchester. If he be not, let him choose.

Edward. O would I might! but heav'n and earth conspire
To make me miserable! here, receive my crown;
Receive it! no, these innocent hands of mine
Shall not be guilty of so foul a crime.
He of you all that most desires my blood,
And will be call'd the murtherer of a king,
Take it. What, are you mov'd? pity you me?
Then send for unrelenting Mortimer,
And Isabel, whose eyes, being turn'd to steel,
Will sooner sparkle fire than shed a tear.
Yet stay, for rather than I will look on them,
Here, here: now, sweet God of heav'n!

[49] *confirm*] All the editions read *conspire*. The allusion seems to be to the several forms observed in the creation of a Bishop, in which the act of *confirmation* comes between *election* and *installation*. S. P.

The old copies concur in reading *conspire* and yet S. P. would change it to *confirm*. Was the creation of Bishops all the mischief that the enraged monarch had to dread from his opposers? Would a king during the height of his resentment give himself the trouble to marshal a set of forms with which, perhaps, none but the understrappers of episcopacy are regularly acquainted? I have no doubt but that the ancient reading is the true one. Go, says Edward, *elect* another prince, *conspire* against the present one, and *instal* his enemies in those high honours, which he has already bestowed on his friends. There are surely other *elections* and other *installations*, besides those of *Bishops*. S.

Make me despise this transitory pomp,
And sit for aye inthroniz'd in heav'n!
Come death, and with thy fingers close my eyes,
Or, if I live, let me forget myself.

Enter BERKELEY.

Berkeley. My lord.

Edward. Call me not lord;
Away, out of my sight—ah, pardon me,
Grief makes me lunatick!
Let not that Mortimer protect my son;
More safety there is in a tiger's jaws,
Than his embracement—Bear this to the queen,
Wet with my tears, and dry'd again with sighs;
If with the sight thereof she be not mov'd,
Return it back and dip it in my blood.
Commend me to my son, and bid him rule
Better than I.   Yet how have I transgrest,
Unless it be with too much clemency?

Trusty. And thus, most humbly do we take our
    leave.

Edward. Farewell; I know the next news that they
    bring·
Will be my death; and welcome shall it be;
To wretched men, death is felicity.

Leicester. Another post! what news brings he?

Edward. Such news as I expect—come, Berkeley,
    come,
And tell thy message to my naked breast.

Berkeley. My lord, think not a thought so villainous
Can harbour in a man of noble birth.
To do your highness service and devoir,
And save you from your foes, Berkeley would die.

Leicester. My lord, the counsel and the queen com-
    mands
That I resign my charge.

Edward. And who must keep me now? must you,
    my lord?

Berkeley. Ay, my most gracious lord, so 'tis decreed.

Edward. By Mortimer, whose name is written here

Well, may I rend his name that rends my heart*!
This poor revenge hath something eas'd my mind.
So may his limbs be torn, as is this paper!
Hear me, immortal Jove, and grant it too!

    Berkeley. Your grace must hence with me to
      Berkeley straight.

    Edward. Whither you will, all places are alike,
And every earth is fit for burial.

    Leicester. Favour him, my lord, as much as lieth in
      you.

    Berkeley. Even so betide my soul as I use him.

    Edward. Mine enemy hath pitied my estate,
And that's the cause that I am now remov'd.

    Berkeley. And thinks your grace that Berkeley will
      be cruel?

    Edward. I know not, but of this am I assur'd,
That death ends all, and I can die but once.
Leicester, farewell.

    Leicester. Not yet, my lord, I'll bear you on your
      way.   [*Exeunt omnes.*

    Enter MORTIMER *junior, and queen* ISABEL.

    Mortimer junior. Fair Isabel, now have we our de-
      sire,
The proud corrupters of the light-brain'd king
Have done their homage to the lofty gallows,
And he himself lies in captivity.
Be rul'd by me, and we will rule the realm.
In any case take heed of childish fear,
For now we hold an old wolf by the ears,
That if he slip will seize upon us both,
And gripe the sorer, being gript himself.
Think therefore, madam, that imports as much,
To erect your son with all the speed we may,
And that I be protector over him;
For our behoof, 'twill bear the greater sway
When as a king's name shall be under writ.

    Queen. Sweet Mortimer, the life of Isabel,
Be thou persuaded that I love thee well,

            * Tears the paper.

And therefore so the prince my son be safe,
Whom I esteem as dear as these mine eyes,
Conclude against his father what thou wilt,
And I myself will willingly subscribe.
    Mortimer junior. First would I hear news he were
        depos'd,
And then let me alone to handle him.
            Enter MESSENGER.
    Mortimer junior. Letters! from whence?
    Messenger. From Killingworth, my lord.
    Queen. How fares my lord the king?
    Messenger. In health, madam, but full of pensive-
        ness.
    Queen. Alas! poor soul, would I could ease his
        grief*!
Thanks, gentle Winchester; sirrah, be gone.
                          [*Exit Messenger.*
    Winchester. The king hath willingly resign'd his
        crown.
    Queen. O happy news! send for the prince, my son.
    Winchester. Further, or this letter was seal'd, lord
        Berkeley came,
So that he now is gone from Killingworth,
And we have heard that Edmund laid a plot
To set his brother free; no more but so,
The lord of Berkeley is so pitiful,
As Leicester that had charge of him before.
    Queen. Then let some other be his guardian.
    Mortimer junior. Let me alone, here is the privy
        seal.
Who's there? call hither Gurney and Matrevis,
To dash the heavy-headed Edmund's drift;
Berkeley shall be discharg'd, the king remov'd,
And none but we shall know where he lieth.
    Queen. But, Mortimer, as long as he survives,
What safety rests for us, or for my son?

---

   * This part of the scene is not intelligible, unless we suppose
that the Bishop of Winchester enters after the queen has thus
spoken, and whispers to Mortimer who takes up the next line,
" Thanks, gentle Winchester, &c."   C.

Mortimer junior. Speak, shall he presently be dis-
   patch'd and die?
Queen. I would he were, so 'twere not by my means.
          Enter MATREVIS *and* GURNEY.
Mortimer junior. Enough; Matrevis, write a letter
   presently
Unto the lord of Berkeley from ourself,
That he resign the king to thee and Gurney;
And when 'tis done we will subscribe our name.
Matrevis. It shall be done, my lord.
Mortimer junior. Gurney.
Gurney. My lord.
Mortimer junior. As thou intend'st to rise by Mor-
   timer,
Who now makes fortune's wheel turn as he please,
Seek all the means thou canst to make him droop,
And neither give him kind word nor good look.
Gurney. I warrant you, my lord.
Mortimer junior. And this above the rest, because
   we hear
That Edmund casts to work his liberty,
Remove him still from place to place by night,
Till at the last he come to Killingworth,
And then from thence to Berkeley back again:
And by the way, to make him fret the more,
⁵⁰ Speak curstly to him; and in any case
Let no man comfort him if he chance to weep,
But amplify his grief with bitter words.
Matrevis. Fear not, my lord, we'll do as you com-
   mand.
Mortimer junior. So, now away: post thitherwards
   amain.
Queen. Whither goes this letter, to my lord the
   king?

⁵⁰ *Speak curstly*] *Curstly* is *shrewishly, ill-naturedly,* or *frowardly.*
As, in *Philaster:*
   " Hadst a *curst* master when thou wentst to school."
Taming of the Shrew:
   " —— her only fault
   Is that she is intolerably *curst.*"

Commend me humbly to his majesty,
And tell him, that l labour all in vain
To ease his grief, and work his liberty;
And bear him this, as witness of my love.
　　Matrevis. I will, madam.
　　　　　　　　　　　[Exeunt Matrevis and Gurney.
　　　　　　　　Manent Isabel and Mortimer junior.

Enter the young PRINCE, *and the earl of* KENT *talking with him.*
　　Mortimer junior. Finely dissembled! do so still,
　　　　sweet queen.
Here comes the young prince, with the earl of Kent.
　　Queen. Something he whispers in his childish ears.
　　Mortimer junior. If he have such access unto the
　　　　prince,
Our plots and stratagems will soon be dash'd.
　　Queen. Use Edmund friendly, as if all were well.
　　Mortimer junior. How fares my honourable lord of
　　　　Kent?
　　Edmund. In health, sweet Mortimer: how fares your
　　　　grace?
　　Queen. Well, if my lord your brother were enlarg'd.
　　Edmund. I hear of late he has depos'd himself.
　　Queen. The more my grief.
　　Mortimer junior. And mine.
　　Edmund. Ah, they do dissemble!　　　　　　[*Aside.*
　　Queen. Sweet son, come hither, I must talk with
　　　　thee.
　　Mortimer junior. You being his uncle, and the next
　　　　of blood,
Do look to be protector o'er the prince.
　　Edmund. Not I, my lord; who should protect the
　　　　son,
But she that gave him life, I mean the queen?
　　Prince. Mother, persuade me not to wear the crown;
Let him be king, I am too young to reign.
　　Queen. But be content, seeing it is his highness'
　　　　pleasure.
　　Prince. Let me but see him first, and then I will.

Edmund. Ay do, sweet nephew.

Queen. Brother, you know it is impossible.

Prince. Why, is he dead?

Queen. No, God forbid!

Edmund. I would those words proceeded from your heart.

Mortimer junior. Inconstant Edmund, dost thou favour him,

That wast a cause of his imprisonment?

Edmund. The more cause have I now to make amends.

Mortimer junior. I tell thee 'tis not meet, that one so false

Should come about the person of a prince.

My lord, he hath betray'd the king his brother,

And therefore trust him not.

Prince. But he repents, and sorrows for it now.

Queen. Come son, and go with this gentle lord and me.

Prince. With you I will, but not with Mortimer.

Mortimer junior. Why, youngling, s'dain'st thou so of Mortimer?

Then I will carry thee by force away.

Prince. Help, uncle Kent, Mortimer will wrong me.

Queen. Brother Edmund, strive not, we are his friends,

Isabel is nearer than the earl of Kent.

Edmund. Sister, Edward is my charge, redeem him.

Queen. Edward is my son, and I will keep him.

Edmund. Mortimer shall know that he hath wrong'd me.

Hence will I haste to Killingworth castle,

And rescue aged Edward from his foes,

To be reveng'd on Mortimer and thee.   [*Exeunt omnes.*

Enter MATREVIS *and* GURNEY *with the* KING.

Matrevis. My lord, be not pensive, we are your friends;

Men are ordain'd to live in misery,

Therefore come, dalliance dangereth our lives.

Edward. Friends, whither must unhappy Edward go?

Will hateful Mortimer appoint no rest?
Must I be vexed like the nightly bird,
Whose sight is loathsome to all winged fowls?
When will the fury of his mind assuage?
When will his heart be satisfied with blood?
If mine will serve, unbowel straight this breast,
And give my heart to Isabel and him,
It is the chiefest mark they level at.

    Gurney. Not so, my liege, the queen hath given this
       charge,
To keep your grace in safety;
Your passions make your choler to encrease.

    Edward. This usage makes my misery encrease.
But can my air of life continue long,
When all my senses are annoy'd with stench?
Within a dungeon England's king is kept,
Where I am starv'd for want of sustenance.
My daily diet is heart-breaking sobs,
That almost rend the closet of my heart;
Thus lives old Edward not reliev'd by any,
And so must die, tho' pitied by many.
O water, gentle friends, to cool my thirst,
And clear my body from foul excrements!

    Matrevis. Here's channel-water, as our charge is
      given;
Sit down, for we'll be barbers to your grace.

    Edward. Traitors, away; what will you murder me,
Or choak your sovereign with puddle-water?

    Gurney. No; but wash your face, and shave away
      your beard,
Lest you be known, and so be rescued.

    Matrevis. Why strive you thus, your labour is in
      vain?

    Edward. The wren may strive against the lion's
      strength,
But all in vain; so vainly do I strive,
To seek for mercy at a tyrant's hand.

    [*They wash him with puddle-water, and shave his
      beard away.*
Immortal powers! that know the painful cares,

That wait upon my poor distressed soul!
O level all your looks upon these daring men,
That wrong their liege and sovereign, England's king.
O Gaveston, it is for thee that I am wrong'd,
For me, both thou and both the Spencers dy'd!
And for your sakes a thousand wrongs I'll take.
The Spencers ghosts, wherever they remain,
Wish well to mine; then tush, for them I'll die.

Matrevis. 'Twixt theirs and yours, shall be no enmity.
Come, come, away, now put the torches out,
We'll enter in by darkness to Killingworth.

Enter EDMUND.

Gurney. How now, who comes there?

Matrevis. Guard the king sure; it is the earl of
Kent.

Edward. O, gentle brother, help to rescue me!

Matrevis. Keep them asunder; thrust in the king.

Edmund. Soldiers, let me but talk to him one word.

Gurney. Lay hands upon the earl for his assault.

Edmund. Lay down your weapons, traitors, yield the
king.

Matrevis. Edmund, yield thou thyself, or thou shalt
die.

Edmund. Base villains! wherefore do you gripe me
thus?

Gurney. Bind him, and so convey him to the court.

Edmund. Where is the court but here? here is the
king,
And I will visit him; why stay you me?

Matrevis. The court is where lord Mortimer remains;
Thither shall your honour go; and so farewell.

[*Exeunt Matrevis and Gurney, with the King.
Manent* EDMUND *and the Soldiers.*

Edmund. O miserable is that common-weal, where
lords
Keep courts, and kings are lock'd in prison!

Soldiers. Wherefore stay we? on, sirs, to the court.

Edmund. Ay, lead me whither you will, even to my
death,
Seeing that my brother cannot be released.

[*Exeunt omnes.*

Enter MORTIMER *junior, alone.*

Mortimer junior. The king must die, or Mortimer
    goes down.
The commons now begin to pity him.
Yet he that is the cause of Edward's death,
Is sure to pay for it when his son's of age;
And therefore will I do it cunningly.
This letter, written by a friend of ours,
Contains his death, yet bids them save his life.
Edwardum occidere nolite, timere bonum est.
Fear not to kill the king, 'tis good he die.
But read it thus, and that's another sense:
Edwardum occidere nolite timere bonum est.*
Kill not the king, 'tis good to fear the worst.
Unpointed as it is, thus shall it go,
That being dead, if it chance to be found,
Matrevis and the rest may bear the blame,
And we be quit that caus'd it to be done.
Within this room is lock'd the messenger,
That shall convey it, and perform the rest:
And by a secret token that he bears,
Shall he be murder'd when the deed is done.
Lightborn, come forth; art thou so resolute as thou
    wast?

Enter LIGHTBORN.

Lightborn. What else, my lord? and far more reso-
    lute.
Mortimer junior. And hast thou cast how to accom-
    plish it?
Lightborn. Ay, ay, and none shall know which way
    he died.

---

* The equivocal line must be pointed thus in the first instance:
    Edwardum occidere nolite timere, bonum est.
In the second:
    Edwardum occidere nolite, timere bonum est. S.
  Sir J. Harington has an Epigram (L. i. E. 33.) " Of writing
with double pointing," which is thus introduced. " It is said that
King Edward, of Carnarvon, lying at Berkeley Castle, prisoner,
a cardinal wrote to his keeper, *Edwardum occidere noli, timere bonum
est,* which being read with the point at *timere,* it cost the king his
life." C.

Mortimer junior. But at his looks, Lightborn, thou
    wilt relent.

Lightborn. Relent! ha, ha, I use much to relent.

Mortimer junior. Well, do it bravely, and be secret.

Lightborn. You shall not need to give instructions;
'Tis not the first time I have kill'd a man.
I learn'd in Naples how to poison flowers;
To strangle with a lawn thrust thro' the throat;
To pierce the wind-pipe with a needle's point;
Or, whilst one is asleep, to take a quill
And blow a little powder in his ears;
Or open his mouth, and pour quick-silver down.
But yet I have a braver way than these.

Mortimer junior. What's that?

Lightborn. Nay, you shall pardon me, none shall
    know my tricks.

Mortimer junior. I care not how it is, so it be not 'spy'd.
Deliver this to Gurney and Matrevis.
At every ten mile end thou hast a horse.
Take this, away; and never see me more.

Lightborn. No!

Mortimer junior. No; unless thou bring me news
    of Edward's death.

Lightborn. That will I quickly do; farewel, my lord.
                           [*Exit.*

Mortimer junior. The prince I rule, the queen do I
    mand,
And, with a lowly congé to the ground,
The proudest lords salute me as I pass:
I seal, I cancel, I do what I will;
Fear'd am I more than lov'd—let me be fear'd;
And, when I frown, make all the court look pale.
I view the prince with Aristarchus' eyes,
Whose looks were as [48] a breeching to a boy.

---

[48] — *a breeching*] *A whipping.* So, in Massinger's *Unnatural
Combat*, A. 1. S. 1
    " Tales out of school! take heed, you will *be breech'd* else."
The Bashful Lover, A. 1. S. 1:
    " You will *be breech'd*, boy,
    " For your physical maxims."

They thrust upon me the protectorship,
And sue to me for that which I desire.
While at the council-table, grave enough,
And not unlike a bashful puritan,
First I complain of imbecility,
Saying it is, *onus quam gravissimum*,
Till, being interrupted by my friends,
Suscepi that *provinciam*, as they term it,
And, to conclude, I am protector now.
Now is all sure, the queen and Mortimer
Shall rule the realm, the king, and none rule us.
Mine enemies will I plague, my friends advance,
And what I list command; who dare control?
Major sum quàm cui possit fortuna nocere.
And that this be the coronation-day,
It pleaseth me, and Isabel the queen.
The trumpets sound, I must go take my place.
Enter the young KING, BISHOP, CHAMPION, NOBLES,
                    QUEEN.

 Bishop. Long live king Edward, by the grace of
  God,
King of England, and lord of Ireland !
 Champion. If any Christian, Heathen, Turk, or Jew,
Dares but affirm, that Edward's not true king,
And will avouch his saying with the sword,
I am the champion that will combat him.
 Mortimer junior. None comes, sound trumpets.
 King. Champion, here's to thee.
 Queen. Lord Mortimer, now take him to your charge.
 Enter SOLDIERS, *with the earl of* KENT *prisoner.*
 Mortimer junior. What traitor have we there with
  blades and bills ?
 Soldiers. Edmund, the earl of Kent.
 King. What hath he done?

The Guardian, A. 1. S. 1 :
 " How he looks ! like a school-boy that had play'd the
  truant,
 " And went *to be breech'd.*"
Shakspeare's *Taming of the Shrew*, A. 3. S. 1 :
 " I am no *breeching* scholar in the schools."
See also Mr. Steevens's Note on the last passage.

Soldiers. He would have taken the king away per
    force,
As we were bringing him to Killingworth.

Mortimer junior. Did you attempt his rescue, Ed-
    mund? Speak.

Edmund. Mortimer, I did; he is our king,
And thou compell'st this prince to wear the crown.

Mortimer junior. Strike off his head, he shall have
    martial law.

Edmund. Strike off my head! base traitor, I defy
    thee.

King. My lord, he is my uncle, and shall live.

Mortimer junior. My lord, he is your enemy, and
    shall die.

Edmund. Stay, villains!

King. Sweet mother, if I cannot pardon him,
Intreat my lord protector for his life.

Queen. Son, be content; I dare not speak a word.

King. Nor I, and yet methinks I should command;
But, seeing I cannot, I'll intreat for him—
My lord, if you will let my uncle live,
I will requite it when I come to age.

Mortimer junior. 'Tis for your highness' good, and
    for the realm's.
How often shall I bid you bear him hence?

Edmund. Art thou king? must I die at thy com-
    mand?

Mortimer junior. At our command! Once more,
    away with him.

Edmund. Let me but stay and speak; I will not go.
Either my brother or his son is king,
And none of both them thirst for Edmund's blood.
And therefore, soldiers, whither will you hale me?
    [*They hale Edmund away, and carry him to be be-*
    headed.

King. What safety may I look for at his hands,
If that my uncle shall be murdered thus?

Queen. Fear not, sweet boy, I'll guard thee from thy
    foes;
Had Edmund liv'd, he would have sought thy death.

Come son, we'll ride a hunting in the park.

King. And shall my uncle Edmund ride with us?

Queen. He is a traitor, think not on him; come.

[*Exeunt omnes.*

Enter MATREVIS *and* GURNEY.

Matrevis. Gurney, I wonder the king dies not,
Being in a vault up to the knees in water,
To which the channels of the castle run,
From whence a damp continually ariseth,
That were enough to poison any man,
Much more a king, brought up so tenderly.

Gurney. And so do I, Matrevis: yesternight
I open'd but the door to throw him meat,
And I was almost stifled with the savour.

Matrevis. He hath a body able to endure
More than we can inflict: and therefore now,
Let us assail his mind another while.

Gurney. Send for him out thence, and I will anger
him.

Matrevis. But stay, who's this?

Enter LIGHTBORN.

Lightborn. My lord protector greets you.

Gurney. What's here? I know not how to construe it.

_ *Matrevis.* Gurney, it was left unpointed for the
[49] nonce;

Edwardum occidere nolite timere,
That's his meaning.

Lightborn. Know ye this token? I must have the
king.

Matrevis. Ay, stay a while, thou shalt have answer
straight.
This villain's sent to make away the king.

Gurney. I thought as much.

Matrevis. And when the murder's done,
See how he must be handled for his labour.
Pereat iste : let him have the king.
What else? here is the keys, this is the lake,
Do as you are commanded by my lord.

[49] *nonce ;*] See Note on *Alexander and Campaspe*, p. 142.

Lightborn. I know what I must do, get you away,
Yet be not far off, I shall need your help;
See that in the next room I have a fire,
And get me a spit, and let it be red hot.
  Matrevis. Very well.
  Gurney. Need you any thing besides?
  Lightborn. A table and a featherbed.
  Gurney. That's all.
  Lightborn. Ay, ay; so when I call you, bring it in.
  Matrevis. Fear not thou that.
  Gurney. Here's a light to go into the dungeon.
  Lightborn. So now must I about this geer, ne'er was
      there any
So finely handled as this king shall be.
Foh, here's a place indeed, with all my heart!
  Edward. Who's there? what light is that? where-
      fore com'st thou?
  Lightborn. To comfort you, and bring you joyful
      news.
  Edward. Small comfort finds poor Edward in thy
      looks.
Villain, I know thou com'st to murder me.
  Lightborn. To murder you, my most gracious lord!
Far is it from my heart to do you harm.
The queen sent me to see how you were us'd,
For she relents at this your misery:
And what eyes can refrain from shedding tears,
To see a king in this most piteous state?
  Edward. Weep'st thou already? list a while to me,
And then thy heart, were it as Gurney's is,
Or as Matrevis, hewn from the Caucasus,
Yet will it melt, ere I have done my tale.
This dungeon where they keep me, is the sink
Wherein the filth of all the castle falls.
  Lightborn. O villains!
  Edward. And there, in mire and puddle have I
      stood
This ten days space; and, lest that I should sleep,
One plays continually upon a drum.

They give me bread and water, being a king;
So that, for want of sleep and sustenance,
My mind's distemper'd, and my body's numb'd,
And whether I have limbs or no, I know not.
O, would my blood drop out from every vein,
As doth this water from my [50] totter'd robes.
Tell Isabel, the queen, I look'd not thus,
When for her sake I ran at tilt in France,
And there unhors'd the duke of Cleremont.

    Lightborn. O speak no more, my lord! this breaks
      my heart.
Lie on this bed, and rest yourself a while.

    Edward. These looks of thine can harbour nought
      but death :
I see my tragedy written in thy brows.
Yet stay a while, forbear thy bloody hand,
And let me see the stroke before it comes,
That even then, when I shall lose my life,
My mind may be more stedfast on my God.

    Lightborn. What means your highness to mistrust
      me thus ?

    Edward. What mean'st thou to dissemble with me
      thus?

    Lightborn. These hands were never stain'd with in-
      nocent blood,
Nor shall they now be tainted with a king's.

    Edward. Forgive my thought, for having such a
      thought.
One jewel have I left, receive thou this.
Still fear I, and I know not what's the cause,

---

    [50] *totter'd robes.*] i. e. *tatter'd*, as we now pronounce it. In every writer of this period the word was spelt as above written, and perhaps, as Mr. Steevens observes, the present broad pronunciation, almost particular to the Scots, was, at that time, common to both nations. (See Note 6 on *King John.*) To the several instances there produced may be added the following :

    Dekker's *Bel-man of London*, Sign. D 4 : —" the turn spits (who " were poore *tottered* greasie fellows) looking like so many hee " divells."

    Bel-man's *Night walkes*, Sign. M 3 : — " By none but the Soul- " diers of these *totter'd* bands, it is familiarly or usually spoken."

But every joint shakes as I give it thee.
O! if thou harbour'st murder in thy heart,
Let this gift change thy mind, and save thy soul!
Know, that I am a king: Oh! at that name
I feel a hell of grief; where is my crown?
Gone, gone; and do I remain?

    Lightborn. You're overwatch'd, my lord; lie down
        and rest.
    Edward. But that grief keeps me waking, I should
        sleep;
For not these ten days have these eye-lids clos'd.
Now as I speak they fall, and yet with fear
Open again. O wherefore sit'st thou heie?

    Lightborn. If you mistrust me, I'll be gone, my
        lord.
    Edward. No, no; for, if thou mean'st to murder me,
Thou wilt return again, and therefore stay.

    Lightborn. He sleeps.
    Edward. O let me not die; yet stay, O stay a
        while.
    Lightborn. How now, my lord?
    Edward. Something still buzzeth in mine ears,
And tells me, if I sleep, I never wake;
This fear is that which makes me tremble thus.
And therefore tell me, wherefore art thou come?

    Lightborn. To rid thee of thy life; Matrevis, come.
    Edward. I am too weak and feeble to resist:
Assist me, sweet God, and receive my soul.

    Lightborn. Run for the table.
    Edward. O spare me, or dispatch me in a trice.
    Lightborn. So, lay the table down, and stamp on it,
But not too hard, lest that you bruise his body.

    Matrevis I fear me that this cry will raise the town,
And therefore let us take horse and away.

    Lightborn. Tell me, sirs, was it not bravely done?
    Gurney. Excellent well, take this for thy reward.
                   [*Gurney stabs Lightborn.*
Come, let us cast the body in the mote
And bear the king's to Mortimer our lord: away.
                        [*Exeunt omnes.*

Enter MORTIMER *junior, and* MATREVIS.

Mortimer junior. Is't done, Matrevis, and the mur-
    derer dead?

Matrevis. Ay, my good lord; I would it were un-
    done.

Mortimer junior. Matrevis, if thou now growest peni-
    tent

I'll be thy ghostly father; therefore chuse,

Whether thou wilt be secret in this,

Or else die by the hand of Mortimer.

Matrevis. Gurney, my lord, is fled, and will, I fear,

Betray us both, therefore let me fly.

Mortimer junior. Fly to the savages.

Matrevis. I humbly thank your honour*.

Mortimer junior. As for myself, I stand as Jove's
    huge tree;

And others are but shrubs compar'd to me.

All tremble at my name, and I fear none;

Let's see who dare impeach me for his death.

           Enter the QUEEN.

Queen. Ah, Mortimer, the king my son hath news,

His father's dead, and we have murdered him.

Mortimer junior. What if he have? the king is yet a
    child.

Queen. Ay, ay, but he tears his hair, and wrings his
    i. ands,

And vows to be reveng'd upon us both.

Into the council-chamber he is gone,

To crave the aid and succour of his peers.

Ah me! see where he comes, and they with him;

Now, Mortimer, begins our tragedy.

      Enter the KING, *with the* LORDS.

Lords. Fear not, my lord, know that you are a king.

King. Villain!

Mortimer junior. How now, my lord?

King. Think not that I am frighted with thy words!

My father's murder'd through thy treachery,

And thou shalt die, and on his mournful hearse

---

   * This speech obviously belongs to Matrevis: it has been given
hitherto by mistake to Mortimer. C.

Thy hateful and accursed head shall lie,
To witness to the world, that by thy means
His kingly body was so soon interr'd.
    Queen. Weep not, sweet son!
    King Forbid not me to weep, he was my father;
And, had you lov'd him half so well as I,
You could not bear his death thus patiently.
But you, I fear, conspir'd with Mortimer.
    Lords. Why speak you not unto my lord the king?
    Mortimer junior. Because I think scorn to be accus'd.
Who is the man dares say I murder'd him?
    King. Traitor! in me my loving father speaks,
And plainly saith, 'twas thou that murd'rest him.
    Mortimer junior. But hath your grace no other proof
      than this?
    King. Yes, if this be the hand of Mortimer*.
    Mortimer junior. False Gurney hath betray'd me
      and himself.
    Queen. I fear'd as much; murder cannot be hid.
    Mortimer junior. 'Tis my hand; what gather you by
      this?
    King. That thither thou did'st send a murderer.
    Mortimer junior. What murderer? Bring forth the
      man I sent.
    King. Ay, Mortimer, thou know'st that he is slain;
And so shalt thou be too. Why stays he here?
Bring him unto a hurdle, drag him forth,
Hang him I say, and set his quarters up.
But bring his head back presently to me.
    Queen. For my sake, sweet son, pity Mortimer.
    Mortimer junior. Madam, intreat not, I will rather
      die,
Than sue for life unto a paltry boy.
    King. Hence with the traitor! with the murderer!
    Mortimer junior. Base fortune, now I see, that in
      thy wheel
There is a point, to which when men aspire,
They tumble headlong down: that point I touch'd,

    * Probably shewing a paper.

And seeing there was no place to mount up higher,
Why should I grieve at my declining fall?
Farewell, fair Queen, weep not for Mortimer,
That scorns the world, and, as a traveller,
Goes to discover countries yet unknown*.

King. What! suffer you the traitor to delay?

Queen. As thou received'st thy life from me,
Spill not the blood of gentle Mortimer.

King. This argues, that you spilt my father's blood,
Else would you not intreat for Mortimer.

Queen. I spill his blood! no.

King. Ay, madam, you; for so the rumour runs.

Queen. That rumour is untrue; for loving thee,
Is this report rais'd on poor Isabel?

King. I do not think her so unnatural.

Lords. My lord, I fear me it will prove too true.

King. Mother, you are suspected for his death,
And therefore we commit you to the tower,
Till farther trial may be made thereof:
If you be guilty, tho' I be your son,
Think not to find me slack or pitiful.

Queen. Nay, to my death, for too long have I liv'd,
When as my son thinks to abridge my days.

King. Away with her! her words inforce these tears,
And I shall pity her if she speak again.

Queen. Shall I not mourn for my beloved lord?
And with the rest accompany him to his grave?

Lords. Thus, madam, 'tis the king's will you shall
hence.

Queen. He hath forgotten me; stay, I am his mother.

Lords. That boots not; therefore, gentle madam,
go.

Queen. Then, come sweet death, and rid me of this
grief.

Lords*. My lord, here is the head of Mortimer.

---

* Exit Mortimer here, attended by some lords.

† These are some other peers, who having gone out with Mortimer, return after his sudden execution. C.

King. Go fetch my father's hearse, where it shall
    lie;
And bring my funeral robes.   Accursed head,
Could I have rul'd thee then, as I do now,
Thou had'st not hatch'd this monstrous treachery.
Here comes the hearse; help me to mourn, my lords.
Sweet father, here unto thy murdered ghost,
· I offer up this wicked traitor's head;
And let these tears, distilling from mine ey es
Be witness of my grief and innocence.

EDITIONS.

(1.) The troublesome Raigne and lamentable Death of Edward the Second, King of England: with the tragicall fall of proud Mortimer. And also the Life and Death of Peirs Gaveston, the great Earle of Cornewall, and mighty favorite of King Edward the Second. As it was publiquely acted by the right honorable the Earle of Pembroke his servauntes. Written by Chri. Marlow, Gent. Imprinted at London by Richard Bradocke, for William Jones, dwelling neere Holbourne Conduit, at the signe of the Gunne, 1598, 4to.

(2.) The troublesome Raigne and lamentable Death of Edward the Second, King of England: with the tragicall fall of proud Mortimer. And also the Life and Death of Peirs Gaveston, the great Earle of Cornewall, and mighty favorite of King Edward the Second. As it was publiquely acted by the right honourable the Earle of Pembrooke his servants. Written by Christopher Marlow, Gent. Printed at London for Roger Barnes, and are to be sould at his shop in Chauncerie Lane, over-against the Rolles, 1612, 4to.

(3.) The troublesome raigne and lamentable death of Edward the Second, King of England: with the tragicall fall of proud Mortimer. And also the Life and Death of Peirs Gavestone, the greate Earle of Cornewall, and mighty favorite of King Edward the Second. As it was publikely acted by the late Queenes Majesties Servants, at the Red Bull in S. Johns-streete. Written by Christopher Marlow, Gent. London printed for Henry Bell, and are to be sold at his shop at the Lame Hospital Gate neere Smithfield, 1622, 4to.

Lightning Source UK Ltd.
Milton Keynes UK
UKHW022005131118
332286UK00007B/144/P